HOLDING THE SHOP TOGETHER

HOLDING THE SHOP TOGETHER

German Industrial Relations
in the Postwar Era

STEPHEN J. SILVIA

ILR PRESS
AN IMPRINT OF
CORNELL UNIVERSITY PRESS
Ithaca and London

First published 2013 by Cornell University Press
First printing, Cornell Paperbacks, 2013

Printed in the United States of America

Library of Congress Cataloging-in-Publication Data

Silvia, Stephen J., author.
    Holding the shop together : German industrial relations in the postwar era / Stephen J. Silvia.
        pages cm
    Includes bibliographical references and index.
    ISBN 978-0-8014-5221-5 (cloth : alk. paper) —
    ISBN 978-0-8014-7897-0 (pbk. : alk. paper)
    1. Industrial relations—Germany.   2. Labor unions—Germany.   3. Labor policy—Germany.   I. Title.
    HD8451.S55   2013
    331.80943'09045—dc23   2013013040

Cloth printing   10 9 8 7 6 5 4 3 2 1
Paperback printing   10 9 8 7 6 5 4 3 2 1

To Jenny,
for holding our shop together

Contents

PREFACE

My big aims in writing this book have been: (1) to integrate into a single volume the economic, historical, legal, political science, and sociological assessments and methods used on both sides of the Atlantic to analyze the major aspects of German industrial relations; and (2) to make innovative arguments using new evidence regarding the trajectory of German industrial relations.

Academics often wax eloquently in the abstract about the superiority of interdisciplinarity and multidisciplinarity, but in practice most stay in their individual disciplinary lanes and focus their scholarship narrowly. Indeed, it is rare to find any study of industrial relations anywhere that discusses both trade unions and employers in a single book, no less one that uses multiple methods drawn from the different tribes of academe. In this book, in contrast, I do take an interdisciplinary approach. I use the tools of a range of disciplines to address the questions that each discipline commonly asks. I then integrate these assessments to gain a broader and deeper understanding of German industrial relations than could be obtained through individual studies undertaken by scholars in each discipline acting in isolation.

The uneven chapter lengths are the most immediate manifestation of the book's interdisciplinary approach. This is most apparent when comparing chapters 3 and 4. I intentionally wrote chapter 3 the way economists write. Consequently, it is relatively short. Chapter 4 takes a historical approach. As a result, it is considerably longer. The other chapters, which incorporate a range of disciplines, fall somewhere in between. I should also note that the first two chapters are in part intended for people new to the topic of German industrial relations. Those more familiar with the topic are likely to be most interested in chapters 3 to 5 and the conclusion, because these feature more novel arguments and original evidence.

Finally, it is worth noting why I chose *Holding the Shop Together* as the title for this book. First, it captures what many of the actors themselves say they are doing. During the hundreds of interviews that I have done over the years with officials at German employers associations and trade unions, many interview partners summed up their efforts by saying that they were simply trying "to hold the shop together" (*den Laden zusammenhalten*) in the face of increasingly difficult circumstances. Second, *Holding the Shop Together* in English (but not in German) contains two words with double meaning that deepen the title's import. First, the word *Laden*, which is commonly translated as "shop," simply means store in German. In English, however, shop can also mean workshop, the traditional focal point of industrial relations. Second, the word "together" can be understood in two ways. One meaning is not letting things fall apart. A second meaning places the emphasis on labor and management working *together* rather than as adversaries. These double meanings turn the title into a nice summary statement of a signature aspect of postwar German industrial relations: the embrace of a mutually accepting "social partnership" by both collective bargaining parties. It also captures the ongoing effort of both labor and management to hold together their organizations and the industrial relations system in the postwar era.

I have been working on the topic of German industrial relations for three decades. Finishing a book on the topic gives me the opportunity to thank many people, some of whom should have been thanked long ago. I would first like to thank my parents Pauline and William Silvia for their extraordinary love and support over the years. They made my career possible, for which I am forever grateful. I would also like to thank their friends Ekkehard and Sybille Feustel. On many occasions, they showed me what *Gemütlichkeit* really means. John Windmuller was an extremely helpful and influential mentor while I was an undergraduate at Cornell University and beyond. Although he is no longer with us, he certainly deserves acknowledgment.

Many German researchers and practitioners have helped me over the years, especially, Wolf-Rüdiger Baumann, Hansjörg Döpp, Wolfgang Goos, Berthold Huber, Otto Jacobi, Thomas Klebe, Hartmut Küchle, Wolfgang Lecher, Karl Molitor, Walther Müller-Jentsch, Klaus Murmann, Hinrich Oetjen, Matthias von Randow, Helmut Schauer, Klaus Schnabel, Hubertus Schmoldt, Friedrich Wilhelm Siebel, Michael Sommer, Wolfgang Streeck, Karsten Tacke, Norbert Trautwein, Gudrun Trautwein-Kalms, Manfred Warda, Wolfgang Weipert, Detlev Wetzel, Jörg Wiedemuth, and Michael Vassiliadis. In particular, I would like to acknowledge the important support that I have received from Reiner Hoffmann and Nik Simon, and thank my great friend, Wolfgang Schroeder, who has provided me with considerable insight into German industrial relations and who was kind enough to read some draft chapters of the book. I would also like to recognize Mike Fichter and David Soskice for all of their help, which was considerable, as well as recently retired social affairs counselor at the US Embassy in Berlin, Joachim Kowalik.

Returning to this side of the Atlantic, the social counselors at the German embassy have all been extremely helpful over the years in providing me with both information and opportunity to meet with the top figures in German industrial and labor relations when they have passed through Washington and keeping me up on what was going on in Germany: Karl Feldengut, Markus Franz, Günther Horzetzky, Michael Mersmann, and Karl Pitz. I would particularly like to thank Marion Knappe for her helpful comments on a draft chapter. Andrew Martin and George Ross, two greats in the field of comparative labor relations, have always been extremely supportive, for which I am extremely grateful. Conversations with Adam Posen of the Peterson Institute were very helpful for framing things in the context of the larger German economy, as were numerous exchanges with individuals in the private sector, in particular, Robert Dugger, Thornton Mattheson, Amy Houpt Medearis, Robert McNally, and Angel Ubide. I would like to thank Dieter Dettke and Jack Janes for all of their substantial support over the years. Special thanks go to Andrei Markovits for his extraordinarily insightful comments on the penultimate draft of this book. I very much appreciate the help I received from my research assistants Heidi Hiebert, Rob Kevlihan, and Mike Stanaitis, as well as the encouragement and support that I received from Louis Goodman.

It has been a great pleasure working with Cornell University Press ILR editorial director Fran Benson and acquisitions assistant Kitty Liu. I have very much appreciated their very helpful advice and guidance.

I am grateful to the numerous funders that supported the research that went into this book. These include the American Institute for Contemporary German Studies, Deutscher Akademischer Austauschdienst, the Friedrich Ebert Foundation, the German Fulbright Commission, the Hans Böckler Foundation, and the National Endowment for the Humanities. I would like to acknowledge the support of my children Christopher, Sean, and Peter, who properly kept me engaged in the daily life of coaching and practices while I was working on the book and supported me daily through their love and encouragement. Above all I am forever grateful to my wife, Jennifer Paxton. Jenny lived through every twist and turn of this book. She gave me sound advice, considerable time, and an extraordinary degree of support. I could not have completed it if it were not for her.

Finally, I would like to let readers know that the bibliography for this book as well as the quantitative data and supplemental tables from the analysis in chapter 3 can be found at http://www.american.edu/sis/faculty/Silvia-Holding-the-Shop-Together.cfm.

ABBREVIATIONS

ADGB   Allgemeiner Deutscher Gewerkschaftsbund (General German Federation of Labor)

AG   *Aktiengesellschaft* (joint-stock company)

ASU   Arbeitsgemeinschaft selbstständiger Unternehmer (Working Group of Independent Entrepreneurs)

AVE   *allgemeine Verbindlichkeitserklärung* (declaration of general applicability)

BA   Bundesagentur für Arbeit (Federal Employment Agency)

BAG   Bundesarbeitsgericht (Federal Labor Court)

BAT   Bundes-Angestellten-Tarif (Federal Collective Agreement for Public Employees)

BAVC   Bundesarbeitgeberverband Chemie (Federal Employers Association of the Chemical Industry)

BCCG   Berlin Center of Corporate Governance

BDA   Bundesvereinigung der Deutschen Arbeitgeberverbände (Federal Organization of German Employers Associations)

BDI   Bundesverband der Deutschen Industrie (Federal Association of German Industry)

BVG   Bundesverfassungsgericht (Federal Constitutional Court)

CDA   Christlich Demokratische Arbeitnehmerschaft (Christian Democratic Employees Group)

CDI   Centralverband deutscher Industrieller (Central Association of German Industrialists)

CDU   Christlich Demokratische Union (Christian Democratic Union)

CGB   Christlicher Gewerkschaftsbund Deutschlands (Christian Trade Union Federation of Germany)

CSU   Christlich Soziale Union (Christian Social Union)

DAF   Deutsche Arbeitsfront (German Labor Front)

DAG   Deutsche Angestellten-Gewerkschaft (German White-Collar Employees Union)

xiv   **ABBREVIATIONS**

DBB	Deutscher Beamtenbund (German Civil Servants Federation)
DEEWC	Directive on the Establishment of a European Works Council
DFV ULA	Deutscher Führungskräfteverband Union der Leitenden Angestellten (German Managers Confederation)
DGB	Deutscher Gewerkschaftsbund (German Trade Union Federation)
DPG	Deutsche Postgewerkschaft (German Postal Workers Union)
ECJ	European Court of Justice
ERA	*Entgeltrahmentarifvertrag* (compensation framework agreement)
ETUC	European Trade Union Confederation
ETV	*Entgelttarifvertrag* (compensation collective bargaining agreement)
EU	European Union
EVG	Eisenbahn und Verkehrsgewerkschaft (Rail and Transportation Employees Union)
EWC	European works council
FBBB	Fachgemeinschaft Bau Berlin und Brandenburg (Trade Group Construction Berlin and Brandenburg)
FDGB	Freier Deutscher Gewerkschaftsbund (Free German Trade Union Federation)
FDP	Freie Demokratische Partei (Free Democratic Party)
GdED	Gewerkschaft der Eisenbahner Deutschlands (Railroad Workers Union of Germany)
GDL	Gewerkschaft Deutscher Lokomotivführer (German Locomotive Engineers Union)
GdP	Gewerkschaft der Polizei (Police Officers Union)
GDR	German Democratic Republic
GEW	Gewerkschaft Erziehung und Wissenschaft (Union of Education and Science Workers)
GGLF	Gewerkschaft Garten, Land- und Forstwirtschaft (Union of Horticulture, Agriculture, and Forestry Workers)
GHK	Gewerkschaft Holz und Kunststoff (Union of Wood and Plastic Workers)
GK	Gewerkschaft Kunst (Union of Artists and Musicians)
GL	Gewerkschaft Leder (Union of Leather Workers)
GLS	generalized least squares

GTB	Gewerkschaft Textil-Bekleidung (Union of Textile and Clothing Workers)
HBV	Gewerkschaft Handel, Banken und Versicherungen (Union of Retail, Banking and Insurance Workers)
HDB	Hauptverband der Deutschen Bauindustrie (Main Association of the German Construction Industry)
IG BAU	Industriegewerkschaft Bauen-Agrar-Umwelt (Construction, Agriculture, and Environment Employees Industrial Union)
IG BCE	Industriegewerkschaft Bergbau, Chemie, Energie (Industrial Union of Mining, Chemical and Energy Employees)
IG BE	Industriegewerkschaft Bergbau und Energie (Industrial Union of Mine and Energy Workers)
IG ChPK	(or IG Chemie) Industriegewerkschaft Chemie-Papier-Keramik (Industrial Union of Chemical, Paper and Ceramic Workers)
IG DruPa	Industriegewerkschaft Druck und Papier (Industrial Union of Printing and Paper Workers)
IG Medien	Industriegewerkschaft Medien (Industrial Union of Media Workers)
IG Metall	Industriegewerkschaft Metall (Industrial Union of Metalworkers)
INSM	Initiative Neue Soziale Marktwirtschaft (New Social Market Economy Initiative)
MTV	*Manteltarifvertrag* (skeleton collective bargaining agreement)
NGG	Gewerkschaft Nahrung-Genuss-Gaststätten (Union of Food, Hotel, and Restaurant Workers)
OEM	original equipment manufacturer
ÖTV	Gewerkschaft Öffentliche Dienste, Transport und Verkehr (Union of Public Services and Transportation Employees)
OT	*ohne Tarif* (no contract)
PDS	Partei des Demokratischen Sozialismus (Party of Democratic Socialism)
RTV	*Rahmentarifvertrag* (framework collective bargaining agreement)
SE	Societas Europaea (European Corporation)
SED	Sozialistische Einheitspartei Deutschlands (Socialist Unity Party)
SEIU	Service Employees International Union

SME	small and medium-size enterprise
SPD	Sozialdemokratische Partei Deutschlands (Social Democratic Party of Germany)
SPE	Societas Privata Europaea (European Private Company)
TdL	Tarifgemeinschaft deutscher Länder (Collective Bargaining Group of the German States)
TEU	Treaty on European Union
TVöD	Tarifvertrag für den öffentlichen Dienst (Collective Bargaining Agreement for the Public Service Sector)
TVG	Tarifvertragsgesetz (Collective Agreements Act)
UFO	Unabhängige Flugbegleiter Organisation (Independent Flight Attendants Organization)
USPD	Unabhängige Sozialdemokratische Partei Deutschlands (Independent Social Democratic Party of Germany)
VDA	Vereinigung der Deutschen Arbeitgeberverbände (Organization of German Employers Associations)
ver.di	Vereinte Dienstleistungsgewerkschaft (United Service Employees Union)
VMI	Verband der Metallindustrie Baden-Württemberg (Association of Baden-Württemberg Metal Industry Employers)
ZAG	Zentralarbeitsgemeinschaft der industriellen und gewerblichen Arbeitgeber und Arbeitnehmer Deutschlands (Central Work Community of German Industrial and Commercial Employers and Employees)
ZDB	Zentralverband Deutsches Baugewerbe (Central Association of the German Construction Trade)
ZVOB	Zweckverbund Ostdeutscher Bauverbände (Eastern German Construction Associations Cooperative)

Introduction

Since the onset of the global financial crisis in late 2008 there has been a boom in positive assessments of the German economy.[1] Little wonder. Remarkably, Germany has managed to bring down unemployment to more than one percentage point below the *precrisis* level and to maintain a current account surplus equivalent to 5 percent of its gross domestic product. This is not the first time that Germany's stock has ridden high. German economic institutions received praise for the "economic miracle" of the late 1950s and early 1960s, the "model Germany" economy that weathered the oil shocks comparatively well during the 1970s, and the "export world champion" economy of the mid-1980s. At other times, however, academics and journalists have been bearish on Germany. High unemployment dogged the German economy for a quarter century, starting in the early 1980s. From the mid-1990s to the mid-2000s, Germany was generally dismissed as the economic "sick man" of Europe. These oscillating appraisals of the German economy raise two questions: Does the current positive assessment of German economic institutions reflect something real, or is it just another speculative bubble? And, what is it about German economic institutions that has drawn the attention of so many over the years? In this book I address these questions by examining a key pillar of the postwar German economy, namely, the industrial relations system.

The industrial relations system holds a prominent place in the German economy. It is strongest where the German economy is strongest. It is responsible for many of the distinctive features of postwar German capitalism. Industrial relations institutions extend into the boardrooms, workplaces, and government to a degree that is unimaginable in most other countries. Collective bargaining determines compensation for a substantial majority of German employees. Trends in German industrial relations, moreover, are reliably indicative of developments in the broader German economy and frequently influence industrial relations developments beyond Germany's borders. All these aspects make the German industrial relations regime an ideal focal point for developing a deeper understanding of the German economy as a whole and its international impact.

The story of postwar German industrial relations is fascinating and reflective of many broader economic, political, and social trends in postwar Germany. Immediately after the Nazi era, employers, workers, and legislators struggled—sometimes as partners and at other times as adversaries— to rebuild a viable industrial relations regime. The cautionary legacy of the demise of German democracy in the 1930s helped to keep the effort focused and constructive. Engagement led to change. Employers supported democracy without reservations for the first time and accepted the unions as equal partners. Trade unionists reached a modus vivendi with capitalism and in the 1960s explicitly embraced white-collar employees. These efforts paid off. From the 1950s through the 1970s, the postwar German industrial relations system flourished and served as an important component of an effective economy and a sound democracy. German trade unions and employers associations embraced "social partnership," that is, acceptance of each other as equal partners that work together constructively to advance the economic and social well-being of German citizens.

The idyllic conjuncture did not last, however. The industrial relations system began to come under stress in the 1980s. The German domestic economy started to falter, and a shift toward individualism in German society, which began in the 1960s, produced a more challenging set of countercurrents for organized business and labor. Many employers associations and trade unions began to experience difficulties recruiting and retaining members. When German unification became a sudden reality, economic and social heterogeneity expanded greatly, amplifying the challenge collective bargaining parties faced to produce collective agreements that were viable and acceptable to all. The legal framework supporting

German industrial relations remained sound, but collective bargaining coverage shrank because of membership losses in some (but not all) employers associations.

Thus, the 1990s and 2000s were decades of experimentation born out of desperation for organized labor and management alike. The unions engaged in a spate of mergers that starkly concentrated the movement in order to shore up its structural integrity. By the turn of the millennium, just two unions accounted for over two-thirds of all German union membership. Both collective bargaining parties experimented with new forms of recruiting and retaining members. Some reforms were bold. Others were incomplete and contradictory. Internecine disagreements and rivalries complicated matters. Large unions continued to lose members. Small occupational unions have increasingly challenged the large ones. The accumulation of daunting challenges has led some to wonder how long organized labor and management will remain influential.

The story is not all negative, however. Labor and management in the chemicals industry have forged an intensive social partnership manifested in scores of supplemental agreements that cover a wide range of topics well beyond collective bargaining. In the late 2000s, the metalworkers union embraced grassroots "social movement unionism," which has its origins in the United States, and began a radical reorganization. This effort has been the first to show promise in reversing membership declines. Employers associations and trade unions have managed to hold on to their leading roles in the German economy and society. They showed that they could still work together in society when they acted effectively to minimize the impact of the global financial crisis. This productive cooperation brought them renewed respect.

Design and Principal Findings of This Book

Five chapters form the core of this book. They can be divided into two parts. The first part presents in two chapters the framework of the German industrial relations system, that is, the laws and the role of the state. The first chapter discusses German labor law and several state institutions that are crucial components of the industrial relations regime. The second chapter investigates Germany's distinctive system of codetermination. The second part, which consists of three chapters, analyzes the principal actors in German industrial relations: the trade unions and the employers associations. The conclusion combines the material portrayed in chapters 1 through 5 into a comprehensive picture and then considers the future of German industrial relations.

In chapter 1, I challenge conventional wisdom in two respects. First, I call into question the assertion that defeat in the Second World War laid the groundwork for Germany's postwar economic "miracle" by clearing out the laws and interest-group bargains that were alleged to have previously constrained economic growth.[2] This is decidedly not the case when it comes to German economic statutes, especially industrial relations legislation. Postwar German labor law is in most respects a refurbished version of the laws of the Weimar Republic and, in some instances, the Second Empire. To the extent that the laws are different, they contain provisions that have strengthened the scope and coverage of the industrial relations regime. The German government enacted these laws by the early 1950s. Thus, a full thicket of laws was already in place before the famous German "economic miracle" took off starting in the mid-1950s, and those laws did not impede growth.

The second shibboleth concerns the importance of the German state in industrial relations. Industrial relations practitioners and politicians routinely declare collective bargaining to be autonomous of the state. Yet, a detailed examination of German labor law in chapter 1 makes plain the indispensible role of the state in buttressing the postwar German industrial relations regime. Laws, regulations, agencies, and courts unobtrusively sustain a framework highly supportive of "autonomous" collective bargaining. Ironically, union officials and employers are generally oblivious to the state's important role. German-style regulation relies on maintaining background "framework conditions" (*Rahmenbedingungen*) conducive to the state's objectives rather than remedial intervention. Unlike in most other high-income countries, the German framework has remained intact, despite considerable buffeting, particularly since the oil shocks of the 1970s. Germany's consensual form of federal democracy, which usually requires the assent of the major established parties and a large share of the states to make major legislative changes, helps account for the stability of postwar industrial relations over the years.[3]

Chapter 2 appraises the uniquely German system of codetermination, which gives employees some say in management decision making. Codetermination has two components: works councils, which are representative bodies of employees in the workplace, and employee representation on supervisory boards. Codetermination has made trade unions especially resilient because it anchors employee participation in the law and provides an added platform for employee influence in a company's affairs besides collective bargaining. Employers' attitudes toward code-termination have always been ambivalent. Most praise it in public and genuinely welcome the opportunity codetermination provides for building a cooperative relationship with employees in the workplace, but some also charge that German codetermination laws are costly and infringe on property rights. Employers have always been especially critical of various forms of parity representation on supervisory boards as a violation of management rights.

Officials from employers associations and trade unions have repeatedly tried to amend codetermination legislation over the years, with occasional success. Most recently, labor spearheaded the passage of a law strengthening workplace codetermination in the early 2000s. In contrast, employers undertook a concerted effort to roll back employee representation on supervisory boards in the mid-2000s, but failed. The results of both efforts illustrate the continuing strong support for codetermination in German politics and society and the enduring resilience of these components of the statutory framework of German industrial relations.

The future of codetermination is not completely secure, however. The biggest threats come not from within Germany but from the European Union. The first is European legislation. Over the years, successive German governments, regardless of political complexion, have ensured that EU commercial laws intended to deepen the internal market do not undermine domestic codetermination. The need to make sure that new European legislation promoting economic integration does not undercut codetermination is no less pressing today. The second threat to codetermination has come from the European Court of Justice. Since the mid-2000s, the ECJ has pursued an aggressive agenda of economic liberalization that has begun to chafe against Germany's codetermination statutes. The incompatibility is likely to intensify in coming years. It is premature, however, to determine the ultimate outcome.

The first part of the book shows that the framework of the postwar German industrial relations system has remained intact and performed effectively. The principal actors—that is, the trade unions and the employers associations[4]—have not fared nearly as well, however. Most have lost a large portion of their memberships over the past two decades. The second part of the book explores why.

Chapter 3 opens the consideration of membership developments by undertaking a quantitative analysis of the unionization rate in postwar Germany. The book's model of union density overturns accepted explanations by introducing new variables. Previous models of unionization in Germany focused exclusively on economic and demographic variables. Chapter 3 includes two additional factors: "social custom" and trade. The notion that social custom—that is, the social expectations and the milieu that influence an individual's decision to join a union—has an impact on unionization has been discussed broadly in the general literature on union density, but it has never been incorporated into a quantitative model of German unionization. *Holding the Shop Together* employs an innovative measure of social custom and finds it to be the most powerful factor correlated with the German unionization rate, establishing empirically the importance of this *sociological* element in German unionization. The quantitative analysis also reveals trade as a percentage of the gross domestic product correlates *positively* with the German unionization rate, which runs counter to much of the qualitative literature on the sources of trade union decline but is consistent with Germany's strong record as an exporter.[5] German unification also correlates positively with unionization, confounding conventional expectations. The results in chapter 3 are consistent with those of the first two chapters. The decline in German trade union density is not the result of a breakdown of labor law or state institutions but rather the deterioration of trade unionism as a social custom.

Chapter 4 undertakes a broader qualitative assessment of the German trade union movement. It builds on the findings of the previous chapter by probing the strategic considerations and actions of trade union leaders in light of postwar sociological and economic trends. The record of the postwar German trade unions is one of remarkable stability and success in their first four decades. Stability did not last, however. From the mid-1990s to the early 2000s, plummeting membership figures in both eastern and western Germany triggered a reorganization of the unions of the Deutscher Gewerkschaftsbund (DGB, German Trade Union Federation) and the Deutsche Angestellten-Gewerkschaft (DAG, German White-Collar Employees Union) through a spate of mergers that was so substantial that it is best understood as the creation of a second postwar German trade union movement. The first was an industrial union movement structured by the principle that each major sector should have one (and only one) trade union. The second is a multisectoral union movement that is dominated by two mammoth organizations that span multiple sectors: Industriegewerkschaft Metall (IG Metall, Industrial Union of Metalworkers) and Vereinte Dienstleistungsgewerkschaft (ver.di, United Service Employees Union).

The second postwar trade union movement achieved fuller economies of scale, resulting in greater organizational stability, but most have not managed to staunch membership decline. The mergers that created the multisectoral movement may have inadvertently precipitated another phenomenon that has proved problematic for larger unions. Small occupational unions, particularly in the transportation sector, have become more prominent players in German industrial relations. Some have used their choke point positions in the economy to extract sizable wage concessions. The success of occupational unions since the latter half of the 2000s has embarrassed the leadership of the multisectoral unions because the large unions have not been able to secure comparable wage gains. The heads of the large unions also fear that the spectacular successes of the occupational unions may stoke demands to break up the multisectoral unions only a few years after they had gone to great pains to create them.

The 2000s were a particularly difficult decade for the German labor movement. A weak economy led to meager results at the bargaining table and declining real incomes. Experiments with peak-level neocorporatism in the form of the Alliance for Jobs failed to produce reforms or any tangible improvements in the labor market. German chancellor Gerhard Schröder responded to the failure of the neocorporatist Alliance for Jobs in his first term of office by largely dispensing with consultation in his second term and enacting legislation designed to liberalize the German labor market. The two largest unions—IG Metall and ver.di—tried confrontation to stave off the labor market reforms but failed. The aggressive tactics generated much rancor within the labor movement, especially between the leaders of the two giant unions and the chair of the third biggest German union, the Industriegewerkschaft Bergbau, Chemie, Energie (IG BCE, Industrial Union of Mining, Chemical, and Energy Employees), who preferred a more conciliatory approach. By mid-decade, IG Metall and ver.di abandoned political confrontation after it had proved ineffectual. It took a leadership change in the federal chancellery and in IG Metall for the labor movement to recover some semblance of its past standing.

The years since the 2008 global financial crisis have not been all bad for German trade unions. Ironically, formulating effective policies to address the crisis and subsequent downturn brought trade unions, employers associations, and the government together, restoring some of the collective bargaining partners' influence. At the end of the decade, the largest unions also attempted to reverse their fortunes by pursuing internal reforms. The strategies were diverse. IG BCE doubled down on the pursuit of intensive social partnership. In contrast, IG Metall began efforts to shore up social customs supportive of union membership by borrowing the rhetoric and techniques of social movement unionism from English-speaking countries.[6] The metalworkers union also adopted several measures designed to strengthen the incentives and resources to recruit and to retain members, particularly at the local level. IG Metall's grassroots strategy has yielded some initial success. In 2012, union membership grew in all categories, including the all-important currently employed and youth subsegments, for the first time in decades. It is still too soon to tell whether a social union movement strategy pioneered in the decentralized and adversarial environment of US plant-level union-recognition elections can succeed over the long haul in an industrial relations system steeped in an ethos of cooperation and with a center of gravity for collective bargaining at the sectoral level. Nonetheless, IG Metall's reform effort is a demonstration of the creativity and resolve still present in the German labor movement. A few local ver.di officials experimented with social movement unionism as well, but the union's fragmented and frozen structure prevented local lessons from percolating upward.

Chapter 5 turns to the other side of the collective bargaining table. It starts with a brief discussion of the prewar establishment and postwar reconstruction of employers associations. It is employers associations' substantially higher density and more complete coverage of the economy rather than a high unionization rate that have given postwar German collective bargaining such broad reach in determining compensation. As a result, density trends among employers associations have been of greatest importance in determining the influence of the postwar system of German industrial relations.

Officials of employers associations tightened their influence over member firms during the 1960s by strengthening the capacity of associations to engage in industrial actions and by using lockouts frequently. Despite these steps, which curtailed the autonomy of individual firms, the associations maintained high membership densities. In the 1980s, external economic developments—namely, Europeanization, globalization, and the introduction of new manufacturing techniques such as "lean production"—challenged employers associations. Large original equipment manufacturers (OEMs) faced much stiffer competition from companies both at home and abroad. They in turn placed pressure on their suppliers by cutting prices and demanding higher quality. The impact of the transmission of this intensified economic pressure from the global to the national level varied depending on the sector. For sectors in which both the OEMs and their suppliers are in the same employers association (e. g., mechanical engineering), the transmission of economic pressure prompted a disproportionately high share of small supplier firms to "flee" their associations, which lowered employers association density. In contrast, high and stable membership in employers associations has prevailed in sectors dominated by large firms with suppliers mostly in other sectors (e. g., chemicals). The empirical findings from the chapter also disconfirm the claim of Schmitter and Streeck that employers associations must choose between maximizing external influence and retaining membership.[7] The chemical industry employers associations increased influence over the member firms but retained members. The employers association in the mechanical engineering sector, in contrast, sacrificed influence and catered heavily to members, but association density in that sector declined nonetheless.

In the conclusion I discuss the implications of the five substantive chapters and compare the findings to other countries. Most striking are the divergent trajectories of the principal components of the German industrial relations system. Germany's consensual politics have effectively protected the legal framework. Trade union membership is declining due in large part to domestic sociological developments. The bifurcation of membership trends among employers associations is the product of international economic integration playing out differently in individual sectors, depending on their structures. The legal framework has provided sufficient support to prevent membership decline from turning into a commensurate loss of influence. The neocorporatist components of the German state, such as the Federal Employment Agency, have helped to preserve the political influence of trade unions and employer associations. Codetermination has also served as a backbone for German industrial relations and in particular the trade unions, because it provides for employees' access, voice, and resources in firms that are guaranteed by statute rather than just union muscle. Codetermination has also intertwined labor and management to such an extent that it is far harder for employers to escape organized industrial relations in Germany than in most other countries. Still, the divergent trajectories raise questions about how much longer the postwar industrial relations system can hold together.

The social partners are not giving up, however. Both have devoted an unprecedented amount of attention and resources to membership recruitment and retention. The largest union is experimenting with US-style social movement unionism. Many employers associations are trying new types of membership, including ones that do not require participation in collective bargaining. It is too soon to tell whether these experiments will reverse membership declines or whether these efforts to save the industrial relations system will wind up destroying it. The surge in experimentation and ongoing uncertainty are among the developments that make contemporary German industrial relations both interesting and important.

Most previous work on German industrial relations has focused on the parts of the German industrial relations system rather than the whole. Many scholars have written about the trade unions.[8] Others have surveyed the labor market, law, or employers associations.[9] This fragmentation of the scholarship is unfortunate because it has become increasingly clear that the various parts of German industrial relations can only be properly understood in context. Only a few authors have produced books on German industrial relations, but those books either predate German unification or consist of descriptive summaries designed primarily for teaching.[10] So, there is room for a comprehensive scholarly treatment of German industrial relations such as this one.

In this book I use multiple methods—specifically, historical institutionalism and statistical analysis—both to evaluate several existing theoretical assertions and to sketch some new causal mechanisms. I do not rely on an overarching theory of industrial relations, capitalism, or interest groups (German or otherwise), but at several junctures I do assess the two most prominent explanations for developments in German industrial relations: "erosion" and "exhaustion."

The erosion and exhaustion arguments share an assertion that there has been a general weakening of all of the components of the German industrial relations system over the last twenty to thirty years. Advocates of the erosion argument claim that German industrial relations functioned well from the immediate postwar years into the mid-1970s because the German economy was relatively sheltered. Thereafter, a series of developments exogenous to industrial relations—the end of full employment, rising private service-sector employment, German unification, and "European integration and globalization since the mid-1980s"—all contributed to the "erosion" of the German industrial relations regime.[11]

Wolfgang Streeck claims in his 2009 *Re-Forming Capitalism* that German industrial relations have become "disorganized." At one point or another in the book, Streeck loosely invokes a wide variety of explanations and mechanisms for this development. These include liberalization, the dialectic, Karl Polanyi's double movement, and a surge in the rapaciousness of German employers. The heart of Streeck's argument, however, comes in part 2, where he focuses on "exhaustion." Streeck references Darwin and asserts that "the mere passage of time" brings down institutions because their efficacy inevitably declines and maintenance costs rise simply because economic and social change make institutions fit less well in their environment. "Positive externalities turn negative" as a result, and institutions ultimately break down. In chapter 10, Streeck asserts that "time's up" for the institutions of the postwar German economy and, in particular, industrial relations. They are now at the point of exhaustion.[12]

The summary of my findings makes clear that I do not think the evidence supports either the "erosion" or "exhaustion" argument. Both obscure more than they reveal because they become black boxes that hinder investigation into the diverse trajectories and causal mechanisms behind membership change in employers associations and unions.

Why German Industrial Relations Matters

Knowledge of the German industrial relations system is essential to comprehending fully many topics beyond its immediate scope. As mentioned at the outset, the German economy cannot be understood without a firm grasp of the industrial relations system. Consequently, any economic analysis of the German economy that does not reflect a solid understanding of German industrial relations is bound to miss the mark. The German economy matters, in turn, because Germany is a powerhouse exporter and a key player in world capital markets. The German economy has been repeatedly held up as a model for others to emulate.[13] The euro crisis, which began in 2009, is just the latest demonstration of the pivotal place of the German economy in both Europe and the world. All indications are that in the future Germany will become even more dominant in the European economy and remain important in the world economy.

Beyond economics, German trade unions and employers associations are powerful actors in German and European society. They are among the most affluent and innovative labor and management organizations in the world. Their influence extends far beyond Germany's borders. Unraveling the puzzle of why many employers associations and unions began to shrink after decades of growth and stability addresses a dilemma confronting many organizations in all affluent democracies.[14] Moreover, several prominent academic theories, such as collective action,[15] neocorporatism,[16] and varieties of capitalism,[17] use German industrial relations either as a prominent part of a critical case or as a thinly veiled sketch model for ideal types, such as "the Rhine model" and the "coordinated market economy." Thus, having a strong understanding of German industrial relations is essential to a wide variety of analyses, both economic and political.

CHAPTER 1

The Enduring Resilience of the Law and the State in German Industrial Relations

In this chapter I examine the role of law and the state in German industrial relations. This is to familiarize readers with the distinctive history and contemporary features of German labor law because they profoundly shape the reckoning of German employees and employers about what are possible and preferable policies in the field of industrial relations. I also make clear that law and the German state have been crucial in supporting and sustaining the postwar industrial relations regime.

I challenge two commonly held perceptions about labor law and the role of the state in Germany. First, some scholars have asserted that the German economy was more successful in the immediate postwar era because losing the Second World War wiped the slate clean of prewar laws and deals between interest groups and the state that hindered growth.[1] An examination of the facts, however, demonstrates that postwar German law and practice in most areas consist largely of borrowings from the Weimar Republic and even the Second Empire. They have been, if anything, more numerous and encompassing than in previous eras. This is certainly true for postwar industrial relations. Second, labor and management practitioners typically stress collective bargaining autonomy and underplay the important role the state plays in providing the prerequisites for that autonomy. Rather, the German state has served as a sturdy trestle supporting the postwar industrial relations regime. Contrary to the erosion and exhaustion arguments discussed in the introduction, the foundations of the law and the state have remained as robust components of German industrial relations.

I am also clearing the field here for one of my larger arguments, namely, that the forces driving membership trends for German trade unions and employers associations differ. Unionization is primarily a sociological phenomenon, whereas employers association membership is principally an economic calculation based on sectoral considerations. State support of German industrial relations is quite important, but it has been a constant; it therefore cannot be held responsible for change in the postwar era.

German Labor Law: A Brief Overview

Germans commonly refer to the start of postwar reconstruction in May 1945 as "hour zero," largely because of the devastating impact of the war and the wholesale scrapping of Nazi state structures. A brief review of the contents and antecedents of statutes delineating freedom of association, collective bargaining, and adjudication of workplace disputes reveals, however, that most of the components of the postwar regime are refurbished versions of prewar institutions, practices, and structures. I begin with a discussion of the freedom of association, which is the bedrock on which both the statutes and the jurisprudence for industrial relations is built. In subsequent sections, I examine the legal provisions undergirding collective bargaining, contracts, labor courts, and the regulation of industrial disputes.

Freedom of Association

In industrial relations, freedom of association (*Koalitionsfreiheit*) means the right of employees to organize trade unions and of managers to form employers associations. This right existed formally even in Imperial Germany, though it was often difficult for employees to exercise it in practice. Most business associations and individual firms in Imperial Germany went to considerable lengths to avoid having to deal with unions. Employers frequently used ties to local police and politicians to harass unionists and to disrupt their organizations. At times the German national government also made life difficult for unionists. Under the leadership of Imperial Chancellor Prince Otto von Bismarck, the German state banned all socialist activities and organizations, including socialist trade unions, from 1878 to 1890.[2] Even after the expiration of the antisocialist laws, government officials at all levels in Imperial Germany frequently subjected unionists to spying, harassment, dismissal, police violence, and sensational trials before biased judges.

The famous statement of Judge Lujo Brentano summarizes the contradictory attitude of the Imperial German state toward trade unions: "Workers possess the freedom of association. If they make use of it, however, they will be punished."[3] In contrast, the German state did not inhibit the creation and operation of business associations during this same period. In fact, it even permitted the formation of cartels.

The First World War substantially changed the configuration of Germany's sociopolitical relations, which helped to advance the legitimization of trade unions. Once war broke out, nationalism trumped cross-national class solidarity for most workers and their organizations, despite considerable rhetoric to the contrary in socialist circles in the years leading up to the conflict. German labor backed the war effort and quickly offered to participate in a "national unity front" to maintain a "civil peace" (*Burgfrieden*) for the duration of the conflict.[4] Labor's initial contribution to the civil peace was a no-strike pledge. In return, employers and the government agreed to stop harassing trade unions and to cooperate with them throughout the war. The highpoint of the civil peace came on 5 December 1916. The imperial government's Third Supreme Military Command headed by Gen. Paul von Hindenburg and Gen. Erich Ludendorff enacted the Auxiliary Patriotic Service Act (Gesetz betreffend den vaterländischen Hilfsdienst). This act recognized unions as legal bargaining agents for workers, opened the public sector to union recruitment, and required the establishment of employee committees in medium- and large-sized workplaces. In return, labor accepted a work requirement for all able-bodied males between seventeen and sixty and a stipulation that employees gain permission from their current employer before changing jobs. Labor leaders hoped that the civil peace would permanently anchor trade unions within Germany's economy and society, but achieving this objective proved elusive.[5]

Germany's defeat in the First World War unleashed considerable turbulence. The kaiser abdicated on 9 November 1918, two days before Germany signed the armistice to end hostilities. On November 10, a mass gathering of Berlin workers' and soldiers' councils elected a five-person council of "people's commissars" as the new government. All of the commissars were social democrats. Three were from the larger and more moderate Social Democratic Party of Germany (Sozialdemokratische Partei Deutschlands, SPD), and two were from the left-wing Independent Social Democratic Party of Germany (Unabhängige Sozialdemokratische Partei Deutschlands, USPD). Friedrich Ebert, head of the SPD, became provisional chancellor.[6]

The kaiser's abdication did not induce union leaders to change their integrationist course, but it did trigger a renegotiation of labor's arrangement with German employers. The unrest of the moment and the social democratic monopoly in the new provisional government put labor in the stronger strategic position. The upsurge of radicalism prompted significant numbers of German employers to abandon their rejectionist attitude toward organized labor and to embrace the reformist trade unions as a way to save capitalism. Many established union leaders feared a full-blown socialist revolution nearly as much as did employers, because it would most likely sweep them and their organizations away along with the institutions of capitalism. Thus, a common interest in preserving the status quo served as a foundation for cooperation and compromise between German labor and management.[7]

On 15 November 1918, business and union leaders acted on their own to start to build a post-Imperial industrial relations system. A delegation of social democratic trade unionists led by the head of the Generalkommission der Gerwerkschaften Deutschlands (General Commission of German Trade Unions), Carl Legien, and a group of prominent businesspeople led by Ruhr industrialist Hugo Stinnes signed a twelve-point pact known as the Stinnes-Legien agreement. The agreement took the form of a private contract rather than legislation because of doubts about the stability and legitimacy of the provisional German government. Most prominently, the Stinnes-Legien agreement recognized independent trade unions as the sole legitimate collective representative of employees, declared collective agreements to be inviolate, permitted the formation of works councils (*Betriebsräte*) in workplaces with more than fifty employees and instituted the eight-hour workday as a standard.[8]

Germany's new republican constitution, drafted in the city of Weimar in 1919, greatly improved the legal anchoring of labor's freedom of association. Article 159 of the Weimar constitution adopted much of the language of the Stinnes-Legien agreement, including the guarantee of the right of employees to form unions. Employers also remained free to create associations. The German state generally respected this freedom of association during the Weimar era, although it did not always defend trade unions and their members from hostile employer actions (e.g., the use of strikebreakers and dismissal of union activists).

Freedom of association soon came to an end after Adolf Hitler rose to power in January 1933. His National Socialist government did permit trade unionists to hold their traditional May Day celebration in 1933, but the motivation was by no means benign. The Nazis used the demonstrations to identify union activists. On the following day, autonomous union representation came to an abrupt end. Nazi officials conducted a massive nationwide sweep, arresting thousands of trade unionists and shutting down all independent labor organizations. In the place of unions, the Nazis set up the subservient Deutsche Arbeitsfront (DAF, German Labor Front).[9] Nazis were far less confrontational with business associations, but they dissolved them nonetheless in 1934, replacing them with the Reichsgruppe Industrie, which had compulsory membership and a subservient relationship with the Nazi state.

After the Second World War, Western occupying powers gradually restored freedom of association, but it was ultimately up to Germans themselves to decide how such freedom should be structured in a postwar republic. From the summer of 1948 to the spring of 1949, a constitutional convention consisting of representatives elected by the parliaments of the western German states (*Länder*) met to draft a provisional constitution, which they called the Basic Law (Grundgesetz). Article 9, section 3 of the Basic Law does not use the word "union" (*Gewerkschaft*), but it explicitly declares: "The right to form associations to safeguard and improve working and economic conditions shall be guaranteed to everyone and to all occupations." This expansive language, which includes all public-sector employees as well as white-collar employees with supervisory duties, exceeds the rights granted in many other countries (e.g., the United States). It should be noted that the general language of article 9, section 3 also gives firms full freedom to form employers associations. The only restriction in the realm of industrial relations is a ban on company-dominated unions. Courts have ruled that company unions deny employees a genuine right to freedom of association.[10]

Mindful of the compulsory nature of most Nazi organizations, court rulings have also interpreted article 9, section 3 of the Basic Law to protect the freedom *not* to be forced to belong to an organization, which in German legal parlance is called "negative freedom of association" (*negative Koalitionsfreiheit*). The doctrine of negative freedom of association forbids compulsory union membership (i.e., a "closed shop" or a "union shop") as a condition of employment, which is permissible in many English-speaking countries. Since the 1960s, court rulings have forbidden collective bargaining agreements that give some benefits to union members only, concluding that these amount to indirect pressure on employees to join a union. This interpretation of article 9, section 3 has deprived unions of a means to neutralize a significant free-rider problem that has deprived them of members and dues.[11] Still, the Basic Law contains the strongest language protecting the rights of both employees and employers to organize ever found in any German constitution.

Collective Bargaining and Contracts

Whereas freedom of association simply guarantees the right of unions and employers associations to exist, a collective bargaining regime goes one step further. It establishes the ground rules for negotiations between employers and trade unions, and—in instances when talks fail—industrial conflict. German jurisprudence has built out the concept of "collective bargaining autonomy" (*Tarifautonomie*) as a predicate of the freedom of association. Collective bargaining autonomy at its foundation should not be equated with the absence of state involvement. The state does provide substantial support for collective bargaining "without, however, involving itself in the substantive issues dealt with around the bargaining table."[12] To draw an analogy, the role of the German state in industrial relations is like that of a fish bowl. The state's role in defining and sustaining the contours of a highly constructed realm of industrial relations is crucial, but it is in the background and often not immediately apparent to actors and observers alike. If it were withdrawn, however, the state's full significance would become immediately apparent to all, just as fish would immediately notice the disappearance of their bowl. The state's supporting role in industrial relations is consistent with postwar Germany's general approach to regulation, which has been to create underlying "framework conditions" (*Rahmenbedingungen*) that tilt the playing field for economic decision making in a constructive direction, but then let private parties interact without interference.[13]

The German state did not always provide supportive framework conditions for collective bargaining. Before the First World War, collective bargaining was a precarious endeavor. Although Imperial Germany had a series of laws regulating working conditions, it had no industrial relations legislation. Collective agreements fell uneasily into the category of private contracts concluded by collective actors. Since cartels were legal in the Second Empire, there was no foundation in law to attack collective bargaining agreements as a restraint of trade, which was a common antiunion tactic in English-speaking countries at the time. Instead, judicial opinions varied widely. Some judges found collective bargaining agreements to be illegal, but others did not. A few judges even ruled that collective agreements were binding on all employees, including non-union members.[14]

The 1916 Auxiliary Patriotic Service Act ended the legal ambiguity surrounding collective bargaining agreements by definitively establishing their legitimacy, but it was only in the immediate post-Imperial years that the German state adopted specific legal ground rules for collective bargaining. The Collective Agreements Order (Tarifvertragsordnung, TVO) of 23 December 1918 laid the procedural foundation for collective bargaining in interwar Germany. The TVO had an unusual pedigree. Large portions of the order (which is quite short) came directly out of the Stinnes-Legien agreement that labor and management had crafted on their own six weeks earlier. The short-lived provisional German assembly passed it. The German government, working under the Weimar constitution, absorbed the TVO into German law. The new collective bargaining regime shifted most negotiations out of the workplace and into the hands of employers associations and the trade unions negotiating regionally for individual sectors, which helped to professionalize them and to reduce workplace-level conflict. It quickly took root and proved successful when it was used, but external circumstances reduced its application.[15]

The great inflation of 1923 compelled the German government to introduce a system of binding state arbitration as an option for settling labor disputes. This option gave the labor ministry the power to set compensation unilaterally, so long as the collective bargaining parties had agreed to submit themselves to it after negotiations had reached an impasse. During the mid-1920s, unions frequently resorted to state arbitration, taking advantage of a sympathetic labor ministry to achieve better contract results than could have been attained without intervention. Autonomous collective bargaining atrophied as a result. In 1928, poor economic conditions led the labor ministry to begin imposing settlements far less favorable to employees. In subsequent years, when economic conditions went from bad to worse as a result of the Great Depression, state arbitration awards became even more meager. The unions still used the arbitration regime, albeit reluctantly, because soaring unemployment undercut their capacity to wage successful strikes. In 1931, Chancellor Heinrich Brünning scrapped state arbitration. The horrendous unemployment of the time completely undercut union bargaining power, and real wages plummeted. When the Nazis came to power in 1933, they eliminated collective bargaining altogether when they wiped out autonomous trade unions.[16]

After the war, it took several years to reassemble a collective bargaining regime. The legislative components were once again put into place by a provisional government. On 9 April 1949, the assembly of the three united economic zones of western Germany passed the Tarifvertragsgesetz (TVG, Collective Agreements Act). The postwar German government subsequently adopted it as federal law. Just as in many other instances during the postwar reconstruction of Germany, the lawmakers decided to adhere very closely to the old law when drafting the new one. As a result, the structure, language, and even the name of the 1949 Collective Agreements Act echo the 1918 Collective Agreements Order. One portion of the Weimar collective bargaining regime was pointedly dropped, however. The Allies banned binding state arbitration under article 2, section 1 of Control Council Law 35 because of the bad experience with the practice during the Weimar Republic. The new Federal Republic of Germany followed suit.[17]

The Collective Agreements Act is short. It has only 1,600 words in the original German. Article 1 defines a collective agreement as a written contract that regulates the rights and duties of the collective bargaining parties concerning the "content, conclusion and termination of employment relations." Article 2 states that collective agreements are legally binding and only employers associations, individual employers, and trade unions are eligible to make collective agreements (*tariffähig*). Germans call a contract between a union and an employers association that covers all member firms of the association a "regionwide" collective bargaining agreement (*Flächentarifvertrag*). A regionwide agreement has been the most common contractual arrangement in German industrial relations. A regionwide agreement is binding on all employers association and union members in the sector and district specified in the contract. There is nothing like a regionwide collective bargaining agreement in English-speaking countries. The closest thing is pattern bargaining. Both pattern bargaining and regionwide bargaining have the same objective—that is, the elimination of competition on the basis of wage costs among firms in the same sector—but pattern bargaining is organized around firms rather than regions.

The typical sector has a set of regionwide districts for the purposes of collective bargaining. The number of districts varies from sector to sector, depending on the specific profile of that sector (e.g., the size of firms and regional concentrations of production facilities). Most sectors have between eight and twelve districts. For each sector, formal negotiations to produce a new set of regionwide agreements take place separately in the individual regional districts. In practice, however, the union leadership typically picks one district to serve as the "pilot." The lead negotiations take place in the pilot district, and, if talks break down, strikes normally occur there too. Union officials are strategic in selecting the district where a strike can be most effective economically and where the rank and file are motivated and capable.

Both the union and the employers associations in individual sectors generally prefer that all the other districts copy the results reached in the pilot district with little or no change, in order to avoid one region gaining a cost advantage over the others. The union and the confederation of employers associations for each sector have mechanisms designed to facilitate the spread of the pilot agreement to the other districts. The procedure for ratifying a regional contract within most unions typically includes approval by the union's national collective bargaining committee as a step, which makes rogue ratification of a regional contact impossible. The means of achieving nationwide uniformity on the employers' side of the table differ in several respects from those of the unions, reflecting crucial dissimilarities between employers associations and trade unions.

Employers associations are not mass organizations, their members are firms rather than individuals, and their membership typically numbers only in the hundreds or low thousands for each district within a sector. As a result, employers associations rely far more heavily than unions on direct and informal means, such as e-mail and telephone calls, to gain a sense of membership preferences. Reaching consensus has frequently proved to be much harder for employers. The greater difficulty is not surprising. Employers association membership is far more heterogeneous than that of trade unions. Member firms range from small shops to multinational enterprises. Some members are bitter rivals; others are linked along supply chains or engaged in joint ventures. In practice, the leadership of the national confederation for each sector takes a principal role in setting and executing the strategy for each collective bargaining round, but it does so only after extensive consultations with key members, both large and small. Since the 1990s, the national bodies of employers associations in many sectors have strengthened coordination by assembling a national collective bargaining advisory group with representatives from leading regional associations in the sector and requiring the national sectoral organization to be on hand during negotiations in pilot districts. The purpose of these groups is to improve communication and buy-in and to decrease the likelihood that member firms will balk at a compromise reached at the bargaining table.[18]

It should be noted that, in some sectors, the union and the national confederation of employers associations have tolerated differences in regional agreements. In most instances, the differences have been too small to produce significant regional divergences in labor costs. There are two prominent exceptions, however. First, in 1973, IG Metall's regional district in Baden-Württemberg agreed to a pilot framework agreement with the North Württemberg–North Baden mechanical engineering employers association that tightly regulated assembly line work and gave employees expansive break times.[19] No other regional employers association adopted this pilot framework agreement, which put Baden-Württemberg employers at a cost disadvantage vis-à-vis their competitors elsewhere in Germany until this agreement was replaced with a new one in the mid-2000s. Second, since German unification, the compensation agreements for eastern Germany in most sectors have set rates lower than those for the western regions.

TVG article 3 stipulates that all members of unions and employers associations remain bound by any regionwide collective agreement reached when they were members for the duration of those contracts even if they subsequently quit the organization. Firms cannot immediately escape the requirements of a collective agreement simply by leaving an association. This provision enhances the power of collective agreements and augments the stability of the organizations that sign them, in particular, employers associations.

Uniformity in collective agreements does not extend beyond the sectoral level. Labor market conditions differ too greatly from sector to sector, and the institutional architecture of German industrial relations is too fragmented along sectoral lines to facilitate the coordination of collective bargaining across the whole economy. Still, collective bargaining results in some sectors do affect outcomes in others. Each year the settlement achieved by one of the stronger unions (usually the metalworkers) sets the unofficial benchmark for all of the others.

The most common alternative to a regionwide collective agreement used in German industrial relations today is a single-firm contract (*Firmentarifvertrag*), which is often called a "house" agreement. The number of single-firm agreements has grown over the last thirty years, but they are still of secondary importance. In 2007, they only set compensation for 8 percent of all employees in western Germany and 13 percent in eastern Germany. Most house agreements only deviate from regionwide collective agreements at the margins.[20]

Whereas labor and management in most countries rely on a single contract to cover all aspects of their relationship, multiple specialized contracts are the norm in Germany. The social partners use three specialized accords: the compensation collective bargaining agreement (*Entgelttarifvertrag*, ETV, often just referred to as a *Tarifvertrag* or collective bargaining agreement); the framework collective bargaining agreement (*Rahmentarifvertrag*, RTV); and the skeleton collective bargaining agreement (*Manteltarifvertrag*, MTV).

The ETV is the most prominent of the three types of contracts. It sets pay and benefit rates. The media, central bankers, investors worldwide, public officials, and rank-and-file members of both trade unions and employers associations pay most attention to ETVs because they have the most immediate effect on pay and hence labor costs. ETVs are negotiated more frequently than any other type of contract. The duration of a typical ETV is one year, though variance from this norm is not unusual. Longer ETVs are most often the product of a more comprehensive agreement to phase in a new benefit (e.g., weekly working-time reduction), hard times, or the desire to provide more certainty for employers regarding future labor costs. Sometimes union negotiators ask for a thirteen- or fourteen-month contract so that the total wage increase over the life of the agreement is bigger than it would be for a twelve-month accord. This enables union officials to present a percentage increase to their members that is nominally closer to the initial union demand than a twelve-month agreement would allow. ETVs very rarely extend to three years in length, which is the typical duration of a US collective agreement. At times, when economic conditions have been especially unpredictable, the bargaining parties have agreed to ETVs as short as eight or nine months, but this is also quite rare.[21]

The second type of German contract, the framework agreement, defines the job classifications and compensation structure within individual sectors. Jobs are defined by the tasks involved, educational requirements, and experience. Often, the classifications can be quite general, so that the thousands of firms using the same classification scheme can easily adapt them to their specific needs. RTVs are extremely technical and notoriously complex. They are nonetheless quite important because they establish the underlying framework for how work gets done and how one is paid for doing it. They also establish the relative importance of education, work duties, and experience in determining compensation.

In most instances, decades pass before the collective bargaining parties renegotiate framework agreements. The long intervals between negotiations are problematic because as framework agreements age, the occupational specifications they contain grow increasingly out of date. Old agreements have contained occupations that no longer exist (e.g., computer-card key punchers) and failed to provide guidance regarding the duties and pay for whole new classes of employees (e.g., webmasters) and work practices (e.g., group and home work). When the gap between an RTV and actual practice becomes too great, labor and management find that they can no longer put off a more comprehensive revision of the RTV. The collective bargaining parties wrote their first RTVs in the late 1940s and early 1950s. Most sectors in Germany drafted completely new RTVs during the 1960s. The microprocessing revolution of the 1980s prompted the production of a third generation of RTVs approximately a decade later.

Historically, private-sector RTVs had five to eight blue-collar wage groups, within which pay was pegged to either piece rates or hourly work, and three to five white-collar salary groups. Starting in the 1990s, individual sectors have increasingly adopted a single set of job classifications that cover all their employees, be they blue- or white-collar workers. The transition has occurred because automation has made blue- and white-collar work less distinct, class difference has become less salient in postwar German society, and simpler job classification schemes provide more flexibility and are cheaper and easier to manage. Contemporary RTVs typically have five to eight job categories for all employees based on tasks, technical knowledge, and experience. They provide for pay in the form of a monthly salary for all, but employees still receive a premium for doing overtime and extra work.

An analogous transformation occurred in the public sector. The public sector used the Federal Collective Agreement for Public Employees (Bundes-Angestellten-Tarif, BAT) as a framework agreement from 1961 to the mid-2000s. The BAT was a relic from a bygone era of paternalism and bureaucratic complexity. The BAT had over 16,000 attributes to determine compensation. The most important were age, seniority, and family size. Job performance was *not* an attribute. The result was a complex and arbitrary pay determination that did not reward the best performers.

After years of talks, negotiators completed a new framework agreement called the Tarifvertrag für den öffentlichen Dienst (TVöD, Collective Bargaining Agreement for the Public Service Sector) in 2005. The TVöD is a significant departure from the BAT. It eliminates the old demographic categories for wage determination, sets a new lower baseline category (to enable the public sector to bring down costs to the level of private-sector firms providing similar services), and makes performance central to pay, which is a revolution in the German public service sector. The bargaining parties were both satisfied with the TVöD, but the agreement has not been popular with some of the union rank and file, particularly those who no longer receive the supplemental payments specified in the old contract.

The third type of contract, the MTV or skeleton collective agreement, regulates the remaining terms and conditions of employment not covered by an ETV or RTV. MTVs include such things as weekly working time, overtime, maternity leave, sick pay, bonuses, vacation benefits, and severance provisions. Most MTVs consist of a main body followed by a series of independent contracts addressing particular items (e.g., vacation time and pay) attached as appendices. As a rule, an MTV is long and contains very general language because hundreds of firms use them. Managers and works councillors in individual enterprises apply broad provisions of an MTV to meet their specific needs. The parties to collective bargaining typically renegotiate at least some portion of an MTV every three to five years. Besides these three types of contracts, many collective bargaining parties have created special contracts to address particular concerns in several sectors. The most common special contracts provide for employee stock ownership, further education, layoff protection, and supplemental retirement.

This constellation of complementary collective agreements is complex, to be sure, but it does provide for more flexibility than is immediately apparent. After all, contracts differ significantly from sector to sector. The nested arrangement of contracts permits bargaining parties to focus on different aspects of industrial relations incrementally as need arises. The contracts are also meant to set minimum standards. TVG article 4 contains the so-called favorableness principle (*Günstigkeitsprinzip*) that allows management to *improve* compensation unilaterally above the rates spelled out in a regionwide collective agreement but not to undercut it. Firms may pay more if they wish, and many do so in order to remain competitive within a tight local labor market, to reduce turnover, or to attract the best employees. Employers and works councils may also negotiate a "workplace agreement" (*Betriebsvereinbarung*), which would supplement a collective agreement, in order to codify understandings regarding extra compensation that are specific to a workplace. An agreement with a works council does not fall under the protection of the TVG because works councils are not eligible to be a party to a collective agreement as defined by article 2 of the act. Agreements to provide workplace compensation *below* the contractually specified minima are also permitted, but *only* if the collective bargaining parties both agree.

Article 5 of the TVG provides a means to use the state to expand the reach and stability of the postwar collective bargaining regime. Article 5 authorizes the Federal Ministry of Labor and Social Affairs to issue a "declaration of general applicability" (*allgemeine Verbindlichkeitserklärung*, AVE, aka *erga omnes* declaration), which is a decree that extends the coverage of an existing regionwide collective agreement to *all* businesses in a bargaining district of a sector, including firms that are not members of the employers association. The purpose of a declaration of general applicability is to establish a floor to wages. There are important differences between an AVE and a minimum wage. A nationwide minimum wage typically sets an extremely low floor because it must be geared not to disrupt employment in the most basic unskilled segments of the economy. AVEs, in contrast, set a much more rigorous standard because they are tailored to each sector and include all compensation. In essence, article 5 provides the opportunity to establish prevailing compensation rates specific to individual sectors. It should also be noted that AVEs amplify the reach of sectoral collective bargaining, whereas a nationwide minimum wage reduces it.

AVEs are not automatic. An employer, employers association, or trade union must ask for one. The federal labor minister then decides whether to submit the request to the ministry's collective bargaining committee, which consists of three employers association and three trade union representatives. If the committee approves the AVE (which it usually does), then the labor minister issues it. Article 5 also states that only contracts that cover at least a majority of employees in the bargaining district for the sector in question are eligible to be declared generally applicable. Since the unionization rate in individual sectors and regions of the German economy has rarely ever amounted to a majority of those employed, it is the high density of employers associations that have made most sectors in western Germany eligible for an AVE.

It is important, however, not to overstate the significance of AVEs in German industrial relations. AVEs have never set compensation for more than 5 percent of the labor force. AVEs are rarely if ever used in heavy manufacturing or the public sector in western Germany, because few employers have relied on a business model that depended on undercutting the regionwide collective agreement. That having been said, the very existence of article 5 has dissuaded employers at the margins from trying to gain a competitive edge through lower labor costs. AVEs have been more influential in sectors with large numbers of small firms, such as janitorial services, hotels, restaurants, and the retail trade.

Over the last two decades, AVEs have become a less effective means to police the labor market. First, many eastern German employees and foreign nationals, desperate for work, have accepted without complaint jobs paying far below the minima set in collective agreements from employers. Second, membership density in regional employers associations throughout many sectors in eastern Germany has fallen well below the threshold needed to qualify for an AVE. So, this avenue of redress is often not available there. Third, in a few instances over the last twenty years, the employer representatives on the federal labor ministry's collective bargaining committee refused to approve a declaration of general applicability. Fourth, foreign firms and foreign subsidiaries of German companies primarily in construction and related sectors have increasingly "posted" employees from abroad to work in Germany on fixed contracts paying foreign wages that are well below German rates. This practice falls outside of the purview of TVG article 5.[22]

Germany began to address the erosion of coverage of collective agreements in the mid-1990s. The Christian Democratic–led government under Chancellor Helmut Kohl first spearheaded passage of an EU directive that permitted member states to regulate compensation for posted employees.[23] The government then passed the Employee Posting Act (Arbeitnehmer-Entsendegesetz) in 1996, which extended the German government's power to issue a new type of AVE that would cover foreign-based construction companies working in Germany.[24] Unlike TVG article 5, the Employee Posting Act does not require a collective agreement to cover at least a majority of employees in the bargaining district for the sector in question as a precondition to converting a contract into a generally applicable compensation floor. This solution made it possible for the collective bargaining parties in the construction sector to create contracts that set minimum rates specifically for posted employees, which they have done since 1997. These collective agreements have produced a practical compromise that sets wages for posted employees significantly lower than standard domestic rates but substantially higher than what they had previously received.[25]

The Employee Posting Act set a precedent that drew the attention of those interested in establishing wage floors for other sectors where wages were extraordinarily low but an article 5 AVE could not be used because trade union and employers association membership was too low. Several years of political wrangling ensued because opinions on the matter were divided within both business and labor circles. Many businesses, especially those in the sectors experiencing cutthroat wage competition, favored extending the act, but the peak confederation of employers associations opposed it, in large part because the act cut the confederation out of the new process for declaring contracts generally applicable. Some union officials expressed a preference for a nationwide minimum wage over this system of extending special contracts in only the most hard-hit sectors. In 2006, a "grand coalition" government under the chancellorship of Christian Democrat Angela Merkel finally garnered enough support simply to amend the Employee Posting Act to include six new sectors: janitorial services, private postal delivery, private security, specialized coal mining duties, laundry, and waste management. The amendment still failed to curb cutthroat wage competition because the Employee Posting Act applied only to foreign firms using posted employees in Germany. Consequently, the Merkel grand coalition government followed up with the separate Minimum Working Conditions Act (Mindestarbeitsbedingungengesetz) that applies to domestic firms in low-wage sectors that do not qualify for an article 5 AVE because of low trade union and employers association membership.[26] The Minimum Working Conditions Act, which includes the nursing care, private security, and waste management sectors, borrows the mechanism from the Employee Posting Act that permits the conversion of special collective agreements written by the trade union and employers associations in a designated sector into a generally applicable compensation floor. Since 2009, special sectoral minimum compensation provisions have covered twelve sectors particularly prone to low-wage employment.[27]

Union officials see widening the scope for using AVEs as an important means to shore up collective bargaining coverage. Proposals include eliminating the 50 percent coverage threshold to qualify for an AVE, removing the need to have the labor ministry's collective bargaining committee approve all AVEs, and permitting the extension of AVEs to comparable sectors.[28] For example, at the 2011 convention of the Vereinte Dienstleistungsgewerkschaft (ver.di, United Service Employees Union), ver.di chair Frank Bsirske declared, "Lowering the hurdles for general declarations of applicability; that currently is among our most important demands in advance of the 2013 Bundestag election."[29] The Employee Posting Act and Minimum Working Conditions Act show that the German government can and will take steps to buttress the industrial relations regime. The fact that Christian Democratic chancellors headed the two governments that passed these acts demonstrates that support for the postwar industrial relations regime extends across party lines. In recent years, several German states have passed prevailing-wage legislation (*Tariftreugesetze*) that restricts government procurement only to firms that pay at least the collective bargaining rate. These patches on the German industrial relations regime have slowed the decline in collective bargaining coverage. Their efficacy as long-run solutions remains unclear, however. Maintaining membership density remains a challenge in both unions and employers associations, and in the past five years, courts outside of the industrial relations regime have challenged this sort of legislation as a solution.

Within Germany, the Berlin Administrative Court (Verwaltungsgericht) struck down a 2008 AVE issued for the private postal delivery sector based on a technicality. The court decided that the labor ministry committed a grave procedural error by instituting the AVE without first soliciting the written position of private postal sector firms. The Federal Administrative Court upheld the decision in 2010. The European Court of Justice has also issued a series of rulings curtailing posting directives (i.e., Laval, Luxembourg, Rüffert, and Viking). The broader political arguments surrounding these cases have pitted the freedom of association against the free movement of people, but the actual decisions have been grounded in narrow technicalities, specifically, failures to implement the posting directive to the letter of the law. The German and European posting directives remain on the books. Since employers are always looking to cut costs, new court cases challenging them are likely to arise in the future.[30]

All German collective agreements spell out the parties' binding contractual commitments (*schuldrechtliche Verpflichtungen*) to one another in what is known as the "obligatory" portion of the document. Failure to uphold any obligatory commitments leaves the offending party vulnerable to a damage suit, which can be quite costly, depending on the violation. The most salient obligatory component of most contracts in the manufacturing sector is the so-called peace obligation (*Friedenspflicht*). The peace obligation forbids strikes and lockouts for the duration of the accord. The obligatory portion of German collective agreements also routinely contains a mediation procedure, which begins once a contract expires. This portion of the contract also typically has an "expanded peace obligation" clause that extends the ban on industrial action to the mediation period. If mediation fails, a union is then free to engage in a strike. Contracts with these obligations became the norm in manufacturing during the 1950s.[31]

In practice, the overwhelming majority of collective negotiations in Germany result in an agreement without resort to industrial action, but strikes do happen. Before launching a discussion of industrial disputes, however, it is essential to say something about the bodies that have produced the jurisprudence that regulates them, namely, the labor courts.

Labor Courts

The system of labor courts serves as "the backbone of labor relations and labor law in Germany."[32] The creation of specialized courts to deal with commercial and labor matters in Germany dates back to the late nineteenth century. Previously, civil courts heard labor disputes, but they lacked the expertise to adjudicate properly the expanding number of statutes regulating industry and working conditions. In 1890, the Imperial German government established specialized industrial courts and in 1904 added commercial courts (*Handelsgerichte*) modeled after French *tribunaux de commerce* to hear cases involving commercial activity. These courts used tripartite panels (*Kammer*) of three judges. The chair of each panel was either a professional judge or civil servant. The other two panel members were lay judges (*ehrenamtliche Richter*). One came from the ranks of employees and the other from among the employers. Trade unionists were still dissatisfied with this arrangement, however, because courts at times subordinated the employment relationship to other concerns of enterprises. During the Weimar Republic, organized labor agitated for the creation of specialized labor courts that would be institutionally independent and have enlarged competence. In 1926, the government passed the Labor Courts Act (Arbeitsgerichtsgesetz), which created a new system of labor courts and gave it sole jurisdiction over all legal disputes concerning labor and employment law involving employees. The law borrowed the tripartite model from the industry and commercial courts and established a three-tier structure of local courts, regional appellate courts, and the Imperial Labor Court (Reichsarbeitsgericht) as the court of last instance.[33] Once in place, labor courts played an important role in the industrial relations of the Weimar Republic. The collective bargaining parties and individual actors resorted to them frequently and generally obeyed their rulings.

When Adolf Hitler rose to power, the labor courts were not dismantled, but the Nazis invoked their *Führerprinzip* (leadership principle) to justify rendering them subservient to the political leadership. In practice, Nazi labor courts were heavily biased in favor of employers. This core component of Nazi ideology also sanctioned employers to act unilaterally in a paternalistic fashion in the workplace and admonished employees simply to follow the orders of their superiors. In 1946, the Allied Control Council of the four occupying powers enacted Law No. 21, which reestablished local and regional labor courts with judicial independence. German lawmakers integrated elements of Law No. 21 and the old 1926 act to create a new Labor Courts Act, which passed in 1953 and was amended in 1979.[34]

German labor courts today have the same exclusive jurisdiction over labor and employment law as did the Weimar courts. The system has three tiers: labor courts (*Arbeitsgerichte*) at the local level; state labor courts (*Landesarbeitsgerichte*, LAG), which hear appeals; and the Federal Labor Court (Bundesarbeitsgericht, BAG), which is the court of last instance unless a constitutional question is involved. On those occasions, an appeal to the Federal Constitutional Court (Bundesverfassungsgericht, BVG), which is Germany's supreme court, is possible. European Court of Justice decisions are also binding on all German courts. Local labor courts have retained the tripartite three-judge panels first introduced during the Second Empire. The number of panels in each locality varies, depending on the size of the population. The chair is a full-time judge with a lifetime appointment. The labor minister of each state appoints the lay judges, relying heavily on lists of potential candidates that the trade unions and employers associations suggest. There is no requirement that lay judges have any legal training, and many do not. State labor courts are also composed of tripartite three-judge panels, the difference being that only those with at least five years of experience as a lay labor court judge at the local level are eligible to be appointed to serve on a state labor court.[35]

The 1953 Labor Courts Act added the Federal Labor Court as a single court of last instance above the state level. The BAG started hearing cases in 1954. It was in Kassel until 1999 when it moved to Erfurt, the capital of the eastern state of Thuringia. The Federal Labor Court is organized into several specialized "senates." There are currently ten. Each senate hears cases within a subsection of the labor law and is composed of three full-time judges and two lay judges, one drawn from the ranks of employees and the other from the employers. Thus, full-time judges voting as a bloc possess a majority. The federal labor minister appoints all the judges according to the Federal Republic's general guidelines for selecting judges and, unlike at the lower levels, without consulting employers associations or trade unions. Individual BAG senates hear routine cases. If an appeal addresses a fundamental question of labor law that could set a new precedent, the "full senate" (*grosser Senat*) of the BAG hears the case. The full senate includes the chief justice of the BAG, four full-time justices, the senior chairs of the BAG senates, one lay employee judge, and one lay employer judge. The BAG has continued a tradition first articulated by labor courts of the Weimar Republic that envisions the preservation of "social order" as the principal mission of the industrial relations system and the maintenance of balance between the social partners as the best means to accomplish this end.

The jurisdiction of German labor courts is broad. It covers cases involving employers associations, trade unions, and any dispute between an employer and an employee. The latter include individual cases involving wrongful dismissals, compensation, damages, and complaints regarding the contents of references. Over the last three decades, the number of new cases filed annually has ranged between 350,000 and 660,000. At the end of each year, pending cases have ranged from over 100,000 to over 250,000. The heavy reliance on labor courts to settle individual disputes in German industrial relations has proved to be both extremely slow and highly costly. It even has its own name, "juridification" (*Verrechtlichung*), which is typically used pejoratively. Juridification is by no means new; it was a feature of industrial relations in the Weimar Republic.[36]

In the realm of collective bargaining, both the BAG and BVG have explicitly embraced the "parity principle" (*Paritätsprinzip*) as a guiding doctrine. It holds that neither collective bargaining party should enjoy systematic advantage over the other. In practice, achieving parity entails using "the system of collective bargaining contracts . . . to balance out the structural inferiority of individual employees when making employment contracts."[37] Courts have protected "collective bargaining sovereignty" (*Tarifhoheit*) and autonomy—that is, the right to produce private law in the form of collective agreements—free from state intervention, so long as that private law is consistent with statute and precedent and does not knock out of alignment the balance of power between the social partners.[38] The parity principle has provided considerable stability even in tumultuous economic and political times because courts punish actors that attempt to use labor market muscle to cripple or to destroy their opposite number. The plainest and most frequent manifestation of courts enforcing the parity principle is in the regulation of industrial disputes.[39]

Strikes and Lockouts

As mentioned earlier, the Basic Law only explicitly grants freedom of association, but it says nothing about rights or limits regarding industrial conflict.[40] Courts in the postwar era have filled this void by producing jurisprudence to define the contours of the permissible in industrial disputes. It is now settled law that the German constitution implicitly grants a right to engage in industrial conflict.[41] That right has limits, however. A doctrine of German jurisprudence first developed by prominent legal scholar Hans Carl Nipperdy established "social appropriateness" (*Sozialadäquanz*) and "societal balance" as measures for determining a strike's legality. Newspaper publishers hired Nipperdy to write a brief for a case involving a two-day strike by the printers union in May 1952. The union struck to protest as inadequate the draft of the Works Constitution Act (Betriebsverfassungsgesetz) that was before the Bundestag and to pressure the government to alter the draft legislation to make it more favorable to labor. The newspapers asserted that the strike was illegal and were seeking a damage settlement from the union. Nipperdy contended that strikes must be socially appropriate and balanced to be legal and presented three assessment criteria: (1) the strike must be directed against an employer or employers association; (2) it must be a strike over wages or working conditions; and (3) the goal of the strike must be the conclusion of a collective bargaining agreement between a union and one or more employers.[42]

Nipperdy argued that the newspaper strike met none of these criteria. At the time, the court of last instance was the *Land* labor court of each state, because the Federal Labor Court did not yet exist. *Land* labor courts in all the states except for West Berlin found the Nipperdy argument persuasive and decided in favor of the newspaper publishers. The case became an important precedent.[43]

Labor leaders have groused publicly about this interpretation of German law ever since because it confines the subject of legal industrial action to wages and working conditions, thereby precluding strikes to influence government policies or to affect other decisions at a firm, such as investment. Unionists regularly assert that the Nipperdy criteria do not impinge on labor's "duty" to strike if undemocratic elements ever seize power again in Germany. Fortunately, circumstances have never arisen in postwar Germany that would have led to putting labor's interpretation to the test.[44] Occasionally, unions have staged what have amounted to political strikes in order to influence government policy (e.g., in 1986 during an effort to thwart the amendment of article 116 of the Employment Promotion Act),[45] but they have kept them brief and called them "protests" instead of strikes. Governments typically have not challenged such actions in court. The Nipperdy criteria are the oldest postwar precedent in labor law, but challenges to them persist. A minority view in the German legal community has questioned the Nipperdy approach, arguing that since state regulation has become increasingly important in industrial relations, labor should therefore be permitted to influence it by using industrial action. The Nipperdy criteria have also run afoul of European jurisprudence. In 1998, the Ministerial Committee of the Council of Europe found a ban on noneconomic strikes to be incompatible with article 6, section 4 of the European Social Charter, which addresses collective bargaining rights. To date, however, no cases have arisen in German courts to prompt changes to the doctrine.[46]

The first case that came before the newly created Federal Labor Court in 1954, which concerned the right to strike, provided an opportunity to elaborate on the Nipperdy criteria. The court's ruling, which was handed down in 1955, recognized the strike as a collective and therefore protected action that did not breach an individual labor contract. The ruling included a definition of "legitimate" strikes that not only embraced the Nipperdy criteria of social appropriateness (which came as no surprise because Hans Carl Nipperdy served as the first president of the Federal Labor Court) but also added more qualifications. First, it specified that only parties capable of signing collective agreements as stated in TVG article 2 can engage in industrial disputes, reinforcing the prohibition against political strikes. Second, the court stated that a strike is legal only if it is a last resort (*ultima ratio*) after all other means to settle a dispute have been exhausted. In other words, it is illegal to strike or to lock out employees without first going through established settlement mechanisms (e.g., negotiation and meditation).[47] Third, the 1955 BAG ruling stated that it was essential that the collective bargaining parties maintain an "equality of weapons" (*Waffengleichheit*), which in practice legalized the option of employers to lock out employees. Lockouts, the court argued, give employers an opportunity to counterbalance the tactical advantage unions have because labor leaders get to pick the location and extent of strikes. The court's 1955 ruling gave employers substantial discretion in the use of lockouts. It stated that once a collective agreement and any additional contractual peace obligation expired an employer was free to initiate a lockout even if no employee had yet struck. This is known as an "offensive lockout" (*Angriffsaussperrung*). The ruling also held that employers have no obligation to rehire locked out employees once an industrial conflict ended.[48]

As German society demonstrated greater affluence and confidence in the postwar democracy, new justices replaced old and jurisprudence evolved. In 1971, the BAG added the concepts of "parity of forces" (*Kampfparität*) and "proportionality" (*Verhältnismässigkeit*) as important new refinements of the parity principle that had guided German jurisprudence in industrial relations since the Weimar Republic. The court justified the need for these additional criteria by pointing out that strikes adversely affected others beyond the immediate participants and therefore should be contained as much as possible. In practice, proportionality has three dimensions. First, the size of an industrial conflict should be proportionate to what is necessary to achieve the stated goals in the dispute. Second, no side should aim to destroy the other through industrial conflict. Third, the participants in an industrial action must restore industrial peace as soon and as fully as possible once a dispute is over.[49]

The BAG has used the new criteria to reverse much of the 1955 decision regarding lockouts. In 1971, the court ruled that lockouts merely suspend rather than end the employment relationship; employers therefore must reemploy locked out workers once an industrial dispute has ended before it can hire other employees. In 1980, the court reaffirmed the permissibility of lockouts, but it sought to limit their use through a mathematical formula. The formula itself is somewhat arbitrary; it is largely a product of the specifics of the strike that was the subject of the 1980 case. If less than one-fourth of the workforce in a bargaining district is on strike, an employer may lock out up to one-fourth of the employees in addition to the strikers. For larger strikes, the court argued that the employers needed proportionately fewer lockouts to neutralize a union's tactical advantage. If between one-fourth and one-half of the employees are striking, an employer may lock out employees until a maximum of one-half of the entire workforce is either striking or locked out. If a majority of the workforce is on strike, lockouts are no longer legal. The BAG in the same decision indicated in passing that offensive lockouts were incompatible with the parity principle, but no test case has arisen since to clarify the matter.[50]

The 1980 BAG decision sparked considerable speculative discussion within legal circles about "lockout arithmetic." Experts attempted to use the ratios and reasoning that the court provided to fill in the remainder of the frontier to distinguish proportionate from disproportionate lockouts, but a 1988 BAG decision rejected this exercise. It stated that there is no abstract boundary defining proportionality; each case must be judged on its own merits. The BAG did find that proportionality precludes employers associations from responding to a small strike by locking out huge numbers of employees. Specifically, the court ruled that a nationwide lockout in the printing industry in response to a strike involving fewer than 10 percent of all printing employees was disproportionate. Since the 1980s, lockouts have become extraordinarily rare. As a result, no new jurisprudence has been produced on the topic.[51]

The BAG has also been active in defining permissible behavior regarding strikes. The court allows union leaders considerable discretion over setting the targets, extent, and timing of economic strikes. When selecting targets, union officials pay careful consideration to firm vulnerability, spillover effects, the capacity of local union branches to wage an effective campaign, and the impact on the union's strike fund. The BAG has used the *ultima ratio* principle mentioned earlier to make holding a strike vote using a secret ballot a necessary prerequisite to a "full" (*unbefristet*) strike. Typically only one or two union districts out of a nationwide total of ten to fifteen hold a vote. In the few sectors that have single national contracts, a nationwide strike vote is held. The execution of a strike vote is an internal union matter. Union officials use the process not only to poll the membership but also to maximize internal support and to demonstrate resolve externally. Only union members are permitted to vote, and union officials write and count the ballots. Union officials craft the ballot in a way that leaves no doubt as to the preferred outcome. Union statutes require at least 75 percent of the votes cast to support a walkout in order to proceed with a full strike. Given union officials' control over the process, attaining at least 75 percent has been routine. If a provisional settlement is reached only after a strike has begun, German unions require a second vote. It takes a supermajority of 75 percent to *reject* a settlement, with the logic being that it should take the same percentage of the vote to continue a strike as it takes to launch one. This requirement opens up the possibility that a majority could reject a settlement without the "no" vote reaching the 75 percent threshold required to continue a strike. In such instances (which have been rare) the tentative agreement still proceeds through the ratification process.[52]

The jurisprudence regarding full strikes is relatively straightforward, but it is not so clear regarding other types of strikes. The *ultima ratio* principle makes wildcat strikes illegal, but the Federal Labor Court ruled in 1976 that "warning strikes"—that is, half-day walkouts in the midst of negotiations—are legal even if they depart from the *ultima ratio* principle. The court reasoned that warning strikes accelerate reaching a settlement because their intent is to show resolve rather than to apply economic pressure. After the 1976 ruling, some unions took advantage of the exception granted for warning strikes by developing a tactic called "new mobility." This tactic deploys waves of warning strikes that critics have denounced as crossing the line beyond an expression of resolve. Still, the BAG decided in 1984 and again in 1988 not to ban new mobility tactics because each individual action was of the size and scope of a warning strike. In practice these court decisions have eroded the *ultima ratio* principle.[53] The Federal Labor Court has also tackled the difficult issue of sympathy strikes (*Unterstützungsstreiks*), which are strikes in support of another group of employees who are engaged in an industrial dispute. In 1988, the BAG ruled that sympathy strikes are lawful only when they benefit those for whom the sympathy strikers are striking but not the sympathy strikers themselves. The BAG revisited the question of sympathy strikes in 2007, ruling that proportionality is necessary for such a strike to be legal.[54]

There has been only one recent court ruling that challenges rather than bolsters the status quo. In June 2010, the Federal Labor Court ruled that a foundational concept of postwar German industrial relations—namely, that each workplace should have only one collective agreement—was incompatible with the German constitution's protection of the freedom of association. In practice, the ruling makes it easier for small "occupational unions" (*Berufsgewerkschaften*) to carve out niche positions at choke points in the economy and negotiate contracts that are more generous than those secured by the larger unions. The ruling sent shock waves throughout not only the union movement but also the employers associations. The latter feared more frequent industrial disputes and small unions whipsawing their associations for greater compensation. The employers associations and the larger established unions initially denounced the court's ruling and jointly proposed legislation to reverse it by extending all aspects of any collective agreement covering the plurality of employees in a workplace—including the "peace obligation" that restricts strikes—to all unions and their members in that workplace.[55] The federal government was open to making these changes, but a year after the court ruling, the second largest German union, ver.di, reversed its position and came out against the draft legislation. Ver.di leaders explained that they still supported the principle of "one workplace, one union" but that they did not favor protecting it by making the peace obligation legally binding throughout the German economy. The peace obligation has been the norm in manufacturing, but many of the service sectors under ver.di's jurisdiction do not have it. Ver.di's shift stopped the legislation cold.[56] So far, the impact of the court ruling has been negligible. Moreover, the willingness of the center-right Merkel government to pass legislation aimed at reversing the court ruling is further evidence of the willingness of leading politicians, regardless of party, to take action to preserve the integrity of the postwar industrial relations regime.

Taken in full, courts in postwar Germany have sculpted industrial conflict into a highly controlled exercise of economic muscle to be used solely to settle individual disputes rather than existential struggles between capital and labor. The role of courts in postwar German industrial relations is a prime manifestation of state activism to preserve the status quo. The evidence in this chapter shows a legal edifice that continues to function effectively. It suffers from neither erosion nor exhaustion. Beyond the courts, the postwar German state has bolstered the social partners through the use of tripartite bodies to govern numerous aspects of German society, both economic and noneconomic. These tripartite bodies are therefore worthy of some consideration here.

Tripartite Bodies in Postwar Germany

Germany, like many other northern European countries, frequently uses neocorporatist forms of governance. Distinctive features of the neocorporatist approach include government designation of interest groups (such as employers associations and trade unions) as official representatives of certain segments of society, government consultation with these groups as a part of the decision-making process, and derogation to interest groups of the execution of some traditional government tasks.[57] Tripartite bodies composed of business, labor, and government representatives manage all important aspects of the welfare state. For example, in a tradition dating back to the nineteenth century, Germany uses boards consisting of an equal number of employee and employer representatives to supervise management at each of the more than five hundred providers of social insurance (i.e., accident, health, hospice, and retirement insurance). Every six years, Germany holds "social elections" to fill these seats. In practice, the social partners determine who ends up on these boards. The trade unions generally endorse only as many employee candidates at each provider as there are employee seats available. Other candidates rarely enter the race. The result is a noncontested "peaceful election" (*Friedenswahl*). The employers associations do the same for the employers' seats. Consequently, German trade unions and employers associations have considerable influence over social insurance providers.[58] With the adoption of postal balloting in 1974, participation had been stable at 43 to 44 percent between 1974 and 1993. Participation began to drop thereafter, falling to 30.8 percent in 2005, indicating a deterioration of the social milieu of both business and labor. Participation slipped only marginally further in 2011, dropping to 29.4 percent.[59] The social partners also have designated seats on the German states' media councils, which are neocorporatist bodies that advise state radio and television outlets on programming and the use of the media for the public good, and are regular board members on numerous charities and not-for-profit groups.

The most important corporatist body in the German labor market is not an insurance provider but a parapublic institution: the Federal Employment Agency (Bundesagentur für Arbeit, BA). The BA was created as the Federal Employment Office (Bundesanstalt für Arbeit) in 1969 as a part of the Employment Promotion Act (Arbeitsförderungsgesetz, AFG), but antecedents date back to the Weimar Republic. The BA is an independent agency managed by a board of employee, employer, and government representatives. The BA's duties include job placement (over which it has a monopoly in Germany), the calculation and distribution of unemployment insurance, job creation programs, vocational counseling, and vocational training. The BA has a four-tier structure. Beneath the headquarters in Nürnberg there are ten "regional managements" (*Regionaldirektionen*), 178 "employment agencies" (*Agenturen für Arbeit*) and 610 branches (*Geschäftsstellen*). The principal source of funds for the BA is a payroll tax borne equally by employees and employers. For some time, the BA has also received a supplemental payment out of general revenues to make up for budget deficits, which arise when expenditures exceed the payroll taxes collected.[60]

When unemployment swelled starting in the 1970s, so did the BA. Between 1970 and 1980, the BA's budget increased more than sixfold, from an equivalent of €2 billion (4 billion deutschmarks, $2.6 billion) to €13 billion. From 1980 to 1988, it almost doubled, moving to €23 billion. By the turn of the century, the BA had ninety thousand employees; a substantial portion of the staff consisted of bureaucrats trained only in the intricacies of Germany's complex system for determining individual unemployment benefits. By 2004, the BA's budget had more than doubled again. It stood at €56 billion, which amounted to 20 percent of total public expenditures. To fund this explosive growth, the unemployment insurance tax, which employees and employers pay jointly, rose from 3 percent of payroll in 1980 to 4.3 percent in 1990 and to 6.5 percent in 1993.[61] The unemployment insurance tax remained at that rate until 2007 when the government cut it to 4.2 percent in a bid to stimulate hiring. A series of smaller cuts followed. As of 2011, the tax rate returned to 3 percent. Significant declines in the number of unemployed since 2005 have enabled the BA to avoid massive budget deficits despite the tax cuts.[62]

The tripartite governance structure of the BA gives the social partners control over what is a significant share of total public expenditure. Critics, such as Wolfgang Streeck, assert that trade unions and employers associations have "captured" the BA and subverted its mission to fulfill particularistic needs at the expense of the economy as a whole. A series of publicly subsidized early retirement schemes introduced in the 1980s and 1990s permitted the unions to provide additional benefits to members. Employers used the system to externalize the cost of increasing productivity through labor shedding and to reduce the average age of their workforces. Much of the BA's active labor market funding that poured into eastern Germany after unification was used to purchase services from training and educational outfits with close ties to trade unions. The government tolerated the social partners' abuses because it was exploiting the system too. Relatively generous unemployment insurance benefits bought social peace for some time. During the 1990 federal election campaign, Chancellor Kohl pledged that German unification would not require any major tax increases. Immediately after the campaign, which Kohl's coalition won, the government drew heavily on the BA's funds in an effort to pay for the rising cost of unification while honoring Kohl's campaign promise. This dysfunctional use of the BA did not last. Within a few years, the BA's reserves were exhausted, and the Kohl government introduced a "solidarity surcharge" to income taxes.[63]

A scandal that engulfed the Bundesanstalt in late 2001 and early 2002 provided an opportunity for reform. It came to light that for years the BA had been falsifying data on its success rate in making job placements. In response, the German government assembled a commission of experts in 2002 headed by Peter Hartz, chief of personnel at Volkswagen, to develop a proposal for a comprehensive overhaul of the BA. The Hartz Commission, at the urging of the Gerhard Schröder government, expanded the mandate of the commission to address the problem of unemployment in general.[64] The reforms of the BA, most of which were adopted in 2003 and came into effect in 2004, endeavored to break the bureaucratic culture, to streamline the structure, and to transform the BA into an agile job-placement service. The organization changed its name from the Federal Employment Office to the Federal Employment Agency in order to make the BA sound less like a government agency and more like a private job-placement firm. Changing culture and practice within the BA has been difficult. BA personnel claim that they are far too under-resourced, understaffed, and undertrained to be an effective, consumer-oriented placement agency. Critics point to such claims as indicative of a hidebound bureaucratic mentality that is still prevalent in the agency. Management debacles, such as the purchase of ineffectual software in the mid-2000s, have not helped.[65] Unemployment has come down in recent years, but the bulk of the progress is due to the labor market reforms of the Schröder government and declining unit labor costs vis-à-vis Germany's trading partners in the euro area rather than administrative improvements at the BA. Still, the BA remains as a pivotal institution that maintains the social partners' positions as prominent actors in the German economy and society.

The State as a Source of Support and Stability in German Industrial Relations

In this chapter I have pointed out the central role the state plays in sustaining the German industrial relations system through legislation, courts, and parapublic institutions. This support has remained steadfast despite rotations in governmental power and even in the most difficult of times, such as the 2008 financial crisis. Court rulings starting in the latter half of the 2000s at the national and European levels have posed challenges to the law at the margins, but they evidence neither erosion nor exhaustion. To the contrary, the law and the state still serve as supportive pillars.

In countries where the law and the state have not served as bulwarks (e.g., Japan, the United Kingdom, and the United States), the influence of organized labor and employers associations (vs. individual firms) has declined. In countries where the state has supported the industrial relations system (e.g., France and Spain), trade unions and employers associations have retained influence, despite declining membership. It is not often in traditional taxonomies of industrial relations that Germany is grouped with France and Spain, but when it comes to state support, it is appropriate. There is one important distinction, however. The state has a less visible role in the Federal Republic, which is consistent with Germany's regulatory preference for providing framework conditions rather than more direct forms of intervention.

I reject the canard that losing the Second World War was a gift in disguise because it permitted Germany to liberate itself from the laws, interest groups, and political deals that had supposedly impeded economic growth. The Second World War did not wipe the slate clean. The postwar industrial relations regime actually consists of laws, institutions, and practices resurrected from prewar times, most with only light refurbishment. All this was accomplished by the first half of the 1950s, that is, before the German economic miracle took off. The restoration facilitated rather than hindered growth. This chapter also provides the grain of salt with which to consume organized labor and management's heavy emphasis on collective bargaining autonomy.

The architects of postwar German industrial relations not only returned to the old slate immediately after the end of the Second World War, they quickly began to write more on it by expanding some institutions that existed only in rudimentary form before the war. The most prominent of these is codetermination, which is the topic of the next chapter.

CHAPTER 2

Codetermination

Pillar of Postwar German Industrial Relations

The purposes of this chapter are to acquaint those new to German industrial relations with the history and structures of the distinctly German system of employee participation known as "codetermination" (*Mitbestimmung*) and to demonstrate that codetermination has played a crucial role in preserving the solidity and stability of the German industrial relations system throughout the postwar years.

Codetermination "ranks among the foundational pillars of the German economic order."[1] It is widely seen as "the trademark of a socially regulated, tamed, 'Rhenish capitalism.'"[2] Codetermination is one of the most well-known elements of German industrial relations, but it is frequently misunderstood beyond the German frontier. Codetermination facilitates employees having some influence over decision making in their enterprises. Depending on the issue at hand, codetermination gives German employees rights ranging from information and consultation to a veto over certain workplace decisions. Codetermination does not mean, however, that unions or employees are calling the shots.

Most German managers accept codetermination as part of doing business in Germany, and some even praise it because it has proved effective in promoting peace and cooperation in the workplace.[3] Still, a certain air of controversy has always accompanied codetermination because it places some constraints on "management rights." Employers and unionists have each at times endeavored to change codetermination and on occasion have had success. Deepening economic integration both inside and outside of Europe has generated new questions regarding the utility of this uniquely German set of practices, but it has managed to survive with little evidence of erosion or exhaustion. Incremental adjustments and unwavering state support have been crucial to the resilience of codetermination.

Ironically, trade unionists initially expressed deep disappointment regarding the codetermination laws of the early 1950s because they did not conform to labor's vision of a comprehensive panenterprise network of bodies that could serve as a stepping stone to a planned democratic socialist economy. Yet, within a few years, organized labor had learned the value of the enterprise-centered codetermination that they had received because it added a second system of interest representation grounded firmly in law. Codetermination buttressed the unions and gave employee representatives statutory protection and access to information that they never could have gained through collective bargaining. Codetermination and collective bargaining combine to provide what the Germans call a "dual system" of employee representation that has made the postwar German industrial relations regime especially resilient and stable.[4]

Viktor Agartz, a leading theoretician of the German trade union movement during the 1950s, observed that codetermination was a "compromise out of the most heterogeneous sources."[5] Scholars have traced codetermination's roots back to nineteenth-century republicanism, employer paternalism, accommodationism from the First World War, socialist planning, syndicalism, and Catholic social teaching. Indeed, today's codetermination is not the result of any comprehensive plan. It is instead the product of a series of compromises among actors with divergent motives and interests that have accreted over the decades.[6]

As with the previous chapter, the evidence presented here shows that postwar policymakers relied heavily on prewar statutes as the starting point for crafting codetermination legislation. Moreover, employers, labor, and the state must all be brought into any credible account of why codetermination exists in Germany and how it has developed over the postwar years.

Postwar codetermination consists of two distinct components: employee representation on supervisory boards (*Aufsichtsräte*) of large enterprises, and works councils (*Betriebsräte*).[7] Each provides for representation, but they do so in very different ways and in very different places in a firm. Employee representation on supervisory boards puts a small number of employee representatives on the governing board of an enterprise along with the shareholders' representatives. It gives them access to a firm's inside information as well as the right to participate in making strategic decisions, including investment decisions. Works councils, in contrast, are representative bodies of employees situated at the lowest level of a firm, namely, the workplace. Works councils give employees limited say over big decisions that affect workplaces, such as layoffs or the introduction of new equipment. Both forms of codetermination anchor in law access to considerable resources and powerful protections for employee representatives, which their counterparts in other countries rarely have. The impact of codetermination has been considerable. It has served as a legal and financial backstop for trade unions, and it has deeply entwined managers and employee representatives, which in turn has dampened both labor and management militancy.

Since the two components of codetermination are quite different, in this chapter I look at each separately in successive sections. The concluding section returns to the discussion begun here of the larger significance of codetermination to German industrial relations and the German economy.

Employee Representation on Supervisory Boards

Employee representation on supervisory boards, which is the first component of codetermination, has three variations. Firm size and sector determine which format applies. A brief historical overview serves as the best vehicle to explain the crucial role of codetermination in German industrial relations and why employee representation on supervisory boards takes a patchwork form.

Origins and Establishment of Employee Representation on Supervisory Boards

A modest form of employee representation on supervisory boards was first introduced in the Weimar Republic. A 1922 law required incorporated enterprises (*Kapitalgesellschaften*) with works councils to put council members, or councillors, on the supervisory board (one for small firms and two for large ones). These employees were full voting members of their boards, but shareholder representatives heavily outnumbered them, so their influence was limited.[8] The practice did not last. The Nazis eliminated codetermination soon after they came to power by passing the 1934 Regulation of National

Labor Act (Gesetz zur Ordnung der nationalen Arbeit).[9] Codetermination was antithetical to the paternalistic and hierarchical "leadership principle" (Führerprinzip) that was central to the ideology of National Socialism.

In the immediate postwar years, the belief was widespread that both the captains of industry and capitalism itself were responsible, at least in part, for the Nazis' rise to power.[10] Even many Christian Democrats were convinced that capitalism needed a new set of constraints to preclude a reemergence of fascism on German soil. Many German trade unionists pushed for a sweeping nationalization of heavy industry and finance. They also agitated for an expansion of "economic democracy" as envisioned by Weimar trade union economic expert Fritz Naphtali, which would consist of sectoral, regional, and national planning through a network of codetermination that would include representatives from business, government, and trade unions sitting on a vast constellation of boards, committees, and councils organized hierarchically from the workplace to the national level.[11]

The four occupying allied powers also believed that change in German corporate governance was in order, but they differed considerably over the precise content of the reforms. The leaders of the newly elected British Labour government had some sympathy with the nationalization proposals, but they did not support the German Left's vision of economic planning. US authorities were far more skeptical, particularly given their desire to reduce the cost of occupation through a quick revival of German private production. The rapid onset of the Cold War pushed practical concerns to the fore and highlighted the contrast between market-based and authoritative systems for allocating goods and services. Consequently, economywide planning and nationalization quickly fell from consideration outside of union circles.[12]

Simultaneously, however, experimentation did begin with worker participation as a tool to tame German capitalism. Although opinions varied within and among the British and US occupation authorities regarding the efficacy of placing employee representatives on corporate boards, two advocates of the idea held key positions in the postwar German iron and steel industry: William Harris-Burland and Heinrich Dinkelbach. Harris-Burland headed North German Iron and Steel Control, which the British created in August 1946. Dinkelbach was an executive from the German steel giant Vereinigte Stahlwerke who was put in charge of a temporary trust administration for the steel sector, Treuhandverwaltung Stahl, in the fall of 1946. Both Harris-Burland and Dinkelbach were proponents of codetermination, in large part because they found it more palatable than the radical proposals for nationalization emerging from many of the plant-level movements within the iron and steel sector.[13]

In December 1946, Dinkelbach met with the man who eventually became the first chair of the Deutscher Gewerkschaftsbund (German Trade Union Federation, DGB), Hans Böckler, to discuss plans for breaking up cartels in the German iron and steel sector. At the meeting, Dinkelbach offered to include union representatives on the supervisory boards, and Böckler agreed to pursue the matter. In January 1947, the two men reached agreement on the details for what has become, with a few minor modifications, the system of "parity codetermination" (*Paritätsmitbestimmung*) for the coal, iron, and steel (*Montan*) industries.[14]

Under parity codetermination, the supervisory board overseeing a company consists of eleven members, five representing employees, five representing shareholders, and one neutral party.[15] In one variation, employee representatives suggest the neutral member and the annual shareholders' meeting votes on this recommendation.[16] In another, the shareholders select the board's chair, typically a shareholder representative. Of the five employee representatives, two must come from the firm: one a blue-collar worker and the other a white-collar employee. The firm's works councillors typically nominate these representatives, and the nominees are often leading members of the works council. The DGB, in consultation with the union within whose jurisdiction the enterprise falls and the firm's works councillors, names two additional employee representatives. These are typically top union officials. The DGB also picks the fifth employee representative in consultation with the relevant union, but that person must be an outsider (i.e., neither an employee of the firm nor a union official). Most often, this person is a retired politician who is sympathetic to the labor movement. It should be noted that under parity codetermination, a company's workforce has no direct say over the selection of employee representatives for the supervisory board; union officials and works councillors choose them. Parity codetermination also specifies that the executive committee (*Vorstand*) responsible for managing the company (i.e., the "second board" in the German model of corporate governance) must have three directors with equal authority: an operations director, a commercial/financial director, and a personnel director (*Arbeitsdirektor*). Under parity codetermination for the *Montan* industries, the personnel director must be approved by a two-thirds vote of the supervisory board, which gives employee representatives veto power regarding the choice.[17]

Allied Statute Number 75, which was issued in November 1948, established parity codetermination in the coal, iron, and steel sector, and twenty-three newly reconstituted enterprises initially fell under it. Statute 75 was extremely controversial. When the Allies were drafting it, many German stockholders objected to external employee board members as an injection of "forces from outside of the workplace." Some also claimed that parity codetermination was tantamount to expropriation without compensation and thus a backdoor route to socialism. This property question and internal disagreements led the Western Allies to sidestep making a permanent decision regarding parity codetermination. The statute specified that a future German government should determine the ultimate structure of property rights in the coal, iron, and steel industries.[18]

The Federal Republic of Germany was created on 24 May 1949. On 14 August 1949, the new state held its first elections. A month later, Christian Democrat Konrad Adenauer emerged as Germany's first postwar chancellor. On 20 September 1949, Adenauer presented his government's program, which included drafting new industrial relations legislation. The new chancellor stated, however, that he would prefer that organized labor and management work out a mutually acceptable compromise that could then be converted into law. So, beginning in November 1949, DGB chair Hans Böckler met periodically with Walter Raymond, head of the Bundesvereinigung der Deutschen Arbeitgeberverbände (BDA, Federal Organization of German Employers Associations), and BDA official Hans Bilstein in an effort to craft permanent codetermination legislation. At the end of March 1950, the BDA-DGB talks had reached an impasse. The employers' representatives wished to scale back parity codetermination. Trade unionists, on the other hand, wished to extend parity codetermination to all large firms throughout the economy and to institute supracompany codetermination at the sectoral, regional, and national levels.

On 14 April 1950, German labor leaders made their codetermination demands public. This proved awkward for Adenauer. His party, the Christian Democratic Union, was divided over the issue, but his government had already begun drafting a new codetermination bill that offered employees only one-third of the seats on supervisory boards and no codetermination beyond individual firms. Federal labor minister Anton Storch met with labor and management in June and July but failed to reach a compromise. Once the talks broke down, the cabinet decided to go ahead with the weaker bill. The DGB executive committee (*Bundesausschuss*) responded in July by passing a resolution announcing that it would go as far as calling a strike to block any weakening of parity codetermination. The Adenauer government officially introduced the weak codetermination bill in October 1950. In response, Industriegewerkschaft Metall (IG Metall, Industrial Union of Metalworkers) announced that it would hold a strike ballot. The results of the vote, held in late November, were overwhelming: 97.9 percent supported a strike.

Two months later, Industriegewerkschaft Bergbau und Energie (IG BE, Industrial Union of Mine and Energy Workers) also held a strike vote. The result was 92.8 percent support for industrial action. At the same time, Böckler exchanged a series of letters with Adenauer. Böckler asserted that codetermination strengthened the democratic foundations of the young Federal Republic by adding an additional forum for participation. Adenauer's replies stated that he found Böckler's argumentation unconvincing.[19]

In January 1951, Adenauer held a series of meetings with both union and business representatives in a renewed effort to find a mutually acceptable compromise. Adenauer's attempt at reconciliation failed, so he pursued a Solomonic solution instead. The government split codetermination legislation into two separate bills. The Montanmitbestimmungsgesetz (Coal, Iron, and Steel Codetermination Act) secured parity codetermination for firms with one thousand or more employees in the coal, iron, and steel industries. The second bill, which the new government had already drafted, would establish the rules governing employee representation on the supervisory boards of individual enterprises for all other sectors.

Several factors account for Adenauer's shift to support parity codetermination for the *Montan* sectors: sincere respect and admiration for Hans Böckler, an interest in rewarding the labor movement for supporting Adenauer's anti-Communist foreign policy even to the point of publicly disagreeing with organized labor's close political ally, the Social Democratic Party of Germany (Sozialdemokratische Partei Deutschlands, SPD), and deference to the trade-union wing of the Christian Democratic Union. Most important, however, was Adenauer's estimation that a bruising battle over a single form of codetermination for the entire economy "would have cost too much politically and economically" for the nascent Federal Republic.[20] Limiting the scope of the first bill to the coal, iron, and steel sectors meant that parity codetermination would remain where it already was in place but not become the law of the land for the entire German economy. Adenauer's compromise split the business community between those covered by the act, who opposed it, and the rest, who were relieved that it did not extend to them. The chancellor's divide-and-conquer maneuver generated sufficient support for the proposal in the Bundestag to pass. A total of 105 enterprises were initially subject to the Montan Act (i.e., 71 coal companies and 34 iron and steel firms).[21]

The Coal, Iron, and Steel Codetermination Act was a victory for labor. Tragically, Hans Böckler was unable to see his efforts bear fruit. The first chair of the postwar DGB died unexpectedly on 16 February 1951, eight weeks before the act became law. Hans Böckler's death also came at an inopportune moment. The passage of the Coal, Iron, and Steel Code-termination Act was just the opening battle in a two-round bout. The second confrontation was at least as important as the first. It concerned the contents of the Works Constitution Act (Betriebsverfassungsgesetz), which would set the rules for employee representation on the boards of large firms in the rest of the German economy and for employee workplace participation in the entire private sector.[22]

Business learned from the loss in the first struggle over codetermination legislation. The representatives of German business took the initiative during the drafting of the Works Constitution Act and convinced the government to salt the bill with several provisions designed to contain organized labor's influence in the boardroom. Hans Böckler's successor, Christian Fette, proved incapable of filling the void left by the death of the popular and capable Böckler. The DGB conducted a lackluster campaign to extend parity codetermination throughout the economy that lurched back and forth between lobbying and industrial protest. As a result, organized labor failed to persuade the Adenauer government to amend the Works Constitution Act, which was approved on 11 October 1952.[23]

From the perspective of German trade unionists, the rules governing employee representation on supervisory boards of firms outside of the coal, iron, and steel sectors spelled out in the Works Constitution Act fell far short of the provisions for codetermination in the coal, iron, and steel industry in several respects. The 1952 act provides for what the Germans awkwardly call "one-third parity codetermination" (*Drittelparitätsmitbestimmung*) for firms with five hundred or more employees. The share of seats on the supervisory board for employee representatives is only one-third rather than half. The first two employee representatives must work at the firm, which limits unions' opportunity to place their own officials on boards. Perhaps most important, employee members of the supervisory board do not have veto power over the selection of the enterprise personnel director, which they possess under the *Montan* model of codetermination.[24]

The DGB denounced the Works Constitution Act as a "dark moment for democratic development in the Federal Republic."[25] The portion of the Works Constitution Act governing employee representation on supervisory boards was a defeat for organized labor in two senses. First, the provisions were far weaker than the Coal, Iron, and Steel Codetermination Act. Second, the ineptitude of organized labor's campaign proved demoralizing. It took union leaders years to regain their political footing. German business, in contrast, was elated with its success. The BDA's monthly magazine, *Der Arbeitgeber*, praised the Works Constitution Act because it "retained the basic

elements of the entrepreneurial economy: the entrepreneur's right to decide the economic direction of his workplace and the freedom of economic
initiative."[26]

It is important to note how organized labor dealt with this defeat. Trade
union officials could have chosen to refuse to participate in one-third parity
codetermination out of protest or to challenge the economic order through
destabilization, but they did not. They instead decided to make the best of
what was there. This is characteristic of a defining feature of postwar German industrial relations that Walther Müller-Jentsch has called "conflictual
partnership" (*Konfliktpartnerschaft*).[27] This term captures the relationship between German business and labor well because the two parties regularly
engage in serious conflict, but they share an acceptance of each other as
legitimate partners and a commitment to follow the rule of law. Müller-
Jentsch was thinking primarily about collective bargaining when he coined
the term "conflictual partnership," but the conceptualization easily extends
to the legislative arena as well. Acceptance of partnership and the rule of
law are not to be taken for granted. For example, in the United States, most
businesses and business associations do not recognize trade unions as partners,
and it has been common practice for decades in the United States for employers to violate the labor law in order to keep out unions and "bust" them
if they gain a foothold in a firm.[28] Similarly, employers routinely broke the
law during the Second Empire and in the Weimar Republic. On the other
side of the ledger, soldiers' and workers' councils threatened revolution in the
immediate aftermath of the First World War. The Second World War and
the onset of the Cold War chastened both sides into accepting each other
as partners and playing by the rules, which fortified the fledgling postwar
system of German industrial relations.

Labor's First Drive to Enhance Employee Participation
on Supervisory Boards, 1965–1976

Christian Democrats dominated politics in the first two decades of the Federal Republic. Consequently, the laws governing employee representation
on supervisory boards remained essentially unchanged.[29] Nonetheless, labor
leaders never gave up the objective of extending parity codetermination
throughout the German economy. To the contrary, "the implementation of
parity codetermination throughout the West German economy was perhaps
the most fundamental political goal of the West German labor movement."[30]
The DGB's 1963 Basic Program explicitly called for the spread of parity
codetermination.[31] In 1965, the DGB launched a new campaign to expand

parity codetermination beyond the *Montan* industries. Industry associations, such as the Verband der Chemischen Industrie (Association of the Chemicals Industry), responded vigorously, arguing that parity codetermination would inject an "alien entity" (*Fremdkörper*) into the free market order, and convert "social codetermination" into "socialist codetermination."[32] When labor's traditional political ally, the Social Democratic Party, entered government as a junior partner in a coalition with the Christian Democratic parties in 1966, the DGB began producing draft codetermination legislation. In the following year, Chancellor Kurt Kiesinger tasked Kurt Biedenkopf, a young law professor and rising Christian Democratic politician, with producing a report to assess the performance of codetermination and to suggest reforms. The report of the Biedenkopf commission, which was issued in January of 1970, gave codetermination a largely positive assessment. The report heavily influenced subsequent reforms.[33]

Fresh federal elections in 1969 elevated the SPD to senior partner in a coalition with the laissez-faire Free Democratic Party (FDP, Freie Demokratische Partei). The change of government unleashed a wave of "reform euphoria" among trade unionists. For the first time in the postwar era, labor leaders' more ambitious legislative proposals would get serious consideration. Still, the new government took a measured approach. The chancellor, Willy Brandt (SPD), initially focused his energies on his signature Ostpolitik, which was a new approach to foreign policy designed to improve relations with the Communist countries to the east, including the German Democratic Republic. On the industrial relations front, the Brandt government decided to revise the portions of the Works Constitution Act regulating works councils first rather than tackling the far more politically charged issue of employee representation on supervisory boards, in large part owing to the FDP's fierce opposition to it.[34] Willy Brandt resigned abruptly in the spring of 1974 when it came to light that one of his close aides, Günter Guillaume, was an East German spy. Finance minister Helmut Schmidt (SPD) replaced Brandt as chancellor. The turmoil surrounding the Guillaume affair delayed action on numerous fronts, including board-level codetermination.

Initially, Helmut Schmidt's foremost concern was adjustment to the economic turbulence caused by the 1973–74 oil shock. Labor leaders cooperated on this front by keeping wage demands relatively moderate despite accelerating inflation and considerable grassroots dissatisfaction. In early 1976, the Schmidt government took up the issue of employee representation on supervisory boards in order to reward the trade unions for their restraint at the bargaining table and to fulfill his party's commitment to address the topic before the national election in the fall. Although employee representation on supervisory boards was a crucial element that helped to move German capitalism during the 1950s and 1960s toward a firm embrace of social partnership, some in business circles still harbored resentment toward it because they saw the practice as a constraint on property rights. The view of these critics in the business community mattered because the SDP's junior partner in government, the FDP, relied heavily on the German business community for support.[35]

Crafting a bill that was mutually acceptable to both coalition partners proved to be exceedingly difficult. As could be expected, the final product pleased no one. The Employee Codetermination Act (Gesetz über die Mitbestimmung der Arbeitnehmer), which the Bundestag approved by an overwhelming majority on 4 May 1976, was a compromise. It requires firms outside of the coal, iron, and steel industries with two thousand or more employees to distribute seats on their supervisory boards equally between shareholders and employees. The price for getting the FDP to support the bill was the addition of several provisions that departed from the 1951 *Montan* act to enhance the influence of shareholder representatives. First, the act requires that at least one of the employee representatives be a "middle manager" (*leitender Angestellte*). Typically, this middle manager sides with the shareholders' representatives on contentious issues. Second, if there is ever a tie vote on the supervisory board, the 1976 act gives the board's chair a second vote with which to break the tie. Provisions for selecting the chair favor shareholders. If two-thirds of a supervisory board cannot agree on a chair, the shareholder representatives may select one unilaterally. Third, the employee representatives have no veto over the choice of the personnel director.[36]

The 1976 act disappointed German union officials and employers alike. Union leaders complained that the act was much weaker than parity codetermination in the *Montan* industries. Employers did more than complain; they went to court. In 1977, the BDA, thirty employers associations, and nine individual firms challenged the act as an unconstitutional restraint on property rights, generating considerable ill will with trade unionists. The employers' effort was in vain. On 1 March 1979, the Federal Constitutional Court ruled the Employee Codetermination Act constitutional.[37] The employers accepted their defeat; in keeping with the philosophy of conflictual partnership, they did not fight the expansion of codetermination rights and worked cooperatively with the employee representatives. The employers' decision to stick to the rule of law and to continue to treat organized labor as a partner reinforced the postwar German industrial relations regime.

Economic change has affected the coverage of the acts. As the German economy grew, the number of firms under the jurisdiction of the 1976 act increased from 475 in 1977 to 573 in 1991. The number of covered firms jumped to 709 in 1992, in large part because 107 additional firms came under the act as a result of German unification. The number of enterprises covered by the 1976 act peaked in 2002 at 767; it subsequently edged down, reaching 681 in 2010. In contrast, the number of firms and employees covered by the 1951 Coal, Iron, and Steel Codetermination Act fell dramatically due to sharp contractions in the coal and steel sectors.

Shoring Up Employee Representation on Supervisory Boards

For several decades, German governments have taken incremental measures to shore up codetermination in the coal, iron, and steel sectors. Action was required because these sectors were becoming an ever smaller share of the German economy, and coal, iron, and steel firms had begun to expand into new industries. As a result, some firms no longer had a majority of their economic activities in the *Montan* sectors and wanted to opt out of parity codetermination.

In 1981, the German parliament passed legislation that gave companies that fell under the jurisdiction of the 1951 act an opportunity to opt out, provided they gave six years' notice of the intention to do so. One firm, Mannesmann, gave notice immediately. Thyssen followed suit two years later. Management at Salzgitter and Klöckner also expressed an interest in opting out. As 1987 approached, however, political tensions rose as Mannesmann prepared to exit the 1951 act.[38] The Christian Democratic–Free Democratic government took a stopgap measure by passing a bill extending the notice period by one year while they worked on compromise legislation. In 1988, a new law produced a longer-term fix that largely preserved the status quo in terms of the firms covered by reducing the minimum percentage turnover that a firm must have to fall under the Coal, Iron, and Steel Codetermination Act from fifty to twenty. The 1988 law thwarted Mannesmann's intention to opt out. Small shareholders at Mannesmann, Thyssen, and Klöckner responded by going to court, asserting that the 1988 law amounted to unequal treatment of shareholders. The case ultimately went to the German Constitutional Court. The court saw nothing unconstitutional in the change to a 20 percent threshold.[39]

The efforts to extend the coverage of the 1951 act have slowed the decline, but they have not stopped it. Coverage peaked in the early 1960s when one million employees, or about 4 percent of the workforce, came under its jurisdiction. By 1980, employment in ferrous metal production and mining had fallen by half to approximately 500,000. The sharp decline continued over the course of that decade, as employment fell to 350,000. German unification increased the number of firms covered by parity codetermination from thirty-one to forty-six, and employment reached close to half a million again, but this renaissance proved short lived. In 2009, only 160,000 worked in the coal, iron, and steel sectors, which amounted to 0.4 percent of all employees. By 2011—that is, sixty years after the passage of the *Montan* act—the number of firms it covered had fallen back down to thirty-one (i.e., nine coal companies and twenty-two steel firms). As a result, parity codetermination in the *Montan* industries has little impact in the economy today.[40]

Despite the erosion of the coal, iron, and steel sectors, all three codetermination acts taken together still cover a sizeable share of the German labor force. They have a significant influence on German industrial relations in other ways, too. More than 5,000 individuals, including over 1,700 union officials, currently serve as employee representatives on supervisory boards. Employee representatives receive the same compensation as any other board member. This money, which has grown to as much as €20,000–30,000 per board member per year, has been both a resource and a temptation for employee representatives. The tradition and bylaws of German unions call on officials who are on boards to donate most of their honoraria to the DGB's Hans Böckler Foundation, which supports educational and research projects in the field of industrial relations. The sums have become considerable. Before the financial crisis, annual donations amounted to €25–30 million. Over the decades, the occasional union official has neglected to make the donation. When such cases have come to light, the person in question has typically made back payments. In a few egregious instances, individuals have resigned.[41] Other temptations posed by sitting on supervisory boards have felled union officials, including some at the top. For example, in 1993, IG Metall chair Franz Steinkühler stepped down because of accusations that he had taken advantage of insider information as a member of the Daimler-Benz supervisory board to profit from the company's decisions to acquire the aircraft manufacturer Fokker and to buy back Mercedes stock.[42]

Post-Unification Efforts to Amend Employee Representation on Supervisory Boards: Unions 1, Employers 0

Codetermination reform fell from the agenda for two decades. The fight to pass the 1976 Codetermination Act had been bruising. Few wanted to engage in something similar right away. There was also considerable interest in letting some time pass to see how the 1976 act worked in practice. When Germany unified in 1990, the government simply extended the existing laws and practices of the entire industrial relations regime eastward, including codetermination. Absorbing unification was initially such an overwhelming task that neither business nor labor challenged this decision, but by the mid-1990s both social partners began to pursue codetermination reform once again. In 1996, the Bertelsmann Foundation, which is a philanthropic organization established by the publishing house with the same name, and the Hans Böckler Foundation jointly formed the Kommission Mitbestimmung (Codetermination Commission). The Kommission Mitbestimmung consisted of top representatives from German academia, business, government, and trade unions. For two years, participants engaged in a massive qualitative assessment of codetermination. They commissioned and evaluated reports, interviewed scores of participants and experts, and engaged in a series of discussions. The Kommission Mitbestimmung produced a final report in 1998; it concluded unanimously that codetermination on the whole was still worthwhile. Codetermination has proved flexible and has promoted the "cooperative modernization" of German firms by enhancing the flow of information and deepening of trust between labor and management.[43] The report's recommendations were sparse and vague, however. It called for no major reforms of employee participation on corporate boards. Most suggestions were in the area of supplemental agreements between works councils and workplace management.[44]

A very different reform effort to change the codetermination laws started a few years later. In 2002, Technical University of Berlin business professor Axel von Werder, working in coordination with six law professors and representatives of the business community, launched what became the Berlin Center of Corporate Governance. The BCCG began to hold conferences and issue papers that were highly critical of codetermination. The BCCG and other critics argued that board-level codetermination hinders effective oversight, leads to excessively large boards, slows decision making, produces inefficient compromises regarding firm strategy, deters foreign investment, and makes mergers and acquisitions exceedingly difficult. The BCCG's proposed solution was to end board-level codetermination and to create a "consultation council" composed of employees. The council would have information and consultation rights but no board seats or codetermination rights.[45]

Over the course of 2004, the BDA and the peak confederation for the industry associations, the Bundesverband der Deutschen Industrie (BDI, Federal Association of German Industry), organized a seventy-two person commission drawn largely from their membership to examine codetermination and to issue a report. The report did not go as far as the BCCG proposals because there was significant support for the status quo even among the ranks of the employers, but hardliners ultimately set the tone of the final document. It suggested adopting a "negotiated" model of board-level codetermination. One-third parity codetermination should serve as the default. The social partners would be free to negotiate regarding mutually acceptable changes from that starting point. Simultaneously, the leadership of German business associations engaged in concerted public criticism of the 1951 and 1976 codetermination legislation. In the heat of debate, BDI president Michael Rogowski went so far as to call board-level codetermination "an error of history" that "produced nothing positive."[46]

The DGB quickly rejected the BDA-BDI proposal, asserting that "under the cover of reforms, the BDA and BDI are practicing the dismantling of not only workplace codetermination, but also boardroom codetermination as well as collective bargaining autonomy." The DGB countered with its own reform proposals, which largely consisted of an extension of key elements of parity codetermination beyond the coal, iron, and steel industries, specifically, switching from the board chair having a second vote in cases of ties to the board selecting an additional person to serve as a neutral chair and instituting a two-thirds vote for selecting the management committee's head of personnel, which in practice would give a united front of employee board members the power to veto choices.[47]

Chancellor Schröder, who by the fall of 2004 had found himself at odds with much of the trade union movement over his labor market reforms (see chapter 4), used the controversy over codetermination reform as an opportunity to mend fences with the unions. He defended codetermination in unqualified terms. In an exchange with reporters at the BDI's aerospace industry conference, Schröder declared that employee participation had strengthened Germany. Christian Democratic politicians were split on the issue. For the most part the party leadership around Angela Merkel preferred incremental alterations to the status quo over the proposals contained in the BDA-BDI report, but a few party members close to business backed the BDA-BDI initiative.[48]

Schröder dealt with the political hot potato that board-level codetermination had become by creating a commission in March 2005 to study the issue. Specifically, the commission's remit was "to make proposals for a further development in board-level codetermination that is modern and appropriate to European circumstances, taking current legislation as its starting point." Schröder appointed Kurt Biedenkopf, now in the twilight of his political career after having served as CDU party general secretary in the 1970s and prime minister of Saxony in the 1990s and early 2000s, to serve as chair of the Commission on the Modernization of German Board-Level Codetermination. The commission quickly became known as the second Biedenkopf commission. The nine-person commission had high-powered members. The employers' representatives were BDA president Dieter Hundt, BDI president Jürgen Thumann, and president of the International Chamber of Commerce–Germany and former member of the DaimlerChrysler executive committee Manfred Gentz. The employee representatives were DGB chair Michael Sommer, IG Metall chair Jürgen Peters, and the chair of the enterprise works council for RWE Power AG, Günter Reppien. Three "academic" members rounded out the committee: Kurt Biedenkopf, who had taught law and business at various points in between his political posts; Wolfgang Streeck, who directed the Max Planck Institute in Cologne; and Hellmut Wissmann, who was a retired chief justice of the Federal Labor Court.[49]

The commission met six times during 2005 and 2006. It also formed two expert groups to delve into technical questions. Wolfgang Streeck led the first group. Its mandate was to investigate the economic impact of board-level codetermination in light of recent changes to capital markets. Hellmut Wissmann headed the second group, which was charged with assessing the likely consequences of developments in EU law for German board-level codetermination. The German government changed hands in the fall of 2005 from the SPD and the Greens to a grand coalition of the two Christian parties and the SPD under the chancellorship of Angela Merkel (CDU), but the new government agreed that the commission should continue its work. The commission submitted its report to Chancellor Merkel on 12 December 2006.[50]

At the outset, the commission members agreed that they would attempt to reach a common position, but if this were not possible, the academic members would produce their own report and the employer and employee representatives would be free to write opinions that would accompany that report. A rift opened up immediately regarding the understanding of the commission's remit. The employer representatives insisted that a reduction of the share of employee board members to one-third had to be a part of any reform. They also called for a reduction of employee involvement on boards and an elimination of external union representatives from boards. The academic and employee representatives argued that these demands were beyond the commission's remit because they amounted to a repeal rather than a revision of the 1976 act. Commission chair Kurt Bieden-kopf determined that the employer representatives' demands were indeed beyond the commission's remit, but the employer representatives refused to compromise. Consequently, only the academic commission members wrote the report.

The report included a reminder that the purpose of postwar codetermination legislation had never been to enhance company competitiveness but to provide employees with a means to voice their views regarding management decisions that affected them. The academics judged codetermination to have "succeeded in the task of providing an effective instrument for reconciling differing interests of employees and employers, particularly in economically difficult times." That having been said, the report pointed out that the voluminous academic literature on the economic impact of codetermination is not definitive and, given numerous intractable methodological problems, is unlikely ever to yield authoritative conclusions regarding the economic impact of board-level codetermination but that the balance of the research leans toward a positive assessment.[51] The report also conveys the findings of the commission's expert group that "board-level codetermination is no hindrance to a positive evaluation of Germany as a place to do business." There is no evidence of either a "codetermination discount" in capital markets for German firms or of codetermination hindering foreign direct investment. To the contrary, the report argued that "the cooperative approach of the German system of codetermination has not simply had a positive impact on the motivation and sense of responsibility of employees; it also has important social effects through its contribution to social harmony. Companies can and should take competitive advantage of the productivity provided by cooperation." All in all, "the academic members consider a fundamental revision of the existing legislation unnecessary and that the protection of employee interests provided by the existing regulations remains appropriate."[52]

The report advocated for reform of board-level codetermination in three areas: (1) expansion of opportunities for the social partners to negotiate their own mutually agreeable arrangements, particularly regarding such matters as the size and composition of the supervisory board; (2) inclusion on supervisory boards of employees working outside of Germany; and (3) simplification and removal of contradictions in existing legislation, such as simplifying the election of employee representatives, making explicit that parity composition extends to board committees, clarifying that the determination of firm size includes employment at all entities under control of the enterprise, and requiring the management of a limited liability company (*Gesellschaft mit beschränkter Haftung*, GmbH) to make regular reports identical to the requirement for a joint-stock company (*Aktiengesellschaft*, AG).[53]

The opinions of the employer and employee commission members, which were in section B of the report, did not change over the course of the commission's work. The social partners concurred regarding the inclusion of employees working outside of Germany in boardroom codetermination, but disagreed about how to do it. The employer commission members wanted to make room for foreign-based employees by eliminating union representatives, but the employee commission members rejected that suggestion. Similarly, the social partners both supported permitting the negotiation of mutually agreeable departures from the statutes, but the employer commission members only wanted to allow departures that weakened board-level codetermination, whereas employee commission members wanted the opposite.[54] The media declared the report of the second Biedenkopf commission a victory for unions.[55] Once again, in keeping with conflictual partnership, employers continued to work within the system and to treat organized labor as a partner, even though they came up empty handed.

Chancellor Merkel made her views regarding codetermination clear in 2006 when she declared, "Codetermination is part of our social market economy, which is impossible to imagine doing without, and which has proved itself in Germany." In June 2009, the Merkel government enacted largely unaltered the reforms that the second Biedenkopf commission proposed. During the 2009 federal election campaign, Merkel stated explicitly that she was not interested in pursuing any changes to the codetermination laws in her next government, and she has not deviated from that position. Academics and institutes sympathetic to employers have continued to float reform proposals, but none has resonated in the political realm in the wake of the second Biedenkopf commission. The failed effort to ratchet back board-level codetermination in the mid-2000s demonstrated that the practice retains broad support within the German body politic. Board-level codetermination has also proved to be resilient. *Montan* codetermination has shrunk along with coal, iron, and steel sectors, but the number of firms that fall under the 1976 codetermination law has remained stable at roughly seven hundred for two decades. Still, it cannot be said that the future of board-level codetermination is completely secure. The biggest threat comes not from within but from the European Union.[56]

European Union Law and Employee Representation
on Supervisory Boards

On 8 October 2001, after three decades of discussions and numerous drafts, the European Union passed a European company statute and a supplementary directive on the involvement of employees.[57] These provisions, which took effect in 2004, provide newly established, merged, and reincorporated enterprises with the option of incorporating at a European-wide level anywhere within the European Union. This new category of incorporation is called Societas Europaea (SE). Its aim is to simplify matters for larger firms operating in more than one EU member state. Each SE has a single system for corporate reporting and governance valid throughout the European Union. The SE, however, "does not *de facto* represent a complete European corporate form."[58] The EU statute and directive provide a framework, but individual EU members had to enact national laws to bring them into force, and national legislatures have discretion to tailor the implementation to the national needs and traditions of each country within that framework. As a result, each EU member has its own version of the SE. Reliance on a framework and national transposition is largely the product of the failure to reach consensus regarding a single standard for employee participation. Paul Davies has summarized the arrangement as coming down to "participation: no escape, no export."[59] The directive does require national legislation to allow companies to choose to have either a single board of directors along the lines of Anglo-American corporate law or a two-board system resembling the German model of corporate governance. It also mandates some form of employee consultation but not specifically codetermination.

The critics of board-level codetermination within Germany had hoped that European company law could serve as the thin edge of the wedge in their efforts to pare back board-level codetermination. They expected that large numbers of German firms and foreign subsidiaries would incorporate as SEs in other EU countries with fewer restrictions (such as the United Kingdom), much like the disproportionately high number of incorporations of US firms in Delaware because of the state's lax regulations and low corporate taxes. The Schröder government, which had the responsibility of transposing European company law into German law, was also concerned about the potential for the erosion of codetermination. It chose to make the German transposition of European company law as fully compatible with existing German codetermination legislation as possible. It also endeavored to minimize the likelihood that German SEs could undermine codetermination. For example, the German enabling legislation specifies that if negotiations between central management and firm employees over employee representation on corporate boards reach an impasse at a newly incorporated SE, the SE must automatically adopt the strongest form of codetermination available under German law for a company of its size and sector.[60]

So far, only a very small number of enterprises in Europe have incorporated as SEs, which has disappointed officials of the European Commission and the German critics of board-level codetermination, but it demonstrates the continuing widespread acceptance of codetermination among the vast majority of German business leaders. As of 1 June 2011, there were 817 SEs throughout the European Union, and of those only 183 were "normal" companies with operations and employees. The remaining SEs were "empty" (i.e., no employees), on the "shelf" (i.e., neither employees nor operations), or "UFO SEs" (i.e., there is no information about them). Eighty-seven SEs have been established in Germany, which translates to less than 1 percent of the total number of German AGs. Only twenty-seven of the active German SEs chose the single-board structure. Of the sixty German firms that chose the traditional dual-board structure, roughly half of those firms have adopted codetermination in conformance with the 1976 act, even though they had no obligation to do so. In other words, in total, fewer than sixty German firms have opted out of codetermination.[61]

Similarly, some feared that the 2007 cross-border merger directive would be a threat to board-level codetermination. This directive, which regulates the establishment of companies through cross-border mergers, permits the newly merged company to register in a country without board-level employee representation and thereby avoid it, even when the bulk of its activities and headquarters are not in that country. In practice, however, there are virtually no instances of firms using this loophole. The European company statute also permits enterprises to transfer the headquarters seat across borders. A total of fourteen transfers have happened, four involving Germany. Of these four, three firms have transferred their headquarters *into* Germany and only one has transferred out. In brief, the European company statute has precipitated no flight out of codetermination in Germany.[62]

The European Union is in the process of developing a statute for a new corporate form, the Societas Privata Europaea (European Private Company). The draft SPE statute is more basic than the SE. It currently includes no board-level employee participation and is meant for small and medium-sized enterprises. Progress on the SPE has stalled due to wrangling over the maximum number of employees an SPE may have and a disagreement over whether a firm should be allowed to register in one country while having its administrative office in another.[63]

A potentially bigger danger to board-level participation comes not from the lawmakers but from the European Court of Justice and its decisions regarding the freedom of establishment. German law and the SE legislation have used a "real seat" doctrine of corporate registry. Firms must have their headquarters in the same country where they are registered as a legal entity. Over the past decade, the ECJ has championed a "registered seat" doctrine, which permits a registry and headquarters to be in different countries, which could even include countries outside of the European Union. In some instances, the headquarters location does not have laws mandating board-level codetermination. The number of companies with significant operations in Germany that use such exotic corporate governance models grew from seventeen in 2006 to forty-three by late 2010. These instances taken in isolation have not compromised board-level employee representation in Germany, but the pattern of ECJ decisions that reject discrimination between enterprises with different forms of corporate governance is making defense of distinctly national practices, such as board-level codetermination, more difficult. Taken together, steps by various EU actors have kept alive potential threats to board-level codetermination, but so far none have diluted or displaced the practice in Germany. Concerns remain among codetermination advocates, but their countermobilization has helped to preserve the status quo.[64]

In summary, the postwar German labor movement expended considerable time, effort, and resources to obtain, to maintain, and to enhance employee representation on supervisory boards. Union officials initially hoped to use employee representatives in the boardrooms of large firms to create a "new economic democracy," which would have included comprehensive economic planning.[65] Those dreams were never realized. Nonetheless, employee participation on supervisory boards has been instrumental in creating a consensual, stable, and mutually respectful system of industrial relations by integrating business and labor to a far greater degree than ever before. The immensity of this achievement should not be underestimated. The cooperative tenor of the postwar years stands in sharp contrast to the deeply acrimonious and ideological character of industrial relations in the Weimar Republic. Nonetheless, the recent challenge to board-level codetermination made plain that aspects of codetermination remain contested and that some segments of the German business elite would like to pare it back. Still, in practice, the vast majority of German managers who work at firms subject to board-level codetermination continue to embrace it. Equally noteworthy has been the broad political support for board-level codetermination, which led to the practice being shored up rather than diluted in the 2000s. European statutes and court rulings have at times heightened fears regarding displacement of board-level codetermination in Germany with European alternatives, but there is no evidence of a significant shift away from it.

In the immediate postwar era, German labor leaders valued employee representation on supervisory boards far more highly than the other component of codetermination, namely, works councils. Indeed, many unionists were initially critical of the postwar institutionalization of works councils, fearing that they could become rivals of the trade unions.[66] The DGB criticized the 1952 codetermination act as a setback, in part because of the sections that gave works councils considerable autonomy.[67] Today, works councils and their sister institutions in the public sector, staff councils, play a substantially more significant role in the lives of most German employees than employee representation on supervisory boards ever has, and unions as a rule work closely with works councils, typically in a leading role. How and why did this orphan institution rise in importance over the decades? The next section chronicles this evolution.

Works Councils and Staff Councils

The idea of providing workers with a representative body in the workplace has a long history in Germany that predates board-level codetermination by several decades. Its antecedents can be found in the mid-nineteenth century.

The Origins of Works Councils

Works councils have two quite different institutional progenitors: worker committees and revolutionary soldiers' and workers' councils (*Soldaten- und Arbeiterräte*).[68] Worker committees have a paternalistic, top-down status quo oriented pedigree. The German constituent national assembly, which convened in 1848 at the church of St. Paul in Frankfurt, discussed (among many other things) inserting into a new commercial code a requirement that firms create factory committees (*Fabrikausschüsse*) that would give workers limited consultation rights. Within a few years, the aristocrats in most German principalities reasserted control and crushed the republican movement, snuffing out any immediate hope of reform through legislation. A few employers, such as Zeiss head Ernst Abbe and Heinrich Freese, who ran a venetian blind factory in Berlin, voluntarily created "worker committees" (*Arbeiterausschüsse*) that provided limited information and consultation opportunities for employees in their firms. These employers were exceptional, however. Most nineteenth-century employers rejected any constraints on their decision making from any source. For example, nineteenth-century steel industrialist Carl Ferdinand Freiherr von Stumm declared, "If a factory enterprise is to prosper, it must be organized militarily, not in a parliamentary fashion."[69] In 1887, a leading industry group, the Centralverband deutscher Industrieller (CDI, Central Association of German Industrialists), issued a memorandum that stated bluntly, "The worker is not the partner with equal rights of the employer . . . he is the subordinate of him, to whom he is to be dutiful. . . . The insertion of a standing authority (*regelmässige Instanz*) between employer and worker is not to be permitted." Many unionists also disapproved of worker committees, fearing that employers would use them as company unions. Left-wing Social Democrat August Bebel denounced the committees as a "pseudoconstitutional fig leaf." Still, the early experiments with worker committees influenced future efforts to institutionalize worker representation in the workplace.[70]

The 1891 revision of the Imperial German commercial code (*Gewerbeordnung*) provided the first explicit legal foundation for the establishment of worker committees, but it said nothing about their structure, rights, and responsibilities. Some on the German left concluded that worker committees were harmless; others saw them as little more than "employer police."[71] In 1890, the Bavarian government passed legislation that required mines with at least twenty employees to form employee committees (*Arbeitnehmerausschüsse*). The law, which came in the wake of a strike in 1889, gave the committees limited information and consultation rights regarding social and personnel matters, but it did not grant them the power to call a strike. Prussia passed a similar law for mines that employed at least one hundred people in the immediate aftermath of a strike in 1905.[72]

Employee committees spread as a result of the First World War. The 1916 Auxiliary Patriotic Service Act required the creation of blue-collar worker committees in all workplaces vital to the war effort that employed more than fifty workers and a separate white-collar committee if a workplace had at least fifty white-collar employees. The act gave the employee committees information rights regarding employment matters and provided for review and mediation before a labor court over a narrow range of issues when an employee committee and management had reached an impasse. Still, the act ultimately reserved the final say for management. Many union officials supported the employee committee provision in the Auxiliary Patriotic Service Act, but others criticized it as a "drop of social balm" that was insufficient to calm industrial strife.[73]

The second institutional ancestor of the contemporary German works council is the soldiers' and workers' council. These councils sprung up spontaneously in towns and cities throughout Germany starting in 1918. Russia's revolutionary soviets served as the inspiration for these councils.[74] Friction plagued the relationship between soldiers' and workers' councils and the more established leaders of the German Left within the SPD and the trade unions affiliated with the Social Democratic Party. Whereas most radical councillors were ardent proponents of direct democracy and the councils' right to strike, SPD officials were strong supporters of representative parliamentary government and had little patience for syndicalist councils. The trade union leaders believed firmly in a union monopoly over the right to strike, whereas the councils also claimed this right.[75]

The 1918 Stinnes-Legien agreement discussed in the previous chapter reflected the established Left's preferences. Although it gave employees the right to form a "works council" (*Betriebsrat*) in workplaces with more than fifty employees, the actual powers and role of the new bodies resembled those of an employee committee rather than a soldiers' and workers' council. Many criticized the use of the name "council" instead of "committee" for the new bodies as a bait-and-switch maneuver because the new works councils did not have the expansive powers of soldiers' and workers' councils. The explicit aim of the new works councils was to promote the constructive integration of employees into the process of production.[76]

The first Weimar government passed the Works Councils Act (Betriebsrätegesetz) on 4 February 1920. The act provided a firm legal foundation for the councils and expanded their rights beyond those specified under the Stinnes-Legien agreement. It permitted employees in private and public workplaces with more than twenty employees to elect a works council. The size of a works council increased in proportion with the number of employees at the workplace. (Workplaces with between five and twenty employees did not have works councils but could elect a single "works representative" [*Betriebsobmann*]). Works councillors had to be employees at the workplace for a minimum of six months and be at least eighteen years old. Top managers were not permitted to serve as works councillors nor to vote in the election of a council. Works councillors served one-year terms. The act also required firms with more than one workplace to form a central works council (*Gesamtbetriebsrat*) with members drawn from the works council of each workplace.[77]

The act gave works councils the task of representing the economic interests of the employees. This included a joint say over the content of workplace rules and consultation rights over a limited range of personnel and economic decisions. It also mandated that a council support the employer in achieving the economic objectives of the enterprise, a provision that upset the far left. The act granted works councillors the right to inspect a company's books, but it required works councillors to keep that information confidential. In addition, several provisions in the 1920 act ensured that works councils did not undercut trade unions. Article 8 stated, "The right of economic organizations of manual workers and salaried employees to represent the interests of their members is in no way prejudiced by the provisions of this law."[78] Article 31 permitted unions to advise works councils. Articles 66 and 78 required works councils to uphold, and even to enforce, union collective bargaining agreements.[79]

Most of Weimar's trade union leadership declared the Works Councils Act to be a step forward. The act did not institute the unions' preferred approach (i.e., the legal recognition of union shop stewards as the employees' representatives in the workplace), but with the assistance of the state, trade union leaders were able both to establish a secure indirect presence in many workplaces and to buttress central union authority against more radical strains within the labor movement.[80] Some employers and their associations, in contrast, engaged in hyperbolic criticism of the 1920 Works Councils Act; they claimed that it was indistinguishable from socialism. Others were less critical, recognizing that the act would enable union leaders to bring the militant council movement to heel. The Works Councils Act did deliver the final blow to the workers' and soldiers' councils, which were already on the ropes because of the hostility of employers, established political parties, and trade union leaders. The soldiers' and workers' councils did not fit within the new order because they were incompatible with parliamentary democracy, collective bargaining, and capitalism. The workers' and soldiers' council movement did manage to wage massive protests against the act in front of the Reichstag that resulted in forty-two deaths, but it did not derail the legislation.[81]

Implementing the Works Council Act proved difficult. Many employers complained that unions used works councils as "collective bargaining police" and as an enforcement tool for workplace legislation. Some resisted employee attempts to form works councils. During the period of rampant hyperinflation in 1923, aggressive employers fired militant councillors, which intimidated those who remained. Some firms forced works councils to agree to concessions, violating the act's prohibition on the infringement of trade union activities.[82] Even before the onset of the Great Depression, observers such as C. W. Guillebaud concluded that "a sufficient number of examples was made to intimidate the bulk of the councils and to reduce them to a state of inglorious quiescence."[83] Rivalries among socialist, Christian, and liberal trade union movements played themselves out within many works councils, further undercutting their effectiveness. The Great Depression sapped the little remaining leverage of the works councils.[84]

The Nazis' 1933 Labor Trustee Act (Gesetz über die Treuhändler der Arbeit) transformed works councils into "councils of trust" (*Vertrauensräte*). Each workplace had a single council for all types of employees. Only Nazi Party members could serve as councillors. The Nazis justified the changes as part of their effort to create a classless and harmonious national community. In reality, the councils took a subservient position as a part of the Nazis' paternalistic and hierarchical restructuring of the workplace.[85]

Despite the persistent decline in the efficacy of works councils in the Weimar Republic and the perversion of councils in the Nazi era, a desire for works councils retained deep roots. Workers began to create works councils once more almost immediately after Germany came under Allied occupation. Works councils were instrumental in expediting the resumption of production in numerous plants. At first some works councils even ran whole factories. The motives were twofold, as Volker Berghahn noted: "Many workers had enthusiastically involved themselves in factory administration not only because they were keen to resume production but also because they had hopes of a new beginning after the defeat of Nazism." Many works councillors helped Allied military authorities to "denazify" their companies and local governments by identifying party members and providing evidence of their criminal acts. Works councils also frequently coordinated the distribution of food, clothing, and shelter in war-torn Germany, since they were among the few indigenous institutions in place during the first few months after the war that were able to do so. Local Allied military officers were often grateful for the assistance of the works councils. Still, the occupying powers wished to gain control over production themselves and quickly put a stop to works councils running workplaces. The mushrooming of works councils and their spontaneous actions ultimately prompted the four allied powers to regulate them.[86]

The Creation of Works Councils and Staff Councils in Postwar Germany

On 10 April 1946, the Allied Control Council governing Germany issued Law No. 22, which repealed the 1933 Nazi legislation and established a new

framework for works councils. The occupiers did this without any real af-
finity for works councils—none had a similar domestic institution—but the
councils were too widespread and deeply rooted to abolish. They made the
councils subordinate to the unions. Article 7 of the law explicitly stated that
works councils were to work with the officially recognized trade unions to
achieve their objectives. Union officials quickly converted works councils
into their de facto workplace locals. Since the trade union leadership in
the western occupation zones, made up principally of exiles, was far more
moderate than the works councillors, connecting the works councils to the
trade unions in a subservient position achieved the objective of reining in the
councils without doing so directly.[87]

The USSR was happy with Law 22. The Soviets were rapidly coming to
dominate trade unions in their zone (see chapter 4). Law 22 ultimately gave
them the means to eliminate the independence of works councils, which
had proved troublesome to them. In November 1948, the Communist-
controlled Freier Deutscher Gewerkschaftsbund (FDGB, Free German
Trade Union Federation) voted to fold works councils into the workplace
trade union leadership (*Betriebsgewerkschaftsleitung*) in all workplaces in the
Soviet occupation zone with a unionization rate of at least 80 percent. This
effectively eliminated all works councils in areas under Soviet control.[88]

In the western zones, Law 22 subordinated works councils by formalizing
their existence, but formalization also helped to ensure their survival in a
future industrial relations regime. Union officials were disappointed with
Law 22, despite the power it gave to organized labor, because its brief and
vague formulation gave works councils few competencies. Some German
states subsequently passed their own works council legislation that marginally
expanded the scope of work councils beyond Law 22 before the creation of
the Federal Republic.[89]

The issue of works councils arose again in the early 1950s when the
Adenauer government turned its attention to industrial relations. Trade
unions called for legislation that would greatly expand the competencies
of works councils and secure union control over them. The consensus
position among German employers was that works councils should have a
narrow mandate and be kept strictly independent from trade unions. Once
again, the Adenauer government decided to use the old Weimar Works
Councils Act as a point of departure.[90] Article 80, paragraph 1 of the 1952
Works Constitution Act enumerates essentially the same set of core duties
for works councils as found in the 1920 act, but it enhanced the obligation
of works councillors to maintain loyalty and to promote the well being of
the firm (article 2, paragraph 1), placed greater restrictions on union access

to workplaces (article 2, paragraph 2; and article 46), restricted the scope of the act to the private sector (article 118), and barred works councillors from engaging in political activity in an official capacity (article 74, paragraph 2). The Works Constitution Act also explicitly banned works councils from calling strikes (article 74, paragraph 2), which had been only implicit in the 1920 act, and established a conciliation process for settling disputes (article 76).[91]

Article 14 of the 1952 act established separate elections for blue- and white-collar employees unless both groups voted to hold a joint election. This practice, known as the "group principle," required an allotment of seats on the works council corresponding to the relative proportion of blue- and white-collar employees in the workplace. The intent of the group principle, which remained in force through 2001, was to ensure that white-collar employees would receive fully proportionate numerical representation. Article 15, paragraph 1 states that the councillors "should when possible" come from a representative sample of departments and employment categories of a workplace, including middle management. Article 15, paragraph 2 used similar language regarding gender balance, but a 2001 revision strengthened it to require that "the gender that is in the minority in the workforce must be represented on the works council corresponding to its numerical proportion, if [the council] consists of at least three members." Labor leaders in 1951 denounced the original text, complaining that it segmented the electorate. They alleged that the objective of the segmentation was indirectly to reduce union influence on the works councils.[92]

Despite the setbacks from labor's perspective, the Works Constitution Act did have positive attributes for labor. Lawmakers gave works councils the right to challenge employer decisions and to settle disputes through arbitration over work rules, remuneration scales, working time, overtime, leave, lay-offs, and vocational training (articles 87, 91, 94, 95 and 98). The act preserved the right of works councillors to access internal information regarding the company's economic performance so long as that information is kept confidential (article 79, paragraph 1) and expanded the competency of councils beyond personnel matters to include conditions of employment (e.g., hours, vacations, safety, and health) and economic issues within the firm (e.g., capital investment) (articles 11, 87, and 89–91). A works council may negotiate a workplace accord (*Betriebsvereinbarung*) with the employer regarding supplemental compensation, including company pensions, but such accords may not extend to topics normally covered in collective bargaining (article 77, paragraph 3).[93] Union officials have the right to initiate the formation of a works council, to attend works council meetings in an advisory capacity, and to contest works council elections where there are alleged improprieties (articles 16, 19, 31 and 46). The term for serving on a works council is three years, and there are no term limits under the 1952 Works Constitution Act. The act required employers to provide office space and material support for works councils. In larger workplaces, employers must release a limited number of works councillors from their work duties so that they may do the work of the council full time while receiving their regular compensation from their employer (articles 37, 38, and 40).

At the time, the trade union hierarchy opposed the legislation, arguing that the negatives of the new rules for works councils contained in the Works Constitution Act outweighed the positives.[94] For example, IG Metall executive board member Fritz Strothmann denounced the act as "a barrier between the plant and the union."[95] In contrast, leading German employers and their associations were satisfied with the provisions pertaining to works councils in the Works Constitution Act; only a minority of hardliners in the German business community objected.[96] In the spirit of conflictual partnership, however, organized labor went to work to maximize what they could get out of the legislation as it stood.

After the 1952 Works Constitution Act passed, German trade unions pursued a two-pronged strategy in response to greater council autonomy. On the one hand, officials in the upper reaches of the union hierarchy and outside of the workplace strove to persuade works councillors to cooperate voluntarily with them by providing the councillors with advice, education, and support. On the other hand, union leaders also endeavored to build up a parallel network of their own shop stewards within the workplace to do tasks that only a union representative could do (e.g., recruit members), to support the works councils, and to serve as a voice to contain any outbreak of "workplace egoism" (*Betriebsegoismus*, i.e., putting specific workplace concerns ahead of a union's policy for an entire sector).[97]

German labor has had much more success over the years working with works councillors than setting up effective networks of union shop stewards. Roughly two-thirds of all works councillors have been union members. In most instances, a union endorsement greatly enhances the odds that a candidate will be elected to a works council. Labor leaders have successfully used union endorsements in works council elections to influence the behavior of works councillors.[98]

Labor has been far less successful in constructing an autonomous, influential, and responsible network of shop stewards. Strong contingents of shop stewards are the exception rather than the rule in most German workplaces. Since German law does not recognize shop stewards, they have no special legal status or protection. This leaves shop stewards vulnerable and weak, particularly when compared to works councillors. The law designates the works council as the representative of the employees in the workplace, which has left little for stewards to do beyond union recruitment and publicity. Stewards have responded in two ways. Most have used the post as a stepping stone to a works council seat, which has usually wound up turning the union strategy of using shop stewards to influence works councillors on its head. Works councillors have used their greater access and endorsements for open council seats to gain control over stewards. Most stewards were more than willing to play along. In a few instances (especially during the late 1960s and early 1970s) some shop stewards chose to take radical positions critical of the existing works councillors as a route to get onto the works council. When this happened, the works councillors (who were usually also union members) demanded that the union involved rein in militant stewards. This put the union leadership in a difficult position. Responding to works councillors preserved a good working relationship with them, but it undercut the union's own shop stewards. Given the legal privileges of works councillors and the reality that most of the radical shop stewards were just as critical of the union officialdom, labor leaders almost invariably sided with works councillors at the expense of shop stewards. The result, however, was typically disaffection among some in the workplace with both the works council and the union. Many works councillors avoided the problem altogether simply by wearing two hats and serving as shop stewards as well.[99]

Still, union provision of services and expertise to works councils has proved sufficient to give higher-level union officials the upper hand. German unions have managed not only to defuse works councils as a competitive threat but also to be the leading player in most instances. Works councillors have considerable discretion regarding firm-specific issues, but unions set the agenda above the level of the firm.

In 1955, the German government passed a separate piece of legislation, the Staff Representation Act of the Federation and the States (Personalvertretungsgesetz des Bundes und der Länder), that created staff councils (*Personalräte*), which are the public-sector equivalent of works councils.[100] Staff councils are a postwar innovation.[101] The Adenauer government made staff councils weaker than works councils, which once again disappointed labor. Specifically, staff councils cannot initiate discussions regarding personnel and workplace arrangements but can only object to changes, and unions cannot take staff councils to court for failure to enforce the law. German law requires states to draft their own legislation regarding staff councils, but within the parameters set by the federal government's guidelines. In general, staff councils in state governments have more extensive participatory rights in states traditionally dominated by the SPD.[102]

Distinctions among categories of employees are particularly strong in the public sector. Article 17 of the Staff Representation Act provides for separate electoral slates for three types of employees: blue-collar public servants (*Arbeiter*), white-collar public servants (*Angestellte*), and civil servants (*Beamte*).[103] Segregation ensures that all three types win seats on staff councils, but it also produces fragmentation that all too often hampers effectiveness. Many staff councils spend considerable time on internal mediation before even approaching the workplace manager. Councillors focus disproportionately on pleasing the slice of the workforce that elects them, sometimes even at the expense of the workplace as a whole.[104]

Although practice varies widely from workplace to workplace, a typical works or staff council meets twice a month on its own and once a month with the workplace manager unless something pressing arises. Article 66 of the Staff Representation Act requires monthly meetings with the employer, but the Works Constitution Act does not. The Works Constitution Act mandates at least one public workplace meeting (*Betriebsversammlung*) per quarter and gives works councils the right to call an additional meeting once every six months if circumstances demand it (article 43). A workplace meeting includes the works council, management, and the entire workforce. In practice, many firms forego holding four meetings per year, despite the legal requirement, if the works councillors concur that no meeting is necessary.[105] Every works council must also work with management to assemble and maintain a conciliation panel to hear employee grievances. It consists of an equal number of employee and employer representatives, plus an independent chair. If the two sides cannot agree on a person to serve as chair, the local labor court makes the appointment.[106]

1971 Works Council Reforms

The laws governing works and staff councils remained essentially unchanged for two decades. When the SPD became the senior partner in government in 1969, party leaders made reform of the councils a priority, largely at the urging of trade union leaders, who argued that the 1952 codetermination act did not go far enough to democratize the workplace. A surge of labor militancy, including a huge strike wave in 1969, added considerable momentum to the reform effort. The FDP, which was the junior partner in the government, agreed to take up workplace codetermination in exchange for postponing consideration of a revision of employee representation on supervisory boards, at least until after the next election. On 17 December 1971, after much debate and a delay in the Bundesrat, the government passed revisions to the Works Constitution Act that strengthened workplace-level codetermination.[107]

The revised Works Constitution Act increased workplace rights of both works councils and unions. The 1971 act expanded the requirement for employers to inform and to consult works councils in decisions involving the introduction of new technologies (article 90). It also explicitly required employers planning to undertake major layoffs or substantial changes in working conditions to inform the works council of this "in a full and timely fashion" and to gain the works council's approval of a "social compensation plan" (*Sozialplan*) for affected employees (articles 111 and 112). This social compensation plan must balance employer and employee interests (*Interessenausgleich*). It sets the terms for severance pay as well as retraining and job-placement assistance. Article 106 of the revised act requires any workplace of more than one hundred employees with a works council to establish an "economic committee" (*Wirtschaftsausschuss*) consisting of three to seven members (depending on the size of the workplace) appointed by the works council(s). At least one member of the economic committee must be a works council member, but others do not have to be enterprise employees. Economic experts from the trade unions are frequent appointees. The economic committee is solely an advisory body. It typically meets once a month, and the act requires a representative of the employer to attend. The firm must fully inform the committee of company performance, personnel decisions, and planning. If at least five employees are either below age eighteen or vocational trainees below age twenty-five, the enterprise must also create a Youth and Vocational Trainee Delegation (Jugend- und Auszubildendenvertretung). The delegation focuses on issues pertaining to the specific needs of young employees and coordinates its activities with the works council.[108]

The 1971 revisions to the Works Constitution Act also gave trade unions additional power in the workplace. Union representatives gained full access to the workplace to undertake a task specific to the act so long as they gave management prior notice, respected safety rules, protected trade secrets, and did not disrupt production (article 2, paragraph 2). The act also enhanced the trade unions' rights to promote, monitor, and contest works council elections. Works councillors gained explicit protection to perform activities and functions in the workplace on the union's behalf, particularly with respect to recruitment (article 74, paragraph 3). The revision also permitted works councillors to participate in trade union seminars related to their work at the company's expense.[109] Initially, organized labor expressed disappointment, calling the revisions to the council legislation just a "reformlet" (*Reförmchen*), but scholars have noted and union officials have subsequently acknowledged that the changes to workplace codetermination significantly enhanced the clout of both employees and unions in the workplace.[110]

In 1974, the SDP-FDP coalition revised the Staff Representation Act along lines similar to the 1971 amendments to the Works Constitution Act. Works council legislation had only one significant revision during Helmut Kohl's chancellorship from 1982 to 1998. That revision, which was enacted in 1988, increased protection for small non-DGB employee associations and middle management. It also lengthened the term for works councillors to four years.

2001 Works Council Reforms

When the SPD returned to power in 1998 (this time in coalition with the Greens), revising the Works Constitution Act reemerged on the political agenda, once again at the urging of trade union leaders. Works councils are voluntary bodies. They do not come into being automatically. Employees must form them. Works councils can also go defunct, but that is rare. It has been far more common for employees at startup companies simply never to bother to form a works council in the first place. Union officials were concerned that the share of the German workforce in private employment that had works councils had dropped by eleven percentage points to just 40 percent between 1981 and 1994. In particular, enterprises in the "new economy" of software production and the internet had increasingly become largely "codetermination-free zones." Turnout for elections in the workplaces that had works councils had also dipped, falling from 80 percent in 1984 to 75 percent in 1998. Union leaders wanted to simplify the procedures for forming and electing works councils to reverse these trends.[111]

Union officials had additional concerns. The Works Council Act was written for the typical German workplace of the mid-twentieth century, which consisted principally of full-time employees working in a single workplace for the bulk of their working lives. New firm structures, which made much greater use of temporary employees and outsourcing, have effectively disenfranchised an increasing share of the workforce from participating in works councils. New technologies and production methods have arisen over which the trade unions wanted employees to have some say before they were introduced into the workplace. Union officials argued that separate works council elections for blue- and white-collar employees should be abolished because the nature of blue- and white-collar work and of the employees who did this work had become increasingly similar over the years. Finally, works councillors themselves had complained for years that they were overworked and that they did not have enough resources to represent employees properly. They pushed for a change in the law to address all these problems. Both coalition partners agreed that it was time to revisit the Works Constitution Act and shared a common view regarding the content of required revisions on most points. As a result, the legislative process proceeded relatively smoothly.[112]

German employers and their associations, which saw no need to revise the Works Constitution Act, were highly critical of the draft legislation. Business has had a largely positive view of workplace codetermination, which stands in sharp contrast to board-level codetermination. Numerous studies show that more than 90 percent of large companies and 80 percent of small ones have a positive assessment of works councils.[113] Some employers prefer working with the councils to collective bargaining because the works councils are workplace bodies and hence familiar with issues specific to each enterprise.[114] Still, employers have two big complaints when it comes to works councils: cost and bureaucracy. The Institut der Deutschen Wirtschaft, a research institute funded by the German industry and employer associations, surveyed twenty-nine large enterprises in 1998 and found that firms reported the average annual administrative cost per employee for implementing workplace codetermination to be €560.[115] Employers asserted that the 2001 revision of the Works Constitution Act would add even more to the cost of codetermination. Employers also complained that the requirement to gain approval from works councils for a wide range of investment decisions slows their ability to respond to the market. More balanced academic studies, however, do not substantiate the employers' complaints.[116]

The legislative and political debate over the reforms focused on cost and the potential impact on productivity growth. German business leaders, however, produced few serious counterproposals. In the end, German business focused their lobbying efforts on pension and tax reform, which were also under discussion at the time, and only put up perfunctory opposition to the draft revisions. As a result, the Act on the Reform of the Works Constitution Act (Gesetz zur Reform des Betriebsverfassungsgesetzes) passed in the second half of 2001 with few amendments.[117]

The 2001 act expands the definition of who constitutes a workplace employee to include temporary workers and the employees of subcontractors who have spent at least three months in the workplace (article 4) and gives collective bargaining parties greater power to define what constitutes a workplace. In instances of mergers or acquisitions, the act also requires a transitional arrangement preserving existing works councils (article 1). The act simplifies procedures for elections in workplaces with fifty or fewer employees. It also requires affirmative action regarding promotions for working mothers and, as mentioned earlier, mandates that the gender balance on a works council with at least three councillors reflect the female-male ratio found in the workplace. The reform made the integration of foreign nationals and environmental protection mandatory objectives of the councils and increased codetermination rights regarding the introduction of group work. The 2001 law addressed the issue of the heavy workload of works councillors by increasing the ratio of works councillors to employees, starting with workplaces employing more than one hundred people. It also lowered the employment threshold at a firm for which councillors begin to be released from regular work duties from three hundred to two hundred.[118]

The 2001 reforms have achieved the intended results. In 2009, the percentage of the private-sector labor force employed at enterprises with works councillors was 44 percent, which was four percentage points higher than in 1994. A majority of the total labor force both public and private is employed in a workplace with either a works or a personnel council. Participation in works council elections reached 81.1 percent, which was higher than it had been two decades earlier. The share of women works councillors increased from 19 percent in 1984 to 25 percent in 2010, which corresponds to the percentage of female employment in the workplaces that held elections.[119] Once again, state intervention shored up a key component of German industrial relations.

European Union Law and Works Councils

German works councils still have vulnerabilities. European economic integration and a dramatic increase in transnational investment have changed the environment of workplace codetermination. Increasing numbers of German enterprises have cross-border holdings. Improvements in transportation and communication and the opening of Central European economies after the Cold War have given more firms than ever the option of servicing the

German market profitably from abroad. Proponents of works councils have responded with efforts to spread the practice throughout Europe coupled with a rearguard action to block any threatening European legislation.

The issue first arose in connection with the initial attempt to create a European company statute during the 1970s and 1980s, which ultimately failed. The European Commission's Directorate General on Employment and Social Affairs headed by Henk Vredling drafted a companion directive on "information and consultation of employees in enterprises with complex, in particular, transnational structure." The directive, which in both its 1980 and 1983 versions called for mandatory procedures for informing and consulting employees in large firms, would have supplemented rather than displaced the German system of codetermination. Vociferous opposition to the Vredling directive, primarily from the heads of British and US multinationals, killed it.[120]

The issue arose again in the early 1990s. The 1986 Single European Act and the 1992 Maastricht Treaty on European Union (TEU) advanced European economic integration considerably, stimulating demand for a European company statute and a European law to govern employee participation.[121] At first, deadlock persisted. The European Commission produced a draft European works council directive in 1990 and a revised version in 1991, but it moved no further. The German government rejected it as too weak; the British government dismissed it as too strong.[122]

The TEU's social protocol opened a new way forward. It expanded and codified the European "social dialogue," which has given the social partners at the European level the opportunity to suggest the text for European legislation in the field of social affairs. Initially, Great Britain chose not to be a signatory to the social protocol, which in effect removed the British-German impasse over the issue of employee participation. In 1994, the social partners reached a common understanding regarding employee participation. On 22 September 1994, the European Commission adopted the Directive on the Establishment of a European Works Council (DEEWC, 94/45/EC), which was based on that understanding. The European Commission gave the signatories to the social protocol two years to enact enabling legislation to implement the directive at the national level.[123]

The DEEWC covers "undertakings" employing a minimum of 1,000 employees in total and at least 150 in two signatory countries of the TEU social protocol. Firms that had already created a means to inform and to consult employees that was mutually acceptable to the social partners were allowed to keep it even if it deviated from the requirements of the directive. The directive also gave interested enterprises two years after its passage to negotiate a mutually acceptable alternative method for meeting the objectives of the directive. Some 450 firms created "pre-directive agreements."[124]

For undertakings without predirective agreements, the DEEWC offers two ways to meet the obligation to inform and to consult employees. First, "central management" may negotiate a procedure with the existing institutions representing employees in each of the signatory countries in which it is economically active. Second, it may initiate negotiations to establish a European works council (EWC). Alternatively, discussions to create an EWC must commence if a written request to do so comes from: (1) entities (i.e., either a trade union or a national works council) from at least two countries representing a minimum of one hundred employees each, or (2) one hundred or more individual employees from at least two different countries.

The first step toward forming a European works council is the creation of a "special negotiating body" of employees to meet with central management to work out the details within the framework of the directive. The special negotiating body must have at least one representative from each signatory country where the undertaking is economically active. Countries with larger workforces are to have more than one representative. The focus of these negotiations is typically on the number and national distribution of EWC seats (the directive specifies a maximum of thirty) and the resources the firm will make available to councillors. Representatives from nonsignatory countries (e.g., Japan and the United States) may also be included on an EWC. If an undertaking refuses to bargain, if talks reach an impasse, if negotiations prove fruitless after three years, or upon a two-thirds vote of the special negotiating body, a default EWC model as specified in the directive comes into existence without input from management. National law and practice establish the procedure for selecting European works councillors. They differ from country to country. In 1994, the year the European Union adopted the DEEWC, there were only 52 active European works councils. Two years later, which was the deadline for transposing the directive into national legislation, there were 517, and by 2000 there were 743. Growth in the number of active EWCs slowed thereafter. In 2012, there were over 950 active European works councils representing 18 million employees throughout the European Union. The coverage rate in terms of employment at eligible firms is 38.6 percent.[125] Obstacles to the creation of additional EWCs include limited trade union resources and the reluctance of employers to disclose necessary information.[126]

Once constituted, a European works council has broad information and consultation rights. The directive stipulates that an undertaking with a EWC must hold at least one meeting per year and management must cover the expenses. At the meeting, central management is required to give presentations on business conditions and its activities in the European Union. Central management must inform the EWC of any "extraordinary conditions" that have a significant impact on the interests of employees when they arise. The directive explicitly states that an enterprise must give its EWC an opportunity to comment on any changes that significantly affect employees' interests in a timely fashion. Central management may not present a fait accompli. Organized labor and management in Germany have had few difficulties with the European works council directive because its functions are easily dovetailed with existing German codetermination structures. Still, it is important to note that EWCs do not have "codetermination" powers in the German sense. In other words, there are no management decisions that an EWC can block or delay; it can only express an opinion.[127]

Soon after the adoption of the DEEWC optimists predicted that EWCs would quickly become important players in negotiations between employee representatives and management.[128] Pessimists replied that EWCs would not become major actors in European industrial relations because the DEEWC relies too heavily on coordinating national systems rather than integrating them, calls only for information and consultation, and requires too few meetings.[129] The pessimists have proved more prescient. EWCs have neither accentuated nor curtailed the influence of German works councils in any meaningful way. In 2009, the European Commission adopted a directive designed to "recast" European works councils to address some of the shortcomings that have hampered the councils' effectiveness (2009/38/EC). The 2009 directive clarified the meaning of "information and consultation" in several respects, including making the right of employee representatives to present their views explicit and providing employees with the right to hold follow-up meetings without management participation. The reforms had little impact, however. EWCs remain an epiphenomenal element in German industrial relations.[130]

The Enduring Resilience of Codetermination in German Industrial Relations

Codetermination has proved to be tremendously advantageous to German employees because it gives them a voice in their companies grounded in statute that is much more secure and extends much farther than anything that they ever could hope to secure through trade unions alone. Codetermination in practice has buttressed unions and expanded the resources available to them. Many employers also acknowledge that the voice co-determination provides to employees has deepened loyalty to their firms, which in turn has enhanced company performance. Codetermination has intertwined labor and management, tilting the incentive structure for both labor and management toward social partnership and away from confrontation. The history of codetermination demonstrates once again the extraordinary resilience of the statutory components of the postwar German industrial relations regime. Codetermination has strong public support. All of the significant political parties except for the FDP also support the practice. Efforts since the early 1950s to expand codetermination have at times succeeded; attempts to water it down have all failed.

It is an irony of history that the German labor movement was at first deeply disappointed with most of the codetermination laws when they passed in the 1950s. This is understandable in the context of the times. The laws failed to correspond to labor's long-held vision of codetermination as a vehicle for democratic socialist planning. Still, union leaders decided to use "real existing" codetermination to advance the rights and interests of employees rather than wage an oppositional campaign against business and the state.

Although most German business leaders accept board-level codetermination as specified in the 1952 act, some segments of the business community continue to chafe at parity codetermination, be it the *Montan* version or the 1976 act; but the failed effort in the mid-2000s to roll back parity codetermination and the subsequent reform that strengthened the practice demonstrated the widespread support codetermination retains in German politics and society.

The biggest potential threat to codetermination is at the European level. Germans, however, have been proactive on the legislative front to ensure that the European company statute and works council directive did not undercut codetermination in the Federal Republic. The European Court of Justice has been less accommodating in its rulings regarding the freedom to establish firms, but it has thus far not weakened codetermination in Germany. Corporate governance expert Gregory Jackson summarizes the consensus opinion well: "Codetermination is nearly universally considered to be a stable institution in Germany."[131] Codetermination will remain a central component of German industrial relations for years to come.

The first two chapters of this book have established that postwar Germany's laws and state structures concerning industrial relations have served as a sturdy supporting trestle. Once the postwar industrial relations framework was put into place in the early 1950s, virtually every subsequent successful reform was designed to strengthen the regime. They succeeded. The framework has maintained its integrity and retained widespread legitimacy and support. Courts have at times posed challenges at the margins, but they have been mostly supportive. The evidence does not support claims that the institutional framework of German industrial relations is eroded or exhausted.

Yet, despite the resiliency of the framework, most trade unions and employers associations have found it difficult to recruit and to retain members for at least two decades. In the remainder of this book I endeavor to explain why. Since the findings reported in this chapter and the previous one are prima facie evidence that law and the state are not responsible for the membership declines, in the remainder of the book I explore other potential explanations. Still, the context of supportive laws and the state inform the remainder of this book and are a topic of the concluding chapter. The next chapter starts an investigation into the declining membership of Germany's social partners by undertaking a quantitative analysis of developments in the postwar German unionization rate.

CHAPTER 3

A Quantitative Analysis of Membership Developments in the Postwar German Trade Union Movement

Milieu Matters

In the remaining chapters I endeavor to explain a paradox. Although the supporting framework—the fishbowl, if you will—of postwar German industrial relations has stood up remarkably well over more than six decades, the fish—that is, the employers associations and trade unions—have struggled. Over the last two decades, most trade unions have lost a large proportion of their membership. Similarly, employers associations in Germany's most prominent and prestigious sector—mechanical engineering—have also lost many members. I begin the investigation of this paradox by looking at the unions. I take a quantitative approach and construct a set of time series models of union density (aka, the unionization rate) for postwar Germany. This sort of analysis of German trade unions is relatively recent and rare. A few studies appeared in the late 1980s and early 1990s, but none was done thereafter. Consequently, there is still much to be learned by undertaking additional research of this kind. The models of union density for Germany presented here are the first to include measures of labor's milieu and globalization as independent variables. They are also the first time series models to use data from a united Germany.

Three important new findings result from this analysis. First, a proximate measure of the robustness of Germany's labor milieu stands out as the most powerful variable related to density in postwar Germany. This suggests that there is a strong sociological component to unionization in Germany. Second, trade as a percentage of GDP correlates *positively* with the unionization rate, suggesting that Europeanization and globalization have actually made a significant contribution toward *strengthening* the German labor movement. Third, German unification correlates *positively* with unionization for the years under investigation. Descriptive statistics are consistent with this finding, but they also indicate that this "unification bonus" is a temporary phenomenon. It shrank over time and disappeared in the mid-2000s.

Additionally, an occupational variable and a demographic variable— that is, public-sector employment and foreign employees as a share of the labor force—correlate with unionization with their signs in the expected directions (i.e., positive and negative, respectively). The model also shows significant correlations in the expected directions for two business cycle explanations for developments in trade union density, but their influence is relatively minor.

The body of the chapter contains the membership and density data for the postwar German trade union movement, and I then specify a set of econometric models to account for German union density. I conclude the chapter with a discussion of the impact of the findings on our understanding of German trade unionism.

Union Membership and Density Trends in Postwar Germany

Numerous quantitative and qualitative studies over the decades have focused on factors affecting union membership in a wide range of countries.[1] Union membership has attracted considerable attention because it is the font of labor's political and economic influence. A business can be successful with one employee or a million employees, so long as it is profitable. Unions, in contrast, must have a critical mass of members to be effective. Certainly, small unions ensconced in key positions in an economy can be effective at extracting additional compensation for their members at the margins, and laws can greatly extend the reach of union movements in the labor market (e.g., France), but it is difficult for a union movement to be influential nationally unless it has enough members to maintain at least a cursory presence in most regions and sectors of the economy. Similarly, unions' political clout depends to a considerable degree on the rank-and-file members, material supplies, and financial resources they can deploy to influence the outcome of elections.

Quantitative studies have used two measures as a dependent variable to specify membership developments: change in union membership and density. Change in membership is self-explanatory. Density is the share of employees who are union members, calculated as a percentage of all employees who are legally eligible to belong to a union. Neither variable is perfect. Change in union membership includes trends orthogonal to union strength, such as shifts in the size of the workforce. Union density, in contrast, does control for changes in workforce size, but when using it as a variable, precautions must be taken to avoid autocorrelation and spurious correlations. In this chapter I use union density as a dependent variable because controlling for change in the size of the workforce is essential for any time series analysis of Germany that includes years both before and after unification.[2]

Union membership is the numerator in any calculation of union density. To determine the actual number of union members, it is important first to decide which organizations are unions. In most instances, this is easy, but for a few it is not. The criterion of inclusion used here is whether an organization negotiates collective agreements. All scholars calculating postwar German trade union membership include the members of the affiliated unions of three confederations: the dominant Deutscher Gewerkschaftsbund (DGB, German Trade Union Federation), the small sectarian Christlicher Gewerkschaftsbund (CGB, Christian Trade Union Federation), and the specialized Deutscher Beamtenbund (DBB, German Civil Servants Federation), whose affiliates' members are mostly but not exclusively civil servants. In this chapter I follow the lead of the two top authorities on German trade union data, Bernard Ebbinghaus and Jelle Visser, by including members of affiliates of a fourth confederation, the Deutscher Führungskräfteverband Union der Leitenden Angestellten (German Managers Confederation, DFV ULA).[3] The clientele of the DFV ULA is middle- to upper-level management, which means they typically have supervisory responsibilities. Including the DFV ULA is warranted, however, because upper managers are counted as employees in German statistics, German law permits them to belong to unions, and DFV ULA associations negotiate collective agreements. As a result, it would be inconsistent to exclude DFV ULA members.

The membership data in this study also incorporate unions that have not belonged to a confederation, specifically, the Deutscher Journalistenverband journalists union, Marburger Bund physicians union, Vereinigung Cockpit airline pilots union, Vereinigung Boden airport ground personnel union, Vereinigung Luftfahrt air traffic controllers, and the Unabhängige

Flugbegleiter Organisation flight attendants union. The data also include the police union, Gewerkschaft der Deutschen Polizei, and the white-collar Deutsche Angestellten-Gewerkschaft before they came under the umbrella of the DGB.[4]

Having established which organizations are unions, the next question that arises is which members to count. The most expansive approach, which German industrial relations scholars call "gross" union membership, counts all trade union members, including retirees and the unemployed. Gross union membership is politically salient because it reflects the pool from which labor can mobilize, but it is not appropriate to use it to calculate density. For a measure of density to be sound, all individuals in the numerator (i.e., unionized employees) must also be among the employees counted in the denominator. This means only employed union members, a population scholars call "net" union membership, should be included.[5] Calculating net union membership is a challenge in practice because most German unions do not disaggregate their membership data. Still, it can be estimated. The two largest unions, the Industrial Union of Metalworkers (Industriegewerkschaft Metall, IG Metall) and the United Service Employees Union (Vereinte Dienstleistungsgewerkschaft, ver.di) both report disaggregated data.[6] This is fortunate, because these two unions have consistently accounted for well over half of all German trade union members and taken together serve as a good representative sample of the German trade union movement as a whole because of the sectors from which they recruit members. Consequently, I estimate the number of employed union members for those unions that do not report it by multiplying their gross union membership by the ratio of net to gross union members in IG Metall and ver.di.[7]

Net union membership in postwar Germany has moved through six phases in sixty years (figure 3.1). During the "economic miracle" years of 1950 to 1962, net union membership rose from 5.6 million to just shy of 7 million, which translates into an annual average growth rate of 1.9 percent. The mid-1960s were more difficult for organized labor. Union membership actually fell by 300,000, or 0.75 percent per year, between 1962 and 1968. Boom years followed, however. From 1968 to 1981, active union membership increased from 6.7 million to 8.3 million, or by a mean annual rate of 1.7 percent. Union membership hit a second soft patch during the 1980s. Between 1981 and 1989, it fell by 300,000, or 0.5 percent each year on average, to just over 8 million. German unification generated a one-time spike in union membership. From 1990 to 1991, the movement expanded by 3.4 million, or 42.1 percent, to 11.5 million

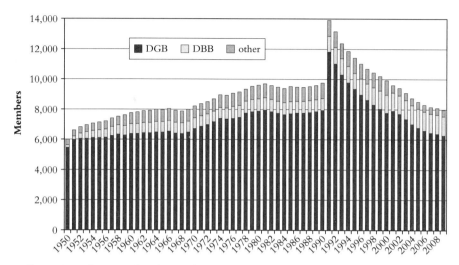

FIGURE 3.1. German trade union membership: Deutscher Gewerkschaftsbund (DGB), Deutscher Beamtenbund (DBB), and other trade unions.

Sources: DGB, DBB, CGB, and Statistisches Bundesamt.

actively employed members. Steep decline characterizes the most recent phase, which is also the longest. Between 1991 and 2009, German unions lost 44.4 percent of their employed membership, or 3 percent per year on average, which amounted to 5.1 million. The pace of the decline has slowed in recent years.

The denominator in a density calculation consists of employees. All individuals in the denominator must be able to belong to a union even if some choose not to do so (e.g., the denominator cannot include the self-employed). The data series that best captures solely the pool of employees who are eligible to belong to a union is "Active employees in the domestic labor market" (*erwerbstätige Arbeitnehmer Inland*). It serves as the denominator. This chapter's density calculation is very close both to the other calculations using a similar methodology and to survey data since German unification.[8]

The course of German postwar net union density differs from the membership trend (compare figures 3.1 and 3.2). Density peaked shortly after trade unions regained full autonomy in 1950, reaching an all-time postwar high of 42.2 percent in 1951, but then it declined steadily for almost two decades (figure 3.2), despite the significant expansion of net union membership (figure 3.1). Union density bottomed out in 1969 at 31.7 percent but then reversed direction, climbing gradually for a decade with only a few setbacks. Density reached a plateau of 35.5 percent in 1979 and then began a long-term decline. The deterioration was gradual for a decade, but then

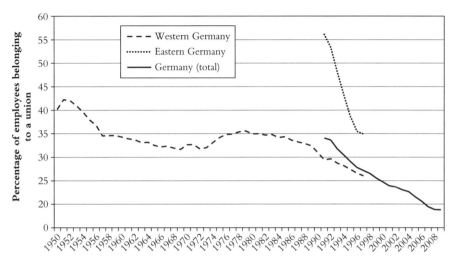

FIGURE 3.2. German trade union density, 1950–2009: Employed union members as a percentage of employees.
Sources: DGB, DBB, CGB, and Statistisches Bundesamt.

it became worse starting in the 1990s. Union density in western Germany reached an all-time low of 26 percent in 1997, the last year for which regionally disaggregated aggregate data exist.

Unification complicates matters. Figure 3.2 presents density data for eastern and western Germany through 1997, and data for united Germany from 1991 onward. Eastern German density data for the early 1990s is reminiscent of the West German pattern from the 1950s, only in an exaggerated form. Easterners initially flocked to the unions; the eastern unionization rate was 56.1 percent in 1991. Eastern union density plummeted quickly thereafter; it fell to 34.9 percent in 1997. The initial influx of eastern union members pushed density for Germany as a whole almost 5 percentage points higher than western density in 1991 (29.4% vs. 24.1%). Thereafter the gap narrowed. By 1997, union density in Germany as a whole was 27.1 percent, which was only 1.1 percentage points higher than in western Germany. The unionization rate declined steadily in united Germany for almost two decades. In 1991 it stood at 34.1 percent. Union density bottomed out in 2008 and 2009 at 18.8 percent.

Model and Variable Selection

Scholars first constructed quantitative models of unionization in the 1960s. The first models were mostly of English-speaking countries, and they typically contained labor market variables related to the business cycle and an occasional political control variable. Later models added occupational and demographic factors, followed by measures of employer strength and globalization. Other scholars devised additional determinants of unionization—such as social custom, that is, a social milieu conducive to union membership—but did not test them empirically in the early days. Quantitative models of German unionization first appeared in the late 1980s. Only a few models exist, and they all have shortcomings. In particular, they frequently use gross rather than net union membership, and they only include business cycle and political variables.[9]

Scholars have used two types of models to investigate the determinants of the unionization rate: time series analyses and panel data. Panel data for western Germany extend back only to the 1980s; for eastern Germany, they begin in the early 1990s. These data are therefore unlikely to capture developments that change only gradually (e.g., milieu strength). As a result, in this chapter I use time series data, which begin in the 1950s. I rely on generalized least-squares (GLS) analyses in order to control for correlation between observations producing misleading inferences.[10]

German unification poses special challenges to undertaking a time series analysis. The German government uses 1991 as a transition year in many data series, reporting figures for both western Germany and Germany as a whole. It is difficult to find separate eastern and western German data series for many variables after 1991. So, all the models in this chapter use data for West Germany up until 1991 and for united Germany from 1992 onward. The models include a dummy variable, which takes the value of "1" starting in 1992 and "0" for the years previous to control for shifts in the data and to capture the impact of German unification. In the results section below, I also report on the results of a regression of a model using data for West Germany for the years 1954 to 1991 to assess the soundness of considering data from West Germany and united Germany to be a single sample.

The Dependent Variable

In this chapter I use union density as a dependent variable for the reasons discussed above. Density data extend from 1949 to 2009, but the data for one of the independent variables—namely, foreign employees—exist only from 1954 onwards. As a result, the number of observations in the model for each variable is 55. Let us now turn to a discussion of hypotheses and their specification as independent variables.

The Independent Variables

The full model tests fourteen hypotheses regarding determinants of union density. Six are economic. The remaining relationships are demographic, institutional, political, and sociological. The model also includes three control variables. Each will be discussed individually. Economic explanations are among the oldest and most frequently used in models assessing union density. So, we will walk through these first.

1. Change in nominal income—that is, the money wage—is the most frequently used variable in unionization studies. The specification of the variable has differed slightly from study to study, but the hypothesized relationship is the same: nominal increases in income produce a "credit effect" for unions that boosts the probability that an employee will be a member. German trade union leaders acknowledged the linkage between the "material usefulness" of unions and recruitment in a 2005 confidential report on strategies to reverse membership declines.[11] I use annual change in nominal net wages and salaries to test this relationship. Net and annual data best capture nominal disposable income because they control for tax increases and adjustments in working time.[12]

2. The inflation rate measured in consumer prices has also been a standard component in models from the very beginning of quantitative analysis of union membership trends. Studies hypothesize that unionization is positively associated with higher rates of inflation because employees perceive inflation as a "threat" and see union membership as a means to protect themselves from that threat.[13] It should be noted, however, that since inflation has been low and has varied relatively little throughout the years in postwar Germany, inflation may not be nearly as salient a variable in Germany as it has been in other countries.

3. Some studies use profits or firm income aggregated at the national level as a proxy for business prosperity.[14] The reasoning here is that prosperous businesses would more readily accept a union because the opportunity cost of production disruptions would be greater and the costs associated with unions would be more affordable. Alternatively, Corneo uses rational choice analytics to support the contention that an increasing surplus earned per employee may engender greater management opposition to unions.[15] This variable is more salient to countries where union recognition is decided at the workplace level, which is not the case in Germany. It is still worth including in this analysis because business prosperity may also affect business attitudes toward unions.[16] I use firm and property income (i.e., the nonlabor share of income) as a percentage of GDP as a variable to assess the relationship

between business prosperity and unionization.[17] Firm and property income is a broad measure to capture most fully the capacity of firms to afford paying higher compensation. Calculating it as a percentage of GDP precludes the necessity to adjust for inflation and also avoids the need to log the variable to compensate for swings in the data over the course of a business cycle.

4. Unemployment is a common independent variable in studies of unionization. The relationship is not simple, however. On the one hand, high unemployment may increase both the hesitancy of employees to unionize and the likelihood that employers will challenge unionization. Union membership, on the other hand, may be particularly attractive to employees in times of high joblessness if they perceive unions as capable of providing some employment protection. The combination of greater vulnerability of employees with the increased attractiveness of employment protection that unions may offer in times of high employment lead Bain and Elsheikh to comment that "the relationship is likely to be relatively weak and characterized by a lag."[18] Subsequent studies taken as a whole are consistent with the assessment of Bain and Elsheikh; some have found a significant negative relationship between unemployment and union membership,[19] but others have not.[20] It has become standard practice in the literature to lag the unemployment variable in keeping with the theoretical justification of Bain and Elsheikh. Lagging also avoids the chance of biasing coefficient estimates owing to endogeneity. As a result, all models here use lagged unemployment as an independent variable.

5. Change in employment is also a frequently used variable for which contradictory hypotheses exist. Ashenfelter and Pencavel reason that employment growth should correlate positively with unionization because it is indicative of a tight labor market.[21] In contrast, Visser and Wallerstein both argue that employment growth could lead to a drop in density, but each identifies a different causal mechanism. Visser invokes a sociological argument, claiming that employment growth leads to "the entry of more people with weak labor market attachments and a low propensity to unionize."[22] Wallerstein uses the logic of marginal cost, pointing out that "the effect of an increased number of potential members on the union's optimal density . . . is unambiguously negative" because "unions in large labor markets must pay a higher price than unions in small labor markets to achieve the same union density. Since the price is higher, unions in large markets purchase less."[23] The specifics of the German case do allow us to distinguish between the arguments of Ashenfelter and Pencavel and those of Visser or Wallerstein, but they do not provide a clear way to sort out whether the causal argument of Visser or Wallerstein is closer to the mark.

6. Trade (i.e., exports plus imports) as a percentage of gross domestic product is the final economic variable. It is not a business cycle measure; it moves owing to factors both inside and outside of the domestic economy. The variable's purpose here is to assess the impact of globalization on union membership. Both Hassel and Blaschke claim that "increased international competition harms unionization by inhibiting wage increases, hardening management attitudes, and intensifying competition among employees, leading to an erosion of solidarity."[24] Wallerstein makes a counterargument: "Perceptions of vulnerability to the vicissitudes of international markets induce the leadership of both business and unions to seek an institutional framework in which compromises can be achieved and conflict can be avoided . . . [which] entails high levels of union density."[25] No previous single-country quantitative study of Germany has included trade as a variable. Blaschke and others who have undertaken cross-national studies have used a trade variable, but they do not permit teasing out information specific to Germany. Investigations of other countries have produced mixed results regarding trade as an independent variable.[26] Given Germany's persistent strong record as an exporter, there is reason to believe that the relationship between trade and unionization may differ for Germany in comparison to countries that do not typically run current account surpluses. Since both multilateral and European-wide economic integration has become progressively stronger over time, we would expect this variable to become more powerful in the later years.

7. In Germany, there is one pair of occupational categories and one pair of demographic groups for which the likelihood of belonging to a union may differ from the general population. The occupations are manufacturing and public service, and the groups are foreign nationals and women.

Many studies conclude that employees in the manufacturing sector have a higher propensity to belong to unions than employees in most other sectors because of the large size and deep division of labor typical of many manufacturing facilities. As a result, numerous scholars of union membership include manufacturing employment as a percentage of total employment as a variable.[27]

8. Some models also include the share of employment in the public sector as a variable. The argument here is that public employers are typically less hostile than private ones to unionization, so the propensity to unionize is higher.[28] This difference in attitude has not been constant over the postwar years. Government officials' position regarding public-sector unionization only became more sympathetic starting in the 1970s. This shift in attitude

may render this variable less effective, particularly for time series populated with data from the 1950s and 1960s.

9. Several analyses of unionization include the percentage of foreign nationals in the workforce as a variable. This makes sense for a study of Germany given the sizable number of employees who are foreign nationals. The expectation is that cultural and social barriers make foreign nationals more difficult to organize.[29]

10. Qualitative studies frequently use anecdotal and demographic data to support the assertion that women have a lower propensity to belong to a union than men do.[30] Lower female unionization rates, however, may be a function of the types of jobs women hold in disproportionately high numbers—that is, part-time or contingent positions at smaller enterprises in the private service sector—rather than an inherent difference in preference. Visser has observed that over the last two decades female union density has caught up with or even surpassed male union density in some countries. This variable may have lost some salience as a result of societal change.[31] Still, it is nothing short of shocking that most quantitative models of union density, particularly studies of countries other than the United States, do not at least include female labor force participation as a variable. This chapter fills that void for Germany.

11. The strike rate is an institutional feature of the industrial relations regime that may also affect the propensity to belong to unions. Strike benefits are a form of insurance. The more frequent an occurrence that has cost, the more likely individuals will insure against it. This line of argument associates higher strike rates with greater union density.[32] It should be said, however, that strikes are relatively rare occurrences in Germany; they tend to be brief and are concentrated in specific regions and sectors. This pattern reduces the likelihood that strikes will be a significant variable in the German case because only a very small share of union members ever need strike benefits.

12. A dummy variable to register the years when the Sozialdemokratische Partei Deutschlands (SPD, Social Democratic Party of Germany) is in power is the first of two political variables considered here. Scholars have argued that a sympathetic party can help increase density by enacting legislation and making administrative decisions favorable to organized labor. The best means to capture this argument is to use a dummy variable that takes a value of "1" whenever the SPD is in the governing coalition at the federal level and "0" when it is not, because the logic here hinges on whether a sympathetic party is in power.[33] The SPD was the lead party in government twice

(i.e., 1969–1982 and 1998–2005). In the two instances when the SPD was a junior partner in a governing coalition (i.e., 1966–69 and 2005–9) SPD politicians controlled key ministries related to industrial relations and the economy. As a result, these years are also coded as "1."

13. Scholars have argued that density may be related to welfare expenditures, and most include it in their models, but they are not unified regarding the causal mechanism behind the measure. Some argue along the same lines as the credit effect for nominal wages, that is, expansive welfare benefits increase union membership because unions receive credit for getting them. A second argument points in the same causal direction using the logic of T. H. Marshall and his adherents. Welfare benefits help to decommodify labor, which expands the "social rights" of workers and reduces the risk involved in unionization efforts. As a result, employees would be more likely to organize when the welfare state is more expansive. Others argue, in contrast, that the welfare and union benefits are substitutes; they therefore are inversely related.[34]

14. In this chapter I also include a measure of the strength of labor's milieu as an explanatory variable for union density. The theoretical justification for using milieu as an independent variable has its roots in a long-standing discussion of the impact of social custom on unionization. The social custom argument begins with the premise that employees' decisions to belong to unions "are influenced by the decisions and pressures of family and friends, co-workers, managers, employers, governments and union organizers . . . Compliance with the norm of membership is seen as deriving from a reputation effect, which in turn, depends on the beliefs and actions of significant others."[35] Social custom is nurtured and passed on within a social milieu. For trade unions, the breadth and vibrancy of this milieu reflects employee class consciousness broadly defined. There have been numerous studies over the years using a variety of approaches that have assessed the size and strength of organized labor's social milieu in Germany. For example, sociologist Ralf Dahrendorf's prescient 1959 analysis of German society concluded that the confluence of the expansion of white-collar work and the labor movement's embrace of Keynesian-style capitalism as a part of its ideological modernization would expand labor's social milieu by allowing for the inclusion of white-collar employees in the traditional blue-collar base.[36] Labor's milieu did indeed expand, which laid the groundwork for the rise in union density during the 1970s.

The tide turned for labor's milieu in the 1980s. A new generation of scholars led by Ulrich Beck detailed a decline in collectivism and the rise in the postmodern "pluralization" of life styles that has contributed to the deterioration of social customs supportive of trade unions.[37] World Values Survey data support these findings and suggest timing consistent with the decline in the German unionization rate. Western German respondents exhibit a significant decline on questions that reflect a preference for collectivism over individualism starting in the early 1980s. A similar decline is registered for eastern Germans during the years after unification.[38] Leading analysts within the German trade union movement have themselves made the connection between social custom and unionization. A 2005 confidential DGB report on strategies to reverse membership decline identified shrinkage of "the importance of the natural labor milieu" as the number one reason why German unions were losing members.[39]

Social milieu and social custom are very difficult to specify. Some studies use panel data (e.g., Visser, "Why Fewer Workers Join Unions in Europe"), but as mentioned, panel data for Germany do not extend far enough back to capture the change in the size and salience of the labor milieu sufficiently. Checchi and Visser attempt to specify social custom in a cross-national time series analysis by using employment ratios for selected occupational and demographic groups as proximate variables, arguing that labor market heterogeneity disrupts the labor milieu. They also use the strike rate and institutional support for workplace representation as additional proximate variables of social custom.[40] The problem with all these variables is that the causal mechanisms involved are far more obviously demographic, economic, and institutional than related to social custom. Doubling them up as social custom measures is not persuasive as a result.

As an alternative, in this chapter I use membership in left-of-center parties as a percentage of the population as a proximate variable for the size of the labor milieu.[41] Party membership is quite distinct from voting preferences because it expresses a willingness of individuals to commit time and resources to sustain a working-class infrastructure and community beyond merely voting for a party. Membership is also a much stronger expression of identity than voting. The left-of-center parties that best give an indication of the health of the labor milieu are the SPD before German unification, and the SPD plus the Partei des Demokratischen Sozialismus (Party of Democratic Socialism, PDS) and then the Linkspartei (Left Party) after unification.[42] No study of unionization has ever included a social milieu measure of this sort. Some have used voting percentages for parties historically associated with labor movements, but those data are more suited to taking the immediate political pulse of the general public than the strength of a milieu.[43]

Without doubt, left-of-center parties are not coterminous with the labor movement, and over the years the German labor movement has had

its differences with left-of-center parties.[44] The relationship between the
SPD and the unions resembles that of blood relatives; it is normally close,
at times fierce disagreements arise, but underlying bonds endure. The relationship between labor and the PDS and then the Left Party has been
circumspect to say the least. The official position of DGB unions during
the Cold War was critical of Communism, and the trajectory of that legacy
only gradually dissipated. On the other hand, a small but significant minority of midlevel union leaders maintained sympathetic positions regarding
East Germany, and several subsequently played key roles in the Left Party
attaining a foothold in western Germany. The SPD has never managed to
secure a position east of the Elbe comparable to its place in the west. The
socioeconomic groups that make up the labor milieu in eastern Germany
have belonged to the PDS and then the Left Party in disproportionately
high numbers. As a result, for united Germany, the combined membership
of the SPD and the PDS/Left Party as a percentage of the population
serves as the best indicator of the size of the milieu supportive of the trade
union movement.

To be sure, left-of-center party membership as a percentage of the population is a proximate measure. Using a proximate variable is the standard
means to specify a broad, abstract concept like social custom/milieu. Checchi and Visser do the same; they just choose different variables. Left-party
membership as a percentage of the population is superior to the proximate
variables of Checchi and Visser precisely because it is a socio-political
rather than a labor market variable. By lagging the milieu variable, this
study avoids the chance of biasing coefficient estimates due to endogeneity and sets change in party membership causally prior to change in union
density.

15. Newer models of union membership and density include lagged
union density as a control variable.[45] A lagged dependent variable serves as
a simple control for the simple yet powerful social science observation that
most often a present outcome will remain unchanged in the immediate
future (i.e., $t_0 = t_1$). To be sure, using a lagged dependent variable runs the
risk of that variable absorbing the effects of other highly trended independent variables, but that is not a problem for this sort of analysis, which is
endeavoring to create as challenging a test as possible of the significance of
individual potentially causal variables. The trend variable is extremely helpful in this regard because it filters out an overall trend from the estimations
of individual independent variables, which improves the likelihood that the
significance of individual variables reflects the specified relationship without

the assistance of unrelated underlying trends.[46] Confidence in the results
for the other individual independent variables will be that much greater if
they consistently exhibit significance in models that also include the lagged
dependent variable.

16. The model also contains a trend variable, which is best practice for
time series to weed out autocorrelation. Including the trend variable increases confidence that the individual variables are actually a measure of the
specified relationship.

Results

Before evaluating the results in detail, it is useful to make two general observations. First, all the models in this chapter have a high adjusted r-squared.
This is not unusual. Several previous cross-national studies (which by definition are far more heterogeneous than a single-case analysis of Germany) that
include lagged density as a variable have an r-squared ranging from 0.80 to
0.95.[47] Unlike those previous models, in this chapter I follow current best
practice of including a separate trend variable, which boosts the r-squared
further. An r-squared is a descriptive statistic that indicates the accuracy of
the estimates of the entire sample. The principal objective of this study, in
contrast, is to draw inferences about individual causal variables. The statistical significance of the individual variables is what is salient here, not the
r-squared results. In fact, a high r-squared is an anticipated by-product of
intentionally constructing a model with a lagged dependent variable, a trend
variable, and numerous independent variables in order to be as rigorous as
possible in weeding out spurious correlations to test the significance of each
individual key causal variable.

Table 3.1 presents the results for the four most salient specifications of
union density in Germany. They cover the years from 1954 to 2009. The
first is a simple business cycle model (column 1), which serves as a baseline. The results for this specification produce no surprises. The credit effect specified as nominal net wage change correlates positively with union
density. Change in employment correlates negatively with density, which
provides support for the arguments of Wallerstein and Visser over that of
Ashenfelter and Pencavel discussed earlier. Change in consumer prices and
the lagged unemployment rate yield insignificant results, which is in keeping with our expectations, given postwar Germany's low inflation rates and
the hypothesized cross-cutting impact of unemployment on density. Firm
income as a share of GDP is insignificant, which is also not surprising,

given that the decision to belong to a union in Germany does not depend on workplace elections. Two control variables—lagged trade union density and the unification dummy variable—did correlate significantly in the business cycle model. The sign of the unification dummy variable is negative in

Table 3.1.   German Trade Union Density, 1954–2009: Generalized Least Squares Estimates

Variables	(1) Business Cycle Model	(2) Full Model	(3) Selected Model	(4) Standardized Coefficients
Nominal Net Wage Change	0.158** (0.047)	0.151*** (0.036)	0.096** (0.031)	0.063** (0.020)
Change in Consumer Prices	0.086 (0.070)	–0.065 (0.067)		
Firm income (% GDP)	0.016 (0.055)	0.052 (0.065)		
Unemployment Rate $_{-1}$	0.069 (0.066)	–0.054 (0.061)		
Change in Employment	0.292*** (0.057)	–0.133* (0.057)	–0.123** (0.039)	–0.051** (0.016)
Trade (% GDP)		0.058** (0.019)	0.048*** (0.010)	0.133*** (0.029)
Manufacturing Employment		–0.079 (0.045)		
Public-Sector Employment		0.478** (0.167)	0.547*** (0.114)	0.281*** (0.059)
Foreign Employment		–0.300** (0.101)	–0.267*** (0.045)	–0.153*** (0.026)
Female Employment		–0.390 (0.255)		
Strike Rate		0.000 (0.000)		
SPD in Government		–0.003 (0.002)		
Welfare Expenditures (% GDP)		0.068 (0.055)		
Milieu (Membership in Left Parties [% Population])		4.767*** (1.277)	5.607*** (0.840)	0.294*** (0.044)
Trade Union Density $_{-1}$	0.941*** (0.042)	0.554*** (0.078)	0.512*** (0.059)	0.502*** (0.059)

(*Continued*)

Table 3.1.   (Continued)

Variables	(1) Business Cycle Model	(2) Full Model	(3) Selected Model	(4) Standardized Coefficients
Unification Dummy	-0.010★★	0.030★★	0.027★★★	0.252★★★
	(0.004)	(0.010)	(0.004)	(0.038)
Trend	0.000	-0.001★★	-0.001★★★	-0.346★★★
	(0.000)	(0.000)	(0.000)	(0.573)
Constant	0.005	0.187	0.020	-0.003
	(0.017)	(0.103)	(0.012)	(0.009)
Adjusted R^2	0.990	0.997	0.996	0.996

Note: Coefficients • (Standard error in parentheses) • Column (4) = Standardized z-beta coefficients

★★★p < 0.001; ★★p < 0.01; ★p < 0.05. N = 55.

the business cycle model, but, as we shall see, its sign changes in subsequent specifications.

The second specification is of the full model containing all of the variables discussed above (column 2). The signs and significance of the five business cycle variables do not change when compared to the baseline model, despite the addition of nine new variables, which provides some confidence that the baseline model is robust.

The single most striking finding here is that the milieu measure yields strongly significant results (i.e., p < 0.001), with its sign in the expected positive direction. It is also notable that trade as a percentage of GDP correlates *positively* with union density. This is consistent with the argument that Germany's open economy and strong export performance help to sustain union membership. In other words, this result suggests that globalization and European economic integration have *helped* bolster German trade union membership.

It is noteworthy that the unification dummy variable remains significant but exhibits a positive sign in the full specification, which indicates that it may have captured more than just factors related to unification in the baseline business cycle specification. The unification variable's positive sign in the full specification suggests that unification made a positive contribution to German union membership. An inspection of the descriptive statistics confirm this positive contribution. Eastern German density was persistently higher than western density from 1990 to 1997, the last year for which there are full data on union membership for each part of Germany (figure 3.2). Forty years of central planning in East Germany, which emphasized industrial production over services and collective solutions to social objectives, appears to have initially left an economic and social structure that remained disposed toward unionization. Moreover, many eastern Germans pursuing wrongful dismissal suits joined and stayed in unions for the duration of their cases, which was often years, because the unions covered their litigation costs. This positive differential did not last, however. As the years progressed, eastern economic and social structures gradually converged with the west. The gap accordingly closed in the mid-2000s.

Of the occupational and demographic characteristics, the share of public-sector employment correlates positively and the share of foreign employment correlates negatively with union density. These signs are as expected. The probabilities of significance for the share of manufacturing and female employment fall short (with p-values of 0.088 and 0.135, respectively). The institutional and political variables (i.e., the strike rate, SPD in government, and welfare expenditures) were also insignificant, but by much wider margins.

Robustness Tests

Two sets of robustness tests further support these findings. The first consists of a regression that only covers West Germany before unification, and the second examines a variable for which there exist only truncated data series, namely, foreign direct investment (FDI).

Running the regression for West Germany before unification is a means to assess whether it is sound to consider a combination of data from West Germany and united Germany to be a single sample. The full model for West Germany contains sixteen variables (including trend and the other control variables, but excluding the unification dummy) for the years 1954 to 1991 (i.e., thirty-seven data points). The regression extends to 1991, which is the first full year that Germany was unified, in order to accommodate lagged variables.

The regression for West Germany pushes the limits of the available degrees of freedom, but it nonetheless holds up reasonably well.[48] Nominal net wage change and employment change remain significantly correlated with union density, and their signs do not change. Trade and the shares of public-sector and foreign employment lose significance, but the milieu variable stays positive and significant. Hence, the results for

West Germany are consistent with the finding that milieu is a significant factor influencing union density. The results for trade, public-sector employment, and foreign employment are ambiguous. They could mean that either of those variables only gained salience in recent years, as discussed regarding trade and public-sector employment, or they simply fell victim to the "small-N problem."[49]

It is worth noting that some quantitative cross-national studies of union membership have used additional variables. These include outward foreign direct investment as a second gauge of globalization.[50] Data exist for German outward FDI, but not for the years prior to 1970. A test of the potential explanatory power of this variable using a truncated data series would give some indication as to whether the absence of this variable from the longer time series results in omitted variable bias. The most rigorous test of this possibility is to add it to the baseline business cycle model rather than the full model because this approach preserves more degrees of freedom. If the results are insignificant, it would suggest that FDI does not play a measurable role in determining union density in postwar Germany. Before discussing the results, it is useful to provide more detail about the variable.

The test uses the United Nations Conference on Trade and Development (UNCTAD) data on Germany's outward foreign direct investment as a percentage of GDP to specify FDI. These data extend back eight years further than the Bundesbank's FDI series, the only other source for German FDI statistics available. The results show the baseline business cycle model to be stable when applied to the truncated dataset, except for the unification dummy, which loses significance in the truncated baseline model but regains it with a negative sign when the FDI variable is added. The FDI variable itself comes up insignificant, which suggests that its absence from the full time series models does not bias the results.

Selected and Standardized Estimates

A selected estimate using the eight consistently statistically significant variables from the full model produces strong results (table 3.1, column 3). Changes in trade as a percentage of GDP, shares of public-sector and foreign employment, social custom/milieu (i.e., percentage membership in left-of-center parties), and lagged trade union density all maintain the predicted sign whenever used in this study. In the selected estimate, they produce strongly significant results (i.e., $p < 0.001$). The confidence level for the significant business cycle variables—that is, nominal wage change and change in employment—is slightly lower (i.e., $p < 0.01$), but it is still strong, and the variables have also performed consistently. The unification dummy variable comes up again in the selected estimate strongly significant and with a positive sign.

Column 4 of table 3.1 presents standardized coefficients in order to assess which independent variables have a greater effect on the dependent variable, despite differences in units and ranges among the variables. Standardization is achieved by calculating z-values for each variable, which normalizes them using their individual standard deviations, and then running a regression. The results show milieu as the causal variable having the biggest impact on union density in postwar Germany, with a standardized coefficient of 0.294. The results suggest that the share of public-sector employment and the impact of unification are also relatively powerful. The foreign employment share and trade follow with standardized coefficients of -0.153 and 0.133, which suggests that they are significant but secondary factors. The standardized coefficients for the two business cycle variables—change in nominal net income and employment change—are the lowest (i.e., 0.063 and -0.051, respectively), indicating significant but relatively small influence on union density.

Milieu Matters

The quantitative analysis presented here shows milieu to be the single biggest factor affecting union density in postwar Germany. This variable was consistently highly significant and the most influential causal variable in the regressions. This suggests that the decline in Germany's labor milieu has figured prominently in the drop in union density. The significance and relatively sizable impact of the shares of public-sector and foreign employment are consistent with previous findings in both the qualitative and quantitative literature.

The positive influence of trade on density is also a new and important finding, but it is not wholly surprising for the German case. Globalization and Europeanization have actually expanded German export markets, particularly in sectors such as mechanical engineering, where unionization is relatively robust, which in turn has helped to bolster density. These findings do run counter to much of the qualitative literature and popular discussion of the effects of globalization on unions, including the erosion argument. They indicate that open economies are not inherently disadvantageous for trade unions. Congruence between a country's comparative advantage and the pattern of unionization can benefit organized labor. Bolstering Wallerstein's argument, economic openness may indeed shift the relative incentives for business and labor toward social partnership.

The positive contribution of unification to union density also runs counter to conventional wisdom, which emphasizes the cost and dislocations of unification for trade unions. It was a temporary phenomenon, which was a product of eastern Germany's initial structural and sociological peculiarities that came to an end in the mid-2000s.

Finally, two business cycle variables—change in employment and nominal net wage change—were also consistently significant. In recent years, neither variable has moved in a direction favorable to organized labor. The negative sign for change in employment is indicative of German labor's inability to break into the new growth sectors of the economy. The findings regarding nominal net wage change suggest that the "credit effect" matters in Germany and that wage restraint in collective bargaining, which has been the norm since the 1980s, has contributed to declining union density. It should be noted, however, that the relatively small impact of both the business cycle variables indicates that a more aggressive approach to collective bargaining or more success in organizing new sectors of the economy by themselves would have had a relatively minor impact on density.

It is worth mentioning that the relative impact of all the other significant standardized variables far exceeds that of the business cycle variables, a finding that turns the expectations of the early literature on its head. In other words, the finding in this chapter suggest that unionization is much more of a sociological than an economic phenomenon. A milieu has deep roots, changes slowly, and is shaped largely from within a society.[51] Trends in labor's milieu are difficult to reverse, which does not bode well for the German trade union movement. It is worth noting that these results also run counter to the erosion and exhaustion hypotheses, which emphasize economic and structural variables.

The correlational analyses that I present here help us to understand better the forces affecting union density in postwar Germany. The findings of this chapter also serve as a foundation for the next chapter, in which I undertake a qualitative analysis of the postwar German labor movement. I examine how actors inside and outside of organized labor have come to understand the trade union movement and its challenges as well as the policy debates and decisions that have influenced the course of the movement in the postwar years.

CHAPTER 4

Trade Unions in Germany

The Two Postwar Movements

In this chapter, I present a qualitative analysis of the postwar German trade union movement. I argue that despite continuity in leadership Germany has effectively had two trade union movements in the postwar era. The first movement was established in the immediate aftermath of the Second World War. Its organizing principle was industrial unionism, that is, for each major sector there is one and only one union. The first movement was remarkably stable and successful for four decades. It was a product of the high era of mass production and the unfolding Cold War. The lessons of the Weimar Republic and the Nazi years also decisively shaped it. The second postwar German trade union movement, which emerged in the early 2000s after a decade of organizational reform, is distinct because it is dominated by multisectoral unions. Since 2001, two unions that span multiple sectors account for more than two thirds of all German union membership. The second movement is the product of internally contested responses to a substantially changed economic, political, and social environment for organized labor rather than erosion or exhaustion.

In this chapter, I examine the construction of the first postwar trade union movement, the years of stability, the transition to the second trade union movement, and the considerable difficulties that union officials in the second movement have faced in their efforts to advance the economic and political interests of employees and their own organizations. I also show that the twenty-first century strategies of the three largest German unions differ greatly. The leaders of the mining, chemical, and energy workers union have pursued an intensive version of social partnership with their employers. The metalworkers union leadership, in contrast, has implemented decentralization and adopted a grassroots social movement approach. The service employees union has done little because its byzantine internal architecture impedes reform.

The Rise and Fall of the Industrial Union Movement, 1949–1989

Many trade unionists and some historians describe the structure of the German labor union movement that formed in the wake of the Second World War as an inevitable product of Germany's transition into a modern, democratic state. Yet a careful analysis reveals that the choice of this institutional architecture in the 1940s was "neither preordained nor inevitable."[1] It was the product of political struggle with both domestic and foreign forces. The result was the creation of a dominant trade union confederation consisting of predominantly industrial unions that had a primary focus on collective bargaining at the sector level and an important but secondary emphasis on lobbying to advance the practical interests of employees within a capitalist economic system.

Reestablishing Trade Unions in Germany

The collapse of the Nazi regime on 8 May 1945 left Germany with a severely damaged economy and a desolate social and political landscape. The Nazis had liquidated all independent political parties and associations, including trade unions, soon after they came to power in 1933 and murdered, imprisoned, exiled, or forced into retirement the leaders of these organizations. Consequently, constructing a sound civil society in Germany in the immediate aftermath of the Second World War was a challenging undertaking. Differences among the four occupying powers—France, Great Britain, the Soviet Union, and the United States—complicated matters further.

The biggest gulf was between the Soviet Union and the other victors of the Second World War. The Soviets took a narrowly instrumental and heavy-handed approach toward the occupation. They favored reestablishing a trade union movement in Germany, but they wanted it to serve as a tool to support Stalinist central planning in the economy and a pro-Soviet governing party in politics. The Soviets acted quickly. They started to help trade unionists sympathetic to their government and ideology to organize in the Soviet occupation zone as early as June 1945.

Soviet authorities attempted to convert their early actions to assist pro-Communist unionists into a permanent institutional advantage by supporting a meeting of trade unionists in Berlin in early February 1946 to form a new union movement. Most attendees were Communists and Soviet sympathizers from the Soviet occupation zone. This gathering founded the Free German Trade Union Federation (Freier Deutscher Gewerkschaftsbund, FDGB). The participants constituted the FDGB as a single centralized labor organization to which members belonged directly. The FDGB had sixteen subdivisions demarcated along industrial lines. The subdivisions were called unions, but they were not in any way comparable to their western German counterparts because they were not autonomous. Within a few months, the Soviets and their eastern German political allies transformed the FDGB into a body subservient to their authority. They designed it to enforce in the workplace the orders of the new pro-Soviet Socialist Unity Party (Sozialist-ische Einheitspartei Deutschlands, SED), which was the product of a forced merger in the Soviet occupation zone between the Communist Party and the Social Democratic Party of Germany.[2] The construction of the FDGB as a "transmission belt" for the SED left western German unionists little choice but to create their own trade union confederation independent of their eastern colleagues.

The growth of trade unions in the three western occupation zones also began early, but the process was considerably different. Even before the first allied troops crossed onto German soil, the Anglo-American General Staff had issued Directive CCS 551, which allowed Germans to create trade unions at the local level provided that the new unions adhered to democratic practices. The postwar architects from Great Britain under Clement Att-lee's Labour Party government and the United States under Democratic president Harry S. Truman were keen to reestablish trade unions and collective bargaining as essential components of a sound German civil society, but they chose to do so only gradually in the belief that a slow pace was the best way to cultivate legitimate local leaders. This bottom-up approach was also intended to repudiate the old subservient Nazi worker organization, the German Labor Front (Deutsche Arbeitsfront, DAF) and the actions of Soviet officials in their occupation zone.

Divisions between the British and Americans on the one hand and the French on the other complicated matters. The French feared that the steps that the British and American authorities were taking would preclude consideration of a French-style multiconfederational model of trade unionism for Germany. As a result, they preferred an even slower pace. Despite their differences, the four-power Allied Control Council did issue several directives regarding industrial relations in 1946. The council drew largely from past Weimar legislation rather than drafting legislation from scratch. Law No. 21 reestablished labor courts, No. 22 permitted the creation of works councils, No. 26 reinstituted the eight-hour day, No. 31 allowed the formation of trade unions and union peak confederations at the zonal level, and No. 35 permitted limited collective bargaining and arbitration. Still, a wage freeze remained in place until 3 November 1948, which severely limited the scope of bargaining. In 1947, the western zones restored the Weimar laws related to unemployment insurance and the state employment agency. The British and Americans permitted unrestricted collective bargaining in late 1948; the French did the same in April 1949.[3]

There was broad consensus among western German unionists that the postwar labor movement should be nonpartisan (i.e., politically active but with no formal affiliation to a political party). This founding dogma, which Germans call "unitary unionism" (*Einheitsgewerkschaft*), was one of the few aspects of postwar German industrial relations that departed from past practice. During the Kaiserreich and the Weimar Republic, unions had grouped themselves into rival Christian, socialist, and liberal confederations.

As is often the case with founding stories, the mythology undergirding this embrace of unitary unionism is thick, particularly in justifying a break with past practice. To this day, German union officials repeat the story in almost ritualistic cadences whenever a neophyte enters their midst. The saga begins during the twilight of German democracy in January 1933. German trade unionists claim that Adolf Hitler was only able to consolidate his control over the German state because the Weimar trade union movement was divided along ideological and religious lines. If the unions had banded together and waged a general strike, so the story goes, they could have driven Hitler out of power and saved German democracy. Instead, union officials failed to unite across confederations and paid dearly as a result. On 2 May 1933, the Nazis seized the initiative. They ordered a massive nationwide raid on all trade union offices, arrested top officials, and shut down all independent labor organizations.[4]

Postwar unionists point to Wolfgang Kapp's abortive 1920 putsch to back up their claim that a general strike could have brought down Hitler. In the former case, the Weimar unions successfully organized a general strike to challenge Kapp's seizure of power. Historians, however, generally cite the amateurish design and execution of Kapp's plot—in particular, the failure to gain any support from the military hierarchy—as the principal explanation for its collapse. Many do add that the resistance of social groups, including organized labor, did play a role in foiling Kapp's coup d'état, but it was secondary at best.[5] The cases of Kapp and Hitler differ in other ways, too. Unlike Kapp, Hitler rose to power through constitutional means. The chances of successfully waging a general strike to remove a chancellor who gained power legitimately would have been far slimmer.

Historians have also shown that postwar unionists' recollection of events conveniently excises some unpleasant truths. At the time, several labor leaders argued that letting Hitler take power would make the Nazis' shortcomings plain to all and thereby shatter Hitler's mystique, clearing the path for the Left to make significant gains in the next election. Other trade unionists "harbored the illusion that the National Socialist state would not be able to do without the unions entirely."[6] These union officials, including several social democrats, made it clear that they would be willing to go some way toward accommodating their organizations to the wishes of the Nazis so long as the unions were allowed to survive.

Still, in spite of its weakness as historical analysis, the postwar founding myth of unitary unionism has proved extraordinarily useful to the labor movement, particularly in the early postwar years. It has constructed for all German trade unionists a positive common heritage and a new crucial social role as guardians of the postwar democracy. In reality, unitary unionism is actually ideologically narrower than its proponents have made it out to be. The embrace of unitary unionism represented a practical marriage between the unions of the two largest confederations of the Weimar era: the Social Democratic Allgemeiner Deutscher Gewerkschaftsbund (ADGB, General German Federation of Labor) and the Catholic Deutscher Gewerkschaftsbund (DGB, German Federation of Labor). Social Democratic trade unionists supported the dogma of unitary unionism as the logical counterpart to their statist conception of socialist politics. Unitary unions could most easily interact with the state as the legitimate representatives of employees. Christian unionists favored unitary unionism because it was compatible with the corporatist dimension of Catholic social teaching. The Social Democratic labor movement was much larger than its Catholic counterpart in both the Second Empire and the Weimar Republic. It is therefore no surprise that unitary unionism in postwar Germany has always exhibited a distinctly Social Democratic accent in practice.

The mythology surrounding this fusion of the two movements accomplished several practical ends. First, combining the remnants of Social Democratic and Christian labor confederations enabled movements enfeebled by twelve years of exile and fascist repression to recover on surer footing. Second, it provided unimpeachable ideological and intellectual justification for the merger to both internal and external skeptics. Third, it made a convincing argument for the exclusion of unionists on the political fringes. The founding story emphasized that all unionists must support democracy if they are to serve as guarantors of the new democratic order. This permitted the new unions to justify barring former Nazi Party members and officials from the DAF. The ban was extended leftward in 1956 when the German constitutional court ruled that the Communist Party of Germany was an undemocratic organization according to the criteria set out in Germany's de facto constitution, the Basic Law (Grundgesetz).[7]

The adoption of unitary unionism substantially enhanced the position of organized labor in postwar German society. It has been a crucial element in providing the labor movement with widespread legitimacy, which it had previously lacked. Unitary unionism has enabled the movement to draw more broadly from the social milieu of employees most likely to join a union because it did not tag the postwar union movement with any specific party. It has also helped to limit labor's political vulnerability. The greater political breadth of the postwar movement made labor a more potent force at the bargaining table and in politics.

Despite the overwhelmingly positive contribution of unitary unionism to the position of labor within German society, it should be noted that it has produced one drawback. Some scholars have argued that the rejection of any direct affiliation with a political party has at times made it harder for union leaders to achieve some political ends (e.g., economic stimulus or strengthening of codetermination rights) because they had no direct ties to a political party. This drawback might not be as large as some imagine, however. For example, the experience of the Trades Union Congress since it founded the British Labour Party has shown that even with close direct ties between movement and party, union leaders often do not get what they want out of politics.[8]

The preponderance of postwar labor leaders have been SPD members. Fealty to unitary unionism, however, has precluded organized labor from explicitly supporting the Social Democrats in elections. Still, the DGB's program and political positions have typically tracked quite closely with those of the SPD, and at times the DGB has stretched the boundary of nonpartisanship to the breaking point. Beyond elections, the unions have also worked closely with the SPD in numerous ways that they have not done with any other party. The postwar German unions do have ties with bodies in other political parties, most prominently, the Christlich Demokratische

Arbeitnehmerschaft (CDA, Christian Democratic Employees Group, aka, the Sozialausschüsse [Social Committees]), which is the labor wing of center-right Christian political parties, the Christian Democratic Union (Christlich Demokratische Union, CDU), and Christian Social Union (Christlich Soziale Union, CSU). The DGB and its unions have always had at least one CDU or CSU member on their executive committees, and prominent Christian democratic unionists endeavor to keep the DGB from becoming too explicitly partisan.

The Centralization Dispute

Fierce debates raged within the German labor movement during the latter half of the 1940s about rebuilding. Disagreement was strongest over the degree of centralization of the new movement and the best means to integrate white-collar employees. Before the Nazis' rise to power, German unions were a bricolage of craft, industrial, and professional unions that had sprung up without any central guidance over the previous five decades. There was consensus after the war that centralization was in order, but opinion varied regarding the degree. Left-wing and centrist unionists (in particular, a group of German unionists who spent the war as exiles in Sweden) would have preferred a single general union for all German employees, with subdivisions along industrial lines akin to those of the FDGB and the emerging Austrian labor movement. On the other hand, the traditionalist wing of the labor movement (including many who spent the war in Great Britain, Switzerland, and the United States) tended to favor a more decentralized system composed of a series of independent industrial unions that would be members of a single peak confederation. In the latter model, the individual unions would be stronger than the labor confederation because only the unions would be allowed to have members, to collect dues, to maintain a strike fund, and to call strikes. The confederation would serve simply as the political representative of the movement when a single voice is preferred, a body to provide common services when economies of scale existed, and a referee for jurisdictional disputes among affiliated unions.[9]

   Hans Böckler, the influential trade unionist who eventually became the first chair (*Vorsitzender*) of the postwar Deutscher Gewerkschaftsbund, supported centralization and was highly influential in making it the official preference of the German labor movement, but both the British and American occupying authorities rejected it. They feared that a single general union would give western German labor far too much power within a still fragile economy and society. Officials in the Manpower Division of the Office of Military Government, United States, saw decentralization as a way to promote grassroots democracy and were concerned that a highly central-ized labor movement could far too easily fall under Communist control. They also rejected centralization because it too closely resembled not only the FDGB but also the old Nazi DAF. The British and the Americans pre-ferred that German unionists hew more closely to a decentralized model of trade unionism, as in Britain and the United States. After some resistance, the western German trade unionists relented, and in December 1945 they "provisionally" accepted a decentralized structure as the model for the post-war labor movement. In May 1948, trade union representatives from the British and American zones formed a bizonal trade union council to plan mergers between the two zones and the creation of a single peak confed-eration. Later that year, union representatives from the French zone joined what became the trizonal trade union council, which was the forerunner of the predominant postwar peak trade union confederation, the Deutscher Gewerkschaftsbund.[10]

Guiding Principles of the First Postwar German Trade Union Movement: Industrial Unionism and Unitary Collective Bargaining

Once it became clear that the Western Allies were not going to permit a single general union, most western German unionists embraced two organi-zational principles. The first was industrial unionism (*Industriegewerkschaft*), that is, union jurisdictions covered discrete sectoral categories (e.g., construc-tion, metalworking, and public service) instead of individual crafts. German trade union officials agreed to sixteen sectoral jurisdictions that were based largely on the demarcations of the ADGB's old industrial unions. The sec-ond was unitary collective bargaining (*Tarifeinheit*), which meant that the main economic activity of each workplace would determine which union would have exclusive jurisdiction, regardless of the specific occupations of individual employees. The two principles, stated briefly, are: one sector, one union; and one workplace, one union.[11]

Although industrial unionism as an organizing principle proved ef-fective in defining the jurisdictions of the blue-collar unions, the logic of industrial unionism was problematic when applied to white-collar employees. A group of white-collar and civil service unionists who had belonged to the Weimar-era Social Democratic white-collar and civil service unions (i.e., Allgemeiner Freier Angestelltenbund, AFA, and Allgemeiner Deutscher Beamtenbund, ADB) founded the German White-Collar Employees Union (Deutsche Angestellten-Gewerkschaft,

DAG) in Hamburg in 1945. The DAG was a unitary, nonpartisan union just like the DGB unions, but it was for white-collar employees from all sectors of the economy, which ran contrary to the precept of industrial unionism. A long debate ensued within the labor movement between blue- and white-collar unionists over the appropriateness of a general white-collar employees union within a labor movement structured along industrial lines.[12]

The representatives of the emerging industrial unions argued for a strict interpretation of the principle of one workplace, one union. In practice this would mean, for example, that a secretary in the chemical industry would fall under the jurisdiction of the chemical industry employees union, but a secretary doing the same job in the mechanical engineering sector would fall under the jurisdiction of the metalworkers union. Under strict industrial unionism, secretaries could never have their own union, because there was no free-standing set of firms in a sector made up primarily of secretaries. DAG officials argued that white-collar employees had far more in common with one another than with the blue-collar workers in their specific companies and industries. Consequently, an independent white-collar union would be more sensitive to white-collar concerns and thereby attract more white-collar members. Furthermore, since most industries at the time employed far more blue-collar than white-collar employees, there would be a bias against white-collar employees in unions organized strictly along industrial lines.[13]

The dispute over industrial unionism culminated in March 1949 when the DAG leadership decided to go it alone. In April 1949, the DAG established itself as a single independent union for public and private white-collar employees in the three western zones, but it did not affiliate with the DGB. Although some critics of the DAG claimed that some of the original DAG leadership harbored right-wing views and hid unsavory pasts, the reasons behind the DAG's decision to strike out on its own "are to be found less . . . in ideological differences between the DAG and DGB than in the fight for members and in the bureaucratic self-interest of the leading DAG officials and those officials from the industrial unions who were most affected by the dispute over white-collar employees."[14] The dispute and subsequent battles in the workplace to recruit members resulted in division and ill-will that persisted for decades.

Western German unionists completed the construction of the postwar labor movement in October 1949, some five months after the establishment of the Federal Republic of Germany. Delegates held a convention in Munich that established the Deutscher Gewerkschaftsbund to serve as the peak confederation for sixteen unitary industrial unions throughout the Federal Republic. The Munich convention also produced a basic program that rejected the Soviet-style system of centralized economic planning being installed in the newly created East Germany, but it emphatically embraced an alternative vision of economic planning through codetermination as a more democratic version of socialism. The Munich program called for the nationalization of heavy industry, transportation, and banking, and the expansion of the welfare state to prevent the emergence of extreme inequalities common to unregulated market economies.[15]

The Organization of Unions in the First Postwar Trade Union Movement

It is important to reiterate that despite the structural position of the DGB atop the organizational pyramid of the German labor movement, it has never been labor's most influential body. The individual unions, rather than the DGB, have always been the most powerful entities in the postwar German labor movement. Since 1952, the DGB has received 12 percent of the gross dues,[16] but it is each union that collects the funds and allocates them to the DGB and not vice versa. Nonetheless, the DGB's functions have included serving as the primary public voice for the German trade union movement, lobbying lawmakers at all levels regarding labor's general concerns, representing German labor in international forums, providing common services to individual unions and their members, and resolving disputes between individual unions.[17] Smaller unions have been the disproportionate users of DGB services because they have not had the resources to provide many services on their own.

Five of the original sixteen DGB affiliates covered manufacturing (table 4.1): the dominant union of the postwar German movement, Industriegewerkschaft Metall (IG Metall, Industrial Union of Metalworkers); the influential Industriegewerkschaft Chemie-Papier-Keramik, (IG Chemie or IG ChPK, Industrial Union of Chemical, Paper and Ceramic Workers); Industriegewerkschaft Druck und Papier (IG DruPa, Industrial Union of Printing and Paper Workers); Gewerkschaft Leder (GL, Union of Leather Workers); and Gewerkschaft Textil-Bekleidung (GTB, Union of Textile and Clothing Workers).[18]

Four unions had jurisdiction in the primary and construction sectors: Industriegewerkschaft Bau-Steine-Erden (IG BSE or IG Bau, Industrial Union of Construction Workers); Industriegewerkschaft Bergbau und Energie (IG BE, Industrial Union of Mine and Energy Workers);

Table 4.1.   Original Affiliates of the Deutscher Gewerkschaftsbund

Union	Abbreviation	Sector
Industriegewerkschaft Bau-Steine-Erden	IG BSE	construction
Industriegewerkschaft Bergbau und Energie	IG BE	mining, energy
Industriegewerkschaft Chemie-Papier-Keramik	IG ChPK	chemicals, paper, ceramics
Industriegewerkschaft Druck und Papier	IG DruPa	printing
Gewerkschaft der Eisenbahner Deutschlands	GdED	railroad
Gewerkschaft Erziehung und Wissenschaft	GEW	education, science
Gewerkschaft Gartenbau Land und Forstwirtschaft	GGLF	horticulture, agriculture, forestry
Gewerkschaft Handel, Banken und Versicherungen	HBV	retail, banking, insurance
Gewerkschaft Holz und Kunststoff	GHK	wood and plastics
Gewerkschaft Kunst	GK	art and music
Gewerkschaft Leder	GL	leatherworking
Industriegewerkshaft Metall	IG Metall	mechanical engineering, iron, steel
Gewerkschaft Nahrung-Genuss-Gaststätten	NGG	food processing, hotels, restaurants
Gewerkschaft öffentliche Dienste, Transport und Verkehr	ÖTV	public service, transportation
Deutsche Postgewerkschaft	DPG	postal service
Gewerkschaft Textil-Bekleidung	GTB	textiles and apparel

Gewerkschaft Garten, Land- und Forstwirtschaft (GGLF, Union of Horticulture, Agriculture and Forestry Workers); and Gewerkschaft Holz und Kunststoff (GHK, Union of Wood and Plastic Workers).

Three unions organized workers principally in the private service sector: Gewerkschaft Handel, Banken und Versicherungen (HBV, Union of Retail, Banking and Insurance Workers); Gewerkschaft Nahrung-Genuss-Gaststätten (NGG, Union of Food, Hotel and Restaurant Workers); and Gewerkschaft Kunst (GK, Union of Artists and Musicians), which was a federation of seven smaller unions and professional associations.

DGB also included four public-sector unions: the mammoth Gewerkschaft Öffentliche Dienste, Transport und Verkehr (ÖTV, Union of

Public Services and Transportation Employees); Deutsche Postgewerk-schaft (DPG, German Postal Workers Union); Gewerkschaft der Eisen-bahner Deutschlands (GdED, Railroad Workers Union of Germany); and Gewerkschaft Erziehung und Wissenschaft (GEW, Union of Education and Science Workers).

The DGB "federal congress," or convention, is the formal supreme governing body of the German labor movement.[19] Over the years, the total number of delegates has ranged between four hundred and six hundred.[20] Representation is allotted to each union in proportion to its membership. Every convention elects the DGB's managing federal executive board (*geschäftsführender Bundesvorstand*), which actually runs the peak confederation on a day-to-day basis. Before German unification, the managing federal executive board had nine members.[21] Each board member is responsible for managing several DGB departments (for example, Economic Policy, Education, International Labor Affairs, Legal Services, Women's Affairs).

The full federal executive board (*Bundesvorstand*) consists of the managing board and the chairs of the affiliated unions. In practice, the full federal executive board is the most powerful DGB body because the chairs of the individual unions are the voting members. Each union chair—regardless of the size of the union—has one vote on the federal executive board to resolve routine matters, but when it comes to personnel and core policy decisions, the leaders of the largest unions usually hammer things out among themselves in advance. The biggest unions thereby have a de facto veto over DGB policy.

An additional body, the DGB federal committee (*Bundesausschuss*), meets annually and is tasked with overseeing the work of the federal executive board. It consists of the federal executive board plus the heads of the DGB's regional districts (*Bezirke*)[22] and seventy members from the affiliated unions. The apportionment of the seventy on the federal committee is based on the size of each union's membership. Since the affiliated union chairs serve on the federal committee themselves and pick their own organizations' members to serve on it, they have a powerful influence over the body. As a result, the federal committee is not nearly as influential as it looks on paper. Over the years, the DGB has repeatedly renamed, consolidated, and restructured the units below the districts.[23] These subdistricts (*Unterbezirke*) have never been influential in determining policy. The purpose of the subdistricts was to provide services to members and to represent organized labor in local governmental and public forums. Initially, service provision was the primary task. Starting in the 1990s, advocacy has become more important.

During the first forty years of the postwar German labor movement, the overarching organizational structure of the German industrial union movement only changed at the margins. The police officers union (Gewerkschaft der Polizei, GdP) became the seventeenth DGB affiliate in 1978. The GdP was founded in 1950. DGB union leaders had originally placed police officers under the jurisdiction of the public-sector union, ÖTV. The DGB initially excluded the GdP from membership because many unionists judged it to be a professional association rather than a trade union and therefore incompatible with industrial unionism. Some left-leaning unionists had also been reluctant to permit the GdP into the DGB fold because of a fear that the police union would bolster conservatives within the trade union movement. Yet by the late 1970s, the arguments for admitting the GdP had become compelling. It was clear that the GdP was the union of choice for police officers. The GdP's political track record fell comfortably into the mainstream of the DGB. The police officers union was relatively small (i.e., 150,000 members), so admitting it would not alter the political balance within the DGB.[24] ÖTV ceded its jurisdiction over the police, which enabled the DGB executive committee to vote to admit the police officers union as an affiliate on 1 April 1978. This made it possible for GdP delegates to participate in the DGB convention a month later.

A second minor change in the organizational structure of the DGB during the first forty years transpired in the twilight days of the Bonn Republic. In 1989, the printers union, IG Dru Pa, merged with the artists and musicians associations organized under Gewerkschaft Kunst. The new union was called the Industrial Union of Media Workers (Industriegewerkschaft Medien, IG Medien). As a result, at the close of the Bonn Republic, the DGB once again had sixteen affiliates, just as it did at the outset.

The DGB also undertook only one substantial ideological modification of its basic program in the first four decades of its existence. At its 1963 Düsseldorf convention, the trade union confederation endorsed Keynesian economics. The DGB did not drop the objectives of economic planning or nationalizing the commanding heights of the economy. It just retooled these objectives by employing a Keynesian approach and vocabulary. The new basic program called for a "macroeconomic planning framework" and "investment guidance."[25] Still, as one prominent observer of German industrial relations put it, the program "conveyed a victory of Keynes over Marx."[26] The symbolic importance of this change was substantial. It signaled an expansion of the Weltanschauung and milieu of organized labor beyond the blue-collar laborer. Employees in the public and service sectors found the change particularly attractive and began to join unions in larger numbers.

The DGB revised its basic program again in 1981. Union officials engaged in considerable self-reflection during the drafting of the 1981 program, but the document itself broke little new ground.[27]

Throughout the history of the Federal Republic of Germany, the DGB has been the predominant labor confederation. During the 1950s, the DGB's share of total union membership fluctuated between 80 and 90 percent. After 1960, this ratio has consistently remained around 80 percent. Looking beyond the DGB and its affiliates, smaller employee organizations not affiliated to the DGB have always existed in postwar Germany. Outside organizations have survived for two reasons. First, some groups of employees from occupations with strong professional identities have objected to the logic of industrial unionism. For example, an alternative confederation known as the Deutscher Beamtenbund (DBB, German Civil Servants Federation) remains outside of the DGB. Most members of DBB-affiliated unions are civil servants. Many German civil servants see themselves and their concerns as distinct from those in other occupations. German civil servants cannot be fired except under the most extraordinary of circumstances (e.g., extreme malfeasance or treason). German law permits civil servants to engage in collective bargaining, but they are forbidden from striking.

Over the years, 8 to 10 percent of all organized employees have belonged to one of the DBB's affiliates. The DBB currently comprises forty sectoral unions and sixteen *Land* associations, which means the typical DBB union is quite small, seldom exceeding fifty thousand. Many civil servants have chosen to belong to their own organizations rather than to one of the DGB's public-sector unions. Ideological considerations, peer pressure, and membership amenities explain this preference. Still, until the last decade, more civil servants had belonged to a DGB union than to a DBB affiliate, again largely for reasons of ideology and practical influence, depending on which organization had more impact in a particular workplace.

Christian trade unions have posed a minor yet persistent second challenge to DGB unions. The birth of the postwar Christian trade union movement is in large part due to a miscalculation by the DGB leadership regarding the border between unitary unionism and partisan politics. In the 1953 federal elections, the DGB all but endorsed the SPD by selecting the slogan "Elect a Better Bundestag" to promote union objectives during the campaign. Since the Christian parties were the senior partner in the governing coalition, the partisan antigovernment slant of the slogan was clear. Some Christian democratic trade unionists objected vociferously. A few unionists who were also members of the Christian parties even threatened to create a rival Christian trade union movement. Chancellor Adenauer intervened, however, to help preserve unitary unionism. He convinced the majority of enraged unionists from the Christian parties to stay in their DGB unions in exchange for a promise from the DGB leadership to refrain from such thinly veiled partisanship in future elections. A very small number of unionists, many of whom were members of the CSU, rejected Andenauer's plea for unity and began to build the alternative Christlicher Gewerkschaftsbund Deutschlands (CGB, Christian Trade Union Federation of Germany), which they formally established in 1955.[28] CGB unions have remained quite small, but they recently attracted the ire of DGB unions by signing contracts with a handful of firms, mostly in eastern Germany, that the DGB unions judge to be substandard.[29] DGB unions have managed to contain this threat through legal actions to strip some CGB organizations of legal status as trade unions.[30] It is likely that the CGB unions will remain on the scene for some time to come, but it is doubtful that they will become anything more than an irritant for the DGB unions.

Performance of the First German Postwar Trade Union Movement, 1950–1989

The first postwar German industrial relations movement was far more comprehensive, integrated, and accepted than those of the Second Empire and the Weimar Republic. What was the impact of greater organizational strength on the system's performance?

From Rubble to Miracle: German Trade Unions in the 1950s and 1960s

Increasingly favorable economic conditions during the 1950s and 1960s laid a solid foundation for unions to make significant advances for their members. The German economy grew briskly. The real gross domestic product (GDP) per capita rose at an average yearly pace of 8.1 percent during the 1950s and 4.8 percent in the 1960s. Unemployment fell from 11 percent in 1950 to 1.3 percent in 1960 and averaged a remarkable 0.9 percent for the decade of the 1960s (table 4.2).

During the early decades, German unions focused on collective bargaining both because of the strong economy and because Christian Democratic domination of federal politics made legislative gains less likely. During the 1950s and 1960s, employees received a full share of increased economic efficiency. Real mean annual income rose by 5.4 and 4.6 percent respectively (i.e., 7.3 and 7.1% nominally), which was just 0.2 percent below average annual productivity growth for each decade (table 4.2). The workweek came

Table 4.2.   Economic Performance: Germany*

| Period | | Percent mean annual change | | | |
	Real GDP per capita	Net income per employee: real (nominal)	Productivity (real GDP per hour worked)	Consumer price index	Unemployment rate
1951–59	8.1	5.4 (7.3)	5.6	1.9	5.1
1960–69	4.8	4.6 (7.1)	4.8	2.5	0.9
1970–79	3.3	2.9 (7.8)	4.1	4.9	2.8
1980–89	1.9	-0.1 (2.8)	2.1	2.9	5.2
1990–99	2.3	0.0 (2.6)	2.4	2.6	7.5
2000–2009	0.9	-0.4 (1.2)	1.1	1.6	8.5

* Federal Republic of Germany: 1951–1990 (West Germany), 1991–2009 (united)

Sources: OECD Main Economic Indicators; OECD Productivity Data Base; income data, Bundesministerium für Arbeit und Soziales, Statistisches Taschenbuch.

Table 4.3.   Strikes and Lockouts in Germany*

Period	Mean annual working days lost to strikes	Mean annual working days lost to lockouts	Mean annual lockout days as a percentage of total days lost	Mean annual working days lost to strikes and lockouts per 1,000 employees[†]
1950–59	983,108	79,118	7.4	67.6
1960–69	218,828	137,138	38.5	16.1
1970–79	783,007	622,465	44.3	56.7
1980–89	340,209	269,889	44.2	30.1
1990–99	337,827	259	0.1	13.1
2000–2009	149,084	382	0.3	4.9

* Federal Republic of Germany: 1951–1990 (West Germany), 1991–2009 (united).
† united Germany as of 1992.

Source: Bundesagentur für Arbeit.

down from forty-eight to forty hours, and thirty paid vacation days became the norm.[31] Capturing economic gains did initially require some resort to economic muscle. During the 1950s, 67.7 working days per one thousand employees were lost annually owing to strikes and lockouts, which was the highest this ratio reached in any postwar decade (table 4.3). Tight labor markets during the 1960s gave unions more leverage at the bargaining table, which helped to bring the working-days-lost ratio down to 16.1 per one thousand employees. A much greater share of those lost days were the result of lockouts rather than strikes (7.4% in the 1950s vs. 38.5% in the 1960s), largely because the leadership of the employers associations decided to adopt a more aggressive stance in collective bargaining (see chapter 5).

Tensions Build: German Trade Unions in the 1970s

In the 1960s, a new generation inspired by the renaissance of leftist politics began to join unions and to serve as union officials. The ascendance in the fall of 1969 of the SPD as the senior partner in the federal government stoked economic and political expectations among both union officials and the rank and file. Economic conditions overheated worldwide as a result of the expansionary policies of the United States (i.e., Lyndon Johnson's Great Society programs and the Vietnam War). These forces combined to set off a strike wave in 1971. It included several wildcat actions and challenges to many incumbent union leaders, who were accused by mostly younger colleagues of being excessively timid at the bargaining table. Political tensions within the movement also became more pronounced between "accommodationist" unions, such as the construction workers, and many within the metalworkers, printers, and public-sector unions, who envisioned the role of organized labor as standing as a "countervailing force" (*Gegenmacht*) to the capitalist forces in society. While in power, the SPD extended codetermination rights (see chapter 2) and expanded several components of the welfare state. The unionization rate began an increase that continued into the early 1980s.[32]

The first worldwide oil shock in 1973–74 brought the long postwar boom to a sudden end, and the second oil shock at the close of the decade presaged big changes to come in the German economic landscape. Real annual GDP growth per capita decelerated to 3.3 percent in the 1970s. Unemployment rose, peaking at 4.7 percent in 1975. Joblessness for the decade only averaged 2.8 percent, but the 1970s proved to be the last decade of low unemployment (table 4.2). The combination of political militancy, rising prices, and still relatively low unemployment contributed to an upsurge in industrial disputes. The ratio of days lost owing to labor conflicts shot up to 56.7 per one thousand employees (table 4.3). Employers stepped up their offensive tactics. An all-time high of 44.3 percent of those days lost were the product of lockouts. Average net income per employee increased nominally by 7.8 percent per year during the 1970s, which was comparable

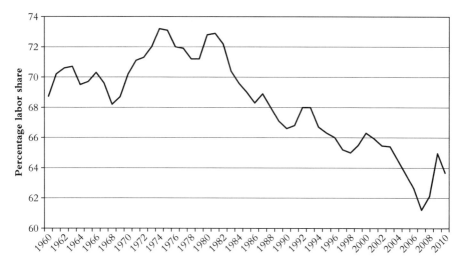

FIGURE 4.1.   Adjusted labor share of national income. Source: Statistisches Bundesamt.

to the nominal results in the 1950s and 1960s, but rising inflation eroded the results down to 2.9 percent in real terms (table 4.2). Labor's share of national income did increase by more than 2 percentage points, averaging 71.7 percent for the 1970s (figure 4.1), but the gap between growth in productivity and income widened to 1.2 percentage points per year.

Twilight of Industrial Unionism: German Industrial Relations in the 1980s

German economic performance took a decided turn for the worse in the 1980s. The average annual growth rate per capita decelerated once again, this time falling to 1.9 percent (table 4.2). The unemployment rate averaged 5.2 percent for the 1980s as a whole, but it had spiked at 9.2 percent in 1985 and never dropped below 8 percent for the remainder of the decade. Average annual productivity growth slowed by almost half, to 2.1 percent per year on average. Nominal mean net income per employee, which is the "credit effect" variable that correlated significantly and positively with the unionization rate in the previous chapter, dropped by 5 percentage points to 2.8 percent per year. Real wages and salaries actually decreased by 0.1 percent per year on average during the 1980s. The gap between developments in productivity and real income widened further to 2.2 percentage points per year. Labor's share of national income slipped to 69.9 percent for the decade (figure 4.1).

German labor responded to the economic difficulties with campaigns to reduce working time. At first, union officials fought among themselves over the best way to reduce working time. IG Metall and the printers union preferred shortening the workweek to thirty-five hours without reducing weekly pay. Employers associations resisted this demand vociferously.[33] Alternatively, IG Chemie advocated an expansion of early retirement. The chemical workers union found support in government. A center-right coalition led by Christian Democrat Helmut Kohl had displaced the Social Democrats from power at the federal level in early 1982. The Kohl government favored early retirement over weekly working-time reduction and passed legislation to promote the former. The unions pushing for weekly working-time reduction pursued their objective anyway through collective bargaining. They developed an iconic public campaign centered on a logo with a smiling yellow sun on a red background with the number "35" in white in the middle. The campaign proved to be an effective tool for mobilizing members. In 1984, IG Metall and the printers union waged one of the most famous strikes in postwar German history. After six weeks, they achieved a breakthrough contract that phased in a 38.5 hour workweek. It took IG Metall ten more years of incremental reductions to achieve a 35 hour workweek. Eventually, all unions campaigned for both variants of working-time reduction. Most unions broke through the 40-hour barrier, but few besides IG Metall managed to get all the way to a 35-hour workweek.[34] Unions were more uniformly successful in negotiating "preretirement" (*Vorruhestand*) programs with employers that tapped into government subsidies to permit employees to retire several years earlier than the statutory age.

Most economists conclude that working-time reduction did not make a substantial contribution to reducing unemployment.[35] Unemployment remained high for a quarter century and did not come down when weekly working time was falling. Some criticized German labor's embrace of working-time reduction not merely as ineffectual but as a wrong turn politically and socially. For example, German intellectual Ralf Dahrendorf commented that the emphasis on working-time reduction marked a transition of German unions from "forward thinking organizations of self-confident future-oriented groups" to "defensive organizations of declining social groups."[36]

The tactics and strategies of industrial relations also began to change in the 1980s. The 1984 strikes masked a steep decline in industrial action during the 1980s. On average, 30.1 working days were lost annually to strikes and lockouts per one thousand employees for the full decade, which is already a substantial decline from the 1970s (table 4.3). Exclude 1984, and the ratio for the remaining years of the decade drops to 2.9. The share of days lost that were a product of lockouts rather than strikes remained just as high as it had been for the previous decade at 44.2 percent, but these lockouts were almost exclusively concentrated in the 1984 strikes. Employers had begun to adopt Japanese "just in time" production practices in the early 1980s, which left them increasingly vulnerable to strikes because they no longer maintained large stockpiles of parts. In 1984, IG Metall explicitly pursued a "minimax" strategy, which consisted of targeting key parts suppliers so that a minimum of strikers (and strike pay) could be used to shut down large numbers of plants through resulting parts shortages. When German labor courts ruled in the midst of the 1984 strike that workers laid off in this way could receive unemployment benefits, the employers relented and made concessions on weekly working time. The employers struck back, however. In 1985 and 1986, they pushed for a change in what was then article 116 of the Employment Promotion Act (Arbeitsförderungsgesetz) to prevent workers indirectly affected by a strike but who would benefit from the results of that strike from receiving unemployment benefits. The unions fought the law, mobilizing several massive protests, but the law passed. After the change to article 116, unions and employers both became wary, and days lost owing to industrial action dropped sharply.[37]

By the end of the 1980s, most of the organizations and practices of the first postwar trade union movement remained intact, but several worrisome developments had already appeared. The sharp deterioration in German economic performance undercut the capacity of German unions to deliver wage increases. Economic pressures led increasing numbers of small enterprises in some sectors to leave their employers associations, which led some to begin to question the utility of regionwide collective agreements. Deterioration of the working-class milieu, which was discussed in the previous chapter, resulted in fewer employees joining unions.

In other words, although few saw it at the time, by the end of the 1980s, the architecture of the first German postwar trade union movement had become quite fragile. When a tempest struck in the form of German unification, the old industrial union model could only weather the storm for a few years before ultimately giving way.

The Metamorphosis to a Multisectoral Trade Union Movement, 1990–2001

The organizational stability that characterized the first four decades of postwar labor relations crumbled in the 1990s. The decade that opened with German unification at first seemed to be an unprecedented chance to strengthen the labor movement because it appeared to provide a rare opportunity for unions to expand quickly in both size and density. Ultimately, however, unification's wrenching impact on Germany's economic, political and social structures proved to be more of a burden than a benefit for organized labor. The old industrial union model, which had already become shopworn in the 1980s, did not survive the trying and tumultuous first decade of German unity. Out of the struggle to reestablish a sound footing for stressed trade unions, a new multisectoral model of unionism emerged.

Eastward Ho!

Unification unleashed feelings of both great joy and deep apprehension within the German population on both sides of the river Elbe. In light of Germany's traumatic history (which included the Nazi era and two failed republics in the twentieth century alone), most Germans both east and west agreed that the most prudent way to unify the country would be to avoid experimentation and to use the institutions, laws, and practices that had a proven track record of success, namely, those of the Federal Republic of Germany. The result was a wholesale eastward extension of West Germany's laws, organizations, and institutional arrangements without amendment, including the entire system of industrial relations.

Simply absorbing East Germany into the Federal Republic averted the need to revise the elaborate networks of economic, political, and social arrangements that were the product of forty years of incremental conflict and compromise in West German industrial relations. In practice, however, what was initially hoped to be a simple institutional transfer has proved stubbornly vexing. Many western institutions, some of which had already demonstrated significant shortcomings even before unification, were ill suited to the new, far more heterogeneous Berlin Republic.

The process of reestablishing independent unions east of the Elbe was fraught with complexity. In late 1989, the top leadership of the FDGB and its unions, which had been subservient to the dominant Socialist Unity Party, resigned. Officials from the lower tiers of the FDGB unions, who were far less "tainted" (*belastet*) by association with the past regime, moved into leadership positions and began to democratize and dismantle the "transmission belt" structures that made the FDGB the implementing body for the SED in the workplace. At first, some western labor leaders considered merging their unions with their eastern counterparts, which in all but a few cases had very similar jurisdictional boundaries. Ultimately, however, only one union, IG Chemie, actually did so. The others rejected that option because most union officials feared that a merger would designate the western unions as the legal and moral successor of eastern trade union officials and thereby would leave the western unions liable for the past actions of the eastern labor movement. Ironically, IG Chemie was in a better position to undertake a direct merger because its history of militant anti-Communism since the 1970s put it above reproach. Most other unions had taken more-or-less sympathetic stances toward the GDR and FDGB during the détente era that began in the 1970s, which made a merger in the newly emerging post-Communist era less attractive. As a result, they chose a different route. The other western trade unions indirectly coordinated the liquidation of their "sister" unions in the east and then recruited eastern members from scratch.[38] This indirect approach, although prudent, did have costs. It complicated the unions' claims to property that the Christian and Social Democratic trade unions owned during the Weimar Republic. Most of these claims were only settled in the second half of the 1990s.[39] Liquidating the eastern unions rather than merging with them also made recruiting eastern members far more costly and labor intensive.

Initially, western German trade unions had great success recruiting new members in the former GDR. By the end of 1991, over four million easterners had signed up. Many easterners initially joined unions because in the GDR union membership was a prerequisite for access to a wide spectrum of benefits (e.g., pensions and vacation homes), and many easterners mistakenly assumed that the same would be true under the new industrial relations order. Large numbers of easterners also believed that being union members would increase the odds of saving their jobs, many of which looked increasingly precarious as market mechanisms were instituted and privatization proceeded at a rapid pace. All told, the initial impact of unification in 1991 at first swelled the ranks of German organized labor by over 40 percent, a proportion far exceeding the eastern share of the population. This membership expansion was not to last, however. Economic and social collapse in eastern Germany cut deeply into eastern union membership rolls. When the unions proved unable to protect most employees from layoffs, increasing numbers of easterners began to exercise their new right not to be trade union members.

Still, the gyrations of unification are not sufficient to explain the decline of Germany's trade unions. To the contrary, the previous chapter showed that unification actually contributed positively to density. Moreover, density had already begun to drop in West Germany more than a decade before unification. In other words, unification was not the source of all of German labor's woes.

Even before German unification, pressure to restructure the western labor movement had been rising. Uneven economic growth over the years had produced extreme membership imbalances among the DGB unions. By 1990, the biggest DGB affiliate, IG Metall, had become over sixty times larger than the smallest, the leather workers union. The top three unions represented 59 percent of total DGB membership, whereas the six smallest DGB unions made up less than 10 percent. These asymmetries caused governance problems. The leaders of small DGB unions often complained that the big unions—in particular, IG Metall—arrogantly used their preponderant size and vast wealth to carve out a de facto veto power within the movement.[40] Officials from the larger unions responded that their actions simply reflected the democratic principle of proportional representation. They complained that the smaller unions were free riders because they were unable to fulfill all the financial and organizational obligations required of DGB affiliates.[41] Jurisdictional disputes among affiliates had also begun to proliferate as new sectors arose that did not obviously fit into the divisions drawn up in the late 1940s (e.g., software production). The DGB's established procedures for resolving jurisdictional disputes proved inadequate in the face of these new challenges.

Eastward expansion was a two-edged sword. On the one hand, it opened the door to explore a more thoroughgoing reorganization of the movement. Many unionists hoped that this first restructuring of the German labor movement since 1949 would be a comprehensive and thoughtful endeavor based on a new strategic vision of what trade unions should be in the post–Cold War world. On the other hand, unification placed a huge cost burden on the unions and forced them to deal with the most traditional of union concerns: wages, hours, employment conditions, and the massive surge in joblessness. Two dimensions came into the discussion of union reform simultaneously: vision and budget. A debate about which vision should guide the German trade union movement unfolded first but soon bogged down. Labor's burgeoning financial crisis vaulted to the forefront and ultimately drove the direction and outcome of the reform.

The Vision Thing: The Unsuccessful Attempt to Reconceptualize Trade Unionism in the 1990s

A decade of intensive organizational reform for German labor began in November 1990. Heinz–Werner Meyer, a former chair of the miners union who had just been elected DGB chair six months earlier, gave the keynote address at the Hattingen Forum, a newly created venue for trade unionists and intellectuals to exchange ideas for renewing the German labor movement. Meyer consciously chose this occasion because a research team made up of union and academic experts was presenting its findings from an exhaustive study on the political, ideological, and structural weaknesses of the labor movement entitled *Beyond the Resolution Register.* Meyer endorsed the study's central conclusion that if unions were to remain a viable force in the twenty-first century, they would need to move beyond their 1940s Fordist conceptualization, which had served them well but was now obsolete. To enhance the appeal of unions to younger, more educated, individualistic, and heterogeneous employees from a dwindling labor milieu, unions would need to launch a wide-open "discourse" within their ranks, become less hierarchical, and adopt participatory reforms in order to transform into organizations that truly activate and engage their members.[42]

Inspired by the message of the Hattingen Forum, DGB officials decided to write a new basic program stating the ideational understanding and policy goals of the German trade union movement from scratch rather than simply amending the existing program, as had been done in the past. DGB staff members began drafting by posing a set of ten "guiding questions" (*Leitfragen*),[43] and invited union members and nonunion members alike to discuss them through a series of written contributions,[44] meetings, and open forums.[45] Despite the DGB's best efforts, little debate ensued, except among top union officials.[46] Top-down commands to commence discourse seldom succeed. Moreover, the wrenching challenges of unification and the untimely death of DGB chair Hans-Werner Meyer in 1994 took much of the energy out of the vision discussion. Meyer's successor, Dieter Schulte, was overwhelmed with the work of unification and proved not nearly as interested in the reform effort as his predecessor had been. Schulte simply let the reform's existing momentum carry it to the end.

The final result of four years of work was a new basic program (which is still in effect) that the DGB approved in Dresden on 16 November 1996.[47] The most controversial element of the basic program was a clause in the penultimate version that implicitly abandoned a socialist vision by explicitly accepting the postwar social market economy as a system that "is better suited than other economic orders for achieving the goals of the unions."[48] The draft did point out that the social market economy is far from perfect—it had neither prevented mass unemployment nor produced social justice—but concluded that its benefits far outweighed its flaws. The clause was controversial because the phrase "social market economy" has two meanings in postwar German parlance. The first is simply shorthand for the postwar German mixed economy, including a relatively generous welfare state. The second meaning, however, is a largely market-oriented understanding of the economy developed by the conservative Freiburg school of economists in the first half of the twentieth century. Most delegates in Dresden could neither bring themselves to embrace uncritically the label "social market economy," given the latter connotation, nor endorse reliance on market forces absent some dimension of political guidance to set the course of the economy. They instead voted to replace "social market economy" with "socially regulated economy," which has decidedly more interventionist overtones.[49]

At one level the controversy over embracing the social market economy seems peculiar because German trade unions have done so in practice if not in principle since the very beginning of the Federal Republic. The change simply would have brought principle and practice into harmony. At a more symbolic level, however, accepting the phrase social market economy in an unmodified form would have represented shedding the last vestige of the leftist transformative tradition of the German labor movement. Turning that page was simply too painful for too many, particularly the aging members of the 1968 generation whose lives had been invigorated by Western Europe's rediscovery of Marx in their youth.[50]

Nonetheless, the details of the new program made considerable strides toward accepting the market as the principal means for governing the economy. It dropped provisions from previous DGB programs calling for the nationalization of key industries, state-led investment guidance, and macroeconomic indicative planning. The delegates did, however, adopt an amendment against the recommendation of the convention's motions committee calling for a further expansion of the welfare state. In a bid to (post)modernize, the basic program also called for greater integration of economic and environmental objectives, a larger role for labor in the coshaping (*Mitgestaltung*) of the society and economy, more thoroughgoing equality for women, and a more socially responsible and democratic Europe.[51]

What was the impact of the 1996 DGB basic program? A successful new basic program for any mass organization, such as a trade union movement or a political party, reconceptualizes ends, means, and identity in such a way that the movement is able to accomplish more and attract additional members. A successful basic program also serves as a mission statement that informs the shape of the institution and the setting of priorities. The classic example of success is the SPD's famous 1959 Bad Godesberg basic program that jettisoned traditional Marxism for Keynesian demand management, thereby demonstrating the modernity of the party and making it attractive to a growing population of white-collar professionals. A failed new basic program, in contrast, dies a quiet death of irrelevance because it either pours old wine into new bottles or is so different that it does not resonate with the membership and they reject it. Whereas the content of the DGB's new basic program is superior to the previous one, it has failed to alter behavior or to attract new members. The 1996 DGB basic program suffers from two problems that often plague these types of documents. It ratifies current practice rather than breaking new ground, and it is often not coherent because it includes contradictory positions to appease multiple constituencies within the labor movement. It is impossible, therefore, to call it a success.

Financial Hardship and Merger Mania

In practice, it was not a strategic vision but rather budgetary concerns and internal jockeying by a few unions that were the most powerful forces shaping the creation of the second postwar German labor movement. Much of labor's financial crisis was a product of German unification. German trade unions and the DGB spent substantial sums extending their organizations eastward in 1990 and 1991. Initially, labor leaders hoped that these expenditures would pay off by increasing memberships and improving economies of scale. It soon became apparent, however, that these hopes would not be realized. The eastward expansion of the labor movement proved to be far more costly than first anticipated. To fill personnel needs, the DGB and its member unions chose to transfer experienced westerners eastward rather than rely on inexperienced easterners. This proved to be terribly expensive. The unions also had to rent offices and set up a communications network from scratch under extremely primitive circumstances. Competition from the private sector for the same resources, which were in short supply, drove up costs.

The massive job losses in the former GDR produced a colossal wave of expensive unfair-dismissal litigation. Since union membership included legal services provided by the DGB as a benefit, DGB expenses soared. Even the most basic case of this type cost five thousand dollars, which exceeded the average eastern member's annual dues payment by severalfold. The litigation boom left the DGB with little choice but to increase its staff of legal experts by 150 (i.e., 40%) between 1989 and 1993. The explosive growth of DGB legal services expenditures helped to push the share of the DGB budget consumed by personnel costs between 1991 and 1994 from 55 to 72 percent.[52]

Many union leaders anticipated (correctly) that the transition to capital-ism in eastern Germany would eliminate many jobs (particularly those in low-end manufacturing sectors). As a result, many unions built organizations that deliberately could service far fewer members than the initial numbers belonging to their eastern branches. Until the shakeout came, however, the unions were hopelessly understaffed yet still overextended financially. Other union leaders, particularly those in the public and service sectors, established a large apparatus in the five new states in the belief that the initial employ-ment and membership levels in their sectors would remain stable, if not grow, because the former GDR had a disproportionately small service sector. By the mid-1990s, eastern job losses far outstripped even the most pessimistic estimates from the early days of unification, and all of the unions suddenly found it difficult to sustain their eastern offices. All of the DGB affiliates except for the police officers union suffered significant membership declines in the east that pinched finances to a greater or lesser degree. Lower eastern wages and a lower ratio of full-time employees to members held the average eastern per capita monthly dues payment to between 50 and 60 percent of that in the west. A few unions, such as HBV, ÖTV, and DAG, had to cut back particularly severely and even to sell property in order to close annual budget deficits that had widened to tens of millions of dollars.[53] The 1993 resigna-tion of Lorenz Schwegler, the chair of the private service sector union HBV, was in part due to the cost of his particularly aggressive eastward expansion. Other unions implemented hiring freezes and pared back perquisites in order to close deficits ranging from the hundreds of thousands to millions of dol-lars. In the end, what labor leaders had at first thought would be a bonanza turned into a burden. All the unions spent far more money setting up and maintaining operations in eastern Germany than they ever collected in dues.

As is common with trade unions and other mass organizations through-out the world, financial exigency rather than persuasive argumentation is the principal catalyst for institutional reform, and considerations of personal fate within the leadership shape its direction. The reform discussions within the union movement were often fractious. They typically advanced through unilateral action rather than consensus. Broadly speaking, starting in the early 1990s, two competing blueprints for the future contours of the German labor movement came into focus. One, for which IG Chemie was the principal proponent, envisioned the creation through mergers of approximately a half dozen self-sufficient "multisectoral" unions.[54] The smaller DGB affiliates and the public-sector unions offered an alternative construction, which they called "cooperative unionism." Cooperative unionism proposed preserving the organizational independence of most unions but doing more activities jointly to achieve greater economies of scale.

Specifically, IG Chemie officials argued that unions will only survive in the twenty-first century if they become self-sufficient providers of high-quality services for an increasingly sophisticated, nonideological professional clientele. The IG Chemie leadership asserted that this would mean transferring to new multisectoral unions the task of providing member services for which the DGB had previously been responsible, such as legal aid and group discounts. The shift to direct provision would permit individual unions to enhance the quality of services provided (which at times had been poor), to tailor the services to the specific needs of their membership, and to strengthen "brand identity" among members and potential members, who join individual unions and not the DGB.[55]

Each multisectoral union would need a membership of at least one million, IG Chemie officials contended, in order to obtain the full economies of scale required to provide a full set of professional services at a reasonable cost and quality directly to members. The only way to achieve this would be through a series of mergers that would eliminate the smaller unions. The IG Chemie leadership added that half a dozen multisectoral unions with one-to-three million members would also have far more political leverage in Berlin and Brussels. Internal labor politics also played a part. IG Chemie had always been a weak number three to the two giant German unions, IG Metall and ÖTV. Moreover, its relative share of gross DGB membership had slipped from 9 percent in 1973 to 7.6 percent in 1994. Mergers would help IG Chemie bulk up.[56]

IG Chemie's vision of self-sufficient multisectoral unionism had numerous detractors. Some accused the IG Chemie leadership of harboring an ulterior motive as it increasingly called for cutting the DGB's budget. Depriving the small unions of the common DGB services on which they depended for survival would force them into mergers with the larger unions. Others argued that IG Chemie's approach would result in mergers based on the personal chemistry of top officials and comparisons of union staff pay scales rather than any organizational or economic logic.[57] Some critics pointed out that the sheer size of the multisectoral unions envisioned by IG Chemie's leadership would actually make recruitment, retention, and representation harder in many sectors because it would be difficult for members to establish and maintain occupational identity with a conglomerate union. Joining a union out of social custom had already deteriorated considerably. A massive, impersonal, and bureaucratic apparatus running a trade union would

alienate large numbers of potential members who would fear that such an organization would be incapable of addressing their individual needs. Large size
would make organizing particularly difficult in smaller workplaces and sectors where shared skills and allegiance to a profession are extremely important.[58] Finally, skeptics expressed concern that multisectoral unionism would
narrow the political horizon of the organization solely to the problems of
the sectors falling under the union's jurisdiction, decreasing the likelihood
leaders and members would be interested in cross-sectoral solidarity beyond
their union during strikes and other campaigns.[59]

The alternative to IG Chemie's vision of multisectoral unionism, cooperative unionism, came in two varieties. One proposal envisioned an alliance among the five traditional public-sector unions: ÖTV, GdED, DPG,
GdP, and GEW. The other was a cooperative relationship among four
moderate-sized private-sector unions known as the "four little tigers":
GHK, GTB, IG Medien, and NGG. A fifth union, HBV, occasionally cooperated with the tigers as well. A joint declaration called "Cooperation
Instead of Merger" served as a provisional statement of the public-sector
group.[60] The four tigers' proposal entitled "Secure Autonomy" was similar
in content.[61] The documents pointed out that "mergers do not bring a
single new member into the DGB" and rejected radical reductions in the
DGB budget, since cuts would impair the ability of small unions to provide services to members. They called for a systematic mutual exchange
of information in order to learn from one another and a "bundling"
of activities in order to save money. In other words, "Cooperation Instead of Merger" and "Secure Autonomy" were not really concrete counterproposals. They were calls for study. It quickly became apparent that
the unions involved did not share a common vision of what cooperation
would mean in practice. Moreover, even if a consensus could be obtained,
cooperation offered few opportunities for savings and would have been a
logistical nightmare. Too many unions would have been involved, and the
transaction costs would have remained high.

Cooperative unionism suffered a severe blow at IG Metall's fall 1995
convention. IG Metall chair Klaus Zwickel broke his union's silence regarding the question of mergers when he stated that he could envision Germany
ultimately ending up with five unions: three for manufacturing, one for private services, and one for public services.[62] Zwickel's statement left no room
for cooperative unionism. By year's end, the IG Metall leadership made its
distaste for the cooperative proposal clear. The head of IG Metall's strategic
planning department, Klaus Lang, stated bluntly that the proposal was simply "a synonym for cost shifting" from the smaller to the larger unions.[63]

The four tigers and HBV then dropped their proposal for cooperation and returned to the idea of direct DGB membership for all members, which Hans Böckler had championed in the 1940s but the American and British occupying powers opposed.[64] Too much time had passed, however. This idea died when labor leaders from the union that would stand the most to lose from the proposal—IG Metall—expressed disapproval.[65]

The decision that put the last nail in the coffin of cooperative unionism came on 1 July 1997. The DGB's federal executive board voted to staunch the single biggest drain on union finances—the provision of legal services—by transferring it out of the DGB and into a newly established autonomous firm, DGB Rechtschutz GmbH (DGB Legal Aid, GmbH). The DGB's holding company, the Vermögens- und Treuhandgesellschaft des DGB (VTG, Property and Trust Corporation of the DGB), would own the new firm, and funding for it would be capped at 40 percent of the DGB's gross dues receipts.[66] The proponents of cooperative unionism saw this vote as a test of the willingness of the larger affiliates, in particular IG BAU and IG Metall, to support services jointly provided by the DGB. In particular, they were interested in the position of IG Metall. When IG Metall voted in favor of the proposal, which took legal services out of the DGB and instituted an expenditure cap, the proponents of cooperation knew that they did not have a majority among union leaders for any of their proposals.

While there was much talk but little action regarding a cooperative model of unionism, the proponents of mergers moved ahead. Once the first serious negotiations regarding mergers began in the early 1990s, they took on a momentum of their own. Between 1995 and 2001, the number of DGB affiliates shrank by half, from sixteen to eight. The mergers can be classified into two categories: (1) larger unions absorbing much smaller ones based in economically declining sectors, and (2) the fusion of several unions from overlapping sectors. All but one of the mergers were of the former type.

The construction workers union (IG BSE) and the agricultural, forest, and garden employees union (GGLF) were the first to complete a merger in the 1990s. On 1 February 1993, the two unions reached a cooperation agreement that established three working groups to iron out the legal, personnel, policy, and structural issues that needed to be settled before a merger could take place. The agreement also set 1995 as the target date for a merger of the two unions. At a special joint convention, the two unions voted on 7 November 1995 to form the Industriegewerkschaft Bauen-Agrar-Umwelt (IG BAU, Industrial Union of Construction, Agricultural, and Environmental Employees).[67] The asymmetry between the two partners facilitated the process unfolding smoothly. IG BSE was six times as large as the GGLF, and the latter organization did not have enough members to remain viable, so there was never any doubt about who was taking over whom.

Around the same time, the chemical workers union engineered a merger with two very different partners, the mining and the leather workers unions. IG Chemie and the miners union (IG BE) announced their intention to merge in December 1991 and approved a cooperation agreement in May 1992.[68] The combination had all the elements of a mercenary May-September marriage. IG BE had been declining for some time along with the German mining sector. By the early 1990s, it had more retirees than actively employed members. The union was attractive to IG Chemie, however, because of its treasury and property. The miners union was among the oldest in Germany. Many of its offices were in prime downtown locations that could fetch premium prices on the real estate market. The miners union also had considerable capital reserves. The mining and chemicals sectors were close enough economically and politically speaking to make the merger plausible.

While the merger between the chemical and mining unions was underway, two other unions—the leather workers union (GL) and the clothing and textile workers union (GTB)—were seeking partners. Job loss had been rampant in both sectors for decades. Each union gambled on German unification, investing as much as possible to regain a critical mass of members, but the eastern clothing, textile, and leather sectors were all but wiped out within the space of a few years. Some suggested that the GL and the GTB merge, since they organized workers in related sectors and the old East German union actually consisted of all three sectors, but bad blood among the leaderships and ideological differences kept this option off the table. The leather workers union was in the worst shape. Its membership had fallen to fewer than 25,000, so its leadership quickly latched on to the most immediately available and willing partner, which was IG Chemie. In June 1993, IG Chemie, IG BE, and GL approved a three-way cooperative agreement. The accord set a timetable. Over the course of 1995 and 1996 the unions each held a convention approving the merger and legally liquidating their organizations. In October 1997, the new Industriegewerkschaft Bergbau, Chemie, Energie (IG BCE, Industrial Union of Mining, Chemical, and Energy Employees) held its founding convention.[69] The new union initially had one million members and 11.7 percent of the membership of the DGB unions. The addition of the GL to the merger irked some because of its transparent opportunism. Leather had little to do with mining or chemicals, and the political gulf between the leftist leadership of the GL and the moderately social democratic IG Chemie was even wider than the one between the GL and the GTB. As a result, the merger simply looked like a case of a big fish swallowing a rather desperate little fish. This naturally worried the other little fish in the trade union pond.

Leaders of the clothing and textile workers union were particularly critical of the IG Chemie-IG BE-GL merger because it eliminated the possibility of the more logical GTB-GL merger. Declining membership and mounting costs left GTB officials little choice but to seek a merger of its own. The GTB and the food and restaurant workers union, NGG, briefly considered a merger. The attraction of the match was that the GTB and NGG were both in consumer goods sectors with predominantly female employment. Moreover, both unions were approximately the same size and had already been cooperating since the 1980s in the production of their monthly magazines. In 1996, the two unions even set 1998 as a tentative date for the merger. In the end, however, the NGG leadership was unable to agree to the organizational compromises that a marriage of equals entailed and backed out of the project.[70]

Once again, the GTB was left without a partner. Both IG Chemie and IG Metall had previously made overtures to the GTB, which GTB heads had rejected. Now the GTB officials had to reconsider both. The GTB leadership took into account five issues when looking for a merger partner: (1) the preservation of institutional structures for clothing and textile employees within a larger organization, (2) enhancement of bargaining leverage, (3) saving the jobs of as many GTB officials as possible, (4) the pay scale for union officials in the new organization, and (5) the size of pensions for retired union officials. IG Metall offered the best deal on all of these fronts, so the GTB turned to the metalworkers union. IG Metall leaders had at first taken a dismissive stance toward mergers because their union was so large already, but once mergers started to mushroom and the union's membership began to plummet, IG Metall officials decided to join in before all the opportunities disappeared. In 1996, the executive boards of both unions approved going ahead with a merger. IG Metall had a mild interest in acquiring the GTB. Automobile companies had increasingly been outsourcing automobile seat production to upholstery firms, which paid their workers at the considerably lower compensation rates set forth in the GTB's collective agreements. IG Metall officials saw a merger with the GTB as an opportunity to close this gap, and they were willing to accommodate the GTB to make it happen. Clothing and textile employers and some employees feared that IG Metall was acquiring the GTB to shut it down. Specifically they feared that

IG Metall would jack up the wage bills in the clothing and textile sectors because the union would be far more concerned with eliminating the pay differential between upholsterers and automobile workers than in preserving employment. The merger went ahead despite these criticisms because the leadership of both unions were committed to it. During 1997, the GTB held a special convention to approve the merger and dissolve itself, and IG Metall held a special convention to add clothing, textiles, and related sectors to its organizational jurisdiction. The two unions officially merged on 1 January 1998.[71]

The tiny wood and plastic workers union, GHK, was also looking for a partner. The jobs of GHK workers most closely resembled those found in the jurisdictions of IG BAU and IG BCE, but GHK leaders decided to merge with IG Metall because it was a better deal for them and their organization. The merger took place in 2000. Critics within the union movement attacked IG Metall's mergers as yet another set of idiosyncratic combinations driven by the narrow objectives of the leaderships involved rather than by larger strategic considerations.[72]

One merger during these years was like no other. It combined five private and public service-sector unions in 2001 to form the Vereinte Dienstleistungsgewerkschaft (ver.di, United Service Employees Union). The project began in the aftermath of the failure of the policy paper "Cooperation Instead of Merger." It gained momentum as the finances of unions deteriorated and mergers began taking place among manufacturing unions. The talks bore fruit in February 1998. Six private and public service-sector unions (including the DAG, which was not a DGB affiliate) issued a provisional "policy platform," which laid out a negotiating process and timetable for forming a single massive public and private service-sector union.[73]

Many experts at the time were doubtful that the project could be completed, given the heterogeneous collection of personalities, policies, and structures existing within the unions.[74] Mergers between one strong and one or two weak unions during the 1990s had proved to be hard enough. Fairly soon into the negotiations, one participant—the small teachers and technicians union (GEW)—dropped out, fearing that its identity would be totally erased in a new mammoth service-sector union.[75] By November 1998, however, the five remaining unions had agreed to set up a series of working groups, which began meeting in 1999. In November 1999, the participating unions held parallel special conventions to begin preparing their organizations for the merger in a coordinated fashion. In December 1999, the unions created a "founding organization" (called Gründungsorganisation ver.di, or GO-ver.di) to coordinate the process.

The union leaderships spent most of the following year hammering out the constitution, structure, and policies of the new union, as well as deciding on the distribution of positions. Throughout the process, the leadership of the largest participant—the public-sector union, ÖTV—was committed to the merger, but local and regional ÖTV officials repeatedly expressed skepticism. Compromises on three matters made the merger possible: structure, leadership, and jurisdiction. Ver.di's constituent unions, including ÖTV, which was much bigger than the other participating unions, accepted the merger as a consensual process among equals. The largest two unions, ÖTV and HBV, did push for substantial organizational integration, but the smaller unions refused because only a highly decentralized structure would preserve some autonomy for each of the constituent unions.

Four deals laid the foundation for the merger. First, the union leaders opted for a "matrix model" that preserves thirteen sectoral units (*Fachbereiche*) from the participating unions. Each unit retains considerable autonomy over collective bargaining and a fixed share of the budget. The new structure also includes unionwide regional offices and nine designated demographic groupings (*Personengruppen*), but these are of secondary importance. Proponents of ver.di's matrix structure assert that it gives the union room to adjust to peculiarities of the more than two hundred sectors and one thousand occupations within its jurisdiction. It is worth noting that critics complain that ver.di is not really a merger at all but simply five unions using the same logo. Franz Kersjes, who was vice-chair of IG Medien at the time of the merger, has since complained, "Many full-time union officials have acted just as before. Unfortunately, with regard to interacting with each other, no new common culture has come into being."[76] Second, ver.di adopted a 50:50 female-male quota for all of its governing committees, which roughly reflects the composition of the membership. No other union in Germany has gone this far to promote gender equality. Third, the participants agreed that Frank Bsirske from ÖTV should become the first chair of ver.di. Bsirske came from a blue-collar background and was the first in his family to attend university. He majored in political science and worked in Hanover's personnel office before becoming a full-time union official. Bsirske, who was forty-two at the time of the merger, projected a youthful, capable, "future-oriented" image. He is also the sole Green ever to rise to the top of a German union. Fourth, ironing out the jurisdictional problems between ver.di and the remaining DGB unions, which had become worse over time, was a prerequisite to DGB approval of the ver.di merger. The participation of the DAG in the merger complicated jurisdictional matters further, because it was not a DGB affiliate and its white-collar members were sprinkled across almost every sector of the economy. Union officials assembled a working group called "2 plus 2 plus 2" because it consisted of two representatives from the DGB, two from the industrial unions, and two from what was to become ver.di.[77]

The group reached an agreement in December 2000 entitled "Bases for Organizational Relations and Cooperation of the DGB Unions on the Occasion of the Founding of ver.di and the Integration of the DAG into the DGB."[78] The understanding states that its purpose is to restore the validity of the basic organizational principle of the postwar German trade union movement, that is, "one workplace, one union." It resolved with a compromise the difficult question of how to handle DAG members who are in non–service sectors. DAG members were permitted either to join the union with jurisdiction over the sector in which they were employed or to become ver.di members. If these members chose to join ver.di, however, the collective agreement of the sector in which they were employed would set their compensation. In other words, the five-decade standoff between the DGB unions and the DAG finally ended. The DGB won.

The document also divided up the jurisdiction of new sectors among individual unions. Ver.di is responsible for telecommunications; IG Metall covers the production of information technology equipment, including software; and IG BCE organizes employees who make film, tape, and CDs. Existing exceptions to this distribution were only allowed "in individual cases and for a transition period." Unions in sectors that traditionally overlapped were to form "sectoral working groups" (*Branchenarbeitskreise*) with the objective of creating a common "orientation to collective bargaining" and eventually a "joint collective bargaining group" (*Tarifgemeinschaft*). The union that had jurisdiction over the sector in question was to "coordinate" collective bargaining. The agreement also called for the creation of an "organization register" to document the claim of individual unions over specific workplaces. All of the parties were satisfied that the December 2000 understanding would serve as a sound basis for dealing with jurisdictional disputes.[79] With all the hurdles successfully traversed, ver.di held its "merging" and "founding" conventions back-to-back in mid-March 2001.[80] With just under three million members at the time of its creation, ver.di became the largest trade union in Germany. (Ver.di eventually ceded first place back to IG Metall in 2005.)

By the spring of 2001, the institutional landscape of the German labor movement was radically different than it had been six years earlier (table 4.4). The DGB consisted of eight unions: two mammoths (ver.di and IG Metall), one medium-sized organization (IG BCE), and five smaller bodies, GEW,

Table 4.4.   Current Affliates of the Deutscher Gewerkschaftsbund

Union	Abbreviation	Sector
Industriegewerkschaft Bauen-Argrar-Umwelt	IG BAU	construction, agriculture, environmental products
Industriegewerkschaft Bergbau, Chemie, Energie	IG BCE	mining, chemicals, energy
Eisenbahn- und Verkehrsgewerkschaft	EVG	railroad
Gewerkschaft Erziehung und Wissenschaft	GEW	education, science
Industriegewerkshaft Metall	IG Metall	mechanical engineering, iron, steel, textiles, wood
Gewerkschaft Nahrung-Genuss-Gaststätten	NGG	food processing, hotels, restaurants
Gewerkschaft der Polizei	GdP	police
Vereinte Dienstleistungsgewerkschaft	ver.di	public and private services

GdP, IG BAU, NGG, and GdED, which had just renamed itself "trans-net" and is now called Eisenbahn und Verkehrsgewerkschaft (EVG, Rail and Transportation Employees Union) after a merger in 2010 with the DBB's small Gewerkschaft deutscher Bundesbahnbeamten und Anwärter (GDBA, Union of German Federal Rail Civil Servants). This remains the current structure of the DGB.

The Emergence of the Multisectoral Trade Union Movement

The relatively sudden and substantial changes to the structure of German organized labor have produced what is best understood as a second postwar German trade union movement in which multisectoral unionism dominates. Two unions—IG Metall and ver.di—now account for 70 percent of all DGB members. Both unions have members from multiple unrelated sectors of the economy. Even the unions at the second tier in terms of size—IG BAU and IG BCE—also comprise unrelated sectors.

Like its predecessor, the second postwar German trade union movement contains exceptions to the predominant organizational model. Two unions, the GEW and GdP, have stabilized as small unions for a professional clientele. The structure of the second postwar German trade union movement has been stable for over a decade, but the ultimate fate of two smaller unions— NGG and EVG—remains an open question. Their sectors are in the throes of change, making their odds of survival uncertain.

The transition from the first to the second postwar trade union movement was the product of contestation, exigency, and fragmentary steps rather than a grand design, but the same can be said about the formation of the first postwar German union movement. The driving force behind the transition to the second postwar labor movement had been a defensive reaction to declining organizational strength. The hope was that structural change—specifically, mergers to achieve diversification and greater economies of scale—would stabilize finances and improve service provision, which would in turn staunch membership decline.[81]

With the creation of ver.di, there is now for the first time another union of comparable size to IG Metall. This changes the balance of power within the DGB in two ways. First, IG Metall is no longer primus inter pares. Second, the want and need for the larger unions to consult the smaller ones has diminished. The larger unions also have less use for the DGB.

The Incredible Shrinking DGB

The future of the DGB as a peak confederation is far from certain. For decades, critics have attacked the DGB as ineffectual.[82] The combination of organizational upheaval and budgetary distress starting in the 1990s left individual union leaders looking for places to cut costs. They quickly turned their gaze to the DGB. The large and increasingly self-sufficient and multisectoral unions no longer needed a peak confederation to provide services and had become less willing to subsidize the remaining smaller affiliates through the DGB. As a result, leaders from the larger unions began to push for stripping the DGB of roles and resources. The 1994 Berlin DGB convention amended DGB statutes an unprecedented forty-two times, in most cases instituting some form of austerity. Convention resolutions reduced the sizes of the managing federal executive board and the federal committee, and pared back the number of local DGB offices. They also cut the size and authority of DGB departments for collective bargaining, education, foreign employees, handicrafts, and technology and eliminated DGB departments for white- and blue-collar employees. The convention did spare the women and youth departments in order not to send the wrong signal regarding the DGB's commitment to these groups.[83]

These changes did not end the DGB's budgetary woes. Falling revenue forced the DGB to cut its operating budget by 17 percent between 1992 and 1997. Over the same period, the DGB trimmed total staff from 2,700 to 2,075 and headquarters personnel from 330 to 210.[84] The DGB ended its financial free fall in 1997 through a decision to move legal services out of the confederation and into a separate restructured entity. In the end, the budget cuts of the 1990s, which were largely ad hoc, reduced the presence and importance of the DGB "out in the field" and within the German labor movement, especially as a provider of services.[85]

At the 1998 DGB convention, the leadership of the DGB and the affiliated unions were determined to improve the coherence of the DGB's organizational restructuring and to bring closure to the reform effort launched earlier in the decade. Specifically, the leaders of the DGB and its affiliates asked the delegates to approve granting the authority to complete the DGB's organizational reform to the federal executive board and to approve transferring the headquarters of the DGB from Düsseldorf to Berlin by 2002. The delegates, protective of the status quo and skeptical after the recent budget cuts, were wary of both proposals. Vague compromise language in resolutions that the convention eventually passed allowed the leadership to claim it had a mandate to proceed.[86]

After the 1998 convention, the DGB chair Dieter Schulte and his staff, with the support of the affiliated union chairs, went quickly to work. In 1998, the DGB held ten workshops with its own officials and a series of meetings with representatives of the individual unions. A consensus gelled throughout the labor movement that the DGB needed to shift focus from the provision of member services and the production of seldom-read social and economic analyses to political work. Specifically, Schulte's staff, informed by the workshops and meetings, identified the three "central tasks" for the DGB: (1) "act as 'the union voice' vis-à-vis the state, business, organizations, parties, etc.; (2) competently influence political and in particular legislative decision-making processes at all levels; and (3) strengthen its capacity to mobilize and stage campaigns." The larger objective behind these goals is to ensure that the DGB be "permanently present in the political decision-making centers and competently be a part of the process."[87]

By establishing the principal tasks of DGB organizational reform as undertaking a transition from service provision to political lobbying, the trade union leadership brought purpose and direction to the endeavor—something that had been noticeably absent during the reform's unruly first stage. The transition to lobbying permitted the DGB to make substantial savings on its largest single cost: personnel. The decision to move the DGB headquarters to Berlin also furthered both dimensions of the organizational reform. It facilitated political monitoring and lobbying at the federal level. It also enabled the DGB to reduce operating costs further by shedding employees who were reluctant to make the move from Düsseldorf, which had been the site of the DGB headquarters since its founding.[88]

The DGB simultaneously increased its monitoring and lobbying activities at the European level, which was in keeping with the logic behind the organizational reform. The DGB had already established an office in Brussels in 1997. In 2000, it added one in Strasbourg and expanded its Brussels office to cover the European Parliament. The individual German unions also increased their activities in Brussels. German union officials rarely miss an opportunity to embrace Europe rhetorically because it resonates well with the antinationalistic leanings of the German Left. In practice, however, most German union leaders have frequently tried to use the European trade union apparatus simply to pressure unions from other countries into adopting stances compatible with German priorities. German unions have taken the lead in promoting European works councils, which began to form in the mid-1990s, but they have been steadfast in ensuring that EWCs do not compromise the authority of German works councils. They have also had considerable success in placing working-time reduction on the agenda throughout Europe.[89]

Still, incompatibilities between the "Latin" trade union structure, which vests ultimate authority in the confederation, and the "Teutonic" model, in which sectoral unions are the dominant players, complicates the European activities of the German labor movement. The structures of the European Trade Union Confederation (ETUC) and the European Union itself are more compatible with the Latin model. For example, German unionists have not been wholly hostile to the "social dialogue" at the European level as spelled out in the social protocol to the Maastricht Treaty, but they have made it clear that they would not support the social dialogue leading to the cession of any significant collective bargaining authority to the DGB, European industry federations of trade unions, or the ETUC. Indeed, the euro crisis has prompted a long-time top staffer at the DGB to warn that talk of a European "economic government" could lead to the introduction of "wage diktats" through the backdoor.[90] The euro crisis has not dissuaded the heads of IG Metall and ver.di from continuing to support European integration, but they are careful to couple these statements with assertions that austerity only worsens economic conditions and that integration must also include greater democratic control.[91]

Be Careful What You Wish For: The First Schröder Government and the Alliance for Jobs

The timing of the plan to convert the DGB into the political arm of the labor movement was fortuitous. In the 1998 German federal election, the unions all but abandoned the postwar principle of nonpartisan unionism. They committed an unprecedented 8 million deutschmarks to a thinly veiled effort to bring a coalition consisting of the Social Democrats and the Greens to power. On 27 September 1998, Germans voted out the center-right parties that had governed for sixteen years. The new "red-green" government headed by the SPD's Gerhard Schröder was the first in the postwar era with both coalition partners left of center. Organized labor had high hopes of reaping substantial returns as a result. Ironically, the seven years of red-green rule proved to be among the most vexing for German labor in the postwar era.

Five months before the election, Schröder said that if elected he would launch an Alliance for Jobs (*Bündnis für Arbeit*). This promise quickly became a centerpiece of the campaign. The Alliance would consist of regular tripartite meetings of top union officials, the heads of the business interest groups, and government officials to develop tangible proposals to reduce unemployment. This would not be the first Alliance for Jobs. Helmut Kohl had briefly created a similar tripartite body with the same name in 1996 after IG Metall chair Klaus Zwickel had suggested it in the previous year. Kohl's Alliance collapsed within months, however. The unions quit ostensibly over new restrictions on sick pay; Kohl's Alliance was also an unlikely prospect because the upcoming federal election already loomed large on the horizon. Union leaders hoped that Schröder's new Alliance for Jobs would be different because the Social Democrats and Greens would be in power, which would make it harder for the employers to avoid compromise. Schröder, moreover, had selected Walter Riester, the very capable deputy leader of IG Metall, as his shadow labor minister. As a result, organized labor firmly embraced the campaign pledge to create a new Alliance for Jobs.[92]

Once the red-green government came to power, however, union officials were ill-prepared to take advantage because they had made attaining a *process*—namely, the Alliance for Jobs—their paramount political objective. There was little consensus or forethought among union officials about how to use a sympathetic government to advance their interests in concrete terms beyond the tripartite talks because they had never undertaken the arduous but necessary work required to hammer out a set of viable political demands.

Union officials did get a few policy changes in the first months of the Schröder chancellorship, but they were relatively minor measures intended to curb erosion at the margins of the German welfare state. The new government made 630-mark-per-month "mini" jobs subject to payroll tax for the first time in exchange for including those employees in the welfare state, and tightened the definition of self-employment to staunch payroll-tax dodging. Additionally, the red-green government passed a modest measure to promote youth employment (Jugendsofortprogramm, JUSOPRO) and undid the cutbacks from 1996 on sick-time pay.[93]

Considerable "megaphone diplomacy" ensued immediately after the election between the social partners in efforts to define the parameters of the new Alliance for Jobs.[94] Much fanfare accompanied the first Alliance for Jobs meeting in December 1998. The chancellor, top ministers, and the social partners agreed to a list of topics and parceled them out into working groups. The Alliance declared job creation the principal objective and agreed to focus on vocational training, tax policy, labor market flexibility, and collective bargaining practices, but the wording was kept so vague that it did not rule out the preferred solutions of either the employers or the unions. The parties made no firm commitments except to participate. They agreed to create a steering group to coordinate the effort and a benchmarking group that would provide research support, including best-practice comparisons from abroad.[95]

The Alliance for Jobs had several ups and downs in the following year. The second meeting in late February accomplished little of substance owing to a contentious collective bargaining round in the mechanical engineering sector that had just concluded. In May, the news magazine *Der Spiegel* featured a cover story entitled "The Plan" that described a leaked proposal from the benchmarking group. The proposal's centerpiece was to increase employment in the private service sector by waiving payroll taxes on low-paid unskilled workers. Neither the employers nor the unions supported the proposal, however. Both sides complained that permanently waiving payroll taxes would be too costly and distort the labor market. It should be noted that few of the social partners' representatives in the Alliance came from sectors that would have benefitted significantly from the tax breaks. To the contrary, the manufacturing sectors would have ultimately covered the cost of the foregone revenue, which may also help to explain the mutual opposition. The union representatives were particularly skittish about waiving payroll taxes. They feared that such a step could be both a precursor to a broader attack on the welfare state and a means to put downward pressure on wage agreements at the low end of the scale. The biggest impact of the leak was on the benchmarking group; it lost influence in the process.[96]

The political complexion of the Schröder government shifted toward the center when the left-wing finance minister Oskar Lafontaine quit the government in the spring of 1999 after a series of confrontations with the chancellor. The cabinet reshuffle improved the mood for the third meeting of the Alliance, which occurred in July 1999. The Bundesvereinigung der Deutschen Arbeitgeberverbände (BDA, Confederation of German Employers Organizations) and the DGB issued a common position paper.[97] The BDA agreed to urge employers to curb overtime, to expand part-time work, and to promote phased-in retirement. The DGB committed the unions to reform collective bargaining to permit greater flexibility but stressed that wage negotiations should not be a part of the Alliance discussions. The final meeting for 1999 was in December. It was the fourth for the Alliance and was highly contentious because IG Metall's Klaus Zwickel insisted on bringing to the table his union's proposal for retirement at age sixty. No progress occurred.

In January 2000, the Alliance met for a fifth time. Both sides gave a little in a joint statement. The union representatives committed to "a longer-term and employment-oriented collective bargaining policy in the forthcoming 2000 bargaining round" in which the "available distributive margin . . . should be primarily used for job-creating agreements." The employers accepted exploration into "new ways for job-creating early retirement on acceptable terms for the persons concerned and without additional costs for the statutory pension scheme."[98] Chancellor Schröder called the new document a "breakthrough,"[99] but in the months that followed, the social partners began to accuse each other of failing to make good on their Alliance commitments. The last Alliance meeting of 2000 was in July. It ended after disputes over providing a sufficient number of jobs for apprentices and employer criticism of the government's plan to reform codetermination. In the fall, two future constituent unions of ver.di, IG Medien and HBV, opted out of the Alliance.[100]

There were two more Alliance meetings in 2001. Schröder praised the Alliance at the March meeting as a "reform motor," while the social partners tossed allegations of broken promises at each other.[101] Nothing of substance was accomplished. The July meeting was much more harmonious, but it had the air of an elegy. The BDA-DGB joint declaration contained a summary of the actions and achievements of the Alliance, including a claim that it created six hundred thousand jobs. When the Alliance met for a final time in early 2002, the first phases of the federal election campaign had already begun. The social partners once again traded recriminations, but little else transpired. The participants did not declare the Alliance dead, but it was clear that there would be no more meetings for the foreseeable future.[102]

Labor's preoccupation with the Alliance for Jobs largely distracted leaders from addressing internal issues. DGB chair Dieter Schulte did acknowledge labor's most pressing problem, however. On a trip to Jerusalem, he partook in the age-old practice of petitioning God by putting a note in the Western Wall of the Second Temple. His note read, "We need more members, Dieter Schulte, DGB Chair." In interviews, Schulte identified the decline of labor's milieu as a social custom as a substantial problem, conceding that no one "naturally becomes a member" anymore.[103] DGB officials hoped to repeat their successful effort in support of Gerhard Schröder with a public relations drive to promote the unions themselves. Shifting over to self-promotion was not as easy as they had hoped, however. The campaign, which included a brief rebranding of the DGB as the "Federation of Unions," failed quickly. Schulte's successor, Michael Sommer, abandoned it when he became DGB chair in 2002. Some regional efforts—such as Schwerin's May Day "Job Parade," which was modeled after Berlin's famous "Love Parade," including flatbed trucks covered with scantily clad dancers and blaring techno music— proved successful, but these were exceptional.[104] Most DGB affiliates did little beyond holding "future conferences" that were internal affairs in which various factions jousted for supremacy over defining the fine points of union doctrine. Such exercises did little to shore up labor's milieu.[105]

Moving from political and organizational to economic developments, the decade of the 1990s was even more difficult for organized labor than the previous one. The German economy grew only slightly faster than in the 1980s; per capita GDP growth averaged 2.3 percent per year (table 4.2). The brief unification boom accounts for the difference. Unemployment became a problem of a whole different order with the addition of eastern Germany. The average for the decade for all of Germany was 7.5 percent, but unemployment peaked in eastern Germany in 1993 at 19.4 percent and remained above 15 percent for the rest of the decade, despite significant job-creation schemes and heavy use of early retirement programs. The average annual increase in productivity was 2.4 percent, which was worse than it seems at first glance, because German unification offered ample opportunities for catch-up productivity growth in eastern Germany.

The coverage of collective agreements began to shrink in the 1990s. In 1995, union contracts in western Germany set compensation directly for 72 percent of all employees. Add those who were affected indirectly and the figure hit 83 percent. By 2000, these numbers had slipped to 63 and 70 percent (figure 4.2).[106] A similar trend unfolded in eastern Germany, albeit from a lower starting point. In 1996, collective agreements set compensation either directly or indirectly for 73 percent of all eastern employees (56% directly). By 2000, this had slid to 55 percent (44% directly). Days lost as a result of strikes and lockouts fell to 13.1 per one thousand employees, which was a new postwar low (table 4.3). A shift in employers' behavior explains

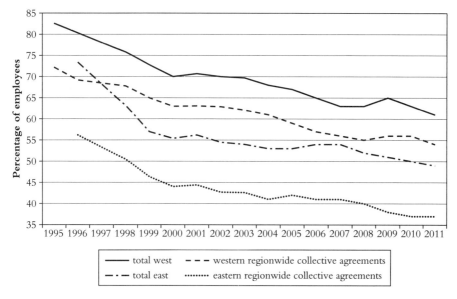

FIGURE 4.2.   Collective bargaining coverage: Percentage of employees.
Source: Institut für Arbeitsmarkt- und Berufsforschung, Enterprise Panel.

the change. The number of days lost to strikes remained virtually the same between the two decades, but the average number of days lost to lockouts each year fell by over 99 percent from 269,889 to just 259. The employers' tactical change, which is discussed in detail in the subsequent chapter, did not help organized labor at the bargaining table. Average nominal income increased by only 2.6 percent per year in the 1990s, which was lower than in any previous decade. The nominal increase equaled the average inflation rate for the decade. Thus, employees' real incomes did not rise at all (table 4.2). Labor's share of national income slipped further, falling to 65.5 percent in 1999 (figure 4.1).

The metamorphosis from the first to the second postwar German labor movement was in its last stages when union leaders engaged in the Alliance for Jobs. As we shall see, the economic, organizational, and political stress tests on the new organizational architecture only intensified in the first decade of the new millennium.

Politics and Policies of the Second Postwar German Trade Union Movement

The German economy performed terribly for much of the first decade of the new millennium, which was also the first decade of the second postwar

German trade union movement. The underlying conditions were not favorable, to be sure. Real per capita GDP grew by an annual average of just 0.9 percent, which was a full percentage point lower than in any other postwar decade (table 4.2). Growth for the decade was abysmal even before the financial crisis. From 2000 to 2007, it averaged just 1.2 percent, despite a mild upturn in 2006 and 2007. Consequently, the mean annual unemployment rate for the decade reached a postwar high of 8.5 percent. Things did improve somewhat in later years. The unemployment rate for Germany as a whole peaked at 10.7 percent in 2005, but then fell to 7.7 percent by 2009. Still, 7.7 percent was worse than the average for the 1990s, and unemployment in eastern Germany remained roughly twice as high as in western Germany.[107] The average annual productivity increase for the 2000s slowed to just 1.1 percent, which was a full percentage point lower than the rate for any previous postwar decade.

Unions resorted to industrial action far less frequently in the inauspicious economic conditions of the 2000s. Mean annual working days lost to strikes and lockouts fell to a postwar low of 4.9 per one thousand employees (table 4.3). Unions were also far less successful at the bargaining table. The nominal annual increase in net income per employee for the decade averaged 1.2 percent, which was another postwar low. In real terms, net income fell on average by 0.4 percent per year (table 4.2). Labor's share of national income fell to 62.5 percent in 2008, which was more than ten percentage points below its peak from the 1970s (figure 4.1). It increased thereafter, but this was largely because the financial crisis cut into returns to capital.

The weak economy affected German politics. The September 2002 German federal election differed from the previous one in several respects. The failure of the Schröder government to reduce unemployment put it on the defensive and behind in the polls at the start of the year. Schröder put himself back on the offensive in February 2002 by expanding the mandate of a commission chaired by the head of personnel at Volkswagen, Peter Hartz, to produce a set of proposals designed to halve the number of unemployed by 2005.[108] The breakdown of the Alliance for Jobs, however, curbed labor leaders' enthusiasm for Schröder. In contrast to 1998, most union officials did little during the campaign beyond the perfunctory. They would only say that Schröder's government was better than his predecessor's. In late spring, DGB chair Michael Sommer even said that he did not think that the red-green government would be reelected. Schröder managed to eke out a victory using the Hartz Commission, opposition to the looming war in Iraq, and effective government assistance after flooding in eastern Germany to sway voters. The political conclusions Schröder drew from his near-death experience were that job creation would be crucial in the next election and that the neocorporatist Alliance for Jobs had failed to deliver. The new approach would be government-led labor market deregulation.

With Friends Like These: Labor and the Second Schröder Government

In November and December 2002, the freshly elected government enacted two laws dubbed Hartz I and Hartz II because they contained the first two sets of recommendations from the Hartz Commission. These laws, which most in the labor movement did not support, restricted the rights of the unemployed to refuse work and still collect benefits, and liberalized the legal use of "atypical work" (i.e., jobs that do not conform to a model of full-time regular employment with a single employer over a long period of time). They served as a prelude to 2003, which proved to be an annus horribilis for organized labor.

In March 2003, the red-green government introduced sixteen bills in the Bundestag that made up a package the chancellor called Agenda 2010. These bills included a provision known as Hartz IV that reduced the maximum duration of the generous unemployment benefit program known as Arbeitslosengeld I (ALG I) from thirty-six months to twelve months for employees under fifty-five and eighteen months for employees fifty-five and older. It also broke the tie to past income when calculating benefits within a less generous program for the long-term unemployed known as Arbeitslosengeld II (ALG II). ALG II benefits would only provide for subsistence and would be set on par with welfare (*Sozialhilfe*).

The Hartz reforms aggravated long-standing tensions within the labor movement. Union officials generally disliked the Hartz reforms and Agenda 2010. Labor leaders asserted that the decision to set ALG II benefits at the level of welfare broke a promise Gerhard Schröder had made, but they split over the best way to respond. The old guard so-called traditionalists within the movement, among them many Marxists, distrusted markets and preferred state allocation of resources and a decommodification of labor through a generous welfare state. Traditionalists tended to be concentrated at second-tier and regional posts within the unions rather than in leadership positions. Traditionalists placed great stock in the old-school tactics of mass highly organized protests and public rhetorical confrontation targeted at top politicians and employers, regardless of the odds of success. Traditionalists called for a massive protest campaign against the Hartz reforms.

Reformers, in contrast, accepted capitalism and embraced a third-way modernization project to get the most out of capitalism for employees. They were willing to agree to labor market reforms and even liberalization if it advanced employees' material welfare. Reformers had no qualms about accepting social partnership between labor and management. They made fewer demands on the state and focused them on improvements in education and infrastructure. Reformers preferred constructive persuasion in private with employers and government as the means to make gains for employees, but they did acknowledge that protests and strikes were at times necessary.

The distribution of traditionalists and reformers was uneven throughout the labor movement. Traditionalists had strongholds in IG BAU and ver.di. The most strongly reformist union was IG BCE. IG Metall was evenly divided; the reformers were concentrated in Baden-Württemberg and North Rhine–Westphalia as well as among works councillors. Traditionalists were somewhat more common in northern Germany and in midlevel positions in the metalworkers union. IG Metall's headquarters had a relatively even mix from each camp. A succession crisis further complicated matters within IG Metall.

In early 2003, IG Metall chair Klaus Zwickel attempted to ensure that Berthold Huber, the head of IG Metall in Baden-Württemberg, be designated as Zwickel's heir apparent before the union's convention in the fall of that year. The step would have been unorthodox. By tradition, the vice-chair in the metalworkers union succeeds the chair. Zwickel's choice to break with past practice was a product of more than solidarity with his fellow Swabian, Huber. The then vice-chair, Jürgen Peters, had gained that post in 1998 despite Zwickel's opposition. Peters, who hailed from Hanover, played an important role in the 2001 negotiations for an innovative contract with Volkswagen. The company committed to create five thousand jobs at a new plant in Wolfsburg if the union agreed to a gross monthly compensation package of five thousand deutschmarks per employee.[109] Peters had the reputation of "looking left while turning right," which meant he often employed militant rhetoric in public but was accommodating with employers in private. Huber, on the other hand, was a reformer who was widely acknowledged to be the union's deep thinker and who had skillfully negotiated path-breaking contracts. Huber's weaknesses were an inability to electrify large audiences and a tendency to be too cerebral. In late 2002, conventional wisdom within IG Metall was that Huber would get the nod. In the wake of the chancellor's Agenda 2010 proposal, traditionalists in IG Metall began to rally around Peters, and the outcome became far less certain.

The endorsement of candidates for top union posts for the fall convention was on the agenda for the April 2003 meeting of IG Metall's federal executive committee. Typically, the executive committee unanimously endorses a single slate of candidates without much fuss. The convention then duly elects the slate. This time, however, the executive committee vote on the endorsement of the next chair resulted in a 20:20 tie. Awkward discussions ensued about creating cochairs, but this quickly fell by the wayside as unworkable. When it became clear that Peters and his supporters would not back down, Huber—who was the younger man by six years—announced that out of "loyalty to the union" he would withdraw his candidacy. The executive committee then nominated Peters as the single official candidate for union chair and Huber as the candidate for vice-chair.[110]

That very month, IG Metall heir apparent Jürgen Peters went on the offensive against the Schröder government. He denounced Schröder's labor market reforms as less supportive of social welfare than the policies of Helmut Kohl and joined with ver.di executive committee member Margret Mönig-Raane in support of a "member petition" (*Mitgliederbegehren*) within the SPD against the reform agenda. SPD party statutes specify that if at least 10 percent of the membership signs a petition in support of an internal referendum, the party must hold it. Peters threatened "a hot May" for the government. In contrast, IG BCE and transnet chairs Hubertus Schmoldt and Norbert Hansen stated that unions should refrain from intervening in an internal party question. IG Metall and ver.di chairs Zwickel and Bsirske had no comment regarding the membership petition.[111]

Top union officials all denounced Agenda 2010 at the 2003 May Day rallies, but some were more confrontational than others. Schröder spoke over a chorus of whistles at a rally at Hessenpark, and later he remarked that he was "disturbed" when he found out that IG Metall officials had distributed the whistles. A week later, Zwickel and Bsirske refused to attend a previously scheduled meeting of union leaders with Schröder, so the meeting was canceled. Reformer Hubertus Schmoldt criticized the decision, stating, "I regret that we wasted an opportunity to influence the contents of Agenda 2010." Conversely, IG BAU chair Klaus Wiesehügel, who was a traditionalist and an SPD member of the Bundestag, called on his colleagues to vote against Agenda 2010, even though it would bring down the government. Jürgen Peters threatened to push for higher wage increases if Agenda 2010 were to pass.[112]

A week after May Day 2003, the DGB issued a twenty-seven-page alternative to Agenda 2010 called "Courage to Change Course." It included a request for €15 billion in stimulus, higher tax rates on property and estates, no change to unemployment insurance, and payroll-tax cuts. The proposal fell flat. Commentators criticized the document as merely a laundry list of thirty-year-old union demands coming out of mothballs. Even IG BCE chair Schmoldt was dismissive, pointing out that the proposal did not engage Agenda 2010 at all and would be "extraordinarily difficult to implement." Ten days later, IG BCE, NGG, and transnet issued their own paper, which was much more moderate.[113]

The SPD leadership headed by Gerhard Schröder decided that the party would hold a vote to determine its position on Agenda 2010 at a conference slated for June 1. Schröder announced that he would personally make the case for these reforms at the meeting. To sway SPD members against Agenda 2010, the DGB and all the member unions except IG BCE organized an "action week" of protests for May 12–17 and a final "action day" on May 24. The rallies changed no minds, however. The next week, Michael Sommer called for a protest pause, claiming, "We have achieved something; the grossest monstrosities are gone," but IG Metall and ver.di leaders refused to go along.[114]

Schröder performed masterfully at the June 1 SPD conference; the delegates voted 90 percent in favor of Agenda 2010. IG Metall lame duck chair Klaus Zwickel acknowledged defeat and called on the unions to back down. IG BCE chair Schmoldt, who had opposed the confrontational approach, was more pointed in his comments: "The basic debate over the for and against of Agenda 2010 is over; for the unions, too. . . . We know too there must be reforms; everything cannot stay as it is. And, the direction that the chancellor proposed for them is correct." Nonetheless, many within the union movement continued to fight in vain as Agenda 2010 moved through the German parliament. The relationship between the Schröder government and organized labor—which had already been frayed owing to the failure of the Alliance for Jobs and Schröder's often disdainful treatment of union leaders, both in public and in private—never recovered.[115]

The year 2003 was equally disastrous for organized labor in its bread-and-butter field, collective bargaining. Jürgen Peters, in his closing days as IG Metall vice-chair, pushed for a strike in the eastern German mechanical engineering and steel sectors to reduce weekly working by three hours to bring it on a par with the western level of thirty-five. Peters was looking for a victory to repair his image, which had been tarnished in the IG Metall succession crisis. He got the opposite. After several months of negotiations, the union launched a strike on June 2. The union was able to reach a quick agreement with steel producers, but not with the employers representatives in mechanical engineering. After two weeks, the union escalated the strike to include eastern automobile parts producers that also supplied western Germany. Within days, the automobile producers began to lay off workers at western plants owing to parts shortages. Western workers protested so vociferously that the union was forced to call off the strike at the end of week three without getting any concessions regarding weekly working time. The collective bargaining archive of the Hans Böckler Foundation judged the June 2003 IG Metall strike in eastern Germany to be the union's biggest failure in five decades.[116]

In the immediate wake of the failed strike, considerable pressure built up within the union for Jürgen Peters to step aside and permit Berthold Huber to become chair. Peters hung on despite the criticism, and in September, the IG Metall convention voted him in as the union's next chair. Peters's mandate was weak. He only received 66.1 percent of the vote in a one-person race, which compares poorly to his predecessors. Undaunted, Peters renewed the attack on the Schröder government in his acceptance speech. He called the Schröder government's policy "nonsensical" and "irresponsible" and vowed, "We say no to this policy and we will continue to do so." Peters went on to call for a "change in policy" (*Politikwechsel*), which also can be interpreted in German to mean a "change in politics."[117]

Berthold Huber, who as the union's new vice-chair was now in charge of collective bargaining policy, also went to work. In February 2004, IG Metall reached a historic agreement with representatives of the mechanical engineering employers association in the town of Pforzheim. The Pforzheim accord expands the instances when company managers may negotiate with their workforce for derogations from a regional collective bargaining agreement beyond short-term financial exigency to include employment protection, job creation, and improved competitiveness. The collective bargaining parties still must approve any workplace agreement before it can go into effect, but the impact of the Pforzheim accord was to loosen, albeit in a controlled fashion, the uniformity of the wage floor set in collective bargaining and to cede some control over wage and benefit determination to the workplace. Both social partners depict the Pforzheim accord as a means to shore up the postwar collective bargaining regime by keeping it attractive in an economy that has become far more open to competitive pressures than in decades past. They hoped that the new flexibility would make firms less likely to leave their employers association. Some other sectors, most notably the chemicals industry, had already implemented controlled decentralization of collective bargaining. Nonetheless, it still was earthshaking when the social partners in mechanical engineering moved in this direction, because that sector is widely seen as the trendsetter for the German economy. An important factor motivating the IG Metall leadership to negotiate the Pforzheim agreement was a pledge that Schröder had made a year earlier in the Bundestag to pursue greater flexibility in collective bargaining through legislation if the social partners in key sectors proved unable to reach an accord on their own.[118]

Union officials from the reformist camp have come to see the Pforzheim agreement as a recruitment tool because larger numbers of employees will have a substantial incentive to work actively with union experts to ensure that they get the most favorable derogation accord possible. In other words, reformers have been willing to trade off some centralization in exchange for greater involvement with the rank and file in the hope that more employees will join the union as a result. Traditionalists, on the other hand, frown on decentralization of collective bargaining, fearing that it will lead to a recommodification of labor and allow employers to drive down wages by playing workplaces off against each other.[119]

Leading unions also began to experiment with a very different form of innovation in 2004. IG Metall and ver.di drew inspiration from the social movement approach to unionization developed by the Service Employees International Union (SEIU) in the United States and activists in other English-speaking countries. This approach adopts elements of the grassroots organization and confrontational tactics of the 1960s United States civil rights movement to recruit members and to get better contracts. Much of the reinvigoration began at the regional level. Detlev Wetzel became IG Metall district manager in North Rhine–Westphalia in 2004. Wetzel had apprenticed as a machine-tool maker and then studied social work in college. Wetzel used Pforzheim's derogation procedure to activate members at firms experiencing economic hardship to become more actively involved in determining their own working conditions. Wetzel called this *Tarif aktiv* (active collective bargaining). Wetzel also engaged employers in economic trouble by working with them to find innovative ways to reorganize production in order to save jobs and to avoid cutting wages. Wetzel named this effort *"besser statt billiger"* (better instead of cheaper).[120]

Local officers in ver.di also began to experiment. Peter Bremme, a ver.di official in Hamburg, spent time in 2003 with the SEIU in Chicago and came away impressed when activist tactics there led the head of the Swedish Securitas security firm to fly to Chicago to negotiate a collective agreement. Bremme maintained his ties with SEIU officials after he had returned to Germany. A few years later, the SEIU sent two veteran organizers to Hamburg to teach Bremme the strategies and tactics of social unionism. He and others in ver.di have applied US social unionism techniques to organize security personnel in Hamburg and to challenge cutthroat employment practices in the retail sector.[121]

At the national level, however, IG Metall, ver.di, and the DGB continued to champion traditionalist tactics to change government policy in 2004, but they made little headway. Several unions and the DGB held demonstrations against the "dismantling of the welfare state," but they had no effect. IG Metall spearheaded an "employees petition for a socially oriented policy" but only managed to get 10 percent of union members to sign it. In June 2004, the red-green government passed the centerpiece of its reforms, the changes to unemployment insurance contained in the Hartz IV legislation. Shortly afterward, SPD majority leader and party chair Franz Müntefering issued an open letter to DGB members in an effort to heal the rift between his party and the unions. Müntefering asked union officials to move beyond the dispute over Agenda 2010. Müntefering's letter irritated many labor leaders; they condemned it as unwarranted interference in their internal affairs. Both Peters and Bsirske rejected his plea.[122]

A much sharper critique of the traditionalists came from within. IG BCE chair Hubertus Schmoldt and his deputy Ulrich Freese issued a scathing open letter, which they posted on their union's web page. They asserted, "A union strategy that relies above all on rejection and obstruction is doomed to failure." They denounced traditionalists for practicing "simplistic populism" when they "push a wealth tax and a higher top tax rate to the center of their policy."[123] Schmoldt and Freese accused the traditionalists of refusing to recognize that economic integration has rendered statist prescriptions to economic problems ineffectual. They observed: "The unions face a process of modernization—to be sure all too often without a clear position. Instead of insight into the necessary change, a contrarian 'no' has frequently dominated. . . . Actually, to date there has been no debate, never mind clarification, about how the unions are to define their self-understanding and their role in times of change." Schmoldt and Freese also charged that traditionalists preferred serving up pat answers to the rank and file even though these fell far short of adequately addressing labor's current problems. They criticized the traditionalists' preference for aggressive mass protests, asserting, "Policymaking through verbal brachial force produces only losers."

Jürgen Peters replied with a letter of his own. He did not make it public, but the contents were leaked to the media. Peters complained that by issuing their letter publicly Schmoldt and Freese were "personally presumptuous, uncollegial, and politically oriented toward weakening the unions in general." Peters stated that he was "deeply disappointed" by "the twisting of the facts" in the letter and found himself "extremely frustrated" that Schmoldt and Freese "also spread the cliché that the unions would refuse sensible reforms." He asserted that the behavior of the IG BCE leadership created the risk that it would "put itself voluntarily on the edge of the political spectrum and isolate itself within the DGB."[124]

Schmoldt and Freese replied in August, rejecting Peters's accusation that they had twisted facts in their previous letter, stating, "You fail to provide examples." They went on to criticize Peters's repeated demand for fundamental policy change "tied to few realistic demands" as an approach that "will make it extraordinarily hard to implement our demand to participate in influencing things." DGB chair Michael Sommers intervened at this point in a bid to cool things down. He acknowledged that he knew that letter writing was "a high art" but that he would like to see the exchanges between union leaders come to an end. Peters and Schmoldt agreed to meet and discuss their differences in private.[125]

The traditionalists staged another round of protests against Agenda 2010. In August 2004, they organized a set of weekly demonstrations in eastern Germany that were intended to invoke the memory of the Monday demonstrations that helped to topple the German Democratic Republic. The turnout was light, however.[126] Consequently, DGB chair Michael Sommer decided to change his approach to one of constructive engagement with the Schröder government. Peters, however, remained critical and maintained his campaign against Agenda 2010 until he retired in 2007.[127]

Fragmentation, Political and Economic

Earlier in 2004 another group of traditionalist trade unionists struck out in a different direction that would have tremendous consequences for German politics. On March 5, thirty midlevel union officials (mostly from IG Metall and ver.di) and SPD members disenchanted by Agenda 2010 met in the DGB's Berlin regional headquarters building on Keith Street to discuss forming a new political party that would have a platform to the left of the SPD. They called their group the Initiative Arbeit und soziale Gerechtigkeit (Labor and Social Justice Initiative). Union leaders Bsirske, Peters, and Sommer all said that they had no interest in cooperating with the group, but this did not dissuade the traditionalists from moving forward. On June 27, the leaders of the Initiative and a similar group called Wahlalternative 2006 (Election Alternative 2006) met in Berlin. On July 3, the two groups announced that they were merging to form the Wahlalternative Arbeit und soziale Gerechtigkeit (WASG, Electoral Alternative Labor and Social Justice). WASG was concentrated in western Germany. A year later, in the run-up to the federal election, WASG formed an alliance with the post-Communist Partei des Demokratischen Sozialismus (PDS, Party of Democratic Socialism), which had its stronghold in eastern Germany. On 16 June 2007, WASG and the PDS officially merged to form Die Linke (The Left, aka the Left Party). The political fragmentation of the Left has been costly for the SPD. In the 2005 federal election, the PDS-WASG electoral alliance received 8.7 percent of the votes; and in 2009, the Left Party garnered 11.9 percent.[128]

The emergence of the Left Party has complicated relations between unions and political parties. Most union officials still see the SPD as a natural ally, but they give deference and respect (at least publicly) to the Greens and, to a lesser extent, the Left Party. Labor behaved quite differently when the Greens first emerged. The social clash in the late 1970s between the older blue-collar union leadership and the younger counterculture college-educated Greens was stark. Union officials refused to talk to the Greens for a decade. Many union leaders feared that Green positions on the environment and nuclear power would jeopardize their members' jobs and that the Greens would undercut the influence of the SPD. Labor's more tolerant approach to the Left Party is in part a product of the lessons learned from the slow rapprochement between labor and the Greens from two decades earlier and generational change within the union movement itself. The rise of the Left Party also made union leaders increasingly sensitive to the potential for internal insurgencies on their left flank, as had occurred in the unions during the late 1960s and early 1970s. Tolerance helped to minimize that risk.[129]

The fragmentation of the German political Left has led the DGB to become more politically neutral and to drop an old political practice. Since the 1950s, the DGB had issued a list of "election touchstones" (*Wahlprüfsteine*) shortly before a federal election to identify the issues most important to the labor movement and indicate indirectly which party organized labor preferred. For the 2005 and 2009 federal elections, however, the DGB and its affiliate unions did not produce election touchstones because the exercise would unavoidably reveal how close the union movement was to each of the three left-of-center parties. In particular, Social Democratic union leaders did not want to take the risk that newly drawn up electoral touchstones would place the DGB closer to the Left Party than the SPD.[130]

DGB reform resurfaced in 2004. The ongoing membership losses and their impact on the DGB budget forced more structural change. The focus was on legal services again. DGB officials had already capped expenditures on the federation's legal insurance program at 40 percent of the entire DGB budget. This move had not solved the problem, however, because demand was still rising. In the previous year alone, the DGB handled over 120,000 cases. Membership declines exacerbated matters because they were reducing the size of the DGB budget by 3 percent each year. To close the gap, the DGB managing executive committee proposed partially privatizing the legal services office so that it could attract business from nonunion members as an additional source of income. The DGB's in-house union was skeptical about the privatization plan and questioned whether the new entity could retain its nonprofit tax status. The DGB leadership implemented the plan nonetheless.[131]

The need for additional budget cuts led union officials to take stock. In May 2004, the DGB managing executive committee called for an external evaluation of the reforms from 1998 to 2002. The report concluded that the goals of previous reforms were only reached in part. In practice, the DGB never became a unified voice of labor to the outside world, mainly because the big unions would not defer to the DGB on matters they deemed important. Leaders of the individual unions also judged the DGB to be ill suited to grappling effectively with Europeanization and globalization. The DGB managing executive committee decided to try to tackle the confederation's organizational deficiencies by creating a medium-term planning project called Projekt Weiterentwicklung Organisationsstruktur (Project for the Further Development of the Organizational Structure).[132]

The DGB's planning project quickly expanded into the Planungsgruppe Weiterentwicklung des DGB (PG WE, Planning Group for the Further Development of the DGB), with DGB executive committee member Dietmar Hexel leading the initiative. The PG WE included representatives from various rungs of the DGB, the affiliated unions, and the DGB's general works council. An adviser from McKinsey Consulting also participated in a private capacity. In January 2005, the PG WE presented to the DGB executive committee a twenty-six-page confidential report entitled "Turnaround!" The frank report stated up front that "the crisis is more severe than is already generally known. . . . The unions face great challenges; it will take decisive action in order to bring about a renaissance of the meaning and usefulness of unions." The report identified five reasons why German unions were losing members: (1) "The importance of the natural union milieu is shrinking; (2) Economic transformation is changing the nature of jobs so that fewer are compatible with union membership; (3) Unions are on a constant defensive. . . . There is a dearth of sufficiently attractive new objectives for which to fight; (4) No concepts exist on which to piggyback for overcoming structural change (welfare state crisis, unemployment, knowledge work, globalization); and (5) The point as well as the material usefulness of trade union membership is shrinking."[133] (It is worth noting that the challenges enumerated in the "Turnaround!" report correspond closely to the quantitative findings in chapter 3.)

The report suggested that there is hope. "The turnaround in membership is doable. . . . The DGB and all unions contain the opportunity for renewal and strategic alternatives within them. . . . There are substantially more suggestions for attempts at solutions than possibilities that can actually be implemented." Structural improvements already underway included unions improving their organizational infrastructures for purchasing and common electronic communication. The DGB put into consideration a structural reform that would do away with standing departments and replace them with single-purpose clusters and competence centers. The report argues that members "want more than collective agreements." In response, unions are developing new work and life initiatives that may improve their image and take them beyond "the traditional milieu."[134] Although the "Turnaround!" report counseled that "a concept of pure austerity cannot solve the crisis of the DGB and its unions but instead leads to further membership losses," top union officials ignored that particular piece of advice.[135] The DGB executive committee approved a medium-term financial plan for the DGB that cut the confederation's budget by 3 percent annually from 2005 to 2007.[136]

Shortly after the January 2005 managing executive committee meeting, Michael Sommer endeavored to reframe the labor movement in postmaterialist terms. He proclaimed that "human dignity" will be at the center of union work, adding, "People strive for freedom, autonomy, security, and they cannot bear it if society is knocked out of kilter. People are not a number, not an expense." Sommer also set a very concrete goal: a reversal of membership decline in 2006.[137] At a subsequent managing executive committee meeting in May 2005, he launched a project to create a working climate index called "Decent Work" (*Gute Arbeit*). The index, which would come out annually, would measure human dignity at work by estimating the percentage of German jobs that are "decent work" using a range of indicators. Its stated purpose is to provide "a very exact instrument in order to distill the mood in the workplaces."[138] The DGB leadership hoped that the Decent Work index would become a staple of economic measure, much like a business climate index, that union officers, journalists, academics, policymakers, and even business people would use. The DGB subsequently hired consultants who developed a survey instrument and protocol. Since

2007, the DGB has issued annual *Gute Arbeit* reports, and many unions have used them in collective bargaining and lobbying. The DGB label on the index, however, made it a hard sell in the business community. Only ten firms became subscribers.[139]

A debate over union policy toward a federally mandated minimum wage also came to a head at the May 2005 managing executive committee meeting. Ver.di had been pushing German labor to demand the enactment of a nationwide minimum wage for several years. Significant occupational and regional gaps in union coverage had always existed throughout the postwar era. Unions were less successful in recruiting employees in service sectors and in more rural areas, for example. Traditionally, the more comprehensive coverage of employers associations closed those gaps when it came to collective bargaining. More recent declines in the densities of some employers associations led to gaps opening up. The problem was particularly pronounced in eastern Germany, but it was also present in the west. Collective bargaining coverage continued to shrink. In 2001, collective agreements either directly or indirectly determined compensation for 70.7 percent of all employees in western Germany and 56.2 percent of those in eastern Germany (figure 4.2). By 2011, coverage had slipped to 61 percent in the west and 49 percent in the east.

Ver.di officials argued that the best solution to declining collective bargaining coverage would be a federally mandated minimum wage. Adopting a minimum wage law would mark a significant change for Germany because it would open the door to direct state regulation of an area that previously had been within the realm of autonomous collective bargaining between the social partners. Union critics of minimum-wage legislation complained that if legislation were to be adopted, it could wind up becoming a wage ceiling as well as a wage floor. They countered that a system of prevailing wages pegged to sectoral collective agreements would be preferable because it would preserve the role of collective bargaining in setting wages. The IG Metall leadership had initially rejected the call for a minimum wage but changed its position when Jürgen Peters became chair. That left IG BCE as the only opponent. In May 2006, IG BCE went so far as to issue a joint communiqué with the federation of chemicals industry employers associations denouncing national minimum-wage legislation. The IG BCE leader's tangles with other union heads over the years left no other union chair willing to accommodate the IG BCE. The DGB federal executive board voted on the matter, and the result was seven to one in support of pursuing minimum wage legislation. Sommer described this outcome as something "that can be lived with."[140]

The political price for unilaterally pursuing labor market reforms caught up with Gerhard Schröder in 2005. When the SPD lost its majority in the North Rhine–Westphalia state elections, Schröder triggered an early federal election that was held in September. The DGB put little effort into the campaign. In the final stretch of the campaign, the Christian Democratic Union committed some unforced errors, and Schröder staged a vigorous rally. The confrontation between Schröder and the unions did have a lingering impact nonetheless. Polls indicated that only 47 percent of trade union members voted for the SPD; 12 percent voted instead for the PDS-WASG alliance. Schröder fell short of securing a third term as chancellor, but his efforts made a grand coalition between the Christian parties and the SPD as a junior partner the most viable option for the next government.[141]

Ironically, Sommer's relationship with the new Christian Democratic chancellor, Angela Merkel, was far better than with Gerhard Schröder, who made a habit of belittling union leaders in both public and private. Sommer contrasted his relationship with the two by saying, "Listening is new." Sommer added that Chancellor Merkel "certainly is not an unconditional friend of the unions," but she is "fair, open, in charge, and knows where our edge of tolerability lies. . . . The chancellor knows that she cannot successfully undertake policies against the unions."[142]

Despite the budding rapprochement between trade union leaders and the CDU, the bitterness that had built up over three very difficult years came pouring out at the 2006 DGB convention in Berlin. Delegates roundly booed and whistled while Chancellor Merkel and Vice Chancellor Franz Müntefering spoke, whereas Oskar Lafontaine, coleader of the Left Party, received repeated applause. Müntefering responded pointedly, saying, "The prescriptions from the 1970s do not go far any more. The world has gone around a few more times since then. . . . Put your whistles away and simply think for a change." A commentator from the *Frankfurter Rundschau*, a newspaper that generally views the labor movement with considerable sympathy, gave the 2006 convention a scathing review:

> What sort of position is the DGB in after its convention? Not better than it was before. . . . Not once in the formulations in Berlin was it to be found how the DGB could come to grips with the problems that have long plagued it. . . . The internal conflicts between traditionalists and modernizers are unresolved . . . no one knows how to address falling membership and declining support among the public. . . . The isolation of the DGB was only too clear in Berlin. . . . In previous years, DGB chief Michael Sommer earned credit through the steadfastness

with which he pursued discussions with all the major political camps against intense resistance among his own ranks. Through this work, which often took place in the background, he was able in individual cases to bring about improvements in the reforms from a trade union view. Yet the main speech that Sommer gave at the federal convention read like an application for an executive committee post in the Left Party.[143]

Instrumental considerations may explain the traditionalist tone of Sommer's speech. Since it is the norm that only one candidate stand for election to any top DGB post at the convention, delegates use their votes to register approval of that candidate. In 2006, 78.4 percent of the votes were in favor of Sommer continuing as DGB chair, which was 15.6 percentage points lower than four years earlier when he was first elected. Had Sommer not applied traditionalist rhetoric in thick coats, his results would likely have been worse. Still, the 2006 DGB convention failed to produce any progress toward addressing the German labor movement's problems. Union membership and density were still dropping; Sommer had failed to reverse these trends by 2006 as he had promised. Real wages and collective bargaining coverage also continued to decline (table 4.2 and figure 4.2). The only bright spot on the horizon was the start of a significant decline in joblessness. Most assessments concluded that Agenda 2010 made a belated but significant contribution toward reducing unemployment.[144] Ironically, however, these were the very reforms that most union leaders had rejected.

In the 2000s, a spasm of fragmentation afflicted public-sector collective bargaining. Traditionally, collective bargaining in the public sector was centralized. German local, state (*Land*), and federal governments bargained jointly with public-sector unions. Germany's weak economic performance since the 1980s and the obligation to limit the public-sector deficit to 3 percent contained in the European Union's 1997 Amsterdam treaty had intensified pressure on public-sector budgets, but the pressure played out differently, depending on the level of government. Personnel represented a much higher share of total costs for the states than for either the federal government or the local governments, which prompted negotiators for the states to demand concessions, particularly increasing weekly working time, because that is where they could make the biggest savings.

Joint public-sector bargaining began to unravel in the early 2000s. The city of Berlin dropped out of the states' common collective bargaining group, the Tarifgemeinschaft deutscher Länder (TdL, Collective Bargaining Group of the German States), because a huge debt rendered it effectively bankrupt. The breakdown of joint bargaining advanced a step further in June 2003 when the TdL took the state governments out of the general public-sector contract governing Christmas and vacation bonuses. In May 2004, the TdL left the working-time contract. Ver.di and the TdL negotiated about working time for over a year to no avail. During the negotiations, several states unilaterally extended the weekly working time for new hires (typically to forty hours). Ver.di staged a few warning strikes in April 2005 but backed away from a full industrial conflict for the moment. The union tried a carrot instead in the form of a new framework agreement.

In October 2005, the federal government, the localities, and ver.di agreed to a new framework agreement for setting salary scales and assessing performance called the Tarifvertrag für den öffentlichen Dienst (TVöD, Collective Agreement for the Public Sector). The TVöD, which replaced the decades old Bundes-Angestellten-Tarif (BAT, Federal White-Collar Employees Collective Agreement), eliminated the distinctions between blue- and white-collar employees and made job performance the principal criterion in determining individual salaries within the same job category. This marked a big change from the BAT, which had used principally seniority and family demographics to set individual salaries. The union hoped the advantages of a new accord would entice state governments to drop their demands for concessions, but the states held firm. Ver.di consequently shifted to a confrontational approach and launched waves of strikes in early 2006. The results were meager. The city of Hamburg reached a settlement with ver.di on March 1. The new accord established a range of working time at between thirty-eight and forty hours and relied on three criteria to establish the working time of each individual: pay grade, age, and minor children. Older employees as well as those in lower pay grades or who had minors at home only work a maximum of thirty-eight hours. Those with none of these attributes work for forty hours.

The rank and file did not like the Hamburg agreement. Only 42 percent voted in favor. The union approved it anyway because fewer than 75 percent voted to continue the strike. The problem with the settlement was that it still privileged demographic components over job performance to set compensation. Both ver.di and TdL officials immediately declared that the Hamburg agreement would not set the pace for other contracts. In May 2006, ver.di gave up on strikes and accepted the unilateral increase in working time. Most states raised weekly working time to either thirty-nine or forty hours. Public-sector bargaining has remained fragmented between the states on the one hand, and the federal and local governments on the other. Nonetheless, the contents of collective agreements at all three levels of government have remained largely the same.[145]

Fragmentation emerged elsewhere in the 2000s. "Occupational unions" (*Berufsgewerkschaften*)—that is, small unions of skilled employees who work at a choke point in the economy—have grown in number and have been increasingly willing to use their strategic positions in order to extract significant wage increases. For example, in late 2007 and early 2008, a DBB affiliate with only 34,000 members, the Gewerkschaft Deutscher Lokomotivführer (GDL, German Locomotive Engineers Union), waged a series of strikes involving only a few thousand members that on several occasions paralyzed the entire German rail-transit system. The union managed to extract a double-digit wage increase, which embarrassed DGB union heads, who for years had negotiated agreements that had failed to keep up even with inflation. The GDL's action was the most spectacular, but it echoed others that small professional associations outside of the DGB waged, such as the pilots association, Cockpit, and the Independent Flight Attendants Organization (Unabhängige Flugbegleiter Organisation, UFO). So far, militancy among occupational unions has been limited mostly to the transportation sector because their key positions in the economy enable them to wage effective strikes with very few employees.[146]

The DAG's inclusion in the ver.di merger is the catalyst for much of the fragmentation. For example, Cockpit used the DAG as its bargaining agent from its founding in 1968 until 1999, but the union went solo in 1999 because the 8,200-member union did not want to be absorbed into ver.di. Similarly, the 100,000-member physicians and nurses association, the Marburger Bund (MB, Marburg Federation), which was established in 1947, also used to cooperate closely with the DAG in collective bargaining. The MB initially continued this relationship with ver.di but broke it off in 2005 because the new TVöD would have sharply reduced physicians' incomes. MB leaders complained that ver.di officials ignored physicians' concerns when negotiating the TVöD with the public employers. After several waves of protests and strikes, the MB got a separate collective agreement in 2005. This trend has continued. On 1 May 2011, firefighters founded the Deutsche Feuerwehr-Gewerkschaft (DFeuG, German Firefighters Union). Why did firefighters form their own union? One local union leader asserted, "We are tired of being the fifth wheel on the wagon at ver.di" and pointed to Cockpit and the MB as examples of groups of professional employees who have benefitted from breaking away from the multisectoral union. It is important to keep in mind that declaring an organization to be a union does not automatically make it one. Municipalities are highly resistant to negotiating a separate collective agreement with DFeuG. This is unlikely to change unless DFeuG can successfully organize a substantial series of demonstrations and strikes the way the MB did, which remains to be seen. Only small groups of employees with considerable professional coherence could successfully found an occupational union.[147]

Analysts have interpreted the increased prominence of these "mini-unions" as an expression of rank-and-file dissatisfaction with the multisectoral unions of the second postwar German trade union movement by those employees who are in a position to dissent. Even within the DGB, the contrast between the mammoth ver.di and the miniscule GEW has been instructive. The creation of ver.di has benefitted the GEW. Teachers and technicians have a choice. They can join either ver.di or the GEW. It is therefore instructive to compare membership trends for the two unions. Ver.di's membership fell by 12.6 percent between 2005 and 2012, while GEW membership has increased by 5.9 percent. GEW members stay with the union because it has a simpler, more accessible structure and is more focused on their specific needs. In other words, multisectoral unionism as a top-down solution to German labor's financial and organizational problems has a big flaw. The greater economies of scale have stabilized the unions' finances, but some employees find the massive impersonal unions unable to address their specific concerns. The growth of occupational unions has already produced considerable consternation among the leaders of the multisectoral unions, even though the numbers involved remain extremely small. Were the trend to accelerate, however, pressure would mount on the established unions to emulate the occupational unions by moving away from the traditional one-size-fits all regionwide collective agreements toward deals covering smaller groups of employees that can exploit choke points in the economy.

In 2007, IG Metall endeavored to combat a different sort of fragmentation. The union opened a nationwide campaign to extend collective bargaining coverage to temporary employees. The use of this sort of worker had grown over the years, particularly in the mechanical engineering sector. IG Metall North Rhine–Westphalia head Detlev Wetzel spearheaded the campaign, which was modeled on his successful *besser statt billiger* effort. The union asked firms to sign "better agreements" (*Besser-Vereinbarungen*) that would allow companies to get derogations from their regionwide collective bargaining contract if they agreed to restrict the use of temps and to pay them at the same rate as permanent employees. The campaign, branded

"Equal Work–Equal Pay," proved effective. At the end of 2008, IG Metall had over four hundred agreements covering 11,000 temp employees. By mid-2011, this had expanded to 35,000.[148]

Invigorating the Grass Roots from Above

The balance of power within the DGB shifted decidedly in favor of the reformers when delegates at IG Metall's convention elected Berthold Huber and Detlev Wetzel as the union's chair and vice-chair in November 2007. Huber quickly made it plain that the focus of his time in office would not be demonstrations against government policies but recruiting new members.[149] In January 2008, IG Metall set up a new department called Members and Campaigns headed by Detlev Wetzel. The task of the department has been to develop new strategies to recruit and to retain members. The effort has two prongs. The first has been to reconceptualize recruitment techniques, borrowing heavily from US-style social movement unionism. The second is a professionalization of recruitment and service provision within IG Metall through a reorganization of the union, better training, and the establishment of concrete goals for the union's local units backed by financial incentives.

The reconceptualization came first. In May 2008, the union's Members and Campaigns department issued a paper called "Organizing." The paper starts by presenting "eight theses on the renewal of union work." The first five theses actually address the changed landscape for organized labor in Germany. "Organizing" argues that the traditional social partnership between labor and management has become "frail" because: (1) employment has become more precarious, (2) collective bargaining coverage has been receding, (3) the welfare state has been hollowed out, (4) German capitalism has become more oriented toward shareholders, and (5) union membership has fallen so much in so many workplaces that employers see less need to negotiate with employee representatives and therefore have not been pushed to take a long-term perspective.[150]

The last three theses begin sketching out changes. Thesis number six calls for "participation and integrative conflict management" in order to "enhance both member loyalty and the appeal of the organization." In practice this means giving union members "voice and influence, not as ritual, but on matters that are important to them." Thesis number seven calls for the union to take into account and to incorporate contingent and part-time employees in workplace activities. Number eight argues that "the historical achievement of integrating works councils into union policies assumes greater importance than ever before" because of the rise of atypical work and the deterioration of the traditional systems of social support. The last thesis continues by making a controversial assertion challenging the traditional de jure separation of trade unionists and works councillors: "In essence, works councils are union representatives from the union in the company. . . . In organizational terms, the highest priority must therefore be accorded to ensuring that they are not only furnished with first-rate advice and support, but also perceive themselves as active trade unionists."[151]

The remainder of the paper develops the reconceptualization further, arguing that "a member-oriented offensive strategy is required as the foundation for trade union renewal." The three guiding principles for this strategy are that it be "member oriented, participation oriented, and conflict oriented." The paper then briefly discusses the SEIU's organizing model, including the Justice for Janitors campaign—which has relied heavily on aggressive public tactics, such as blocking streets and occupying buildings—and how to apply it to Germany. It argues that German labor needs to be more confrontational and participatory, and less legalistic and top-down. Unions need to identify hot issues in the workplace, support members in organizing themselves, encourage members to use conflict constructively to change things, and plan meticulously to increase the odds of success.[152]

Borrowing from the United States has its merits, but there are big differences between the two countries' industrial relations systems. First, the US system is much more inherently adversarial. US law requires unions to gain recognition in a workplace as the official representative of the employees as a prerequisite to collective bargaining. This is what "organizing" in the United States is all about. In most instances, gaining recognition entails a union recognition election, which is typically confrontational. Finding a vehicle to leverage conflict into grassroots participation will be inherently more challenging in Germany because there is no analogous practice to recognition elections. Second, the US system has nothing like works councils. The confrontational US approach runs counter to the more cooperative relationship most works councils have with managers, which matters because works councils are normally critical in union recruitment in Germany, as the "Organizing" paper itself underscores.[153] Third, US-style social unionism requires substantial research to find firms' political and financial vulnerabilities, but German unions have not dedicated significant resources to corporate research.[154] Fourth, the Service Employees International Union—the foremost practitioner of social unionism—dedicates 30 percent of its budget to organizing. This vastly exceeds the investment and commitment German unions have made.[155] Finally, it should not escape notice that the tactics of social movement unionism have not managed to reverse the decline of organized labor in the United States.

IG Metall officials have taken steps toward enhancing the union's grassroots infrastructure. The union is active on a full array of social media venues, including Facebook, flikr, Google+, studiVZ, Twitter, and YouTube. In 2009, IG Metall's youth department copied the US practice of holding a "union summer," which is a retreat to train organizers. The union's youth wing has its own separate assortment of social media sites, and also uses flash mobbing and crowd sourcing techniques at the local level. On 2 October 2011, IG Metall staged a "youth action day" in Cologne that drew twenty thousand.[156]

In 2009, which was also a federal election year, IG Metall launched a campaign called Gemeinsam für ein gutes Leben! (Together for a Decent Life!). The purpose of the campaign was to raise the prominence of issues such as job security, the welfare state, and codetermination in the election through an ad campaign, a "road show" replete with information booths, a website, and a series of rallies. The union also gathered the views of over 480,000 on their vision of a decent life. IG Metall officials have continued to use the campaign after the election to stage rallies, to voice positions on economic and social policy questions, and to recruit new members.[157] The components of the first prong of reforms are all efforts to enhance the capacity of IG Metall to communicate and to reach out, particularly at the local level. IG Metall leaders have become increasingly sensitive to the importance of keeping the union's external activities current with contemporary sensibilities. That said, internal reform has been the prime focus of the Huber-Wetzel leadership team.

IG Metall's leadership began working on the second prong of renewal, organizational reform, in July 2008. In September 2009, IG Metall's Membership and Organizing department presented the first results of that work in the form of a glossy brochure on organizational reform entitled, "Projekt IG Metall 2009." The twenty-four-page document—which drew on internal interviews, questionnaires, an efficiency study, ideas from a steering committee, and input from consultants—argued that if IG Metall is to survive, it must supplement its focus on providing advice and service (Betreuung) to existing members by concentrating on member "acquisition" (Erschliessung). It then proposed to produce the efficiencies and funds to engage in both service and recruitment simultaneously through a thorough restructuring of the union. The brochure suggested two possibilities regarding politics: either the DGB represent IG Metall politically or IG Metall do its own political work and reduce its contribution to the DGB.

IG Metall's more than 160 union locals (*Verwaltungsstellen*) would receive much more responsibility and resources, and would be tasked with focusing on service and recruitment. The managing executive committee would establish a clear set of performance indicators for the locals. These would include recruitment targets and mandates to extend coverage of the union and works councils to regions and sectors where the union has been weak. Performance on the indicators would determine the distribution of internal funds. For example, the brochure proposed that locals keep 60 percent of the dues money from any new recruit for the first year and 40 percent thereafter. IG Metall's middle layer of union districts would have a smaller "hinge" role between the headquarters and the locals. Districts would still be responsible for engaging in collective bargaining, but they would have no involvement in strategic planning.[158]

The Members and Organizing department gave union members only six months to discuss "Projekt IG Metall 2009" because the leadership wanted to have the text of any changes to the union's constitution ready by April 2010, which was the deadline for submissions to be included for discussion at the union's October 2011 convention. Criticism within the organization was muted. Local officials were broadly supportive because the proposal shifted resources to them. It was difficult for anyone to question placing greater emphasis on recruitment and efficiency, given the substantial membership losses of the past two decades. Wetzel's past success in recruiting and mobilizing members also made it hard to criticize the brochure. Still, some traditionalists expressed concern that this new narrow emphasis turns the union into a neutral service provider that differs little from an automobile association. Many traditionalists would prefer that the union return to its traditional self-understanding as a "countervailing power" within a capitalist society and suggest that IG Metall focus attention on building alliances with environmental, women's, and antiglobalization movements. They also would have preferred to see IG Metall set goals first (for example, a push for more working-time reduction) and then change its structure to facilitate fulfillment of those ends.[159]

IG Metall leaders began to implement some elements of "Projekt IG Metall 2009" even before the 2011 convention. The union reduced expenses by €20 million annually through trimming the workforce at its Frankfurt headquarters from 550 to 430, and transferring both personnel and funds to the locals. Following the US model, headquarters encouraged the locals to hire specialized "organizers" to focus solely on recruitment. IG Metall also took the unorthodox step of opening fourteen recruitment offices at universities with the objective of attracting university-educated members through providing advice and assistance with placement in paid internships (*Praktika*) and jobs.[160]

Some have argued that the structure of "Projekt IG Metall 2009" would be better suited to a hierarchical corporation driven by the bottom line than a union, which is a membership organization that is internally pluralistic and depends on dialog to formulate positions that have widespread support within the organization. Streamlining IG Metall along the lines proposed in the report also eliminates sites for developing alternative ideas and solutions. Some expressed fears that narrowing opportunities for voice within the union could discourage future local experimentation and even accelerate rank-and-file flight.[161]

By 2011, the reform efforts began to yield tangible results. Union membership stabilized for the first time in over two decades. IG Metall's October 2011 convention rewarded Huber and Wetzel by reelecting them by majorities comparable to their election four years earlier (i.e., 92.6% and 83.8%, respectively). One reform proposal, however, fell nine votes short of the two-thirds majority needed to implement it. It called for reducing the size of the union's managing executive committee from seven to five. Enough delegates feared the loss of additional voices at the top to reject the change, which was a minor setback and somewhat of an embarrassment for Huber and Wetzel.[162]

Recent events have made clear the limits on grassroots organizing within IG Metall; local officials challenge union personnel preferences at their own peril, even when it comes to positions outside the union itself. At the Daimler-Benz plants in Berlin, Kassel, and Stuttgart-Sindelfingen, several alternative candidates ran in the 2010 works council elections against individuals on the union's approved list and won. The alternative candidates were IG Metall members, but they were critical of the incumbent councillors. Some alternative candidates also disparaged the framework collective bargaining agreement that union chair Berthold Huber had negotiated a decade earlier when he was head of the Baden-Württemberg district of the union. After the elections, IG Metall pursued disciplinary proceedings against the alternative candidates. The union banned some from serving in union posts and expelled others. Many inside and outside of the labor movement protested the decisions.[163] Disciplining dissident works councillors highlights one of the challenges inherent in the union's decentralization effort. If IG Metall had not meted out punishments, incumbent local union officials and works councillors throughout the union would conclude that the IG Metall leadership would not stand behind them when the going got tough. The price, however, of defending the incumbents was to expose the limits of grassroots empowerment for all to see. Loyalty can still trump competence and local support.

The worldwide financial crisis, which began in the fall of 2008, had a surprisingly positive impact on IG Metall's reform efforts. The union had already implemented some portions of organizational reform, for example, setting performance indicators regarding recruitment and linking them to local funding. Initially, some IG Metall leaders feared that the crisis could cripple the reform because massive employment losses would make it impossible for local officials to meet their recruitment targets and they might sour on the whole process as a result.[164] Instead, the dramatic economic downturn sparked an extraordinarily cooperative form of "crisis corporatism" among the government, the employers associations, and the unions.

Thomas Haipeter, director of the Research Department on Working Time and Work Organization at the Institute Work and Qualification, observed, "The coordinated initiatives of the 'social partners,' particularly in the metal industry, were developed virtually overnight. . . . Firm-level emergency coalitions . . . proved to be a particularly effective technique to decouple, in the short run, employment from the economic downturn."[165] A common theme in the workplace discussions was that the social partners, works councils, and government all needed to pull together in order to "hold the shop together."[166] As a result, "German trade unions . . . experienced a remarkable comeback in terms of public reputation, and acknowledgement by employers' federations and the federal government."[167]

The German government's decisions to expand dramatically the use of short-time work (*Kurzarbeit*) and several other emergency labor market measures to preserve employment during the crisis actually helped the union to recruit.[168] Coordinating short-time work (which most firms did in cooperation with the company works council and local union officials) put works councillors and union officials in direct contact with thousands of employees, including many nonmembers with whom they otherwise would not have interacted. Union officials were also able to have constructive conversations with employers that otherwise would have been unlikely. IG Metall also organized "taskforce crisis intervention" in late 2008. The taskforce assembled more than two hundred experts from the union's *besser statt billiger* program to help employees devise plans to save jobs. The union supplemented the job preservation policies by agreeing to postpone a wage increase scheduled for May 2009 for firms that did not lay off employees. Germany's quick initial recovery from the economic crisis, which was driven by demand from Asia and Latin America for producer goods, helped IG Metall by stabilizing employment, which was a prerequisite to the union staunching membership losses.[169]

It is worth noting that IG Metall's more aggressive organizing tactics have begun to draw the ire of the employers associations. The president of the federation of mechanical engineering employers associations, Martin Kannegiesser, complained that mobilization drives intended to promote recruitment would produce precariousness at work that could damage the sector. Kannegiesser also criticized the "style of public confrontation" of the union's new organizing strategy as completely contrary to the cooperative social partnership that was so effective in the global financial crisis. Kannegiesser expressed concerns that "such one-sidedness is dangerous for collective bargaining autonomy" and "problem-solving capacity."[170]

IG Metall's early success has spurred other unions to begin modest experiments of their own. In January 2011, IG BCE under the leadership of a new chair, Michael Vassiliadis, launched a campaign called "We Make Decent Work!" The campaign resembles IG Metall's "Together for a Decent Life!" effort. It sets an agenda of improving working conditions and endeavors to engage the rank and file through blogs and social media. Simultaneously, union leaders asked local officials to submit proposals for innovative projects to improve recruitment or membership engagement. For 2011, IG BCE funded forty projects totaling €2 million.[171] In contrast to IG Metall, IG BCE's campaign does not include an aggressive organizational restructuring, permanent sizable incentives for recruitment, or any confrontational rhetoric vis-à-vis employers. IG BCE has instead pursued intensive social partnership with the chemical industry employers association, which has included scores of "social partnership agreements" covering topics extending well beyond wages and working conditions.

Ver.di launched a reform effort around the same time as IG Metall, but with starkly different results. The 2007 ver.di convention passed a resolution asking the union's executive committee to develop a program to combat membership losses. After a six-month "discussion and development process," ver.di officials "conceptualized" the program. In May 2008, ver.di's executive committee issued a sixteen-page discussion paper entitled "Opportunity 2011" and approved it in September 2008. Like "Projekt IG Metall 2009," "Opportunity 2011" sets out recruitment and closing gaps in the union's coverage within its jurisdiction as goals and identifies strengthening the "membership orientation" of the organization as the way to achieve them. "Opportunity 2011" defines membership orientation as "a matter of the organization having to stick firmly to the question: What does this do for membership development and retention?" as well as "strengthening the self-consciousness and capacity of as many members as possible to act independently" by opening up union decision making to more participation and fortifying the connections between the works councils and the union in the workplace.[172]

"Opportunity 2011" casts a transition to membership orientation as beneficial for full-time union officials because it would transform their work from "a paramedic, who helps everywhere he is needed and called" to a "process manager." It also flags potential difficulties, conceding that the condition of ver.di is "still far from optimal" for making a transition to greater membership orientation because many union officials are either set in their ways or judge any change primarily by its impact on their personal power. The paper acknowledges that including the rank and file in more decisions "can lead to conflicts and contradiction." It counsels that "such conflicts must be discussed in earnest" but offers nothing more on how to deal with them.[173]

The remainder of "Opportunity 2011" focuses on organizational reform. On the one hand, it stresses the need to build up workplace groups and networks to engage in "systematic personnel development" and to create sophisticated databases including "workplace atlases" to identify workplaces with employees ripe for recruitment. On the other hand, it repeatedly bemoans the failure of officials in many union locals simply to make entries into the union's existing Member Information and Service System database, which raises questions regarding the capacity of ver.di actually to execute the more ambitious data analyses the paper proposes. The final section of "Opportunity 2011" takes up the touchy matter of ver.di's internal structure. It criticizes a 2004 agreement that set fixed percentages for the shares of dues distributed among the union's sectoral and hierarchical units as "unfair," because the dues distribution per member now varies widely from unit to unit since some have shrunk far more than others. "Opportunity 2011" gingerly calls for more flexibility in redistributing resources and ends on a hopeful note by declaring that there has already been "a noticeable shift of accent" among ver.di officials away from internal politics and toward the members and their workplaces.[174]

The internal reaction to "Opportunity 2011" within ver.di was quite critical. The officials of some union districts responded that they already have a membership orientation. Others within ver.di attacked the paper as "nothing new," and "ill suited for democratic discussion" because its content and language reflects "the world of modern management and personnel leadership theories." Critics also complained that "Opportunity 2011" is off the mark because it invokes a "faux problem" of union officials behaving rigidly. Ver.di's Women and Equal Opportunity department criticized "Opportunity 2011" as failing to consider gender implications sufficiently in the analysis.[175]

In contrast to "Projekt IG Metall 2009," "Opportunity 2011" has borne all the hallmarks of an exercise doomed to fail. Unlike the IG Metall effort, "Opportunity 2011" has no real champion in the upper echelons of ver.di. Moreover, ver.di's rigid matrix organizational structure makes it extraordinarily hard for innovation and innovators to rise within the union. The process has also been extraordinarily slow. Once the discussion paper was approved, ver.di's executive committee commissioned polls regarding the "general goals" of "Opportunity 2011." In July 2010, ver.di completed a "target-group analysis" of "reachable nonmembers." Four years after starting the project, the only concrete achievements ver.di has to show are a revision of continuing education programs to bring the content more into line with the *political* positions of the union and reorganizing the union's webpage to make it easier to navigate for first-time users. Organizing has yet to become commonplace in ver.di. In 2010, the European Trade Union Institute undertook a survey of public- and private-sector works councillors and shop stewards in ver.di's jurisdiction in the city of Hamburg. A majority of the works councillors indicated that they made no efforts to recruit members. Fewer than 10 percent of the works councils and only 15 percent of the union's own shop stewards reported that they recruited "intensively." At ver.di's 2011 convention, Frank Bsirske admonished the delegates regarding the results of the Hamburg survey, and union officials indicated that they would continue "Opportunity 2011," but the convention made no significant changes to the union's byzantine matrix structure and took no concrete steps to upgrade ver.di's commitment to recruitment.[176]

The consequences of ver.di's failure to develop a viable strategy to reverse membership decline have been stark. Ver.di's net membership loss was 23.4 percent between its founding in 2001 and the end of 2010, which compares poorly to the 17.4 percent decline for IG Metall during the same period, and comes despite far heavier employment losses in the mechanical engineering sector than in services. Even if ver.di ultimately does produce a viable plan to recruit more members, there will be significantly fewer people to implement it. Membership losses forced ver.di's leadership to reduce the union's workforce by 28.8 percent from 5,200 to 3,700 over the first decade of its existence. Staff cuts helped to reduce ver.di's annual budget deficit from €90.5 million in 2001 to €10.5 million in 2010, but the union remains in the red.[177]

A factor contributing to membership decline at ver.di is the failure of the union to improve the material standing of service-sector employees. Chapter 3 of this book demonstrated a significant correlation between nominal gains in income and union density. A study from before the financial crisis showed that ver.di did no better at the bargaining table than the five constituent unions had done before the merger.[178]

Ver.di's approach to the global financial crisis was far more traditional and one dimensional than IG Metall's. It was also reminiscent of the confrontations between ver.di and the Schröder government. For example, at a speech in September 2010, ver.di chair Bsirske stuck both middle fingers in the air and said, "This refers to the bankers at Hypo Real Estate," which was an insolvent bank that the German government took over in 2009. In terms of policy, ver.di leaders called for a long laundry list of actions that stood no chance of ever becoming law. These included a large stimulus package, a thorough reregulation of the financial sector, several steep tax increases for the affluent, and changes that would largely undo the Hartz and Agenda 2010 reforms. Some union officials even proposed reviving the drive for weekly working-time reduction with no reduction in weekly pay.[179]

The financial crisis, if anything, further undercut the relative position of the DGB vis-à-vis the member unions. The crisis prompted the DGB to return to traditional nostrums. In May 2009, the union confederation held an ineffectual "capitalism congress" to dissect the financial crisis. A subtitle in the *Süddeutsche Zeitung* summarized the meeting well: "Unionists Discuss Capitalism in Berlin but Find No Alternative." Even before the crisis began, dissatisfaction with the DGB from within the trade union leadership had flared up once again. In the spring of 2008, Berthold Huber pushed DGB reform back on to the agenda. Huber spoke of the need for reform in general terms, but the heart of the matter was again financial. In November, the chairs of the DGB affiliates approved a plan to reduce the size of the DGB managing executive committee from five to four and to eliminate a 0.46 percent annual dues transfer to the confederation to maintain a "solidarity fund."[180] The May 2010 DGB convention implemented these and other organizational reforms. The tone of the 2010 convention was much more civil than that of the gathering four years earlier. Ironically, relations between union leaders and Chancellor Merkel have been much better than they ever were with Chancellor Schröder. Merkel had dinner with Berthold Huber before the convention and said kind words about Michael Sommer in her speech to the delegates. The convention approved a new DGB constitution, but it contained no notable changes.

The DGB remains an awkward entity. It has neither the power nor the resources to be influential, yet abolishing it would be going a step too far in the eyes of most, because the individual unions occasionally need a common voice, a referee, a body to interact with other trade union confederations, and a representative in Brussels and at international gatherings, such as the economic summits of the Group of Twenty (G-20) heads of government and state. As a result, the DGB is likely to continue to atrophy but never quite disappear in coming years.

The year 2010 was significant for organized labor. It was the first time in a quarter century that the gross unionization rate had not fallen; it remained stable at 18.8 percent. Gross DGB membership did fall, but only by 72,000, which was the first time since 1991 that it was less than 100,000. Optimism was not overly ebullient, however. After all, the density results are barely more than half as high as they had been in labor's glory days of the late 1970s and early 1980s.

A Tale of Two Movements: German Trade Unionism in the Postwar Era

There have been two trade union movements in postwar Germany. The first was an industrial union movement. It was a product of the economic conditions and political struggles of the immediate postwar period. The first movement helped to provide stability and prosperity to German employees for four decades, but it increasingly began to experience difficulties, starting in the 1980s as nominal wage results became more meager and the milieu supportive of trade unions began to deteriorate. The reaction of labor leaders to their challenges can hardly be characterized as an expression of exhaustion. Union officials' first response to the deterioration of the labor milieu was dramatic structural reforms. The 1990s was a decade of organizational metamorphosis. A series of mergers among rapidly shrinking organizations produced a second postwar trade union movement that consists of a small number of dominant multisectoral unions as well as a few small mostly occupational unions.

The change to the second German labor movement restored some organizational stability to the unions, but they proved insufficient to stem membership losses. Hard times, internal division, and unrelenting membership declines during the first years of the new millennium diminished the unions' economic and political clout. Income increases no longer correspond to productivity growth. Labor's share of national income has fallen sharply. Small occupational unions have embarrassed the new multisectoral unions by showing them up at the bargaining table. The transition to vast and impersonal multisectoral unions has arguably even contributed to a further deterioration of labor's milieu. The political fragmentation of the Left has rendered it increasingly difficult to influence. Labor leaders' inability to convert the Alliance for Jobs into concrete improvements in both the German economy and the trade union movement was a failure that left the movement vulnerable and unable to affect the subsequent Hartz and Agenda 2010 reforms.

In the last five years, however, some German union officials have come to recognize the limitations of structural concentration as a response to declining membership and have begun to experiment with decentralization and grassroots empowerment. These undertakings borrow heavily from the logic and tactics of US-style social movement unionism. It remains too soon to tell whether IG Metall's restructuring to promote grassroots social movement unionism will ultimately pay off, particularly in a country with a deep-rooted tradition of cooperative industrial relations, but the first signs are mostly positive. Still, a big risk for IG Metall is that the trend toward individualism and the deterioration of labor's milieu have rendered too many employees simply uninterested in unionization. Another big risk is that IG Metall's own staff will rebel against policies that have sent some headquarters and district personnel out into the locals and that punish locals that fail to meet recruiting targets with stiff budget cuts.

It is also too soon to tell whether IG Metall's approach will spread. The counterexample of ver.di shows how challenging moving to social movement unionism can be. Ver.di's rigid matrix structure for distributing power and resources within the union has hampered the ability of its leaders to build on isolated internal grassroots experiments with social movement unionism within their ranks to launch a more comprehensive organizational reform. The third biggest DGB union, IG BCE, has taken a starkly different tack. It has pinned its survival on intensive social partnership with the employers associations in the chemicals industry. This intensive social partnership has built up a considerable degree of organizational security for the union, but it has not succeeded in warding off membership decline. Between 2001 and 2010, IG BCE shrunk by 21.7 percent, which is only 1.7 percentage points less than the decline at ver.di. IG BCE's recent experimentation with modest versions of decentralization is likely insufficient to turn around membership losses there.

In the postwar system of German industrial relations, there is no significant matter that union officials can hope to address successfully without consideration of the role and response of employers associations. In many areas of industrial relations, employers associations are the single most important actors. Employers associations are also central players in the German economy. In the next chapter I undertake a detailed analysis of German employers associations. I discuss their formation, restoration, postwar development, and current challenges. I evaluate divergences in the forms of social partnership in key sectors of the German economy and the larger implications of the interplay between trade unions and employers associations for the future of German industrial relations.

CHAPTER 5

Employers Associations

From Regaining Credibility to Retaining Relevance

Employers associations have been prominent in German industrial relations for over a century, and they remain central actors today. Employers associations and unions are counterparts, but they differ in many respects, the most important of which is that a member of an employers association is a firm or a unit of a firm (e.g., a branch plant) rather than a person. This dissimilarity has numerous ramifications.

Joining an employers association is a business decision rather than a personal choice. Internal dynamics also vary substantially between unions and employers associations because they are organizations of differing magnitudes. Unions are mass organizations; the largest have millions of members. Employers associations are not. Membership in a regional employers association for any given sector is typically around one hundred and rarely exceeds one thousand. Employers association governance is much more direct and personal as a result.

Another important difference between unions and employers associations in the postwar years is that employers associations have been far more successful at recruitment than unions. Estimates place employers association density at twice that of trade unions during the postwar years. Employers associations, moreover, come far closer than unions to achieving comprehensive coverage, both sectorally and geographically (although eastern Germany has been a chronic weak spot). Unlike unions, employers associations have done well organizing the service sectors. As a result, the postwar German industrial relations regime has the reach that it does because of the recruitment record of employers associations, not the organizing prowess of the unions. This also explains why declining employers association density since the mid-1980s in one major sector of the economy—mechanical engineering—has drawn the close attention of industrial relations observers and participants alike.

The density trends for employers associations do not shadow those for organized labor. The best estimates show that employers association density was approximately 75 percent from the 1950s to the 1980s. Density has declined since the mid-1980s in the mechanical engineering sector, but it has remained high and stable in both the chemicals industry, the second most important sector of the German economy, and the public sector, which is also large. Divergence also manifests within individual sectors. In mechanical engineering, large firms still belong as a rule to the employers associations, but small and medium-size enterprises (SMEs) increasingly do not. In this chapter I suggest that a structural difference between sectors—namely, the relative importance of SMEs—explains why density has declined in some sectors but not in others.

Organizational trends also differ between employers associations and trade unions. There was no massive wave of employers association mergers during the 1990s and early 2000s akin to those among the unions. Instead, employers associations have incrementally moved away from a uniform system of wage determination by creating new forms of membership and expanding the flexibility of collective agreements. These innovations have sparked debates among practitioners and scholars alike regarding their implications for the relative power of employers associations and trade unions, as well as the future of German industrial relations.[1]

In this chapter I continue the assessment of the erosion and exhaustion hypotheses. In brief, I find innovation and diversity predominating among leading German employers associations rather than exhaustion or erosion. I also evaluate an influential theory of organizational behavior for employers associations from the work on "organized business interests" by Philippe Schmitter and Wolfgang Streeck. They argue that there is a tradeoff between the two principal objectives of business associations: maximizing membership, which Schmitter and Streeck call "the logic of membership," and exerting external influence, which they name "the logic of influence."[2] They postulate that an association's influence is greater the more it can deliver member consent (particularly from among its more skeptical members). Yet submission to negotiated solutions makes membership less attractive to firms because "in a liberal society, individuals, especially resourceful, well-connected businessmen, may not be 'in the market' for associational control over their behavior—even if it is demonstrably in their long-term interests."[3] The evidence presented in this chapter shows that the relationship between the logics of membership and influence does not always take the form of the tradeoff that Schmitter and Streeck anticipate.

Studying employers associations has a dynamic of its own. Most employers associations are far less forthcoming with data than are unions. Only the employers associations in the mechanical engineering sector regularly publish membership data. As a result, it is impossible to create a quantitative model for employers associations to assess density trends analogous to the one for unions constructed in chapter 3. Consequently, in this chapter I use descriptive statistics and qualitative research for evidence.

To deepen our understanding of employers associations, particularly for those readers who are new to this subject, it is essential to know their origins. I therefore begin with a brief history of employers associations in Germany. I then continue with a more detailed analysis of developments since German unification.

History of Employers Associations in Germany

German business first began to organize collectively in the latter half of the nineteenth century. The principal motivations to form business associations were to resist unionization and to ward off restrictive or costly legislation. As a result, scholars frequently refer to these early organizations as "counterassociations" (*Gegenverbände*). Early association benefits typically included access to a common strike-insurance fund, coordination in the use of lockouts, and a ban on taking business from other members of the organization during strikes.[4] In the late 1800s, coordination among business associations was largely idiosyncratic. Lobbying failures and a massive 1903–4 textile strike in Crimmitschau—which the employers won, but at considerable cost—prompted employers to reorganize their associations into more functionally specialized bodies to improve the quality and professionalism of their efforts. The restructuring culminated in 1913 when German employers associations consolidated under a single peak confederation called the Vereinigung der Deutschen Arbeitgeberverbände (VDA, Organization of German Employers Associations).[5] The First World War broke out a year later. During the war, employers associations and organized labor agreed to a truce at the behest of the imperial government. The truce functioned well, but it did little to prepare either side for the tumultuous interwar years.[6]

The sudden collapse of the Second Empire, Germany's surrender, and the chaotic transition to democracy in November 1918 changed the political landscape fundamentally. Employers and their associations did their best to cope. An accommodationist faction of employers led by industrialist Hugo Stinnes forged a modus vivendi with the labor movement that was codified in a twelve-point accord signed by Stinnes and the head of the Social Democratic trade union confederation, Carl Legien, on 15 November 1918. The Stinnes-Legien agreement guaranteed trade unions the legal right to organize and to bargain collectively, banned company-supported unions, established a standard arbitration process, and called for the creation of "worker committees" in every workplace with fifty or more employees. The agreement also set up the Zentralarbeitsgemeinschaft der industriellen und gewerblichen Arbeitgeber und Arbeitnehmer Deutschlands (ZAG, Central Work Community of German Industrial and Commercial Employers and Employees). The ZAG had equal numbers of business and trade unionists on its governing board. Its mission was to strive for "common solutions to all economic and social policy questions that affect industry and trade, as well as all legislative and administrative actions that concern it." The ZAG's proponents had high hopes for the organization. They wanted it to become Germany's de facto economic parliament, but this was not to be. Only moderate employers and unionists ever participated in the ZAG, and the body collapsed in 1924 amid economic and political turmoil that arose during the early 1920s, especially as a result of hyperinflation, French occupation of the Ruhr region to collect reparations, and militant employers extending the workday in their facilities beyond eight hours. Practical critics found the ZAG to be too distant and slow to address immediate workplace problems. For those who saw the world through the lens of class struggle, the ZAG was a collaborationist body.[7]

Despite the disappointment, difficulties, and distrust surrounding the ZAG, collective bargaining made some inroads as a means of wage determination. By the early 1920s, collective bargaining agreements set wages and benefits for 14.2 million employees. This was a marked increase from only 1.8 million in 1914, but it still amounted to less than half of the labor force. Most German employers during the interwar years distrusted unions, in particular unions affiliated with the Social Democratic Party, and preferred to determine compensation unilaterally. Collective bargaining became less important toward the end of the Weimar Republic as tumultuous economic conditions led labor and management to turn increasingly to a state-run system of compulsory arbitration to set wages and benefits.[8]

Historians are split regarding the role of German business in the rise of Adolf Hitler. Some see business interests as central players and ardent supporters, whereas others depict them as divided, reluctant, and of secondary importance.[9] Once Hitler rose to power in 1933, internecine struggles for control broke out within many business associations between Nazi supporters and skeptics. In most instances neither side was initially strong enough to push the other out. The leadership of most business associations offered to restructure their organizations to accommodate Nazi preferences but endeavored to preserve institutional independence from the party and state. The new regime judged the compromise offers as insufficient. The Nazi policy of "institutional conformity" (*Gleichschaltung*) did not permit autonomy for any group in society. In 1934, the National Socialist regime dissolved all German business associations and created the Reichsgruppe Industrie, with compulsory membership for all enterprises, as one of a series of uniform corporatist *Reichsgruppen*. The new organization fell under the direct control of the Ministry of Economic Affairs and the National Economic Chamber. The Nazis did not round up the leaders of German business associations the way they did trade union officials. They hoped that the business leaders would choose to work for and with the new Reichsgruppe. Most did. Some were reluctant, but others had few qualms until the very end when it became clear that Germany was going to lose the war.[10]

Many in the business community were among the elite who joined the Nazi Party in significant numbers and helped to advance its aims. This included refusing to employ Jews and others the Nazis deemed undesirable. Most major companies held major defense contracts. Once war broke out, it is beyond dispute that most large German businesses cooperated fully in the war effort, which in some instances entailed using forced labor from Nazi death camps. Some did this out of ideological conviction. For others, simply the quotidian pressures of meeting production deadlines under wartime conditions and a wish to conform within a brutal totalitarian system led to the banality of evil playing out on an unprecedented scale. Thus, by war's end, the German business community was deeply implicated in the actions of history's most horrific and criminal regime.[11]

Finding Footing: Employers Associations in the Immediate Postwar Years

In the immediate postwar years, the Nazi legacy (including the collaborationist role of many managers), the restrictions of occupation, and a desire to regain legitimacy as quickly as possible led all but the most militant fringes of German business to abandon the traditional antiunion model for employers associations. The core mission of employers associations thus became collective bargaining.[12]

Immediately after the war, the explicitly anticapitalist Soviet Union and skeptical left-of-center governments in Britain and the United States actively prosecuted German capitalists. Many managers were arrested and tried for offenses ranging from collaborating with the Nazis to crimes against humanity. The Allies broke up eight of the most notorious industrial combines, including the I. G. Farben chemical manufacturing conglomerate and the Krupp steel and armaments firm. The four powers also issued a series of regulations to rein in the power of German business.[13]

The Western Allies forbade the formation of employers associations until late 1946 or early 1947, depending on the zone.[14] The Soviet authorities took the additional steps of banning all business associations in their occupation zone and summarily jailing several top business officials. The Soviets also relied heavily on *Demontage* (i.e., dismantling entire German factories and shipping them to the Soviet Union for reassembly) as a form of reparation, which particularly unnerved German employers and employees alike.[15]

While the Soviet authorities maintained a punitive policy against business, the Western Allies quickly adopted a more accommodating stance. This change was the product of rapidly shifting circumstances. It was only after the occupation of Germany began that British and American authorities fully realized the tremendous financial burden and the huge security problem that an economically prostrate Germany would be in the emerging Cold War struggle against the Soviet Union. The best way out was to revive the German economy, but this could only be done with the cooperation of German business. Cooperation, in turn, could only be obtained if the Western occupying powers stopped breaking up companies and prosecuting German capitalists as war criminals and instead allowed them to form associations.[16]

The Western Allies also received support for a softer approach toward western German business from an unlikely source, namely, western German workers and their unions. For most workers, protecting their jobs had priority over punishing all but the most egregious capitalist war criminals. Since the occupation began, they had been willing to bargain even with collaborationist employers if this was the only way to preserve employment. From the earliest days of occupation, this practical cooperation between western German workers and their employers to save jobs from any threat—be it Soviet authorities bent on dismantling their workplaces or western officials endeavoring to liquidate industrial combines—helped greatly to develop mutual trust that contributed to improving German labor relations in the immediate postwar era.[17]

To be sure, clashes of culture and class had by no means disappeared. Many of the original top officials in the reestablished employers associations were former military officers. They quickly gained a reputation for taking a martial approach, which frequently caused friction with trade unionists. Still, trade unionists were supportive when the Western Allies once again permitted employers to form associations in their zones. This reaction perplexed some American observers who did not consider the advantages for unions of strong employers associations to discipline individual firms and to elevate the scale of collective action above the level of the firm. The three Western occupying powers initially only permitted employers associations to form slowly and locally, just as they had done with the unions, but the speed and breadth of amalgamation quickly accelerated in order to help improve the coordination of the economy and to keep pace with the unions' reconstruction efforts. Employers association representatives soon began to meet with trade unionists and to advise government officials on labor policy and social service administration.[18]

Regional employers associations were first allowed to form sectoral federations across the US and British zones in May 1947. The Western Allies did not hold a unified position regarding the optimal degree of centralization for postwar German business. Officials from the United Kingdom preferred a single set of business organizations akin to British practice. The US authorities and many Germans favored segmenting business associations functionally into employers associations, industry associations, and chambers of industry and commerce, as the Germans had done before the Second World War. The status quo ante prevailed.

On 2 June 1948, the sectoral federations of employers associations in "Bizonia" (i.e., the American and British occupation zones) founded a provisional peak confederation, and on 28 January 1949, twenty-three sectoral federations and eight state associations reconstituted it with a tighter and fuller structure. On 14 October 1949, the employers named this body the Vereinigung der Arbeitgeberverbände (Organization of Employers Associations), which closely resembled the name of the peak confederation established in 1913. On 15 December 1949, the employers associations from the French zone joined in with their counterparts from Bizonia. On 15 November 1950, representatives from almost fifty sectoral federations of employers associations and eleven state associations with a membership comprising roughly 60 percent of all the eligible firms in the Federal Republic employing 80 percent of the workforce changed the peak confederation's name to the Bundesvereinigung der Deutschen Arbeitgeberverbände (BDA, Federal Organization of German Employers Associations).[19]

How does the organization of employers associations and unions compare? Employers in the Federal Republic have always maintained more fragmented and multilayered industrial relations structures than has organized labor. Sectoral federations of regional employers associations (e.g., Gesamtverband der metallindustriellen Arbeitgeberverbände [Gesamtmetall, General Association of Metal Industry Employers Associations]) are not as centralized as their opposite numbers, the German trade unions. In a few sectors, such as construction, there is more than one national organization. Most sectoral federations have anywhere from five to sixteen affiliates that cover the different regions of the country. Fragmentation continues in a few sectors even below the level of the regional employers association. The regional employers association in the mechanical engineering sector of North Rhine–Westphalia, Metall NRW, is an extreme case. Metall NRW, which is a regional employers association affiliated with Gesamtmetall, is itself a federation of twenty-six local associations. In total, more than five hundred distinct associations and federations of associations at all levels fall under the umbrella of the BDA.

The BDA's position at the top is not indicative of its relative power, however. The fifty-two sectoral federations, which are currently BDA affiliates, are the strongest set of players, but the regional sectoral employers associations below the affiliates do have significant points of leverage. In most instances, the regional employers associations in each sector collect dues and control the dispersal of funds, even to the sectoral federation to which they belong. The sectoral federation typically develops the collective bargaining strategy—including the content and timing of counteroffers, and whether and where to use lockouts—which gives the sectoral federations the upper hand, but this authority has its limits. The leaders of the regional employers associations are usually deeply involved in formulating strategy and must approve all significant actions. Regional associations and individual firms are also the organizations that actually execute most of the federation's plans.[20]

Why are German employers far less centralized than the unions? Employers association members are more heterogeneous and hierarchically arranged than union members could ever be, which goes a long way toward accounting for the difference. Most sectors are made up of firms of all sizes and levels of sophistication. This affects employers associations in three ways. First, employers in the same association or sectoral federation are often locked into zero-sum relationships, which make cooperation difficult. Many compete with each other for the same customers. Some buy from others within the same association (e.g., automobile parts suppliers and assemblers), which means they constantly struggle over prices. Second, heterogeneity makes association governance difficult. In terms of numbers, the small firms far outnumber the large ones in most sectors. In terms of employment and economic clout, the big companies predominate. No matter the governing procedure, at least some members of an association will perceive themselves as relatively disadvantaged.[21] Third, several employers association officials complain that many member firms, particularly the smaller ones, are quite parochial. Owner-managers from small firms are known to express distrust of "those others over the hill," even other employers. The heavily fragmented system allows many employers to be the big fish in a large number of small ponds. Too many are loath to give up that status.[22]

Power and influence are not distributed evenly among the sectoral associations either. Some sectoral associations are much more powerful than others. In general, manufacturing affiliates have dominated BDA governing boards, reflecting "not only the heavier financial burden borne by them in the BDA, but also and more significantly the leadership role of manufacturing and processing enterprises in determining wage and salary patterns" in the Federal Republic. Gesamtmetall has always been the single most important sectoral federation because of its size. When weighted in terms of employment, Gesamtmetall has always accounted for at least 40 percent of the BDA. Gesamtmetall has also provided a comparable share of the BDA budget. Gesamtmetall has used its relative weight to lay claim to the lion's share of posts (in particular the top ones) and to influence policy in the BDA. The Bundesarbeitgeberverband Chemie (BAVC, Federal Employers Association of the Chemical Industry) has been the second most influential BDA affiliate.[23] The relative size and strength of the individual sectoral employers associations largely mirrors that of the trade union in the same sector, with one exception, that is, services public and private. There is no equivalent of ver.di among the employers associations (i.e., a single large employers association representing all public and private service firms). The BDA restricts its membership to private employers only. BDA representation for the private service sector is fragmented; there are over twenty independent employers associations rather than just one.

Restoring Legitimacy: Employers Associations in the 1950s

The economic environment in the 1950s was well suited to facilitate the newly reestablished German employers associations taking root. The real mean increase in the gross domestic product per capita for the decade was an astonishing 8.1 percent per year (table 4.2). Productivity expanded at an equally impressive average annual rate of 5.6 percent, while inflation remained moderate at 1.9 percent per year on average. Unemployment was at 11 percent at the start of the 1950s, but it came down fast. By 1956, it had fallen to 4.4 percent, and by decade's end, German joblessness was at 2.6 percent.

Employers associations quickly spread throughout the whole economy. Most sectors had at least a few firms with substantial resources that were willing to foot a disproportionately large share of the bill for an association. Bankruptcy was relatively infrequent in the booming economy, which provided a stable membership base. Firms maintained multiple interconnections through banks, regional politics, and social organizations. No attractive alternative options to associations existed at the time. There were differences among sectors. Some but not all of the regional employers associations had relatively small local membership pools, which discouraged free riding because it was visible to all when a firm did not join. Strong employers associations arose in most sectors of the economy (e.g., banking, chemicals, and mechanical engineering). A few sectors, however, did have trouble recruiting (e.g., clothing production and hospitality). Sectors suffering more difficulties typically had relatively large numbers of small firms and fewer large firms willing to bankroll an association. In one instance (i.e., construction) an industry formed two confederations because of the stark differences in the sector between large and small firms.[24]

It quickly became standard practice for the employers associations and the trade union in each sector of the economy (banking, mechanical engineering, retail, etc.) to negotiate a set of regionwide collective bargaining agreements (*Flächentarifverträge*). For each collective bargaining round, the union involved selects a pilot district where the main negotiations take place. The pilot district is where the collective bargaining parties focus on reaching a settlement and engage in industrial action, if it comes to that. Talks still take place in the other districts, but they are largely pro forma. During the talks, the negotiators on the employers' side in the pilot district typically consult with representatives from the other regional employers associations in the sector regarding the contents of the negotiations. Once an agreement is reached in the pilot district, all the other districts copy the results from the pilot district, with perhaps a few minor deviations at the margins to take into account local circumstances, and then they submit it to the members for a ratification vote. The result is a set of regional contracts for each sector with essentially the same contents that provides a common nationwide compensation floor for each sector while formally preserving a federal structure. This sort of arrangement did exist for some sectors in the Weimar Republic. The big difference in the postwar years has been that high employers association density gives the regionwide collective bargaining agreements far greater reach in setting compensation for the economy. That having been said, unlike in some other northern European countries past and present, there is no formal mechanism in Germany for wage coordination across sectors. Typically, the settlement in mechanical engineering or chemicals sets an informal target for the unions in all of the other sectors negotiating compensation contracts that year, but the contents vary considerably from sector to sector.

On the political scene, the 1950s were a decade of probation and experimentation for German employers associations, the sectoral federations, and the BDA.[25] Suspicions regarding the business community lingered as a result of the wartime record, but the political environment in the early postwar years was not completely hostile. The political success of the center-right Christian Democratic Union, which placed Konrad Adenauer in the federal chancellery and promarket Freiburg school economist Ludwig Erhard in the economics ministry, gave employers sympathetic personages in the highest levels of power. The intensification of the Cold War, especially the outbreak of the Korean conflict in 1950, helped German employers to regain ground quickly because demand for German products soared and fears of a comparable conflict between the Germanys made more salient the essential position of business in military readiness. As a result, the BDA and its affiliates were able to muster enough influence to contain codetermination rights (as seen in chapter 2).[26] Nonetheless, the legacy of widespread Nazi collaboration constrained business, effectively eliminating a policy of union avoidance for employers associations. Hence, a new policy consensus, which could serve as the foundation of the employers associations' postwar work, needed to be developed.

In 1953, as part of the effort to formulate this new policy consensus, the BDA produced a basic program in preparation for the second German federal election entitled *Reflections on the Social Order* (*Gedanken zur Sozialordnung*).[27] *Reflections on the Social Order* remains the single best statement of the ideological principles of postwar German employers associations and serves as a touchstone to this day.[28] The 1953 basic program identified cooperative labor-management relations within an open "social market economy" as the best means to promote freedom, democracy, and prosperity.[29] The document's pragmatic acceptance of trade unions marked a significant break from the overtly hostile position of many employers and their associations during the Second Empire and the Weimar Republic. The basic program also emphasized individual initiative and private property. It called for the role of the state to be limited to providing the framework conditions for a sound economy and society and serving as a referee to enforce contracts and to ensure fair play in negotiations between the social partners.

The internal debate over the 1953 basic program was intense at times because some employers were still hostile toward trade unions, and others hesitated to embrace a more laissez-faire "social market economy." After all, significant portions of German business had been relying on state intervention in one or another form since the formation of the protectionist "iron and rye" coalition in the 1870s. Still, a solid majority of employers voted to adopt the new basic program. Once the German economy had begun to prosper under a new, more market-oriented and neocorporatist framework, *Reflections on the Social Order* attained near universal adherence.[30]

When the famous German "economic miracle" began to emerge in the mid-1950s, employers and their associations gained further confidence and acceptance. Nonetheless, industrial disputes were common in the early days of the Federal Republic as the collective bargaining parties took the measure of each other and the new social order. From 1950 to 1959, more days were lost owing to industrial action than in any other postwar decade. The data show that unions triggered industrial actions far more often than employers associations. Only 7.4 percent of the days lost during the 1950s were the result of lockouts (table 4.3). The postwar industrial relations system proved capable of managing rapid growth and autonomous collective bargaining effectively. Mean real net income expanded briskly at 5.4 percent per year on average, which stimulated domestic demand but did not exceed productivity growth.

Employers association officials pursued internal consolidation during the 1950s, which included curtailing member autonomy. A difficult steel strike in Bavaria in 1954 revealed that most employers associations were ill prepared to engage in industrial conflict effectively. In response, organized business took several steps. Sectoral federations of employers associations began to create nationwide wage-policy committees to coordinate collective bargaining. In 1956, the BDA required all affiliates to create a strike fund. The bolstering of association control also included setting limits on what firms could concede in collective bargaining. Punishment for transgressing these limits could be severe. For example, in 1955, the BDA and Gesamtmetall successfully pressured the supervisory board of the Duisburg Copper Foundry to dismiss the firm's business manager because he had agreed to reduce the workweek to forty hours well before consensus had been reached among the heads of the sectoral federations of employers associations to permit this concession.[31] Raising the relative importance of the logic of influence through greater association control did not trigger "association flight" (*Verbandsflucht*) or "association avoidance" (*Verbandsvermeidung*) in the 1950s because exiting from the dense network of interconnections among firms that were common at the time would have been perilous for any recalcitrant employer and no attractive alternative arrangements existed. Still, asserting discipline should not be confused with opposition to the postwar state of affairs. The new commitment of employers associations to collective bargaining in place of union avoidance remained firm.

The Employers Strike Back: The Rise of Lockouts as a Tactic in the 1960s

Macroeconomic and labor market performance was once again outstanding in the 1960s, which redounded to the postwar industrial relations system. Growth decelerated somewhat, which was inevitable once the postwar recovery was largely complete, but real GDP per capita still rose by a brisk 4.8 percent per year (table 4.2). Inflation accelerated slightly but remained moderate at a mean annual rate of 2.5 percent for the decade. Productivity growth was once again strong (i.e., 4.8% per year). Real net income kept pace, increasing by 4.6 percent per year on average, without exceeding productivity, which was quite an accomplishment for any industrial relations regime in a decade during which unemployment averaged 0.9 percent.

In the 1960s, tight labor markets and a rise in self-confidence led German employers to adopt more belligerent, strategically savvy collective bargaining tactics in order to contain wage costs in a full-employment economy. In 1963, Baden-Württemberg's metal industry employers associations, under the new aggressive leadership of Daimler-Benz personnel director Hans-Martin Schleyer, with the full support of the new hard-line head of Gesamtmetall, Herbert van Hüllen, provoked a strike in the metals industry in part to field test assertive collective bargaining tactics. Once the strike began, employers launched the first concerted lockout campaign in the postwar era. A total of 120,000 workers struck, and in response over four hundred firms locked out 250,000 employees (i.e., more than twice the number of strikers). The conflict, which lasted twelve days, ended in a settlement brokered by federal economics minister Erhard that fell far short of the union's objectives.[32] In the wake of the 1963 metal industry conflict, lockouts became the norm during industrial disputes throughout the German economy. The average number of working days lost owing to industrial actions per one thousand employees fell sharply during the 1960s in comparison to the previous decade, dropping from 67.6 to 16.1, but the share of lockouts among those days increased substantially. They accounted for 38.5 percent of all days lost owing to industrial actions, up from 7.4 percent in the previous decade (table 4.3).

The 1963 industrial action was also an opportunity for the metal industry employers associations and their national federation, Gesamtmetall, to impose even greater discipline over member firms in a tight economy, shifting the balance further within employers associations toward the logic of influence over the logic of membership. The tightening grip manifested itself most spectacularly when eighteen members of the Verband der Metallindustrie Baden-Württemberg (VMI, Association of Baden-Württemberg Metal Industry Employers) refused to comply with the VMI's request to lock out their employees. VMI responded by expelling thirteen of the eighteen transgressors from the employers association. The impact on the expelled firms was severe. They lost the right to participate in the affairs of the association, forewent the possibility of serving on tripartite quasi-governmental bodies, no longer had access to the strike-insurance fund, which left them vulnerable to strikes, and could not rely on the network of employers organizations for assistance when dealing with banks, other businesses, and government officials. Sectoral federations outside of mechanical engineering also began to shore up their defense by deepening collective bargaining policy coordination during the 1960s and early 1970s. Strong labor market conditions led some local union officials to attempt to create supplemental plant-level accords that went beyond the sectoral regionwide agreements. Employers associations responded by stiffening the punishment of companies that allowed such arrangements.[33]

The BDA, at the behest of Gesamtmetall and other member federations, expanded its disciplinary reach further during the mid-1960s. The BDA's Committee to Coordinate Wage and Collective Bargaining Policy (Ausschuss zur Koordinierung der Lohn- und Tarifpolitik) formalized a secret "taboo catalog" that spelled out in some detail forbidden collective bargaining concessions. Other sectoral federations of employers associations had already produced their own taboo catalogs. The BDA master taboo catalog, which focused on working-time and other nonwage issues, was an attempt to add coherence and consistency to the sectoral efforts.[34] Intensifying the relative emphasis on the logic of influence did *not* reduce membership of the employers associations in mechanical engineering sector members, contrary to the Schmitter and Streeck hypothesis, which I summarized at the start of this chapter.[35]

The German government added to the forces pushing wage determination in the direction of centralization when it took a decidedly Keynesian turn. In December 1966, the two center-right political parties, the Christian Democratic Union and its Bavarian sister party the Christian Social Union, formed a "grand coalition" government with the Social Democratic Party of Germany. The new economics minister, the SPD's Karl Schiller, spearheaded the enactment of legislation designed to give the government the equipment it needed to implement Keynesian demand management. The government also created a neocorporatist forum called Concerted Action for periodic consultations on economic issues among top representatives of government, business, and labor. These innovations pushed both social partners toward thinking about collective bargaining in more macroeconomic terms. Ironically, when SPD gains in the 1969 federal election enabled the party to become the senior partner in government, the Keynesian turn quickly reached its limit because the SPD formed a coalition with the laissez-faire Free Democratic Party, which was particularly allergic to Keynesianism. Concerted Action never became the influential body for serious deliberation over economic policy that the SPD and trade unions wanted. The tripartite forum quickly metamorphosed into ritualistic sessions at which labor and management representatives would read formal policy papers at each other.[36]

The BDA approved a new basic program, whose title translates as "Free Social Order Today and Tomorrow," in 1968. The document was largely a critique of Keynesianism.[37] In contrast to its predecessor, it had little resonance and was the last basic program the peak confederation ever wrote. The BDA began instead to produce shorter and more focused position papers on the big issues of the day as they arose.

Managing Militancy: Employers Associations in the 1970s

The German growth rate eased to 3.3 percent on average during the 1970s (table 4.2), but this compared favorably with Germany's major trading partners during a difficult decade. The industrial relations system was continuing to deliver largely as intended. Unemployment averaged only 2.8 percent in the 1970s. The mean annual inflation rate did accelerate to 4.9 percent, which was relatively high but still admirable given the two oil shocks of the decade. Increases in real net income were decent (i.e., 2.9% per year), but a significant gap between income and productivity growth, which averaged 4.1 percent per year, opened up for the first time. The relatively strong performance of the economy under adverse conditions led the federal government under the leadership of Helmut Schmidt (SPD) to proclaim the German economy to be a model, and the moniker stuck.

Hans-Martin Schleyer became president of the BDA in 1973. In his new position, Schleyer continued a confrontational approach, which was reminiscent of the old counterassociation model of employers associations. A *New York Times* article called Schleyer a "caricature of an ugly capitalist."[38] The BDA attacked the SPD-led government as a "trade union state" that was too beholden to the wishes of organized labor. The BDA fought tirelessly against the expansion of the welfare state, worker protections, and codetermination rights. When the SPD-FDP government expanded codetermination in 1976, the BDA unsuccessfully challenged the law in court as a violation of property rights. Still, the BDA and its affiliates remained committed to existing elements of codetermination and collective bargaining.

In 1977, BDA president Schleyer was also elected president of the peak confederation for industry associations, the Bundesverband der Deutschen Industrie (BDI, Federal Association of German Industry).[39] Talk of merging the industry and employers associations at all levels was widespread, although there was also a general awareness of how difficult such an undertaking would be. A traumatic event, which still reverberates in German politics to this day, derailed the endeavor. On 5 September 1977, the Red Army Faction (RAF) left-wing terrorist group kidnapped Schleyer as part of a larger plot to free three convicted RAF members from prison. Schleyer was an obvious target for two reasons beyond being a valuable individual for a potential prisoner exchange. First, as the head of both the BDA and the BDI, Schleyer personified German business. Kidnapping him struck a symbolic blow against capitalism. Second, Schleyer had a fascist past. In the 1930s and 1940s, he had been an active midlevel Nazi Party official and served as an officer in the Schutzstaffel (SS).

The deaths of three RAF members on 18 October 1977 in Stuttgart's Stammheim Prison (which were officially declared suicides) prompted the kidnappers to kill Schleyer a day later.[40] Schleyer's death briefly debilitated both peak business confederations and painfully demonstrated two major shortcomings of organizational centralization. It heightened the attractiveness of the organization as a target for its opponents, and it increased the risk of organizational paralysis if something were to happen to a top leader. As a result, discussion of a systemwide merger of German employers and industry associations fell from the agenda. Schleyer's successors steered the employers associations back toward an unambiguous embrace of social partnership.

A sharp change in economic conditions during the 1970s gave the leaders of employers associations greater incentive to pursue organizational innovation further. An upsurge in wage pressure resulting from the first oil shock in 1973 and 1974 prompted Gesamtmetall to establish a "negotiating circle" in 1976 in order to improve the coordination of collective bargaining among the regional employers associations in the mechanical engineering sector. The negotiating circle consisted of a small number of representatives from the largest regional associations. Its job was to serve as a brainstorming team to develop the objectives and tactics for future collective bargaining rounds.[41] Employers continued to use lockouts liberally in the 1970s, particularly during a massive wave of strikes in the early years of the decade, thus demonstrating a high degree of organizational discipline and the continuing preeminence of the logic of influence in guiding the actions of the associations. Between 1970 and 1979, the number of days lost owing to industrial action was more than three times higher than it had been in the previous decade. An average of 44.3 percent of the total number of days lost were the result of lockouts rather than strikes, which is a postwar high (table 4.3). Despite the unprecedented emphasis on the logic of influence, membership density in employers associations in the mechanical engineering and chemicals sectors remained high and steady at roughly 75 percent in terms of employment (figures 5.1 and 5.2), which again runs contrary to the expectations of Schmitter and Streeck that there is a tradeoff between recruitment and exercising the internal discipline necessary to exert external influence.

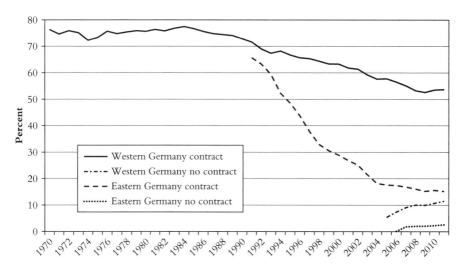

Figure 5.1. German mechanical engineering employers association (Gesamtmetall) density: Employment at member firms as a percentage of employment in mechanical engineering.
Source: Gesamtmetall and Statistisches Bundesamt.

The leaders of some employers associations did begin to have second thoughts regarding the utility of industrial conflict and started to pursue a different, more accommodationist approach toward industrial relations during the 1970s. The sectoral federation for the chemicals industry was the first to attempt to change the dynamic. Confrontation had resulted in numerous production disruptions and stoked militancy in the chemicals sector. In 1970, the BAVC produced a "social policy program" made up of positive suggestions for the future structure of industrial relations. The chemical employees union, torn by internal ideological strife, rejected the program. A year later, the militant leadership of the union provoked a strike, which it lost.[42] The failure opened the way for union moderates to seize control and to reconsider the BAVC offer. Progress was cautious at first, but by 1975, the BAVC and IG Chemie took the first step toward cooperative social partnership when they agreed to create the Unterstützungsverein der chemischen Industrie (UCI, Chemical Industry Support Association). The purpose of the UCI was to provide supplemental support for laid-off and older chemical workers.[43] The construction sector established a similar arrangement. The sectoral federations of employers associations in the clothing and textile industries also grew increasingly close to the clothing and textile employees union during the 1970s as a result of their common pursuit in Bonn and

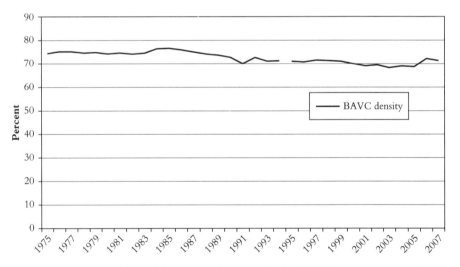

FIGURE 5.2. German chemical industry employers association (BAVC) density: Employment in member firms as a percentage of employment in chemicals and related sectors. Note: definition of employment in the rubber, plastics, and mineral oil producing sectors changed in 1995, which reduced density by 0.8 percent.
Source: BAVC and Statistisches Bundesamt.

Brussels of protectionism for their sectors.[44] Thus, by the end of the 1970s, two types of relationships between unions and employers associations had emerged: the accommodationism of the chemicals, construction, and textiles sectors and the more aggressive approach practiced by both labor and management in the mechanical engineering and printing industries.

Over the first three decades of the Federal Republic, the institutional architecture of the employers associations hardly changed. The only significant alterations were the creation of committees within many sectoral federations to help coordinate collective bargaining across regions, the consolidation of taboo catalogs at the federal and national levels, the requirement that all associations maintain strike funds, and the development of the infrastructure to support the regular use of lockouts in labor disputes. The logic of influence had reached its zenith. Collective agreements had become increasingly uniform within each sector; only a few regional variations persisted at the margins. Membership density remained high nonetheless.

Suffer the Little Ones: Tensions within Employers Associations during the 1980s

Circumstances changed sharply in the 1980s. German economic performance deteriorated. The mean annual growth rate slipped to a lackluster 1.9 percent. Productivity growth slowed by almost half when compared to the previous decade to an average of 2.1 percent per year (table 4.2). Germans suddenly found their country listed toward the bottom in most tables on economic performance. Domestic demand stalled as unemployment rose to an average of 5.2 percent and real net income per employee actually fell by 0.1 percent per year on average. Many German firms increasingly looked abroad to find new demand for their products because the domestic market was so weak. This strategy worked at first. German exports and imports combined reached the equivalent of 50 percent of GDP for the first time in 1980, and by 1985 they topped 61 percent. Business leaders and politicians loudly proclaimed that the Federal Republic was the "export world champion," even though Germany's growing current account surpluses were as much a manifestation of weak domestic demand as they were of export prowess. A soft domestic market and greater competition from both inside and outside of Europe prompted many German employers in tradable goods sectors to undertake a massive reorganization of production.

German firms began to adopt new manufacturing methods—such as "just in time" parts delivery and lean production—imported principally from Japan. The new techniques cut costs and enhanced quality but simultaneously reduced the ability of employers to resist strikes and to wage lockouts because the new practices accelerated the speed and intensity of the impact of production disruptions on the supply chain. German unions quickly began to take advantage of firms' new vulnerability by staging much smaller strikes against key suppliers. These strikes were less costly to the unions but just as devastating in their effect. Employers associations in the mechanical engineering and printing sectors used lockouts heavily in 1984 in their failed effort to stop working-time reduction below forty hours per week. Consequently, the share of days lost owing to industrial actions that were the result of lockouts during the 1980s was 44 percent, which was just as high as it was in the 1970s. Managers, however, all but abandoned lockouts after the 1984 strike because the ill will they produced within the workforce had become extremely damaging to firms.

Maintaining a balance between large enterprises and SMEs within German employers associations became increasingly difficult as centrifugal pressures intensified. Decades of collective bargaining had raised base wage rates and expanded the scope of German regionwide collective agreements, which greatly reduced the options available to small enterprises interested in economizing on labor costs. This problem became much worse after the 1984 conflict over working time. Over the next ten years, unions pressed for further weekly working-time reduction throughout the economy. Large firms were in a far better position than smaller ones to use investment and flexible work arrangements to defray the cost of shorter workweeks. As a result, the collective agreements of the late 1980s and early 1990s became far more onerous for small firms than large ones.[45] Holding the shop together became increasingly difficult for employers associations.

As competition among the major transnational corporations both inside and outside of Europe intensified, large internationally active German original equipment manufacturers, such as Daimler-Benz or Siemens, put more and more pressure on their local suppliers to cut costs and to increase quality. The OEM squeeze on suppliers in the mechanical engineering sector made it increasingly difficult to maintain a single regionwide set of collective bargaining agreements that were acceptable to both small and large firms.[46]

Beyond the matter of cost, many small and medium-sized employers were disappointed with the quality of the legal and personnel advice they received from their associations. Many complained that the associations had become "encrusted bureaucracies" that were primarily oriented toward catering to larger companies.[47] Employers association governance also arose as an issue for SMEs. The repeated use of peak-level "summits" between the heads of sectoral federations and trade unions starting in the mid-1980s in order to reach agreements regarding working-time reduction angered many in the regional employers associations because these practices cut them completely out of the decision-making process.[48] A few SME managers, mostly from the mechanical engineering sector, went one step further and began to organize in protest. For example, the Wetzlar Circle within Hessen Metall and the independent Arbeitsgemeinschaft selbstständiger Unternehmer (ASU, Working Group of Independent Entrepreneurs) formulated passionate critiques of what they called the "collective bargaining cartel."[49]

Greater numbers of managers began to question the utility of belonging to an employers association, particularly in sectors like mechanical engineering where large numbers of small and medium-sized enterprises served as suppliers for a handful of OEMs. The new, more open and integrated economic environment made bucking the system a much more viable option for SMEs, because they now had access to markets and to capital both at home and abroad that were unavailable in the 1960s and 1970s. As a result, employers association density began to drop in mechanical engineering from a peak in the mid-1980s (figure 5.1). This decline was not universal, however. Density remained stable in the chemicals industry (figure 5.2) where large firms dominated the sector and most suppliers were in other sectors, mainly raw materials.

In stark contrast to the mechanical engineering sector, social partnership was in full flower in the chemicals industry. During the 1980s, the heads of the chemical employees union and the BAVC met with increasing regularity to discuss a wide range of topics beyond routine collective bargaining. IG Chemie and the BAVC agreed to an early retirement scheme and took the revolutionary step of eliminating the century-old differences in job classification and compensation between blue- and white-collar employees.[50] The BAVC also started a process of creating "social partner agreements" with the chemicals industry trade union. These agreements are typically joint statements, although a few have been issued by just one of the collective bargaining parties. The social partnership agreements began "to shape decisively the cooperative social climate between the collective bargaining parties."[51] These agreements form the centerpiece of what is best understood as intensive social partnership between the employers association and the union. The most prominent agreements of the 1980s concerned environmental protection, equal opportunity, and vocational training. An increase in the flexibility of the regionwide collective agreement accompanied the expansion of the issues that the social partners tackled. Hence, in this case, contrary to the expectations of Schmitter and Streeck, BAVC leaders paid no price in terms of membership for expanding the influence of their federation through intensive social partnership. In fact, their efforts can actually be seen as improvements, rather than tradeoffs, that have enhanced the attractiveness of joining a chemicals industry employers association.

Two observations are important to make regarding employers associations in the Federal Republic on the cusp of unification. First, there is no evidence that German unification affected density trends. To the contrary, the decline in association density in the western mechanical engineering sector began in the *middle* of the 1980s, that is, *before* German unification. Moreover, the decline in the west has continued but never really accelerated in the years since unification (figure 5.1).[52] In the chemicals industry, density has been high and stable both before and after unification (figure 5.2). Neither trend suggests that unification had a causal impact. Second, diverging density trends in these sectors indicate that blanket explanations, such as erosion or exhaustion, are inadequate. The interplay of globalization and sectoral structure—that is, the relative importance of small firms—provides a better explanation of why density began to decline in mechanical engineering but not in the chemicals sector during leaner and more open economic times. The OEMs pressured SMEs in mechanical engineering, and the latter responded with flight out of their common associations. Integrated chemical companies responded to international market pressures by reorganizing internally and pressuring raw materials suppliers outside of the chemicals sector, which did not precipitate association flight from the chemicals industry employers associations.

Employers Associations in a United Germany

Unification could have provided a perfect pretext for a comprehensive change in the structure of employers associations. Ironically, it had the opposite effect in the early years. The leaders of Germany's business associations came out in favor of extending their organizational structure eastward without change. They also supported transferring to the east without amendment all of the laws, organizations, and institutional arrangements of the Federal Republic, including the entire industrial relations system. At the outset, they also supported the objective of achieving wage parity between eastern and western Germany as quickly as possible.[53]

Why did the western business mainstream reject institutional experimentation and suggestions to allow eastern Germany to become a low-wage region? First, the legacy of four failed political regimes on German soil during the twentieth century made most Germans hesitant to tinker with the only one that had worked. Transferring the western institutional arrangements without changing them was also consistent with the policy the German government was pursuing across the board, and the employers associations went along with it, in part to preserve their influence. Second, both collective bargaining parties anticipated that prices and taxes in eastern Germany would soon rise to western rates. Compensation could not diverge excessively in a single market without problematic results, such as mass westward migration. Third, most western employers and their associations feared that a low-wage eastern Germany could threaten the profitability of existing facilities in the west. Fourth, pushing for a deregulated and low-wage eastern Germany was politically untenable because critics would denounce the German business community as being more interested in exploiting eastern Germans than helping them.[54]

Although the arguments in favor of organizational continuity were compelling, realities, both within and beyond German unification, led this approach to fall short more often than not and to produce unintended consequences that hampered rather than helped eastern Germans to find a firm economic and political footing.

The Failed Effort to Preserve Continuity in the Face of Change: Employers Associations in the 1990s

German employers associations were especially quick to extend their institutions eastward, outpacing the unions by several months. Spreading the institutional architecture of employers associations eastward was far easier than extending the trade unions, because the employers associations were relatively small organizations and there was nothing like them in the formerly Communist German Democratic Republic (GDR). It proved far more difficult for employers associations to take root, however. Data for the eastern mechanical engineering sector show a sharp decline in density from 65.6 percent in 1991 to 18.1 percent in 2004, followed by a slow slide to 15.2 percent by 2011 (figure 5.1). Why? Density started out high because the Trust Holding Agency (Treuhandanstalt), which was a public entity that the German government created to manage all of the former GDR's assets while they were being privatized, had a policy that required firms under its management to belong to employers associations. Once the assets were sold, continuing membership in an employers association became the decision of the new owners. Many new owners let membership lapse because the collective agreements set wages well above productivity in eastern Germany during the first ten years after unification.[55] Important structural differences between east and west also help to explain the lower propensity of employers to join associations in eastern Germany. Newer and smaller firms are far less likely to belong to an employers association, and eastern Germany had a much larger share of new and small firms than western Germany.[56] This structural difference does not explain the steady *decline* in density over time, however, because the ratio of large to small firms in eastern Germany has remained relatively stable since the mid-1990s.

An important explanation for the especially fast decline in density in eastern Germany is the sudden exposure to international markets. As the Treuhandanstalt executed a rapid privatization, eastern German firms faced competition not only from western Germany but also from southern and eastern Europe and the Far East. Cutting costs wherever possible became a priority. This included dropping out of employers associations to save on membership dues and wage costs.[57] It is worth noting that, in contrast to organized labor, unification *never* gave a boost to nationwide density for employers associations in mechanical engineering (compare figures 3.2 and 5.1). Density in the mechanical engineering sector started off lower in eastern than in western Germany, and the gap simply widened over time.

A provision in German labor law regarding declarations of general applicability for collective agreements also helps account for the pattern of steady decline in collective bargaining coverage for western Germany. Article 5 of the 1949 Collective Agreements Act permits the federal government to issue a "declaration of general applicability" (*allgemeine Verbindlichkeitserklärung*, AVE; aka an *erga omnes* declaration), which is a government decree that extends the coverage of an existing collective bargaining contract to all businesses in a bargaining district of a sector, including firms that are not members of the employers association. The coverage of each declaration must be coterminous with an existing collective agreement (e.g., the mechanical engineering sector's collective agreement for Thuringia). Thus, article 5 provides the possibility of establishing a prevailing compensation floor specific to a region and sector. There are restrictions on the use of AVEs. Article 5 states that the only contracts that may be declared generally applicable are those that cover at least a majority of employees in the bargaining district for the sector in question. The labor ministry allows the use of either union membership figures or the number of employees at firms that are members of the employers association to establish whether a contract covers a majority of employees. Since the unionization rate of individual sectors and regions of the German economy has rarely ever amounted to a majority of those employed, it is typically the density of employers associations that determines whether an AVE is an option. AVEs are not automatic. An employer, employers association, or trade union must request one. The federal labor minister then decides whether to submit the request to the ministry's collective bargaining committee, which consists of three employers association and three trade union representatives. If the ministry's collective bargaining committee approves the AVE, then the labor minister may issue one.

Only a tiny fraction of contracts are ever declared to be generally applicable. Nevertheless, the possibility that it could happen made collective agreements de facto compensation floors, because employers paying below the collective bargaining rate did not deviate too far from it in order to avoid becoming the target for a union campaign to get a single-firm contract or triggering a request for an AVE. The weakness of both social partners throughout much of eastern Germany, however, all but eliminated the risk of individual firms that are not employers association members being saddled with either an AVE or a single-firm contract. As a result, eastern managers at mechanical engineering firms gradually but steadily dropped their membership in their local employers associations.[58]

Overall economic performance during the 1990s was weak (table 4.2). The economy grew slightly faster on average than in the 1980s (i.e., 2.3% per year), but growth remained too anemic to generate substantially more domestic demand or jobs. The collapse of the eastern German economy ratcheted up unemployment. Joblessness was stuck at around 15 percent in the east. Unemployment was also a problem in western Germany, particularly in the northern half of the country. Unemployment averaged 7.5 percent for Germany as a whole during the 1990s. Real productivity growth was only slightly improved versus the 1980s, averaging 2.4 percent annual growth. This performance is much worse than it appears at first glance, however. Productivity growth should have been much higher, given the numerous one-off opportunities for big productivity increases in the wake of German unification. Real net income did not grow at all during the 1990s (table 4.2).

Once the German economy began to falter in 1992 after a short-lived unification boom, dissatisfaction among the membership of employers associations in the mechanical engineering sector rose to acute levels. Eastern member firms were particularly incensed that the newly established employers associations in eastern Germany, at the advice of western employers' representatives, had signed a four-year collective agreement in early 1991 that called for eastern wages and salaries—which were at 62.6 percent and 58.5 percent of the western rates respectively—to increase in a series of steps until they reached parity with the west in April 1994. In 1993 alone, eastern wages were scheduled to rise by 26 percent. The prospect of such steep wage increases triggered a hemorrhage in the membership of Gesamtmetall's eastern affiliates.

In response, employers associations in the mechanical engineering and steel sectors shook the very foundations of the postwar German collective bargaining order by taking the unprecedented (and by most accounts illegal) step of unilaterally "cancelling" the regionwide agreements with IG Metall for eastern Germany in early 1993, two years before they were due to expire. This action, however, did *not* signal that German employers or their associations were departing from their postwar policy of acceptance of collective bargaining and social partnership. The eastern mechanical engineering employers instituted a 9 percent wage increase for 1993 and informed IG Metall officials that 1994 would be open to collective negotiation. Still, this act of brinksmanship provoked a bitter two-week strike in Brandenburg and Saxony. Saxon prime minister Kurt Biedenkopf moderated two mediation sessions that laid the groundwork for a compromise.

The eastern employers associations agreed to rescind the cancellation of the contracts and promised never to do it again. IG Metall acceded to extending the phase-in of wage parity by two years to 1996, which cost employees 2 billion deutschmarks ($1.2 billion) in foregone wages. The union also accepted the addition of a "hardship clause" to the eastern German collective agreements that permitted troubled firms to petition the collective bargaining parties to consider a reduction in wages and benefits below the contractually established minima. Only firms that could prove that they were experiencing temporary economic difficulties but were otherwise sound were eligible. Both collective bargaining parties had to approve before a hardship clause could go into effect. The hardship clause was a concession that IG Metall officials feared could undercut the viability of regionwide collective agreements. As a result, the union interpreted the qualification criteria strictly to keep its use to an absolute minimum.[59] In the late 1990s, the collective bargaining parties added a "reorganizing clause" (*Sanierungsklausel*) to the regionwide collective agreements in western Germany, but IG Metall used the same rigor to minimize the number of firms that used it in practice.[60]

Germany's economic downshift and a much more intensely competitive European and global economy made holding the shop together far more difficult for employers associations than in the 1980s. Linkages among local firms had become much less important while interconnections beyond the German market had grown much stronger. The alternative of going without association membership had become viable for many firms for the first time. The traumatic 1993 collective bargaining round and the now decade-long decline in density led the leadership of employers associations in the mechanical engineering sector to switch gears and start to place a greater emphasis on the logic of membership in an effort to staunch declining density.

Critics charged that Gesamtmetall elites miscalculated when they agreed to the multiyear eastern contract in 1991 because they had failed to consult beyond a narrow circle of managers from large enterprises. Consequently, Gesamtmetall officials took great pains to consult with many more managers, in particular those from SMEs, before developing a position for the 1994–95 collective bargaining round. Gesamtmetall leaders took what they heard and formulated a far more aggressive approach to collective bargaining. The result was a five-point opening position that included a demand to build more flexibility into the regionwide collective agreement, plus an item that was very popular among employers: the linkage of wage increases with reductions in other areas of compensation. IG Metall's initial demand, in contrast, was for a simple 6 percent wage increase.

Gesamtmetall's hard-line strategy backfired. After several months, talks reached an impasse. On February 24, a strike began in Bavaria, which was the pilot district for the round. Within a week, over 21,000 employees had walked out. On March 2, the leadership of Bayern Metall voted to respond to the strike with lockouts, but its leaders quickly discovered that they could not find any member firms willing to lock out employees. The leaders of the employers associations had thought that by listening to the militant voices from among their ranks that they were in tune with their membership. They had in fact overlooked the silent majority of managers for whom good relations with their employees were essential for business success. Bayern Metall officials were unwilling to discipline the firms that refused to participate in lockouts, as was common practice in the past, because there were simply too many and they feared accelerating flight from their organization if they tried. Five days later, the employers association capitulated to the union, granting it a two-year contract with wage increases that amounted to 4 percent for each year and no reductions in other areas.[61] The attempt to please militant members by enhancing the influence of the employers associations had failed.

The Bavarian settlement triggered a massive wave of criticism from both inside and outside the mechanical engineering sector. The presidents of the BDI and Assembly of German Chambers of Industry and Commerce denounced the settlement as excessive. Industry associations in the mechanical engineering sector publicly discussed undertaking collective bargaining on their own rather than relying on Gesamtmetall and its affiliates. Gesamtmetall threatened to dissolve itself if the IG Metall leadership refused to discuss reforms to the regionwide collective agreement. Both the president and managing director of Gesamtmetall ultimately stepped down but failed to go through with the dissolution threat when the union did not comply. At the June 1995 membership meeting, Gesamtmetall reconstituted the central negotiating committee to improve its representativeness by creating five regional negotiating groups linked to the committee. Representatives from the regional groups were more fully incorporated into the collective negotiations taking place in the pilot district than had been the case in the past.[62]

The new Gesamtmetall leadership also tried to change the larger structure and tone of collective bargaining in the wake of the 1995 Bavaria strike, but the effort failed. Gesamtmetall president and managing director Werner Stumpfe proposed a "new partnership" with IG Metall that would include working together to produce a common set of economic data upon which to base negotiations and the reduction of the cycle of high demands and low counteroffers. Stumpfe hoped that reforms would make the process of wage determination more efficient and tamp down the ritualistic aspects, such as marathon negotiating sessions and settlements only at the last possible minute, that had made membership in employers associations less attractive to newer firms. Over four years in the second half of the 1990s, Gesamtmetall also issued three "declarations" calling for decentralization of the regionwide collective agreements.[63] Gesamtmetall and IG Metall met a few times to discuss changes, but ultimately the political will on both sides proved insufficient and nothing changed.[64]

In eastern Germany, dire economic straits, plummeting membership numbers, and frustration with IG Metall's strict interpretation of the hardship clause led regional employers associations in the mechanical engineering sector to push beyond the status quo. Easterners led the way. The Verband der Metall- und Elektro-Industrie in Thüringen (VMET, Association of the Mechanical Engineering Industry in Thuringia) established the separate Allgemeiner Arbeitgeberverband Thüringen (AGVT, General Employers Association Thuringia) to provide a full range of employment-related services, but no collective bargaining, for firms both inside and outside of the mechanical engineering sector. Verband der Sächsischen Metall- und Elektroindustrie (VSME, Saxon Mechanical Engineering and Electronics Association) followed suit a year later and set up the Allgemeiner Arbeitgeberverband Sachsen (AAS, General Employers Association Saxony) modeled after the AGVT. Associations like the AGVT and AAS are commonly known as "*ohne Tarif*" (OT, "no contract") organizations. They were rare at the time but not unprecedented.[65]

There are two forms of OT. One is simply a separate type of membership within the same organization. OT members do not participate in collective bargaining. The second form of OT is the establishment of a parallel organization, like the AGVT or AAS, that does not engage in collective bargaining. Even in the latter case, typically the same managers run both organizations. The woodworking industry employers association pioneered the OT option in the late 1980s, and the textile employers association, Gesamttextil, set up an OT organization in 1993. The proponents of the OT option claim that it accomplishes several things. It keeps firms dissatisfied with a sector's collective agreement as dues paying members. In fact, some associations charge OT members higher dues because they typically require more one-on-one service to develop their personnel policies. OT proponents also maintain that the option applies pressure on unions to keep wage settlements moderate because it makes the specter of mass association flight more credible. Finally, OT supporters assert that OT attracts "never been" members; they claim that some may even join the full association if they are satisfied with the OT services and a closer look reduces their anxiety about collective agreements.[66]

The creation of the AGVT and AAS did not initially please most officials from Gesamtmetall and the other regional employers associations in the mechanical engineering sector. Most were of the view that OT associations left firms defenseless when dealing with IG Metall and feared that OT associations could undermine their own organizations if firms switched to them en masse. The tax status of OT associations has also been an issue. Employers associations receive not-for-profit tax treatment because they are engaged in collective bargaining, which courts have deemed as protected under the German constitution. Consulting on employment matters, in contrast, is simply a service and therefore taxable. Heads of employers associations have feared that dabbling with OT membership could jeopardize their organizations' tax status.[67] Despite the qualms, Gesamtmetall did not expel their eastern affiliates or demand that they liquidate their OT organizations if they wished to remain members in good standing. Gesamtmetall officials were well aware of the association flight that VMET and VSME were experiencing. The trend continued in 1996. Gesamtmetall affiliate Nordmetall, which spans both eastern and western Germany, set up an OT organization called Arbeitgeberverband Nord (AGV Nord, Employers Association North). These measures did not stop density declines, however.

The contrast between the mechanical engineering and the chemicals sectors during the 1990s could not have been starker. Social partnership in the chemicals sector was becoming stronger than ever. The chemical industry employers association, BAVC, continued creating social partnership agreements with the chemical employees union on an ever broader range of topics, including competitiveness, demographic change, and drug abuse. The social partnership agreements thereby expanded the association's logic of influence by widening the scope of concerns involving the social partners and intensifying social partnership. Starting in 1994, the BAVC and IG Chemie also began to produce a series of innovative accords containing "flexi-instruments" to provide firms with greater discretion in implementing regionwide collective agreements. These instruments are known as "opening clauses" (*Öffnungsklauseln*) because they authorize reopening the regionwide contract to add company-level side accords that permit paying less or working longer than is specified in the regionwide contract. Opening clause accords in the chemicals industry have included a weekly working-time "corridor" that can range between thirty and forty hours, a 10 percent wage cut for firms in economic distress willing to institute a firing freeze, temporarily lowering wage rates for new employees, and a "working-time bank" through which overtime hours can be saved and then later used for additional vacation time, training, or early retirement.[68]

Given all the harsh criticism of regionwide collective bargaining agreements emanating from the mechanical engineering sector, the heads of the employers associations in the chemicals sector felt obliged to make their very different perspective on the subject heard. In 1996, the BAVC and its thirteen regional associations issued a document called the Rheingau Declaration, which explicitly stated their unwavering commitment to the use of regionwide collective agreements: "There is no general crisis of the region-wide collective agreement in Germany. . . . BAVC and IG Chemie have as federal collective bargaining parties repeatedly declared their support for the regionwide collective agreement and its further development. . . . No-contract employers associations are no model for the chemical industry. Such 'OT-associations' are weak employers associations and the result of unsuccessful collective bargaining policy."[69] The not-so-veiled swipe at the competence of the collective bargaining parties in the mechanical engineering sector at the end of the quotation tells only part of the story. The structural difference between the sectors is a far more powerful explanation for the divergence in density trends than policy errors.

The membership trends in the two sectors continued to move in different directions during the 1990s. Despite considerable efforts to accommodate members, association density in the western German mechanical engineering sector in terms of employment fell by just under ten percentage points from 72.9 percent in 1990 to 63.3 percent in 1999 (figure 5.1). Density in the eastern German metals sector plummeted from 65.7 percent in 1991 to 30.6 percent by the end of the decade, which was well below the minimum share needed to apply to the government for a declaration of general applicability. In contrast, the collective bargaining parties in the chemicals industry had made the collective agreements more flexible, but they had also strengthened the logic of influence in the sector through social partnership agreements. Density in the chemicals industry remained stable at between 71 and 73 percent during the 1990s (figure 5.2). These trends again run counter to the assertion of Schmitter and Streeck that there is a tradeoff between internal organizational discipline and membership density.

Industrial conflict declined significantly in the 1990s (table 4.3). Mean annual days lost owing to industrial actions per one thousand employees fell by over one half to 13.1, which was lower than in any previous decade in the postwar era. The bulk of the decline was a result of the disappearance of the lockout. Lockouts as a share of total days lost to industrial conflict fell from 44.2 percent in the previous decade to an astounding 0.1 percent. The refusal of rank-and-file employers to use the tactic because it was so disruptive to harmonious workplace relations accounts for the sudden abandonment of what had been for decades the principal weapon of employers associations in industrial disputes.

Other employers associations besides the mechanical engineering sector came under stress during the 1990s. The construction sector experienced a sharp boom-and-bust cycle as a result of German unification. Structurally, the German construction sector resembles mechanical engineering much more than the chemicals industry. Most enterprises are small, but there are a handful of large firms. Large firms routinely hire small ones as subcontractors, much like the OEM-SME relationship in mechanical engineering. There is one significant difference between the two sectors that is salient here. The construction sector is far less exposed to international competition than mechanical engineering. As a result, a brief analysis of employers associations in the sector will provide additional evidence regarding the significance of firm size and interrelationships in determining the unity and density of employers associations while controlling for international exposure.

The gulf between these two types of construction firms is so great that the sector has two independent associations, the Hauptverband der Deutschen Bauindustrie (HDB, Main Association of the German Construction Industry), which concentrates on the larger firms, and the Zentralverband Deutsches Baugewerbe (ZDB, Central Association of the German Construction Trade), which focuses on smaller enterprises. Still, for decades, the two employers associations had bargained jointly with Industriegewerkschaft Bauen-Agrar-Umwelt (IG BAU, Construction, Agriculture, and Environment Employees Industrial Union) to produce a federal framework agreement that regional employers associations in the sector had routinely adopted with few changes. A big difference between the mechanical engineering and construction sectors is the long history of cooperative industrial relations in the latter. Strikes had been a rarity.[70] This changed when the bottom fell out of the eastern German construction market once the unification boom ended in the mid-1990s. In 1997, the Fachgemeinschaft Bau Berlin und Brandenburg (FBBB, Trade Group Construction Berlin and Brandenburg), which had been the local employers association for both the HDB and ZDB, cut its ties with the two established sectoral federations in order to negotiate a cheaper collective bargaining contract than the federal framework agreement.[71]

The leadership of IG BAU tried to draw a line. They rejected the FBBB's demands as a threat to postwar practice and called a strike vote for late June. The strike commenced on June 30, but it did not bring the FBBB to heel. It instead caused the regional construction associations in Mecklenburg–West Pomerania and Thuringia to break away as well to form an independent employers association for small construction firms in eastern Germany. IG BAU reached a new agreement for eastern Germany with the HDB and ZDB to put pressure on the FBBB to accept the federal framework agreement, but to no avail. The strike dragged into September. IG BAU took two lines of attack against the FBBB. It signed agreements with individual Berlin firms, and it attempted to get the labor courts to declare the FBBB ineligible to negotiate as a collective bargaining party. Both steps proved inadequate. The breakaway eastern employers associations established a rival confederation that is now called the Zweckverbund Ostdeutscher Bauverbände (ZVOB, Eastern German Construction Associations Cooperative).[72] The eastern German construction sector illustrates the salience of size as a variable affecting the dynamics of employers associations. Employers associations in sectors with large numbers of small supplier and subcontractor firms are particularly susceptible to flight or to fragmentation (which is flight in an organized form) during lean economic times.

Which case is most indicative of the general trend of employers association density, chemicals or mechanical engineering and construction? There is no direct measure, but the federal employment agency's calculation of the percentage of employees covered by regionwide collective bargaining agreements can serve as a good indirect estimate of employers association density for the whole economy, because contract coverage is almost exclusively a function of association membership. This data series, which begins in the mid-1990s, indicates that flight from employers associations was actually worse in western Germany as a whole than in the western mechanical engineering sector. In 1995, regionwide collective agreements covered 72.2 percent of all employees in western Germany, but by 2000, this had fallen by 9.2 percentage points to 63 percent (figure 4.4). Density in the western mechanical engineering sector fell by only 3.4 percentage points over the same period (figure 5.1). The slide was bigger for the eastern economy as a whole when compared to the west. Coverage dropped by 12.2 percentage points from 56.2 percent to 44 percent. In contrast to the west, density in the eastern mechanical engineering fell the farthest (i.e., by 14.5 percentage points). These data show that association flight was the dominant trend. The chemicals sector makes clear, however, that the trend was not universal.

Divergence and Experimentation: Employers Associations in the First Decade of the Twenty-first Century

German economic performance was abysmal during the first decade of the twenty-first century. Real GDP grew at an annual average rate of only 0.9 percent (table 4.2). To be sure, the global financial crisis, which began in the fall of 2008, reduced the average growth rate for the decade somewhat. Still, growth for the years before the financial crisis was also anemic. Between 2000 and 2008, the German economy expanded on average by only 1.5 percent each year. Productivity growth slowed to a mean annual increase of just 1.1 percent between 2000 and 2009. Domestic demand dwindled as real net income *fell* on average by 0.4 percent *per year*, and mean unemployment was 8.5 percent, which was a full percentage point higher than in the 1990s. The employment picture did begin to improve in the latter half of the decade, but joblessness had only receded to 7.3 percent for Germany as a whole in 2008 before climbing back to 7.9 percent in 2009. The poor economy was not conducive to industrial action. The number of days lost per one thousand employees fell to a postwar record low of 4.9. Lockouts remained extremely rare (table 4.3).

The employers associations in the chemicals and mechanical engineering sectors continued to move in opposite directions. The BAVC and the chemical employees union expanded the relative importance of the logic of influence in the sector by qualitatively deepening their cooperative efforts. By October 2007, the BAVC and the chemical employees union had completed forty social partnership agreements. Each social partnership agreement further limited the discretion of the membership, but intensified social partnership by addressing significant problems member firms faced. The social partners decided to take things to a grander scale for the forty-first agreement. The two parties worked with the Wittenberg Center for Global Ethics to draft the first joint code of ethics for a sector. In an exercise dubbed "the Wittenberg process," the BAVC and the chemical employees union held a series of workshops to develop a code that focused on five themes: entrepreneurial success, ecological sustainability, mutual respect in the workplace, fair trade, and effective development of human capital. On 14 August 2008, the BAVC and the chemical employees union held an elaborate signing ceremony for the ethics code that included a speech by German president Horst Köhler. The social partners have used the document, which is entitled "Exercising Responsibility in the Social Market Economy," as the foundation for a series of workplace dialogs to ensure that employees in the chemical industry integrate the code's contents into their actions at work. They also envision establishing a social partner training academy to inculcate the ethics spelled out in the code. The underlying purpose of the whole project is to educate the newest generation of chemicals industry managers about the benefits of social partnership so as to ensure that intensive social partnership continues to flourish.[73]

Collective bargaining continued to function smoothly in the chemicals sector, and both employers association and union officials maintained their explicit support for regionwide collective agreements. Despite the intensification of the logic of influence through the social partnership agreements, membership in the associations with collective bargaining remained high. In 2007, density in terms of employment was 72.2 percent, which was two percentage points higher than in 2000.

The landscape changed much more dramatically during the 2000s for employers associations in the mechanical engineering sector. Employers associations doubled down on the logic of membership. The focus turned to providing firms with greater flexibility regarding employment conditions and labor costs, even if that weakens the relative authority of Gesamtmetall and the regional engineering employers associations themselves vis-à-vis the member firms. The employers associations pursued this objective on two fronts: reforming regionwide collective agreements and creating parallel OT associations.

The collective bargaining parties made three substantial changes to regionwide agreements in the mechanical engineering sector during the 2000s. They adopted a unitary compensation framework agreement, broader language for opening clauses, and working-time accounts. A unitary compensation framework agreement eliminated the distinctions in compensation for white-collar and blue-collar employees in mechanical engineering. Traditionally, white-collar employees received a monthly salary whereas blue-collar workers were paid either by the hour or the piece. White-collar employees typically had higher incomes. Since the 1980s, the distinction between much blue-collar and white-collar work on shop floors had collapsed, as introduction of microprocessors revolutionized production. The class distinctions reflected in the old divided compensation frameworks had also long since attenuated. Both labor and management agreed that moving to a unitary framework for compensation would be a step forward because it would greatly simplify calculating payrolls and provide greater fairness by ensuring that employees doing essentially the same task and subject to the same physical stress would be paid at the same rate. The chemicals sector had made this transition already in the 1980s. There was consensus on the essentials in mechanical engineering, but completing the agreement took more than a decade.[74]

Talks to produce this new *Entgeltrahmentarifvertrag* (ERA, compensation framework agreement) began in the early1990s. The parties lost several years experimenting with "process-oriented" forms of bargaining that involved numerous meetings at multiple levels but failed to produce viable contract language. When IG Metall vice-chair Walter Riester left to become federal labor minister in September 1998, the process stalled. Talks resumed in the fall of 2000. The logistics of a transition posed concerns, but cost remained the principal hurdle. Employers were concerned that IG Metall would attempt a backdoor increase in compensation through the process. White-collar employees worried that their salaries would be reduced to blue-collar levels to make ERA affordable. The collective bargaining parties agreed to a framework in 2002 and finally reached a mutually acceptable compromise on the details in June 2003. They phased in ERA over three years. ERA sets a baseline salary for each job using a point system with five criteria: knowledge and skill, independent decision making, scope of duties, communication requirements, and supervision. Employees in demanding or dangerous jobs receive a premium. Employees also receive performance-based salary increases. The collective bargaining parties hoped that ERA would make regionwide collective agreements in the mechanical engineering sector more attractive to firms by providing a simpler compensation system geared to the concerns of contemporary employers.[75]

A second reform to the regionwide agreements in the mechanical engineering sector followed less than a year later. It has been by far the most significant. In a side agreement of the 2004 collective bargaining settlement, the collective bargaining parties assented to a "controlled decentralization" of regionwide collective agreements through a broader use of opening clauses.

The accord is called the Pforzheim agreement because that is the name of the town where the final negotiations took place. The Pforzheim agreement permits an employer to implement a temporary reduction in compensation below the minima set in a regionwide collective agreement if such steps can be shown to preserve or create employment or to boost competitiveness at the firm. In order to qualify for an exception, managers must present their plan and their firm's books to representatives from both the employers association and the union. The collective bargaining parties must approve a plan before an employer can implement it.

IG Metall officials had resisted this sort of reform for years. They only became more accommodating after Chancellor Schröder threatened publicly to pass legislation to decentralize collective bargaining if labor and management failed to do it on their own.

Employer complaints about the size of the 2004 wage settlement all but drowned out mention of the Pforzheim agreement in the media when it was signed, yet within a year, several hundred firms began to use it.[76] The Pforzheim agreement quickly began to receive widespread praise from both labor and management as a "preventative opening clause" that permits preemptive action to secure employment and competitiveness.[77] The Pforzheim agreement has also expanded the relationship between an employers association and member firms that use it beyond that of principal and agent in collective negotiations to that of client and consultant, which has benefitted the association.[78]

The bargaining parties reformed the structure of regionwide collective agreements in the mechanical engineering sector for a third time in as many years in 2005 by adding working-time accounts as an option available to firms and their employees. These accounts permit employees to bank overtime hours and use them later for additional vacation time, vocational training, or even early retirement. No prior approval from the collective bargaining parties is necessary to introduce working-time accounts.[79]

On the one hand, the three big changes to the regionwide agreements in the mechanical engineering sector during the mid-2000s—the new unitary compensation framework agreement, the Pforzheim agreement liberalizing contract derogations, and the addition of working-time accounts—were momentous and have proven their worth. All three are widely accepted and used. They have made regionwide agreements in the mechanical engineering sector much more flexible.[80] On the other hand, these changes merely brought the mechanical engineering sector up to the point that the social partners had reached in the chemical industry a decade earlier. During these same years, however, mechanical engineering employers moved in the opposite direction of the BAVC in terms of association influence. While the BAVC and its affiliates were intensifying association influence by expanding social partnership agreements with IG BCE, the employers associations in the mechanical engineering sector were ratcheting down influence by expanding the OT option.

In the early 2000s, a debate raged within Gesamtmetall over OT membership. Supporters argued that OT membership was beneficial because it constrains labor's wage demands by making association flight easier in the wake of large settlements. They added that the end result would actually be to preserve the associations with collective bargaining. OT opponents countered that OT would lead to higher settlements, because employers would sort themselves out according to their ability to pay. Smaller, more economically tenuous firms would disproportionately prefer OT membership; whereas the larger and economically stronger enterprises would stay in the traditional associations. The union would take advantage of this self-sorting by being more aggressive at the bargaining table.[81]

Ultimately, facts on the ground settled the policy debate. By 2004, every employers association in the mechanical engineering sector had either created an OT association or permitted OT membership. Gesamtmetall officials, anxious to preclude the emergence of a rival confederation of OT associations, as had happened in the eastern German construction sector, asked for a special membership meeting in January 2005. At the meeting, Gesamtmetall's affiliates unanimously approved a change to the sectoral federation's statutes that would permit OT associations also to become Gesamtmetall affiliates.[82] Eight OT associations then joined. By the end of 2005, these associations in western Germany had over 1,400 members that employed over 160,000 (i.e., 5.4% of total employment in the western mechanical engineering sector). The numbers were smaller in eastern Germany (figure 5.1).

The Bundesarbeitsgericht (BAG, Federal Labor Court) brought greater certainty and clarity to the use of the OT option through a 2006 ruling. The court ruled that nothing in the Collective Agreements Act forbids individual employers associations from offering both traditional and OT memberships. It added, however, that firms switching from traditional to OT membership may no longer participate in association discussions about collective bargaining policy and still must adhere to the traditional association's agreements that were completed while they were full members, even after they left, until new agreements superseding the old ones came into force. The court has subsequently reaffirmed the latter ruling several times.[83] There has been no decision, however, on the tax status of OT associations and mixed associations with mostly OT members.[84]

Beyond the realm of collective bargaining, German enterprises and employers associations were cautious participants in the ill-fated Alliance for Jobs discussions (see chapter 4). Employers and their associations were also supportive of Gerhard Schröder's Hartz and Agenda 2010 reforms to liberalize the German labor market, but they successfully avoided making their support an issue. They also deftly managed to back the reforms without it being seen as support for the Social Democratic chancellor.[85] In the mid-2000s, employers and their associations engaged in an intensive but ultimately unsuccessful effort to pare back codetermination rights (see chapter 2) and continued lobbying on a wide range of topics.

Gesamtmetall broke new ground in 2000 when it provided the financial support for Initiative Neue Soziale Marktwirtschaft (INSM, New Social Market Economy Initiative). INSM is an effort to expand employers' "soft power" in society. The surprising aspect of INSM is not its purpose, which is to promote promarket reforms, but rather its conceptualization and implementation. Gesamtmetall turned over the task of creating INSM to the Berlin political communications firm Scholz & Friends. As a result, INSM has the look and feel of a contemporary public relations shop. INSM produces materials designed for the media. These include "testimonials" by prominent "ambassadors" from the business world, instant "professor panels" on salient topics, issue briefs by well-known experts that can be used to fill out stories, and rankings of a myriad of things, including cities, regions, universities, and conditions for startup enterprises. INSM has proved quite successful in placing stories and is active in social media.[86] Gesamtmetall has maintained an arm's-length relationship with INSM, which has bolstered the latter's credibility. Gesamtmetall just pays the bills, which come to a little over €8 million per year. This relationship is likely to remain unchanged so long as INSM is effective.

Still, a decade of innovation to make employers associations in the mechanical engineering sector more attractive to members had no impact on the pace of density decline, but the addition of OT membership makes the picture somewhat more complex. Between 2000 and 2009, density for the traditional associations in terms of employment dropped faster than ever. It fell by more than 10 percentage points from 63.3 percent to 52.6 percent in western Germany before rebounding slightly to 53.7 percent in 2011 (figure 5.1). On the other side of the coin, by 2011, OT membership in western Germany had risen to 11.5 percent, which more than made up for the density decline in the traditional associations between 2000 and 2011. It is unclear whether OT membership accelerated the density decline in the traditional sector, kept firms as dues paying members that otherwise would have left altogether, or had no effect. Yet, by 2011, even the density of traditional and OT members in the mechanical engineering sector combined was almost 10 percentage points lower than density in the chemicals industry. Developments in the eastern mechanical engineering industry, in contrast, were unambiguously negative. Density fell by 13.7 percentage points from 28.9 percent in 2000 to 15.2 percent in 2009 and stayed flat through 2011. The drop was not as steep as it had been in the 1990s, but this may because 15 percent is the de facto bottom, given that it is the policy of most large German OEMs to join the regional employers association wherever they have operations. Eastern OT membership in 2011 amounted to only 2.6 percent of the total eastern labor force in the sector. Hence OT membership fell well short of making up for the decline in the traditional associations in eastern Germany. More deeply embracing the logic of membership—that is, reforms that enhance discretion for members even at the expense of organizational discipline—did not yield more members in the mechanical engineering sector, which runs counter to the expectations of Schmitter and Streeck of a tradeoff between membership retention and external influence.

In contrast to mechanical engineering, the proxy measure of employers association density for the entire Germany economy (i.e., the federal employment agency's measure of the percentage of employees covered by regionwide collective agreements) indicates a deceleration of association flight (figure 4.4). Between 2000 and 2011, coverage in western Germany fell by 9 percentage points (i.e., from 63 to 54%). This is a much slower pace of decline than the 9.2 percent drop over just five years in the latter half of the 1990s. Coverage in eastern Germany declined by 6 percentage points (i.e., from 44 to 37%), which is also a much slower pace than the 12.2 percentage-point fall between 1996 and 2000. These data add to the evidence that the structure of a sector is the primary determinant of the degree of association flight. The big expansion of the flexibility of regionwide collective bargaining agreements in the mechanical engineering sector had no discernible effect on employers association membership; the declines in the sector were worse than those in the economy as a whole.

The primacy of the structure of a sector as an independent variable for explaining employers association density is also apparent for the public sector. The public sector is relatively large (i.e., 2.4 million employees) and has a relatively small number of large employers (i.e., the federal, state, and local governments) that employ an overwhelming share of the workforce. The public sector, moreover, is virtually immune to foreign competition. Given the structural characteristics of the public sector, one would expect density in the public sector to be high, and it is. The discussion of public-sector collective bargaining in chapter 4 showed that employers association bargaining had been highly centralized and every government had been involved until the 1990s when Berlin dropped out because of its bankruptcy. Public-sector collective bargaining fragmented briefly in the mid-2000s when several state governments pulled out of the joint negotiating structure but, like the chemicals industry, there has been no association flight in the public sector.[87]

The 2008 global financial crisis precipitated a deepening of cooperation among employers associations, firms, trade unions, and works councils. Strikes all but disappeared. The social partners exchanged wage moderation for employment guarantees. Business and labor in the mechanical engineering sector lobbied successfully for a "cash for clunkers" program to stimulate automobile sales. All of the social partners in the private sector pushed for the expansion of the short-time work program (*Kurzarbeit*), designed to preserve employment through the government topping up the incomes of employees working half-time by 20 to 30 percent. This approach permitted firms to retain their skilled employees—many of whom have company-specific skills—during the financial crisis and thereby avoid the transaction costs of finding and retraining new employees once the crisis ended. These are the same firms that tend to be members of the traditional employers associations. Short-time work combined with a handful of other active employment measures proved effective in containing unemployment. Germany has also benefitted through its exports of producer goods more than any other European country from the relatively strong economic performance of China, India, and Brazil in the wake of the financial crisis. The euro crisis has, if anything, further fortified cooperation among the social partners.[88]

The Effects of Industry Structure and Trade Exposure on Employers Association Density

Developments on the employers' side of postwar German industrial relations are far more heterogeneous than previous studies have registered. Some sectors exhibit substantial declines in employers association density (e.g., construction and mechanical engineering), but others have maintained stability (e.g., chemicals and the public sector). The structural articulation of firms within a sector is the single most important factor determining whether employers associations will thrive or fail. Sectors with relatively large numbers of small firms where intrasectoral contractor-subcontractor relationships predominate are much more likely to suffer from association flight than sectors in which large integrated employers predominate and suppliers are mostly in other sectors. Stable density in the internationally active chemicals industry combined with the extreme difficulties with association flight in the construction sector, which is largely sheltered from foreign competition, stand as evidence consistent with the suggestion that intraindustry structure is a powerful determinant of association flight whereas exposure to international competition is not.

Developments for employers moved in a decidedly different direction than those for either the legal and state framework or the trade unions. The consensus politics of postwar Germany not only protected labor law and the state, but it also allowed for periodic reforms to shore them up. Sociological change (i.e., the deterioration of labor's milieu) undercut union density. Economic change hit employers associations most forcefully, but it played out differently in each sector, depending on its internal structure.

The evidence in this chapter calls into question the theoretical speculation of Schmitter and Streeck regarding a tradeoff between the logics of membership and influence. When the relative emphasis within employers associations shifted between catering to member wishes for greater discretion and enhancing external leverage through tightening organizational discipline over members, which happened at several points during the postwar years in the chemicals and mechanical engineering sectors, membership density rarely moved in the direction that Schmitter and Streeck predicted.

Research on employers associations unfortunately remains underdeveloped. Future efforts investigating employers associations in additional sectors would be extraordinarily helpful because they would test the robustness of these findings and perhaps suggest additional mechanisms for understanding patterns of employers association structure and density.

Conclusion

Integrating the Pieces and Looking toward the Future

The five substantive chapters in this book have covered a great deal of ground, much of it in considerable detail. The purpose of the conclusion is to take a step back from the trees to look at the forest that is postwar German industrial relations. I do so in three ways. First, I integrate the results of the previous chapters into a comprehensive picture of German industrial relations. Second, I compare the German industrial relations system to the systems of three major economies. Third, I consider the future of German industrial relations.

A Comprehensive View of German Industrial Relations

The German industrial relations system has two components: the framework and the actors. The framework consists of the law and the state. The principal actors are the trade unions and the employers associations. It is useful at the outset of this conclusion to summarize what we have learned about these components from the five previous chapters.

German labor law and the state have proved to be remarkably resilient throughout the postwar years. They effectively provide a framework that integrates the actors constructively into the economy. Collective agreements are responsible in economic terms (i.e., they do not generate higher inflation or unemployment) and set the tone for compensation in the economy as a whole. Industrial action is rare. When it occurs, it typically settles disputes quickly and without inflicting permanent damage on the economy. The law does not favor one side over the other. Labor courts remain effective. Codetermination legislation facilitates peaceful and productive exchanges between managers and their employees in the workplace and the boardroom. Codetermination has its critics, but it retains widespread support in German society. Codetermination and collective bargaining complement each other.

The industrial relations framework has remained effective and relevant. It has stood up well to threats and tumult, including German unification and European integration. The law and the state have not been static. They have been renewed and revitalized several times over the past six decades. The aim of virtually every reform has been to maintain or to enhance the strength and integrity of the regime.

Why has the postwar framework of laws and the state proved to be so resilient? First, the chastening legacy of the Nazi era has served as a powerful moderating force to this day. Second, organized labor and management understand themselves to be social partners in a "conflictual partnership" rather than enemies. The postwar concept of social partnership has so thoroughly entwined both labor and management within the postwar industrial relations regime that acting to disrupt or to destroy it would have costs greater than benefits for most. Third, unitary and nonpartisan trade unionism has proved effective in convincing the political parties— in particular, the catch-all Christian Democratic and Social Democratic parties—that the postwar German industrial relations regime is beneficial to their interests.

To return to a metaphor from the first two chapters, the framework of the postwar German industrial relations system has proved to be a sturdy trestle. This framework shows no signs of exhaustion. The law, the labor courts, and the institutions of codetermination are stable and still function well. When threats of erosion have arisen, policymakers have intervened to shore things up (e.g., the numerous reforms to codetermination). To be sure, collective bargaining coverage has waned, but it is not because of shortcomings in the law or the state. It is because of declines in the membership of the social partners, which have deeper root causes.

Employers associations and the trade unions had several impressive decades immediately following the Second World War, but of late most have not fared nearly as well as the industrial relations framework. The reasons differ from actor to actor, however. Trade union density plateaued in the 1980s and then dropped precipitously, starting in the 1990s. Trade unions have suffered largely because of the deterioration of the labor milieu as a result of a trend in German society away from collectivism and toward individualization. In other words, sociological change has played the most powerful role in organized labor's decline.

A previously unrecognized economic factor—trade measured as a share of Germany's gross domestic product—has been shown to be *positively* correlated with trade union density. This finding makes intuitive sense because Germany's export-oriented sectors are also where German trade unions are the strongest, but it runs counter to the conventional wisdom found in the literatures on trade unions and globalization. The positive impact of increased trade on unionization was too small, however, to counterbalance the negative effect of the deterioration of the labor milieu.

German labor leaders seized on two successive responses to declining trade union density. The first was a series of mergers from the mid-1990s to the early 2000s, whose collective impact is best understood as the creation of a second postwar trade union movement. The leitmotif of the first postwar movement was industrial unionism. Multisectoral unionism is the hallmark of the second. The transition from industrial to multisectoral unionism within the space of a decade restored organizational stability to the trade union movement, but it did not staunch density declines. In fact, it left the new unions more vulnerable than ever to competition from small occupational unions, particularly those that organize skilled employees at key choke points in the economy. Whether occupational unions are simply a passing byproduct of the transition from the first to the second postwar trade union movement or the harbingers of a third far more decentralized movement remains to be seen. Most evidence points to the former situation, but the latter prospect should not be dismissed out of hand.

The second response to continuing density declines began in the late 2000s. It has been an embrace of a North American import—social movement unionism—in a bid to reinvigorate the sociological foundation of German trade unionism. I have suggested that the labor leaders pursuing this second response are on the right track because the erosion of the labor milieu was the principal source of density decline. The metalworkers union has been at the forefront here, and its efforts have yielded some promising preliminary results. Still, it is too soon to tell whether this strategy, which was born in the highly decentralized and confrontational environment of North American industrial relations, will succeed in a coordinated economy marked by social partnership. So far, only the metalworkers union has produced a credible approach to reversing membership decline. Ver.di's failure to thrive in the crucial services sector is a significant setback for German labor. The chemical workers union's longstanding embrace of intensive social partnership has enabled the union to extend its influence within its sector further than any other union, but this strategy has not helped slow membership loss. Despite the considerable resources and savvy of IG Metall, it would simply be too much to expect it to reverse singlehandedly the deterioration of Germany's labor milieu. Yet it is hard to imagine a successful reinvigoration of organized labor in the Federal Republic without a revitalization of that milieu.

The story of the German employers associations is more complex. Employers associations are more structurally important than trade unions in postwar German industrial relations because they have the higher density in terms of employment. Consequently, the robustness of employers associations determines collective bargaining coverage in the economy. The dynamics of these associations differ from those of the trade unions because they are organizations of firms, not of individuals. Intensified economic competition is part of the story here, but it plays out differently in different sectors, depending on the configuration of each individual sector.

Mechanical engineering and construction have a relatively large number of small firms that have dense vertical linkages within the same sector with a small number of large firms. Intensified competition, which can have either foreign or domestic origins, has led large firms to pressure their smaller suppliers to cut costs. Many small suppliers have responded by quitting their employers associations to save on compensation costs. Employers association density has fallen as a result. The picture is quite different in the chemicals industry. Large capital-intensive firms predominate. Labor cost has been a far less salient issue. As a result, the employers associations in that sector have managed to preserve membership density. Does decline or stability predominate among German employers associations? Evidence suggests that it is the former. Between the mid-1990s and the present, private-sector collective bargaining coverage fell from roughly 80 percent to 60 percent in western Germany, and it slipped from 70 percent to 50 percent in eastern Germany. Adding in the public sector, which is heavily unionized, brightens the picture somewhat. It raises the coverage levels for the entire economy in both the east and the west by approximately five percentage points. Summarizing the situation, regionwide sectoral collective agreements still set compensation for a majority of German employees, but they are not as hegemonic as they once were.

Over the past two decades, the leaders of many employers associations have not stood idly by. To preserve membership levels, they developed new types of membership that typically do not include collective bargaining. They have also pushed to make collective bargaining agreements more flexible through the insertion of opening clauses. These strategies for organizational survival may have merit, but they do risk undercutting the coverage and power of collective agreements.

What is the relationship between the framework and the actors? To carry the analogy of the trestle a bit further, if the framework is the trestle, the actors could be seen as vines on the trestle. Most of the vines have grown weaker over the past three decades. The solid support of the trestle has been instrumental in keeping the vines alive, but they have become thinner and are producing less fruit in terms of members, as the soil (i.e., the labor milieu for the unions and the economy for employers associations) has become weaker. No matter how sturdy the trestle, the fate of the vines ultimately depends on that soil.

No conclusion on any postwar German theme would be complete without an assessment of the impact of German unification. Each of the previous chapters has addressed aspects of German unification, appropriate to its focus, in some detail. The data viewed as a whole present a complex picture of both continuity and rupture in the wake of German unification. On the one hand, unification has had a surprisingly small impact on membership trends for both employers associations and unions. The decline in employers association density for the mechanical engineering sector began before unification and did not noticeably accelerate in the years immediately following it. Density in the chemicals sector for Germany as a whole has remained remarkably unchanged both before and after unification. We have seen through quantitative analysis that unification actually gave trade union density a positive boost for about a decade.

The qualitative narratives present a somewhat different picture of German unification. The impact of German unification looms large. Organized labor's budgetary travails that precipitated the organizational transition from the first to the second postwar trade union movement were largely the product of German unification. "Without contract" membership and opening clauses did not originate in eastern Germany, but eastern conditions stimulated their development. Issues related to unification occupied a good share of the time of union leaders, employers association officials, and policymakers.

It is noteworthy that the quantitative "forest" shows continuity in spite of German unification, whereas the qualitative "trees" exhibit rupture.

One potential explanation for the disparity between the quantitative and qualitative accounts is the way the size disparity between eastern and western Germany plays out in these two forms of evidence. Western Germany is simply much bigger than eastern Germany. Western Germany had 80 percent of the population and produced 90 percent of the GDP at the time of unification. Continuity should therefore not be too surprising in assessments relying on quantitative indicators at a national scale. A second explanation is that the two forms of data capture different things. The quantitative evidence reflects membership developments, whereas the qualitative narratives are more about organizational structure and policy choices. Moreover, anecdotes and experiences play a prominent role in shaping the understandings of individuals, and German unification produced plenty of disruptive experiences. Policymakers and the media also understandably focus on the new and the problematic, which can make their relative importance appear larger than they actually are. Finally, eastern Germany served as an incubator for many of the collective bargaining parties' recent policy innovations largely because there was no entrenched status quo there and the economic conditions were much more dire. So, much that is new emanated from there.

Despite the increased difficulties of the collective bargaining parties in recent decades, the 2008 global financial crisis demonstrated that the postwar system of German industrial relations can respond effectively in an emergency. Employers, employers associations, unions, works councils, and the state pulled together to develop and to implement an effective set of programs to combat unemployment, the most prominent of which was the expansion of short-time work. Trade unions and employers associations supplemented short-time work with exchanges of wage-and-benefit concessions for employment guarantees. Works councillors cooperated closely with managers and local trade unionists to implement the new measures. As a result, Germany's success in containing unemployment stood out among affluent countries. Germany was once again a model.

In summary, the postwar German industrial relations system has continued to perform largely as intended. Regionwide sectoral contracts still set the direction for compensation developments for the larger economy. The industrial relations framework has remained sturdy over the years, but the regime is less encompassing now than it was three decades earlier because many employers associations and most unions have become weaker, albeit for different reasons.

For well over a century, German business has relied on coordination for success. Before the Second World War, coordination came in the form of cartels that managed production and excluded labor. The cartels were discarded in the postwar years in favor of more inclusive forms of coordination, such as social partnership in industrial relations. Social partnership has helped German firms to become some of the most successful in the world and German employees to rank among the most affluent. It has also been a crucial component of the political success of the Federal Republic. Social partnership made possible the deliberation, coordination, and shared sacrifice that helped Germany to weather the global financial crisis better than any other high-income country. Declines in union and employer association density give pause, because these organizations are the key interlocutors that have made effective coordination possible in the postwar years, which has been crucial to Germany's economic success.

One-word summations of trends for large and complex social formations like the German industrial relations system can have merit when they hit the mark because they provide simplicity and focus, but, given the facts presented in the past five chapters, it would be a mistake to attempt to do that here. The evidence shows that the components of German industrial relations are moving in different directions with different dynamics for different reasons. Actors across the German political spectrum still solidly support the framework, but sociological developments challenge organized labor. The mix of large and small firms and the interconnections among them at the sectoral level have a big impact on the success of employers associations in retaining members. In brief, German industrial relations' components have their own dynamic and direction. It is unlikely that the framework and the actors will all fall down, or all stay standing. It will not play out that way. Other countries contain complexities, too. It is helpful, therefore, to look beyond Germany for a moment to get a sense of how things might unfold.

A Brief Cross-National Comparison

This exercise of integrating the analyses of the components of German industrial relations into a whole has revealed that the key features to watch are the continued resilience of the framework, divergent developments among the employers associations, and union reform efforts. It has also made clear the importance of gaining a sense of where the limits and tipping points lie for the most salient trends. A helpful way to pursue this inquiry further is to compare German industrial relations to those in three other relatively large affluent countries, namely, France, Japan, and the United States. These three countries are pertinent because each is much further along than Germany in the unfolding of at least one trend that is of interest here.

French trade unionism is characterized by a very low union density and a continuing legacy of heavy reliance on the state for material support and legislation. Estimates place current French union density at 7 percent, which is well below half of the German rate. Nonetheless, 90 percent of French employees are covered by collective agreements because French law mandates that medium and large enterprises hold annual negotiations regarding compensation with union representatives at the company level, and the French state has broad powers to extend collective agreements to cover entire sectors at the request of one collective bargaining party. France has a unitary system of sectoral business associations rather than parallel sets of industry and employers associations. Membership density in terms of employment is high and steady at approximately 75 percent.[1]

The French case shows that aggressive state intervention can be an effective way to ensure widespread coverage of collective agreements even when the membership density of a social partner is low. It should be noted that coverage in France would remain high even if business association density declined. French legislation is compatible with the German tradition of collective bargaining autonomy, because the state is not involved in setting the terms of the collective agreements. French law could actually be seen simply as a far more muscular version of article 5 of the German collective bargaining act, which permits the state to declare collective agreements generally applicable.

An expansion of state power along French lines to extend collective agreements is nevertheless unlikely in Germany. During the lengthy discussions over expanding the use of minimum and prevailing wages, German employers and their associations expressed opposition to adopting French-style legislation. These contentious discussions did lead to legislation instituting a framework for the social partners to negotiate prevailing wages for a dozen traditionally low-paying, low-skill occupations. These measures have curbed some of the worst instances of low-wage employment in Germany, but they have not appreciably reversed the trend of declining collective bargaining coverage. Most employers and their associations fiercely oppose expanding the number of occupations covered.[2]

French unionists have a tradition of resorting to mass political protest at times to advance their aims. It is unlikely that German trade unionism would ever develop a culture of protest comparable to that of France, or that German politics would be receptive to it, as the failure of German trade unions to influence the course and content of the Hartz and Agenda 2010 reforms amply demonstrated. It is telling that German unionists have looked to English-speaking countries rather than to France for best practices. This indicates that Germany is unlikely to move in a French direction, even though the French have developed a viable means to maintain widespread coverage of collective agreements despite an extraordinarily low union density.

In Japanese industrial relations, the firm rather than the state plays the dominant role. Enterprise unions are common and strikes are rare. Japanese industrial relations promote enterprise-level labor-management-producer coalitions. The principal objective is success in the marketplace in order to maximize what is available for distribution.[3] The relationship between works councils and firms in Germany can at times resemble Japanese enterprise unionism, but the substantially more robust statutory powers and protections granted to works councils, combined with the more authoritative position of trade unions as autonomous actors in Germany, have kept German industrial relations from going down a Japanese road. Moreover, German industrial relations retain a strong focus on the sectoral level through reliance on regionwide contracts rather than on the firm as in Japan. Still, if trajectories for the framework and actors continue to diverge, German industrial relations could increasingly come to resemble Japanese practice because unions and employers associations would no longer be powerful enough to stave off the powerful pull of "workplace egoism" (*Betriebsegoismus*) latent in the relationship between a works council and enterprise management.

The United States is relevant to this discussion of German industrial relations for two reasons. First, collective bargaining coverage has also fallen significantly in the United States, and US unions have experimented the most with social movement unionism as a strategy to reverse membership declines. During the latter half of the 1950s, collective agreements either directly or indirectly set the wages of four out of ten Americans. Today, the number is one in ten. To be sure, it is important not to forget the significant differences between Germany and the United States. The United States has never had as coordinated a system of collective bargaining as most European countries do. The United States never had anything like regionwide collective bargaining either. Collective bargaining coverage in Germany today still is not as low as it was in the United States at its high point. This does not mean, however, that a comparable decline cannot happen. The travails of the social partners in eastern Germany demonstrate the depths to which membership can fall. The United States also provides a picture of what industrial relations with low membership figures might look like.

Second, the largest German unions have begun to experiment with social movement unionism, which has included exchanges with union officials in several English-speaking counties, workshops, seminars, and pilot projects, as

well as more thoroughgoing organizational reforms. German trade unionists' decision to delve into the experience and lessons of social movement
unionism makes sense, given the salience of milieu to trade union density, but
optimism regarding the results would be premature, to say the least. Social
movement unionism has produced some spectacular isolated successes in
North America, but it has never managed to reverse the downward spiral of a
national labor movement.[4] This does not mean it cannot be done, but it does
indicate that considerable additional innovation would have to be involved
if social movement unionism were ever to become a reliable strategy at a
national level. Success is not certain, but the German labor movement is one
of the few labor movements remaining that has both the talent and resources
to take a heretofore unreliable prototype like social movement unionism and
possibly convert it into a more viable formulation.

The Future of German Industrial Relations

At the close of this book, I would like to consider briefly a final question:
Are those engaged in upholding the German industrial relations system on a
quixotic mission doomed to fail? Stated another way, will there still be trade
unions and employers associations in Germany one hundred years hence?
The answer to this admittedly highly speculative formulation is far from
certain. Engaging in a thought experiment like this can only produce the
most tentative of answers, to be sure. If someone had asked this question
one hundred years ago, most would have likely answered yes. Yet, for twelve
years of the twentieth century in western Germany and for sixty-seven years
in eastern Germany, there were no independent trade unions or employers associations. If someone had asked that same question seventy-five years
ago, the answer would have been no because at that time, the Nazis ruled
Germany. Nevertheless, the postwar years subsequently proved to be among
the most successful for German industrial relations. Still, this exercise has
merit because it raises consideration beyond short-term developments to the
question of the survival of the regime and its actors.

Despite strong state support, most employers associations and unions have
been losing members steadily for a long time. If the causes of membership
decline were ineptitude or inadequate state support, it would be relatively
easy to reverse the trend: find better leaders and pass new laws. Certainly, the
leaders of German employers associations and trade unions have made their
share of mistakes, but these mistakes are not the source of these organizations'
troubles. The source is the larger sociological and structural changes that
I discussed previously, such as the rise of individualism and intensified

economic competition. Still, the future of German employers associations and trade unions lies at least in part in their own hands. As the previous chapters have shown, these organizations have already begun experimentation to revive their fortunes. If they are to succeed, these efforts must not just continue. They must accelerate. The example of France shows that states can effectively preserve the role of organizations even when their memberships have shrunk dramatically, but survival owing to heavy state support rather than a solid membership base evokes a certain amount of pathos, a pathos that the leaders and members of German employers associations and trade unions would surely like to avoid.

Current trends, on the one hand, point toward the German social partners getting weaker rather than stronger. There are no signs that individualization is going to abate in Germany any time soon. Economic competition will most likely further intensify. Economic and political developments in the European Union are by no means supportive of social partnership. On the other hand, there are no obvious substitutes for the existing industrial relations regime. The soundest component of the regime, the state, has already begun to play a bigger role. The increased use of statutory minimum wages is one example of this. If used in moderation, state intervention should help to compensate for the membership declines of the social partners, but state support will never be a cure-all. Moreover, due caution must be observed. The failed experiment with state arbitration in the Weimar Republic shows how easily well-meaning interventions designed to preserve the status quo can wind up going wrong.

Germany has its own set of limitations in making effective decisions in difficult times, as the euro crisis has amply demonstrated. That having been said, the commitment to holding the shop together is still very much alive among the social partners and state officials. That commitment will enable the German industrial relations system to continue to play an important role in the German economy and society for some time to come.

NOTES

Introduction

1. For example, *American Prospect*, December 2011; *Bloomberg Businessweek*, 30 September 2010; *Economist*, 14 April 2012; *Financial Times*, 12 April 2011; *Die Zeit*, 1 May 2012; Bill Clinton, *Back to Work: Why We Need Smart Government for a Strong Economy* (New York: Alfred A. Knopf, 2011); Confederation of British Industry, *Future Champions: Unlocking Growth in the UK's Medium-Sized Businesses* (London: CBI, 2011); Steven Rattner, "Learning from the Germans," *Foreign Affairs* 90, no. 4 (July/August 2011): 7–11; and Bert Rürup and Dirk Hinrich Heilmann, *Fette Jahre: Warum Deutschland eine glänzende Zukunft hat* (Munich: Hanser, 2012).

2. For example, Mancur Olson, *The Rise and Decline of Nations: Economic Growth, Stagflation, and Social Rigidities* (New Haven: Yale University Press, 1982), 75–76.

3. Arend Lijphart, *Patterns of Democracy: Government Forms and Performance in Thirty-six Countries* (New Haven: Yale University Press, 1999), 249.

4. Other actors include individual employees and employers, but their significance is minor.

5. For example, Clyde Summers, "The Battle in Seattle: Free Trade, Labor Rights, and Societal Values," *University of Pennsylvania Journal of International Economic Law* 21, no. 1 (Spring 2001): 61–90; and Barbara Shailor, "A New Internationalism: Advancing Workers' Rights in the Global Economy," in *Not Your Father's Labor Movement: Inside the AFL-CIO*, ed. Jo-Ann Mort (New York: Verso, 1999).

6. Peter Bremme, Ulrike Fürniss, and Ulrike Meinecke, eds., *Never Work Alone: Organizing—eine Zukunftsmodell für Gewerkschaften* (Hamburg: VSA, 2007); and Michael Crosby, *Power at Work: Die Rückgewinnung gewerkschaftlicher Macht am Beispiel Australiens* (Hamburg: VSA, 2009).

7. Philippe C. Schmitter and Wolfgang Streeck, "The Organization of Business Interests: Studying the Associative Action of Business in Advanced Industrial Societies," MPIfG discussion paper 99/1 (unpublished), March 1999.

8. See, for example, Andrei S. Markovits, *The Politics of the West German Trade Unions: Strategies of Class and Interest Representation in Growth and Crisis* (Cambridge: Cambridge University Press, 1986); Walther Müller-Jentsch, *Gewerkschaften und Soziale Marktwirtschaft seit 1945* (Ditzingen: Reclam, 2011); Theo Pirker, *Die blinde Macht: Die Gewerkschaftsbewegung in der Bundesrepublik*, 2 vols. (Berlin: Olle & Wolter, 1979); Michael Schneider, *Kleine Geschichte der Gewerkschaften: Ihre Entwicklungen in Deutschland von den Anfängen bis heute*, 2nd ed. (Bonn: Dietz, 2001).

9. For example, Berndt Keller, *Einführung in die Arbeitspolitik: Arbeitsbeziehungen und Arbeitsmarkt in sozialwissenschaftlicher Perspektive*, 7th ed. (Munich: Oldenbourg, 2008); Wolfgang Schroeder and Bernhard Wessels, eds., *Handbuch Arbeitgeber und*

Wirtschaftsverbände in Deutschland (Wiesbaden: VS, 2010); and Manfred Weiss and Marlene Schmidt, *Labour Law and Industrial Relations in Germany*, 4th ed. (Alphen aan den Rijn, Neth.: Wolters/Kluwer, 2005).

10. Volker R. Berghahn and Detlev Karsten, *Industrial Relations in West Germany* (Oxford: Berg, 1987); and Walther Müller-Jentsch, *Soziologie der industriellen Beziehungen: Eine Einführung* (Frankfurt/Main: Campus, 1986); Walther Müller-Jentsch, *Strukturwandel der industriellen Beziehungen: Industrial Citizenship zwischen Markt und Regulierung* (Wiesbaden: VS, 2007).

11. Reinhard Bispinck, Heiner Dribbusch, and Thorsten Schulten, "German Collective Bargaining in a European Perspective: Continuous Erosion or Re-Stabilisation of Multi-Employer Agreements?" paper presented at the 9th European Congress of the International Industrial Relations Association, Copenhagen, 28 June–1 July 2010, 2; Anke Hassel and Thorsten Schulten, "Globalization and the Future of Central Collective Bargaining: The Example of the German Metal Industry," *Economy and Society* 27, no. 4 (November 1998): 486–522; Anke Hassel, "The Erosion of the German System of Industrial Relations," *British Journal of Industrial Relations* 37, no. 3 (September 1999): 483–505; and Jelle Visser, "More Holes in the Bucket: Twenty Years of European Integration and Organized Labor," *Comparative Labor Law and Policy Journal* 26, no. 4 (Summer 2006): 494.

12. Wolfgang Streeck, *Re-Forming Capitalism: Institutional Change in the German Political Economy* (Oxford: Oxford University Press, 2009), part 2, esp. 121–46. For a review, see Stephen J. Silvia, "Things Fall Apart: Contemporary Analyses of German Economic and Political Developments," *Comparative European Politics* 8, no. 34 (December 2010): 481–89.

13. For example, Michel Albert, *Capitalism vs. Capitalism* (New York: Four Walls Eight Windows, 1993); Andrei S. Markovits, ed., *The Political Economy of West Germany: Modell Deutschland* (New York: Praeger, 1982); and Lowell Turner, *Democracy at Work: Changing World Markets and the Future of Labor Unions* (Ithaca: Cornell University Press, 1991).

14. For example, Stanley Presser and Mark Chaves, "Is Religious Service Attendance Declining?" *Journal for the Scientific Study of Religion* 46, no. 3 (September 2007): 417–23; Robert D. Putnam, *Bowling Alone: The Collapse and Revival of American Community* (New York: Simon and Schuster, 2000); and Susan E. Scarrow, "Party Members and Political Participation," in *Oxford Handbook of Political Behavior*, ed. Russell J. Dalton and Hans-Dieter Klingemann (Oxford: Oxford University Press, 2007).

15. Olson, *Rise and Decline of Nations*.

16. Philippe C. Schmitter and Gerhard Lehmbruch, eds., *Trends toward Corporatist Intermediation* (Beverly Hills, CA: Sage, 1979).

17. Peter A. Hall and David Soskice, eds., *Varieties of Capitalism: The Institutional Foundations of Comparative Advantage* (Oxford: Oxford University Press, 2001).

Chapter 1

1. For example, Mancur Olson, *The Rise and Decline of Nations: Economic Growth, Stagflation, and Social Rigidities* (New Haven: Yale University Press, 1982).

2. Hajo Holborn, *A History of Modern Germany, 1840–1945* (Princeton: Princeton University Press, 1969), 285–87; and Michael Schneider, *Kleine Geschichte der Gewerkschaften: Ihre Entwicklung in Deutschland von den Anfängen bis heute* (Bonn: Dietz, 1989), 51–54.

3. Wolfgang Däubler, *Das Arbeitsrecht 1: Leitfaden für Arbeitnehmer*, 5th ed. (Reinbek bei Hamburg: Rowohlt, 1982), 48. Quotation as cited in Andrei S. Markovits, *The Politics of West German Trade Unions: Strategies of Interest Representation in Growth and Crisis* (Cambridge: Cambridge University Press, 1986), 32.

4. Schneider, *Kleine Geschichte der Gewerkschaften,* 114–18.

5. Dieter Schuster, *Die deutsche Gewerkschaftsbewegung*, 6th ed. (Cologne: Druckhaus Deutz, 1980), 42–43.

6. Holborn, *History of Modern Germany*, 515–16.

7. Gerard Braunthal, *Socialist Labor Politics in Weimar Germany* (Hamden, CT: Archon, 1978), 35; and Boris Stern, *Works Council Movement in Germany*, Bulletin of the United States Bureau of Labor Statistics 383, miscellaneous series (Washington, DC: Government Printing Office, 1925), 66.

8. Gerald D. Feldman and Irmgard Steinisch, *Industrie und Gewerkschaften, 1918–1924: Die überforderte Zentralgemeinschaft* (Stuttgart: Deutsche Verlags-Anstalt, 1985), 136.

9. Schneider, *Kleine Geschichte der Gewerkschaften*, 215–25.

10. Däubler, *Das Arbeitsrecht 1*, 58–60; and German Bundestag, *Basic Law for the Federal Republic of Germany* (Berlin: German Bundestag, 2010), https://www.btg-bestellservice.de/pdf/80201000.pdf.

11. Bundesarbeitsgericht, "Pressemitteilung Nr. 21/11," 23 March 2011; *Frankfurter Rundschau*, 24 March 2011; Wolfgang Streeck, "Gewerkschaften als Mitgliederverbände: Probleme gewerkschaftlicher Mitgliederrekrutierung," in *Beiträge zur Soziologie der Gewerkschaften*, ed. Joachim Bergmann (Franfurt/Main: Suhrkamp, 1979), 83–84; and Hans-Eckbert Treu, *Dualistisches System der Interessenvertretung und Einheitsgewerkschaftsprinzip: Eine Studie über das Verhältnis von Gewerkschaft und Betrieb* (Frankfurt/Main: Rita G. Fischer, 1980), 68–72.

12. Carl Mischke, "Industrial Action in Germany," *Industrial Law Journal* 13, no. 1 (1992): 13.

13. Christopher S. Allen, "Ideas, Institutions and Organized Capitalism: The German Economy Twenty Years after Unification," *German Politics and Society* 28, no. 2 (Summer 2010): 140.

14. Stephen J. Silvia, "Working Conditions," in *Modern Germany: An Encyclopedia of History, People, and Culture, 1871–1990*, vol. 2, *L-Z*, ed. Dieter K. Buse and Juergen C. Doerr (New York: Garland, 1998), 1092–93.

15. Markovits, *Politics of West German Trade Unions*, 32; and Thomas Blanke, Rainer Erd, Ulrich Mückenberger, and Ulrich Stascheit, *Kollektives Arbeitsrecht: Quellentexte zur Geschichte des Arbeiterrechtes in Deutschland* (Reinbek bei Hamburg: Rowohlt, 1975).

16. Markovits, *Politics of West German Trade Unions*, 34–35.

17. Michael Kittner, *Arbeits- und Sozialordnung: Ausgewählte und eingeleitete Gesetztexte*, 22nd ed. (Cologne: Bund, 2001), 1394.

18. Volker R. Berghahn and Detlef Karstens, *Industrial Relations in West Germany* (Oxford: Berg, 1987), 26–30.

19. Markovits, *Politics of West German Trade Unions*, 227–32.

20. Institut für Arbeitsmarkt- und Berufsforschung, *IAB-Betriebspanel 2007* (Nürnberg: IAB, 2008); Leo Pünnel and Martin Quecke, *Was man vom Arbeitsrecht wissen sollte*, 19th ed. (Neuwied: Luchterhand, 2002), 27.

21. WSI Tarifarchiv, http://www.tarifvertrag.de.

22. Reinhard Bispinck, "Allgemeinverbindlichkeitserklärung von Tarifverträgen—vom Niedergang zur Reform?," *WSI-Mitteilungen*, no. 7 (2012): 496–507.

23. Directive 96/71/EC, 16 December 1996.

24. Bundesministerium für Justiz, juris, http://gesetiz-im-internet.juris.de/aentg_2009/BJNR079900009.html.

25. Reinhard Bispinck and Johannes Kirsch, "Minimum Standards between Collective Agreements and Statutory Provisions," special issue: "Industrial Relations in Germany: An Empirical Survey," *WSI-Mitteilungen* 56 (2003): 44–45.

26. Bundesministerium für Justiz, juris, http://www.gesetze-im-internet.de/miarbg/BJNR000170952.html.

27. Bundesministerium für Arbeit und Soziales, Pressedienst, 13 May 2011; and *N24*, 14 July 2010.

28. *Frankfurter Allgemeine Zeitung*, 21 September 2011.

29. Wolfgang Däubler, "Reform der Allgemeinverbindlichkeitserklärung: Tarifrecht in Bewegung?" *WSI-Mitteilungen* 65, no. 7 (July 2012): 508–16.

30. *Stern*, 18 January 2010; Bundesverwaltungsgericht, VG Berlin 4 A 439 07; European Court of Justice, C-438/05, 11 December 2007; C-341/05, 18 December 2007; C-346/06, 3 April 2008; C-319/06, 19 June 2008; Diamond Ashiagbor, "Collective Labor Rights and the European Social Model," *Law and Ethics of Human Rights* 3, no. 2 (2009), article 5; A. C. L. Davies, "One Step Forward, Two Steps Back?: The Viking and Laval Cases in the ECJ," *Industrial Law Journal* 37, no. 2 (2008): 126–48; and Alicia Hinarejos, "Laval and Viking: The Right to Collective Action versus EU Fundamental Freedoms," *Human Rights Law Review* 8, no. 4 (2008): 714–29.

31. Hagen Lesch, "Schlichtung: Reichen die alten Mechanismen aus?" *Unternehmen und Gesellschaft*, no. 4 (2005).

32. Manfred Weiss, "Labour Dispute Settlement by Labour Courts in Germany," *Industrial Law Journal* 15, no. 1 (1994): 14.

33. Ibid., 3–4.

34. Markovits, *Politics of West German Trade Unions*, 36.

35. Pünnel and Quecke, *Was man vom Arbeitsrecht wissen sollte*, 197–98.

36. Markovits, *Politics of West German Trade Unions*, 418–19; Rainer Erd, *Verrechtlichung industrieller Konflikte: Normative Rahmenbedingungen des dualen Systems der Interessenvertretung* (Frankfurt/Main: Campus, 1978); and Manfred Weiss and Marlene Schmidt, *Labour Law and Industrial Relations*, 4th ed. (Alphen aan den Rijn, Neth.: Kluwer Law International, 2008), 156–61.

37. Mischke, "Industrial Action," 13.

38. Thomas Blanke, "Koalitionsfreiheit und Tarifautonomie: Rechtliche Grundlagen und Rahmenbedingungen der Gewerkschaften in Deutschland," in *Die Gewerkschaften in Politik und Gesellschaft der Bundesrepublik Deutschland: Ein Handbuch*, ed. Wolfgang Schroeder and Bernhard Wessels (Wiesbaden: Westdeutscher Verlag, 2003), 161.

39. Renate Jaeger and Siegfried Bross, "The Relations between the Constitutional Courts and the Other National Courts, Including the Interference in This Area of the Action of the European Courts," Report of the Constitutional Court of the Federal Republic of Germany, Conference of European Constitutional Courts, 12th Congress, Warsaw, 16–17 May 1999.

40. Five German states do guarantee the right to strike explicitly in their constitutions: Berlin, Bremen, Hesse, Rhineland-Palatinate, and the Saar (Mischke, "Industrial Action," 1).

41. Jens Kirchner and Eva Mittelhamm, "Labour Conflicts," in *Key Aspects of German Employment and Labour Law*, ed. Jens Kirchner, Pascal R. Kremp, and Michael Magotsch (Berlin: Springer, 2010), 199.

42. Kittner, *Arbeits- und Sozialordnung*, 1347; and Xenia Rajewsky, *Arbeitskampfrecht in der Bundesrepublik* (Frankfurt/Main: Suhrkamp, 1970), 36–51, as cited in Markovits, *Politics of West German Trade Unions*, 44.

43. H. Otto, *Münchener Handbuch zum Arbeitsrecht* (Munich: C. H. Beck, 2009), section 285, para. 40–43.

44. Kittner, *Arbeits- und Sozialordnung*, 798–99.

45. See Stephen J. Silvia, "The West German Labor Law Controversy: A Struggle for the Factory of the Future," *Comparative Politics* 20, no. 2 (January 1988).

46. Kittner, *Arbeits- und Sozialordnung*, 1404; Weiss and Schmidt, *Labour Law*, 207–8; and Wolfgang Däubler, "Das Grundrecht auf Streik—eine Skizze," *Zeitschrift für Arbeitsrecht* 4, no. 1 (January–March 1973): 200.

47. Mischke, "Industrial Action," 11; Bundesarbeitsgericht, "Arbeitsrechtliche Praxis" (AP) no. 1 re Grundgesetz Art. 9, Industrial Action, 28 January 1955; and Markovits, *Politics of West German Trade Unions*, 45–46.

48. Däubler, *Arbeitsrecht*, 67–68.

49. Weiss and Schmidt, *Labour Law*, 212–13.

50. Markovits, *Politics of West German Trade Unions*, 47–48.

51. Däubler, *Arbeitsrecht*, 68.

52. Markovits, *Politics of West German Trade Unions*, 43.

53. Bundesarbeitsgericht, 1 AZR 605/75 Art. 9, Abs. 1 GG, 17 December 1976; 1 AZR 342/83 Art. 9 GG, 12 September 1984; 1 AZR 651/86 Art. 9, GG, 21 June 1988; and Weiss and Schmidt, *Labour Law*, 204–5.

54. Bundesarbeitsgericht, 1 AZR 468/83, Art. 9 GG, 5 March 1988; 1 AZR 396/06. Art. 9, Abs. 3 GG, 19 June 2007; and Weiss and Schmidt, *Labour Law*, 206–7.

55. *Frankfurter Allgemeine Zeitung*, 23 June, 20 July, and 9 September 2010; *Frankfurter Rundschau*, 23 June 2010; *Die Zeit*, 1 November 2010; *Süddeutsche Zeitung*, 14 January 2011; Bundesarbeitsgericht, Beschluss des 10. Senats vom 23.6.2010—10 AS 3/10 and 10 AS 3/10; Gewerkschaft Deutscher Lokomotivführer, Hauptvorstand, "14 Eckpunkte-Papier: Argumentationshilfe zur Tarifpluralität," Frankfurt/Main, 21 February 2011; Detlev Hensche, "Wider der Tarifeinheitsfront," *Blätter für deutsche und internationale Politik* 54, no. 8 (August 2010): 13–17; and Olaf Wittenberg, *Tarifeinheit im Betrieb: Ein Auslaufmodell?—Spartengewerkschaften auf der Überholspur* (Hamburg: Diplomica, 2009).

56. *Frankfurter Allgemeine Zeitung*, 8 June 2011; and *Frankfurter Rundschau*, 26 May 2011.

57. For more on neocorporatism, see Peter J. Williamson, *Corporatism in Perspective: An Introductory Guide to Corporatist Theory* (Newbury Park, CA: Sage, 1989), 203–24.

58. Bundesministerium für Gesundheit und Soziale Sicherung, "Organisation und Selbstverwaltung der Sozialversicherung in Deutschland," http://www.bmgs.de/downloads/u_soz_02OrganisationSelbstverwaltung.pdf.

59. *Frankfurter Allgemeine Zeitung*, 17 June 1999; Bernhard Braun, Tanja Klenk, Winfried Kluth, Frank Nullmeier, and Felix Welti, *Modernisierung der Sozialversicherungswahlen* (Baden-Baden: Nomos, 2008); and Deutsche Rentenversicherung Bund, "Ergebnisse der Listenwahl bei der deutschen Rentenversicherung Bund," http://download.sozialwahl.de/fileadmin/user_upload/pdf/Ergebnisse/Sozialwahl_2011_Ergebnisse_gesamt.pdf.

60. Before 2004, the institutions of the top three tiers of the BA had different names. From top to bottom, they were: Head Office (Hauptstelle), State Employment Office (Landesarbeitsamt), and Employment Office (Arbeitsamt). Eric Owen Smith, *The German Economy* (London: Routledge, 1994), 196–97; and Deutsche Rentenversicherung Bund, "Sozialwahl 2011," http://sozialwahl.adlexikon.de/Sozialwahl.shtml.

61. Helmut Reuther, *Soziale Marktwirtschaft im Schaubild* (Bonn: Transcontact, 1990), 60.

62. *Handelsblatt*, 8 September 2004.

63. Wolfgang Streeck, "From State Weakness as Strength to State Weakness as Weakness: Welfare Corporatism and the Private Use of the Public Interest," *Max-Planck-Institut für Gesellschaftsforschung*, Working Paper 03/2, March 2003.

64. For a summary of the broader Hartz reforms and the subsequent "Agenda 2010," see *Frankfurter Rundschau*, 5 May 2003 and 7 July 2004; *Der Spiegel*, 19 May 2003; and Michael Fichter, "Reforming the Labor Market: Chancellor Schröder's Got His Hartz Set on It," *AICGS Advisor* 2002, http://www.aicgs.org/wahlen/hartzcomm.shtml.

65. *Frankfurter Rundschau*, 20 February 2002 and 26 May 2004; *Handelsblatt*, 7 August 2004; *Der Spiegel*, 24 June 2002 and 3 September 2005; *Die Welt*, 28 August 2002; and *Die Zeit*, 3 August 2003.

Chapter 2

1. Leo Kissler, Ralph Greifenstein, and Karsten Schneider, *Die Mitbestimmung in der Bundesrepublik Deutschland: Eine Einführung* (Wiesbaden: VS, 2011), 15.

2. Ibid., 15.

3. For example, *Financial Times Deutschland*, 21 October 2004; *Handelsblatt*, 21 October 2004; and *Stuttgarter Nachrichten*, 20 October 2004.

4. Klaus Koopmann, *Vertrauensleute: Arbeitervertretung im Betrieb* (Hamburg: VSA, 1981), 15; and Kathleen A. Thelen, *A Union of Parts: Labor and Politics in Postwar Germany* (Ithaca: Cornell University Press, 1991).

5. Volker Gransow and Viktor Krätke, *Viktor Agartz, Gewerkschaften und Wirtschaftspolitik* (Berlin: Verlag Die Arbeitswelt, 1978), 106; and Walther Müller-Jentsch, "Geschichte der Mitbestimmung, 1848–1916: Wie die Gewerkschaften zur Mitbestimmung kamen," *Mitbestimmung* 53, no. 12 (December 2007): 52–57.

6. Bertelsmann Stiftung and Hans-Böckler-Stiftung, eds., *Mitbestimmung und neue Unternehmenskulturen: Bilanz und Perspektiven—Bericht der Kommission Mitbestimmung* (Gütersloh: Verlag Bertelsmann Stiftung, 1998), 29; Abraham Schuchman, *Codetermination: Labor's Middle Way in Germany* (Washington, DC: Public Affairs Press, 1957); and Hans Jürgen Teuteberg, *Geschichte der industriellen Mitbestimmung in Deutschland* (Tübingen: J. C. B. Mohr, 1961).

7. The traditional German model of corporate governance includes two boards. The supervisory board (*Aufsichtsrat*) consists of representatives of shareholders and, in larger firms, of employees. It meets about four times a year. Its duties are to select, to advise, and to oversee corporate management. The top management team makes up the second board, which is called the executive committee (*Vorstand*). The executive committee undertakes day-to-day management of a firm, and its chair is the company's chief executive officer. The supervisory board hires, evaluates, and if need be fires members of the executive committee. Codetermination covers the supervisory board only. See Eric Owen Smith, *The German Economy* (London: Routledge, 1994), 300.

8. Walther Müller-Jentsch, "Die Mitbestimmung für eine neue Wirtschaftsordnung nutzen," *Mitbestimmung* 54, nos. 1/2, (January/February) 2008: 47–51.

9. Bundesministerium für Wirtschaft und Arbeit, *Mitbestimmung: Ein gutes Unternehmen—Alles über die Mitbestimmung und die wesentlichsten Gesetzestexte* (Berlin: BMWA, 2003), 22–23.

10. The scholarly debate remains less settled. See David Abraham, *The Collapse of the Weimar Republic: Political Economy and Crisis*, 2nd ed. (New York: Holmes and Meier, 1986); and Henry Ashby Turner, *German Big Business and the Rise of Hitler* (Oxford: Oxford University Press, 1985).

11. Alex Demirović, "Demokratie, Wirtschaftsdemokratie und Mitbestimmung," in *Wirtschaftsdemokratie: Alternative zum Shareholder-Kapitalismus*, ed. H. J. Bontrup, J. Bischoff, A. Demirović, J. Huffschmid, Julia Müller, and Michael Schumann (Hamburg: VSA, 2006), 54–92; and Fritz Naphtali, *Wirtschaftsdemokratie: Ihr Wesen, Weg und Ziel* (Berlin: Verlagsanstalt des ADGB, 1929).

12. Volker Berghahn, *The Americanisation of West German Industry, 1945–1973* (Cambridge: Cambridge University Press, 1986), 206–7.

13. Ibid., 213; and Wade Jacoby, "'Ization' by Negation?: Occupation Forces, Codetermination, and Works Councils," paper presented at "American Impact on Western Europe: Americanization and Westernization in Transatlantic Perspective" conference at the German Historical Institute, Washington, DC, 25–27 March 1999), 19.

14. Gesetz über die Mitbestimmung der Arbeitnehmer in den Aufsichtsräten und Vorständen der Unternehmen des Bergbaus und der Eisen- und Stahlerzeugenden Industrie (MontanMitbestG) vom 21. Mai 1951 (BGBl. I 347) zuletzt geändert durch Gesetz vom 31. Oktober 2006 (BGBl. I 2407, 2434).

15. Larger enterprises may have fifteen or twenty-one members on the supervisory board.

16. If an impasse is reached in this process, the parties use a lengthy mediation process to resolve it.

17. Walther Müller-Jentsch, "Mitbestimmungspolitik," in *Die Gewerkschaften in Politik und Gesellschaft der Bundesrepublik Deutschland: Ein Handbuch*, ed.

Wolfgang Schroeder and Bernhard Wessels (Wiesbaden: Westdeutscher Verlag, 2003), 453–54.

18. Berghahn, *Americanisation of West German Industry*, 217.

19. Ibid., 221–25; and Theo Pirker, *Die blinde Macht: Die Gewerkschaftsbewegung in der Bundesrepublik*, vol. 1, *Vom "Ende des Kapitalismus" zur Zähmung der Gewerkschaften* (Berlin: Olle & Wolter, 1979), 197–98.

20. *Handelsblatt*, 31 March 1987.

21. *Mitbestimmung*, May 2011; Pirker, *Die blinde Macht*, 188–95; Andrei S. Markovits, *The Politics of West German Trade Unions: Strategies of Interest Representation in Growth and Crisis* (Cambridge: Cambridge University Press, 1986), 79; and Erich Potthoff, *Der Kampf um die Montan-Mitbestimmung* (Cologne: Bund, 1957).

22. Markovits, *Politics of West German Trade Unions*, 80–81.

23. Herbert Giersch, Karl-Heinz Paqué, and Holger Schmieding, *The Fading Miracle: Four Decades of Market Economy in Germany*, rev. and updated ed. (Cambridge: Cambridge University Press, 1994), 86–87.

24. Michael Schneider, *Kleine Geschichte der Gewerkschaften: Ihre Entwicklung in Deutschland von den Anfängen bis heute* (Bonn: Dietz, 1989), 267–68.

25. Quoted in Markovits, *Politics of West German Trade Unions*, 81.

26. *Arbeitgeber*, 15 July 1952.

27. Walther Müller-Jentsch, *Konfliktpartnerschaft: Akteure und Institutionen der industriellen Beziehungen* (Munich: Rainer Hampp, 1993), 8.

28. For example, Morris M. Kleiner, "Unionism and Employer Discrimination: An Analysis of 8(a)(3) Violations," *Industrial Relations* 23, no. 2 (March 1984): 234–43; and Morris M. Kleiner, "Intensity of Management Resistance: Understanding the Decline in Unionization in the Private Sector," *Journal of Labor Research* 22, no. 3 (Summer 2001): 540–40.

29. Michael Kittner, *Arbeits- und Sozialordnung: Ausgewählte und eingeleitete Gesetztexte*, 27th ed. (Cologne: Bund, 2002), 971–73.

30. Markovits, *Politics of West German Trade Unions*, 133.

31. Deutscher Gewerkschaftsbund, *Grundsatzprogramm des Deutschen Gewerkschaftsbundes* (Düsseldorf: DGB, 1963), 16.

32. Walther Müller-Jentsch, "Arbeitgeberverbände und Sozialpartnerschaft in der chemischen Industrie," in *Handbuch Arbeitgeber- und Wirtschaftsverbände in Deutschland*, ed. Wolfgang Schroeder and Bernhard Wessels (Wiesbaden: VS, 2010), 410.

33. Deutscher Gewerkschaftsbund, *Mitbestimmungsgesetz DGB: Entwurf eines Gesetzes über die Mitbestimmung der Arbeitnehmer in Grossunternehmen und Grosskonzernen* (Düsseldorf: DGB, 1968); and Sachverständigenkommission zur Auswertung der bisherigen Erfahrungen mit der Mitbestimmung [Biedenkopf commission], "Mitbestimmung im Unternehmen. Bericht der Sachverständigenkommission zur Auswertung der bisherigen Erfahrungen mit der Mitbestimmung," BT-Drucksache VI/334, 1970.

34. Markovits, *Politics of West German Trade Unions*, 117; and Wolfram Weimer, *Deutsche Wirtschaftsgeschichte: Von Währungsreform bis zum Euro* (Hamburg: Hoffmann und Campe, 1998), 217.

35. Berghahn, *Americanisation of West German Industry*, 240; Kittner, *Arbeits- und Sozialordnung*, 907; and Markovits, *Politics of West German Trade Unions*, 133.

36. Until 2009, the volume of company sales determined whether a company had a board with twelve, sixteen, or twenty members. A revision of the law now permits departures from these numbers if both employee and employer representatives on the board agree. The 1976 Employee Codetermination Act also restricts union influence by limiting the number of employee representatives that can come from outside of the firm to two in cases where a company has a total of six or eight employee representatives, and three in firms that have ten employee representatives on the supervisory board. Most firms prefer smaller boards. In 2010, 65% had a twelve-person board, 16% had sixteen, and the remaining 19% have twenty members. See *Mitbestimmung*, May 2011; and Gesetz über die Mitbestimmung der Arbeitnehmer (BGBl. I 1153), zuletzt geändert durch Gesetz vom 30. Juli 2009 (BGBl. I 2479, 2491).

37. *Frankfurter Allgemeine Zeitung*, 2 March 1979; and *Blick durch die Wirtschaft*, 5 March 1979.

38. Mario Helfert, "Betriebsverfassung, neue Rationalisierungsformen, lean Production," *WSI-Mitteilungen* 45, no. 8 (August 1992): 505–10; Gerhard Leminsky, *Mitbestimmen: Wie wir in Zukunft arbeiten und leben durch Mitgestaltung und Management des Wandels*, Graue Reihe no. 105 (Düsseldorf: Hans-Böckler-Stiftung, 1996); and Bernhard Nagel, Birgit Reiss, and Gisela Theis, *Neue Konzernstrukturen und Mitbestimmung* (Baden-Baden: Nomos, 1994).

39. *Mitbestimmung*, May 2011; Kittner, *Arbeits- und Sozialordnung*, 973–76; Smith, *German Economy*, 304–5; and Karl Lauschke, *Die halbe Macht: Mitbestimmung in der Eisen- und Stahlindustrie 1945 bis 1989* (Essen: Klartext, 2007).

40. *Mitbestimmung*, May 2011; and Ursula Wendeling-Schröder, "Mitbestimmung auf Unternehmensebene," in *Gewerkschaftsjahrbuch 1993*, ed. Michael Kittner (Cologne: Bund, 1993), 461–71.

41. *Financial Times*, 30 August 2006; *Handelsblatt*, 22 October 1976; and *Die Zeit*, 10 March 1978.

42. *Der Spiegel*, 24 May 1993.

43. Bertelsmann Stiftung and Hans-Böckler-Stiftung, *Mitbestimmung*, esp. 113–14.

44. Bertelsmann Stiftung and Hans-Böckler-Stiftung, *The German Model of Codetermination and Cooperative Governance* (Gütersloh: Verlag Bertelsmann Stiftung, 1998), 27–33.

45. *Manager-Magazin*, April 2003; *Mitbestimmung*, September 2003; *Süddeutsche Zeitung*, 19 September 2003; *Die Welt*, 24 July 2004; Berliner Netzwerk Corporate Governance, "Corporate Governance und Modernisierung der Mitbestimmung. 12 Thesen zur 'Modernisierung der Mitbestimmung'" (2003), http://www.bccg.tu-berlin.de/main/publikationen/12-Thesen-Papier.pdf; and Axel von Werder, "Modernisierung der Mitbestimmung," unpublished working paper, Berlin: Center of Corporate Governance, 26 November 2003.

46. *Frankfurter Rundschau*, 26 October and 10 November 2004; *Stern*, 13 October 2004; *Süddeutsche Zeitung*, 9 October 2004; *Die Welt*, 24 July 2004 and 22 October 2004; and Bundesvereinigung der Deutschen Arbeitgeberverbände und Bundesverband der Deutschen Industrie, "Mitbestimmung Modernisieren: Bericht der Kommission Mitbestimmung," unpublished policy paper, Berlin, 2004,

http://www.arbeitgeber.de/www/arbeitgeber.nsf/res/547B1EE4EA194F30C12
574EF0053DBFF/$file/Mitbestimmung_Modernisieren.pdf.

47. *Mitbestimmung*, January/February 2007; and Deutscher Gewerkschaftsbund
Bundesvorstand, "Stellungnahme des DGB Bundesvorstandes, Abt. Mitbestimmung
und Rechtspolitik zu dem Bericht der 'Kommission Mitbestimmung von BDA und
BDI," unpublished paper, Berlin, 12 November 2004, http://www.boeckler.de/pdf/
dgb_stellungnahme_umitbest_2004_11.pdf.

48. *Die Welt*, 22 October 2004.

49. Hans Böckler Foundation, "Results of the 'Biedenkopf Commission'—
the Government Commission on the Modernisation of Employee Board-Level
Representation in Germany: An Executive Summary by the Hans-Böckler-Founda-
tion" (Düsseldorf: Hans-Böckler-Stiftung, 2007), 1–2 and 7.

50. Müller-Jentsch, "Die Mitbestimmung für eine neue Wirtschaftsordnung
nutzen," 50–51.

51. The commission report includes a good overview of the literature regarding
the economic impact of codetermination. The best single review of the literature is
Uwe Jirjahn, "Ökonomische Wirkungen der Mitbestimmung in Deutschland: Ein
Update," Hans-Böckler-Stiftung, Wirtschaft und Finanzen Arbeitspapier [Econom-
ics and finance working paper] 186, February 2010.

52. Kommission zur Modernisierung der deutschen Unternehmensmitbestimmung, "Bericht der wissenschaftlichen Mitglieder der Kommission. Mit Stellung-
nahmen der Vertreter der Unternehmen und der Vertreter der Arbeitnehmer," report,
Berlin, December 2006, http://kohte.jura.uni-halle.de/recht/Kommissionsbericht_
Endfassung.pdf, 13–21.

53. Ibid., 21–48.

54. Ibid., 57–80.

55. *Frankfurter Allgemeine Zeitung*, 21 December 2006; and *Manager Magazin*, 22
December 2006.

56. Hans Böckler Foundation, "Results of the 'Biedenkopf Commission,'" 7;
Die Welt, 15 October 2009; and Juergen Donges, Johann Eeckhoff, Wolfgang Franz,
Clemens Fuest, Wernhard Möschel, and Manfred J. M. Neumann, *Unternehmensmit-
bestimmung ohne Zwang*, Stiftung Marktwirtschaft Schriftenreihe, vol. 47 (Berlin:
Stiftung Marktwirtschaft, 2007), http://www.stiftung-marktwirtschaft.de/uploads/
tx_ttproducts/datasheet/KK_47_Unternehmensmitbestimmung_2007.pdf.

57. Council Regulation 2157/2001/EC and Council Directive 2001/86/EC.

58. Michael Stollt and Norbert Kluge, "The Potential of Employee Involvement
in the SE to Foster the Europeanization of Labour Relations," *transfer* 17, no. 2 (May
2011): 182.

59. Paul L. Davies, "Workers on the Board of the European Company?" *Industrial Law Journal* 32, no. 2 (June 2003): 87.

60. *Personalführung*, June 2007; *Die Welt*, 23 October 2004.

61. European Trade Union Institute, worker-participation.edu, http://www.
worker-participation.eu/European-Company/SE-COMPANIES-News/Facts-
and-Figures; *Böckler impuls*, 18/2009; and Hans-Böckler-Stiftung, press release, 23
April 2010.

62. Robbert van het Kaar, "The European Company (SE) Statute: Up against Increasing Competition?" *transfer* 17, no. 2 (May 2011): 197.

63. European Private Company, www.europeanprivatecompany.eu/news.

64. Kaar, "The European Company (SE) Statute," 198–200; and Hans-Böckler-Stiftung, *Böckler impuls*, 2/2011.

65. Quoted in Gransow and Krätke, *Viktor Agartz*, 106.

66. Thelen, *Union of Parts*, 2–5.

67. *Quelle*, May 1952, 225; and June 1952, 329–30.

68. C. W. Guillebaud, *The Works Council: A German Experiment in Industrial Democracy* (Cambridge: Cambridge University Press, 1928), 1.

69. Müller-Jentsch, "Geschichte der Mitbestimmung: 1848–1916."

70. Müller-Jentsch, "Mitbestimmungspolitik," 451.

71. Rudolf Herbig, *Notizen: Aus der Sozial-, Wirtschafts- und Gewerkschaftsgeschichte vom 14. Jahrhundert bis zur Gegenwart* (Frankfurt/Main: Union, 1980), 146.

72. Werner Milert and Rudolf Tschirbs, *Von den Arbeiterausschüssen zum Betriebsverfassungsgesetz: Geschichte der betrieblichen Interessenvertretung in Deutschland* (Cologne: Bund, 1991).

73. Kittner, *Arbeits- und Sozialordnung*, 430.

74. Peter von Oertzen, *Betriebsräte in der Novemberrevolution* (Düsseldorf: Droste, 1963).

75. Klaus Schönhoven, "Germany to 1945," in *European Labor Unions*, ed. Joan Campbell (Westport, CT: Greenwood, 1992), 151. The best studies of the soldiers' and workers' councils are Eberhard Kolb, *Die Arbeiterräte in der deutschen Innenpolitik 1918–1919* (Düsseldorf: Droste, 1978); Ulrich Kluge, *Soldatenräte und Revolution: Studien zur Militärpolitik in Deutschland 1918/19* (Göttingen: Vandenhoeck and Ruprecht, 1975); and Reinhard Rürup, ed., *Arbeiter und Soldatenräte im rheinisch-westfälischen Industriegebiet: Studien zur Geschichte der Revolution 1918/19* (Wuppertal: Hammer, 1975).

76. Kittner, *Arbeits- und Sozialordnung*, 431; and Müller-Jentsch, "Mitbestimmungspolitik," 460.

77. Bureau of Labor Statistics, United States Department of Labor, "German Works Council Law," *Monthly Labor Review* 10, no. 5 (May 1920): 1252–53.

78. Ibid., 1251.

79. Thelen, *Union of Parts*, 68.

80. Ibid.

81. Jacoby, "'Ization' by Negation?" 10; Ronald F. Bunn, "Employers Associations in the Federal Republic of Germany," in *Employers Associations and Industrial Relations: A Comparative Study*, ed. John P. Windmuller and Alan Gladstone (Oxford: Oxford University Press, 1984), 171.

82. Müller-Jentsch, "Mitbestimmungspolitik," 460; and Kurt Brigl-Matthiass, "Das Betriebsräteproblem in der Weimarer Republik," in *Die Betriebsräte in der Weimarer Republik*, vol. 2, ed. R. Crusius, G. Schiefelbein, and M. Wilke (Berlin: Olle & Wolter, 1978), 76.

83. Guillebaud, *Works Council*, 225.

84. Thelen, *Union of Parts*, 70.

85. Hans Jürgen Teuteberg, "Ursprünge und Entwicklung der Mitbestimmung in Deutschland," in *Mitbestimmung: Ursprünge und Entwicklung*, ed. Hans Pohl (Wiesbaden: Franz Steiner Verlag, 1981), 41.

86. Berghahn, *Americanisation of West German Industry*, 212; Jacoby, "'Ization' by Negation?" 26; Klaus-Dieter Henke, *Die Amerikanische Besetzung Deutschlands* (Munich: R. Oldenbourg, 1995), 619; and Klaus Koopmann, *Gewerkschaftliche Vertrauensleute: Darstellung und kritische Analyse ihrer Entwicklung und Bedeutung von den Anfängen bis zur Gegenwart unter besonderer Berücksichtigung des Deutschen—Metallarbeiter-Verbands (DMV) und der Industriegewerkschaft Metall (IGM)* (Munich: Minerva-Publikation, 1979), 338–40.

87. Jacoby, "'Ization' by Negation?" 26.

88. Wolfgang Däubler, *Arbeitsrecht: Ratgeber für Beruf, Praxis und Studium*, 4th ed. (Cologne: Bund, 2002), 73.

89. Carolyn Eisenberg, "The Limits of Democracy: US Policy and the Rights of German Labor, 1945–49," in *America and the Shaping of German Society, 1945–55*, ed. Michael Ermath (Oxford: Berg, 1993), 64–65; and Thelen, *Union of Parts*, 72–73.

90. For example, Berghahn, *Americanisation of West German Industry*, 230; and Thelen, *Union of Parts*, 74.

91. Kittner, *Arbeits- und Sozialordnung*, 431–32.

92. Wolfgang Däubler, Michael Kittner, Thomas Klebe, and Peter Wedde, *Betriebsverfassungsgesetz: Kommentar für die Praxis mit Wahlordnung und EBR-Gesetz* (Cologne: Bund, 2010), 128–37.

93. Some works councils and employers skirt the restrictions on workplace accords by agreeing to an informal "workplace arrangement" (*Betriebsabsprache*). Such arrangements are not legally binding, however. Markovits, *Politics of West German Trade Unions*, 50.

94. Thelen, *Union of Parts*, 77.

95. Quoted in Koopmann, *Gewerkschaftliche Vertrauensleute*, 431.

96. Arno Krüger, *Walter Raymond: Arbeitgeberpräsident der ersten Stunde* (Cologne: Bachem, 1996), 27–28.

97. Müller-Jentsch, "Mitbestimmungspolitik," 461.

98. Thelen, *Union of Parts*, 107.

99. Wolfgang Streeck, *Industrial Relations in West Germany: A Case Study of the Car Industry* (New York: St. Martin's, 1984), 28–30; and Wolfram Wassermann, "Gewerkschaftliche Betriebspolitik," in Schroeder and Wessels, *Die Gewerkschaften*, 416–17.

100. It is important to note that the public sector has no employee representation on supervisory boards because there are none in the public sector, save for a small number of partially or wholly state-owned enterprises.

101. For a history of staff councils, see Klaus Kübel, *Personalrat und Personalmassnahmen: Zur Beteiligung des Personalrats bei der Einstellung und Entlassung von Mitarbeitern* (Giessen: Verlag der Ferberschen Universität-Buchhandlung, 1986); Hartmut Kübler, *Der Einfluss des Personalrats: Empirische Studie am Beispiel der Gemeinden und Städte Baden-Württembergs* (Stuttgart: Boorberg, 1981); and Fritz Ossenbühl, *Grenzen der Mitbestimmung im öffentlichen Dienst* (Baden-Baden: Nomos, 1986).

102. Kübel, *Personalrat und Personalmassnahmen*, 36; and Däubler, *Arbeitsrecht*, 336–37.

103. In Germany, public servants (e.g., municipal trash haulers) work for the government but may strike. Civil servants (e.g., ministry personnel), in contrast, are a special category of government employee who receive special benefits and protections but cannot strike legally.

104. Berndt Keller and Rainer Schnell, "On the Empirical Analysis of Staff Councils: Structural Data and Problems of Interest Representation," in "Industrial Relations in Germany: An Empirical Survey," special issue, *WSI-Mitteilungen* 56 (2003): 16.

105. Däubler, *Arbeitsrecht*, 87–88.

106. Volker R. Berghahn and Detlef Karstens, *Industrial Relations in West Germany* (Oxford: Berg, 1987), 112–14.

107. Weimer, *Deutsche Wirtschaftsgeschichte*, 217.

108. Däubler, *Arbeitsrecht*, 125.

109. Thelen, *Union of Parts*, 100–102.

110. Thelen, *Union of Parts*, 99–100; and Weimer, *Deutsche Wirtschaftsgeschichte*, 217.

111. *iwd—Informationsdienst des Instituts der deutschen Wirtschaft*, 22 November 2001; Müller-Jentsch, "Mitbestimmungspolitik," 469; and Anke Hassel, "The Erosion of the German System of Industrial Relations," *British Journal of Industrial Relations* 37, no. 3 (September 1999): 483–505.

112. Martin Behrens, "The New Works Constitution Act in Practice," in "Industrial Relations in Germany: An Empirical Survey," special issue, *WSI-Mitteilungen* 56 (2003): 56–57; and Wolfgang Schroeder, "The Revision of the Works Constitution Act," paper presented at the Twenty-fifth Annual Conference of the German Studies Association, Washington, DC, 5 October 2001.

113. *Handelsblatt*, 17–18 November 2000; *Manager-Magazin*, January 2004; Bernd Martens and Matthias Michailow, "Konvergenzen und Divergenzen zwischen dem ost- und westdeutschen Management: Ergebnisse einer Befragung von Leitern mittelständischer Industrieunternehmen in Ost- und Westdeutschland," *SFB 580-Mitteilungen*, no. 10 (November 2003): 13–56; Horst-Udo Niedenhoff, *Die Praxis der betrieblichen Mitbestimmung: Zusammenarbeit von Betriebsrat und Arbeitgeber, Kosten des Betreibsverfassungsgesetzes, Betriebsrats- und Sprecherausschusswahlen* (Cologne: Deutscher Instituts-Verlag, 1999), 64–65; and Sigurt Vitols, *Unternehmensführung und Arbeitsbeziehungen in deutschen Töchtergesellschaften grosser ausländischer Unternehmen: Studie des Forums Mitbestimmung im Auftrag der Bertelsmann Stiftung und der Hans-Böckler-Stiftung* (Gütersloh: Bertelsmann Stiftung, 2001).

114. Claus Schäfer, "WSI Surveys of Works and Staff Councils: An Overview," in "Industrial Relations in Germany: An Empirical Survey," special issue, *WSI-Mitteilungen* 56 (2003): 3; Bundesvereinigung der Deutschen Arbeitgeberverbände, *Für ein beschäftigungsförderndes Mitbestimmungs- und Tarifrecht*, 2nd ed. (Berlin: BDA, 2003), 9; and Rolf Reppel, "Unternehmenskultur und Mitbestimmung," in *Praxis Unternehmenskultur: Herausforderungen gemeinsam bewältigen*, vol. 1, *Erfolgsfaktor Unternehmenskultur*, ed. Bertelsmann Stiftung and Hans-Böckler-Stiftung (Gütersloh: Verlag der Bertelsmann Stiftung, 2001), 103–28.

115. *iwd—Informationsdienst des Instituts der deutschen Wirtschaft*, 22 October 1998.

116. Martin Höpner, "Unternehmensmitbestimmung und Mitbestimmungs-kritik," Beitrag zur Diskussionsveranstaltung, "Die Zukunft der Unternehm-ensmitbestimmung," [Contribution to discussion proceedings, "The future of enterprise codetermination"], working paper, Max-Planck-Institut für Gesell-schaftsforschung, Cologne, 23 April 2004, 5.

117. *Financial Times Deutschland*, 14 January 2001, 14 February 2001; *Frankfurter Rundschau*, 24 June 2001; *Der Spiegel*, 9 February 2001; and *Die Zeit*, 27 October 2000.

118. *Frankfurter Rundschau*, 24 June 2001; *Die Welt*, 24 June 2001; and Bundes-regierung, "Gesetz zur Reform des Betriebsverfassungsgesetzes vom 23. Juli 2001," *Bundesgesetzblatt*, pt. 1, 1852; *Bundesgesetzblatt*, pt. 1, 2518, 25 September 2001; and *Bundesgesetzblatt*, pt. 1, 3443, 10 December 2001.

119. Behrens, "New German Works Constitution Act," 64; Peter Ellguth and Susanne Kohaut, "Der Staat als Arbeitgeber: Wie unterscheiden sich die Arbeits-bedingungen zwischen öffentlichem Sektor und der Privatwirtschaft?" *Industrielle Beziehungen* 18, nos. 1–2 (2011): 11–38; Ralph Greifenstein, Leo Kissler, and Hendrik Lange, "Trendreport Betriebsratswahlen 2010: Zwischenergebnisse kurz nach der Wahl," unpublished working paper, Düsseldorf: Hans-Böckler-Stiftung, July 2010, http://www.boeckler.de/pdf_fof/S-2010-338-2-1.pdf; Gerhard Leminsky, "Ent-wicklungspotentiale der Mitbestimmung," in *Umbrüche und Kontinuitäten: Perspek-tiven nationaler und internationaler Arbeitsbeziehungen—Walther Müller-Jentsch zum 65. Geburtstag*, ed. Jörg Abel and Hans Joachim Sperling (Munich: Rainer Hampp, 2001), 149; Wolfgang Rudolph and Wolfram Wassermann, *Gestärkte Betriebsräte: Trendre-port Betriebsratswahlen 2006*, Arbeitspapier 137 (Düsseldorf: Hans-Böckler-Stiftung, 2007); and Schäfer, "WSI Surveys," 3.

120. Tom Spencer, "Where Is Public Affairs Going?" *Journal of Public Affairs* 1, no. 1 (2001): 82.

121. Brian Bercusson, "The European Social Model Comes to Britain," *Indus-trial Law Journal* 31, no. 3 (September 2002): 209.

122. Kittner, *Arbeits- und Sozialordnung*, 535.

123. NB, signatories to the Social Protocol also include members of the European Economic Area, which extends beyond the European Union. Great Britain became a signatory in 1997. Kittner, *Arbeits- und Sozialordnung*, 535–36; and Commission of the European Communities, "Directive on the Establishment of a European Works Council or a Procedure in Community Scale Undertakings and Community-Scale Groups of Undertakings for the Purposes of Informing and Consulting Employees" (Council Directive 94/45/EC of 22 September 1994).

124. Commission of the European Communities, "Report from the Com-mission to the European Parliament and the Council on the Application of the Directive on the Establishment of a European Works Council or a Procedure in Community-Scale Undertakings and Community-Scale Groups of Undertakings for the Purposes of Informing and Consulting Employees," COM (2000) 188 final (Brussels: Commission of the European Communities, 2000), 6.

125. Romuald Jagodziński, "EWCs after 15 Years: Success or failure?" *transfer* 17, no. 2 (May 2011): 206–9.

126. Torsten Müller, Hans-Wolfgang Platzer, and Stefan Rüb, "Transnational Company Policy and Coordination of Collective Bargaining: New Challenges and Roles for European Industry Federations," *transfer* 16, no. 4 (November 2010); and European Trade Union Institute, http://www.ewcdb.eu/search_results_ewc.php.

127. Däubler, *Arbeitsrecht*, 79–81; and Kittner, *Arbeits- und Sozialordnung*, 535–38.

128. For example, Manfred Bobke and Torsten Müller, "Chancen für eine Neugestaltung des Systems der Arbeitsbeziehungen auf der europäischen Ebene," *WSI-Mitteilungen* 48, no. 10 (October 1995): 654–61; and Hans-Wolfgang Platzer and Klaus-Peter Weiner, "Europäische Betriebsräte—eine Konstitutionsanalyse: Zur Genese und Dynamik transnationaler Arbeitsbeziehungen," *Industrielle Beziehungen* 5, no. 4 (1998): 388–412.

129. For example, Berndt Keller, "European Integration, Workers' Participation and Collective Bargaining: A Euro-Pessimistic View," in *Convergence of Divergence?: Internationalisation and Economic Policy Responses*, ed. B. Unger and F. van Waarden (Aldershot, UK: Avebury, 1995), 252–78; and Wolfgang Streeck, "The Internationalization of Industrial Relations in Europe: Prospects and Problems," *Politics and Society* 26, no. 4 (1998): 429–59.

130. Jagodziński, "EWCs after 15 Years," 210–11.

131. Gregory Jackson, "Contested Boundaries: Ambiguity and Creativity in the Evolution of German Codetermination," in *Beyond Continuity: Institutional Change in Advanced Political Economies*, ed. Wolfgang Streeck and Kathleen Thelen (Oxford: Oxford University Press, 2005), 244.

Chapter 3

1. Examples for the United States include: Orley Ashenfelter and John H. Pencavel, "American Trade Union Growth: 1900–1960," *Quarterly Journal of Economics* 83, no. 3 (August 1969): 434–48; John R. Commons, David J. Saposs, Helen L. Sumner, E. B. Mittelman, H. E. Hoagland, John B. Andrews, and Selig Perlman, *History of Labor in the United States*, vols. 1–4 (New York: Macmillan, 1918); John T. Dunlop, "The Development of Labor Organization: A Theoretical Framework," in *Insights into Labor Issues*, ed. R. A. Lester and J. Shister (New York: Macmillan, 1948); Richard B. Freeman and James L. Medoff, *What Do Unions Do?* (New York: Basic, 1984); and Barry T. Hirsch and John T. Addison, *The Economic Analysis of Unions: New Approaches and Evidence* (Boston: Allen & Unwin, 1986). For Germany, examples include: Klaus Armingeon, "Trade Unions under Changing Conditions: The West German Experience, 1950–1985," *European Sociological Review* 5, no. 1 (May 1989): 1–22; Joachim Bergmann, Otto Jacobi, and Walther Müller-Jentsch, *Gewerkschaften in der Bundesrepublik*, 2 vols. (Frankfurt/Main: Aspekte, 1978); Andrei S. Markovits, *The Politics of West German Trade Unions: Strategies of Interest Representation in Growth and Crisis* (Cambridge: Cambridge University Press, 1986); Claus Schnabel, "Determinants of Trade Union Growth and Decline in the Federal Republic of Germany," *European Sociological Review* 5, no. 2 (September 1989): 133–45; and Jelle Visser, "Trade Union Decline and What Next: Is Germany a Special Case?" *Industrielle Beziehungen* 14, no. 2 (2007): 97–117.

2. Two authors have led the way in time series analyses of union membership in Germany: Claus Schnabel and Klaus Armingeon. The studies for which Schnabel was either author or coauthor (i.e., Schnabel, "Determinants of Trade Union Growth and Decline"; Schnabel, "Trade Union Growth and Decline in the Federal Republic of Germany," *Empirical Economics* 12, no. 2 (June 1987): 107–27; and Alan Carruth and Claus Schnabel, "Empirical Modelling of Trade Union Growth in Germany, 1956–1986: Traditional versus Cointegration and Error Correction Methods," *Weltwirtschaftliches Archiv* 126, no. 2 (1990): 326–46) use percentage change in union membership as the dependent variable. Armingeon, "Trade Unions under Changing Conditions," in contrast, uses both percentage change in union membership and density as a dependent variable.

3. Bernhard Ebbinghaus and Jelle Visser, *The Societies of Europe: Trade Unions in Western Europe since 1945* (New York: Grove's Dictionaries, 2000).

4. The sources for union membership are the reports (*Geschäftsberichte*) of the CGB, DBB, DGB, and their respective member unions as well as independent unions; Ebbinghaus and Visser *The Societies of Europe*; Bernhard Ebbinghaus, "Die Mitgliederentwicklung deutscher Gewerkschaften im historischen und internationalen Vergleich," in *Die Gewerkschaften in Politik und Gesellschaft der Bundesrepublik Deutschland*, ed. Wolfgang Schroeder and Bernhard Wessels (Wiesbaden: Westdeutscher Verlag, 2003), 174–203; Michael Kittner, ed., *Gewerkschaftsjahrbuch* (Cologne: Bund, various years); Walther Müller-Jentsch, *Basisdaten der industriellen Beziehungen* (Frankfurt/Main: Campus, 1989); Walther Müller-Jentsch and Peter Ittermann, *Industriellen Beziehungen: Daten, Zeitreihen, Trends 1950–1999* (Frankfurt/Main: Campus, 2000); Hans-Ulrich Niedenhof and Wolfgang Pege, *Gewerkschaftshandbuch: Daten, Fakten, Strukturen* (Cologne: Deutscher Instituts-Verlag, various years); and Statistisches Bundesamt, *Jahrbuch für die Bundesrepublik Deutschland* (Wiesbaden: Hohlhammer, various years).

5. Unfortunately, earlier studies of German unionization (i.e., Armingeon, "Trade Unions under Changing Conditions"; Carruth and Schnabel, "Empirical Modelling of Trade Union Growth"; and Schnabel, "Determinants of Trade Union Growth and Decline") include nonemployed members in their data, which distorts their results.

6. Ver.di is the product of a merger of five unions in 2001. I use data from ver.di's largest predecessor, the Union of Public Services and Transportation Employees (Gewerkschaft Öffentliche Dienste, Transport und Verkehr, ÖTV) for the years before 2001.

7. For a summary and analysis of twenty-six quantitative studies of unionization from the 1960s to the mid-1990s, see Claus Schnabel, "Determinants of Trade Union Membership," in *International Handbook of Trade Unions*, ed. John T. Addison and Claus Schnabel (Cheltenham, UK: Edward Elgar, 2003).

8. Bundesministerium für Arbeit, *Statistisches Taschenbuch* (Bonn/Berlin, various years), series 2.6, *erwerbstätige Arbeitnehmer Inland*. The data include West Berlin from the outset and the Saar starting in 1957.

Ebbinghaus and Visser, *The Societies of Europe*, make the same choices regarding the numerator and the denominator. As a result, my estimate of German union density is very similar to theirs. There is one difference, however. In this study I use series

2.6 as reported by the German labor ministry and Muller-Jentsch, *Basisdaten der industriellen Beziehungen,* for the entire postwar period. Ebbinghaus and Visser estimate the number of active employees for the 1950s using another data set, because they report being unable to find the data for series 2.6 that cover the 1950s. The resulting differences between the two data series are minor. See also Amsterdam Institute for Advanced Labour Studies, Institutional Characteristics of Trade Unions, Wage Setting, State Intervention and Social Pacts (ICTWSS) database at Amsterdam Institute for Advanced Labour Studies, "ICTWSS: Database on Institutional Characteristics of Trade Unions, Wage Setting, State Intervention and Social Pacts in 34 Countries between 1960 and 2007," http://www.uva-aias.net/208.

An alternative calculation of density could include the unemployed in both the numerator and the denominator. Adding the unemployed further complicates the calculation of density and muddies density as a measure of the macroeconomic power of unions in the labor market. As a result, I calculate density using the employed only.

9. Armingeon, "Trade Unions under Changing Conditions," 1–22; Carruth and Schnabel "Empirical Modelling of Trade Union Growth," 326–46; and Schnabel "Determinants of Trade Union Growth and Decline," 133–45.

10. Most quantitative analyses of developments of union membership, regardless of country or dependent variable, use ordinarily least squares (OLS) models. This is unfortunate, because time series analyses are prone to violating the assumptions underlying a sound OLS analysis. OLS assumes that the stochastic terms of all observations in the model are uncorrelated with each other (i.e., there is no autocorrelation). A time series model, however, analyzes observations taken from the same sample over time. We can be fairly certain that the randomness of our observations in year t are correlated to the randomness of our observations in year t+1 when we are looking at the same sample. A generalized least squares (GLS) model, in contrast, actually calculates the stochastic terms. The results are more robust than a simple OLS regression because they are adjusted for expected autocorrelation, which decreases the chance of committing Type I error due to autocorrelation. The data for all regressions in the chapter are subject to a Prais-Winsten transformation.

11. Planungsgruppe Weiterentwicklung des DGB, "Turnaround!: Vorschläge der Planungsgruppe Weiterentwicklung des DGB—Vorlage für die Klausur DGB-Bundesvorstand, am 25.01.2005 (nur für den internen Gebrauch)," unpublished document, DGB, 2005, 5.

12. Armingeon, "Trade Unions under Changing Conditions," 4; Ashenfelter and Pencavel, "American Trade Union Growth," 436; Carruth and Schnabel, "Empirical Modelling of Trade Union Growth"; and George Sayers Bain and Farouk Elsheikh, *Union Growth and the Business Cycle* (Oxford: Blackwell, 1976), 63. The data source is Bundesministerium für Arbeit, *Statistisches Taschenbuch* (Bonn/Berlin, various years), series 1.14, excel files, *Nettolöhne und–gehälte,* http://www.bmas.de/DE/Themen/Arbeitsmarkt/Arbeitsmarktstatistiken/Statistisches-Taschenbuch/statistisches-taschenbuch-2011.html.

13. For example, Bain and Elsheikh, *Union Growth and the Business Cycle,* 64.

14. For example, Schnabel, "Determinants of Trade Union Growth and Decline," 64.

15. Giacomo Corneo, "Social Custom, Management Opposition, and Trade Union Membership," *European Economic Review* 39 (1995): 275–92.

16. Kathleen Thelen, "Why German Employers Cannot Bring Themselves to Dismantle the German Model," in *Unions, Employers, and Central Banks: Macroeconomic Coordination and Institutional Change in Social Market Economies*, ed. Torben Iversen, Jonas Pontusson, and David Soskice (Cambridge: Cambridge University Press, 2000), 173–204.

17. Bundesministerium für Arbeit, *Statistisches Taschenbuch* (Bonn/Berlin, various years), series 1.11, excel files, *Unternehmens- und Vermögenseinkommen,* http:// www.bmas.de/DE/Themen/Arbeitsmarkt/Arbeitsmarktstatistiken/Statistisches-Taschenbuch/statistisches-taschenbuch-2011.html.

18. Bain and Elsheikh, *Union Growth and the Business Cycle*, 66.

19. For example, Bain and Elsheikh, *Union Growth and the Business Cycle*; Sabine Blaschke, "Union Density and European Integration: Diverging Convergence," *European Journal of Industrial Relations* 6, no. 2 (2000): 224; Daniele Checchi and Jelle Visser, "Pattern Persistence in European Trade Union Density: A Longitudinal Analysis 1950–1996," *European Sociological Review* 21, no. 1 (2005): 1–21; and Michael Goldfield, *The Decline of Organized Labor in the United States* (Chicago: University of Chicago Press, 1987), 173.

20. For example, Schnabel, "Determinants of Trade Union Growth and Decline"; Joelle Sano and John B. Williamson, "Factors Affecting Union Decline in 18 OECD Countries and Their Implications for Labor Movement Reform," *International Journal of Comparative Sociology* 49, no. 6 (2008): 479–500.

21. Ashenfelter and Pencavel, "American Trade Union Growth," 436–37.

22. Visser, "Trade Union Decline," 104.

23. Michael Wallerstein, "Union Organization in Advanced Industrial Democracies," *American Political Science Review* 83, no. 2 (June 1989): 488.

24. Blaschke, "Union Density," 219; and Anke Hassel and Thorsten Schulten, "Globalization and the Future of Central Collective Bargaining: The Example of the German Metal Industry," *Economy and Society* 27, no. 4 (November 1998): 486–522.

25. Wallerstein, "Union Organization," 490. See also Sano and Williamson, "Factors Affecting Union Decline," 492.

26. For example, Blaschke, "Union Density," 232; Larry J. Griffin, Holly J. McCammon, and Christopher Botsko, "The 'Unmaking' of a Movement?: The Crisis of US Trade Unions in Comparative Perspective," in *Change in Societal Institutions*, ed. D. M. Klein and J. Glass (New York: Plenum, 1990), 169–94; and Bruce Western, "A Comparative Study of Working-Class Disorganization: Union Decline in Eighteen Advanced Capitalist Countries," *American Sociological Review* 60, no. 2 (April 1995): 194.

27. For example, Blaschke, "Union Density," 221; Schnabel, "Determinants of Trade Union Growth and Decline," 138; Visser, "Trade Union Decline," 107; and Wallerstein, "Union Organization," 490.

28. For example, Visser, "Trade Union Decline," 108; and Bruce Western, "Unionization and Labor Market Institutions in Advanced Capitalism, 1950-1985," *American Journal of Sociology* 99, no. 5 (March 1995): 1325.

29. For example, Blaschke, "Union Density," 221; Carruth and Schnabel, "Empirical Modelling of Trade Union Growth," 330; and Schnabel, "Determinants of Trade Union Growth and Decline," 138.

30. Visser, "Trade Union Decline," 108.

31. Jelle Visser, "Union Membership Statistics in 24 Countries," *Monthly Labor Review* 129, no. 1 (January 2006): 46–47.

32. Sano and Williamson, "Factors Affecting Union Decline."

33. Schnabel, "Determinants of Trade Union Growth and Decline," 138.

34. T. H. Marshall, *Citizenship and Social Class and other Essays* (Cambridge: Cambridge University Press, 1950); Checchi and Visser, "Pattern Persistence," 4; and Schnabel, "Determinants of Trade Union Growth and Decline," 138.

35. Checchi and Visser, "Pattern Persistence," 2. See also, Allison L. Booth, "The Free Rider Problem and a Social Custom Model of Trade Union Membership," *Quarterly Journal of Economics* 100, no. 1 (February 1985): 253–61; Jean Hartley, "Joining a Trade Union," in *Employment Relations: The Psychology of Influence and Control at Work*, ed. J. Hartley and G. M. Stephenson (Oxford: Blackwell, 1992); and Jelle Visser, "Why Fewer Workers Join Unions in Europe: A Social Custom Explanation of Membership Trends," *British Journal of Industrial Relations* 40, no. 3 (September 2002): 403–30.

36. Ralf Dahrendorf, *Class and Class Conflict in Industrial Society* (Stanford: Stanford University Press, 1959).

37. For example, Ulrich Beck, *Risikogesellschaft* (Frankfurt/Main: Campus, 1986); Ulrich Beck and Elisabeth Beck-Gernsheim, *Individualization, Instiutionalized Individualism and its Social and Economic Consequences* (London: Sage, 2002); Stefan Hradil, *Sozialstrukturanalyse in einer fortgeschrittenen Gesellschaft: Von Klassen und Schichten zu Lagen und Milieus* (Opladen: Westdeutscher Verlag, 1987); Reinhard Kreckel, *Politische Soziologie der sozialen Ungleichheit*, vol. 3, rev. and expanded ed. (Frankfurt/Main: Campus, 2004); and Gero Neugebauer, *Politische Milieus in Deutschland* (Bonn: Dietz, 2007).

38. David Peetz, "Are Individualistic Attitudes Killing Collectivism?" *transfer* 16, no. 3 (August 2010): 383–98; and World Values Survey, www.worldvaluessurvey.org.

39. Planungsgruppe Weiterentwicklung des DGB, "Turnaround!" 4.

40. Checchi and Visser, "Pattern Persistence," 4–6.

41. In this chapter I use population as the denominator in the calculation of the left-party variable in order to capture the relative size of the labor milieu within German society as a whole. Although minors and non-German nationals may not vote, they can join both unions and the political parties in question here and are counted among the membership. Consequently, the population of eligible voters is not a better denominator.

42. This measure of labor's milieu does not include the Greens or the labor wing of the Christian parties. Even though most Green Party members would self-identify as left of center, the milieu of the Greens is quite different from that of the labor movement. The Greens have roots primarily among the privileged university-educated "postmaterialist" youths who organized the postwar environmental and peace movements. See Ronald Inglehart and Christian Welzel, *Modernization, Cultural Change, and Democracy: The Human Development Sequence* (Cambridge: Cambridge University Press, 2005).

The measure of milieu used here also does not include the membership of the Christlich Demokratische Arbeitnehmerschaft (CDA, Christian Democratic

Workers Group). A case could be made for including CDA membership, since the postwar German labor movement is a product of a merger of the Christian Democratic and Social Democratic labor traditions. Nonetheless, CDA data are not included for three reasons. First, there are no annual data on CDA membership for any substantial stretch of time. Second, the available CDA membership data never show a membership that breaks out of the tens of thousands, which is a relatively small fraction of left-of-center party membership. Third, the extant data show a development that mirrors that of the left-of-center parties. As a result, the impact of adding CDA membership on the data series would be unlikely to alter the relationship.

Even if the data existed, there would be conceptual problems in including CDA membership in this measure. First, the CDA is neither a party nor an independent organization. It is a caucus within a party. The opportunities and incentives to join it differ substantially from that of a political party. See Herlind Gundelach, "Die Sozialausschüsse zwischen CDU und DGB: Selbstverständnis und Rolle 1949–1966," (PhD diss., Rheinishe Friedrich-Wilhelms-Universität zu Bonn,1983); and Hanns Jürgen Küsters and Rudolf Uertz, eds., *Christlich-Soziale im DGB* (St. Augustin: Konrad-Adenauer-Stiftung, 2010).

43. For example, Checchi and Visser, "Pattern Persistence," 6.

44. Stephen J. Silvia, "The Forward Retreat: Labor and Social Democracy in Germany, 1982–1992," *International Journal of Political Economy* 22, no. 4 (Winter 1992/93): 36–52.

45. For example, Ashenfelter and Pencavel, "American Trade Union Growth"; Bain and Elsheikh, *Union Growth and the Business Cycle*; Checchi and Visser, "Pattern Persistence"; Sano and Williamson, "Factors Affecting Union Decline"; Schnabel, "Determinants of Trade Union Growth and Decline"; Western, "A Comparative Study"; and Alison L. Booth, "A Reconsideration of Trade Union Growth in the United Kingdom," *British Journal of Industrial Relations* 21, no. 3 (November 1983): 377–91.

46. Christopher H. Achen, "Why Lagged Dependent Variables Can Suppress the Explanatory Power of Other Independent Variables," paper presented at the annual meeting of the Midwest Political Science Association, Chicago, April 27–29, 2000.

47. For example, Sano and Williamson, "Factors Affecting Union Decline," 492; and Wallerstein, "Union Organization," 491.

48. For all the data in this chapter and the tables showing the results of the West German and FDI specifications, see "Holding the Shop Together: Supplemental Material," www.american.edu/sis/faculty/Silvia-Holding-the-Shop-Together.cfm.

49. Gøsta Esping-Andersen, "Multiple Regressions in Small-N Comparisons," in *Capitalisms Compared*, ed. Lars Mjøset and Tommy H. Clausen (Oxford: Elsevier JAI, 2007).

50. For example, Blaschke, "Union Density," 222; Corneo, "Social Custom," 291; and Sano and Williamson, "Factors Affecting Union Decline," 491.

51. Marc Howard Ross, "Culture in Comparative Political Analysis," in *Comparative Politics: Rationality, Culture, and Structure*, ed. Mark Irving Lichbach and Alan S. Zuckerman, 2nd ed. (Cambridge: Cambridge University Press, 2009), 156.

Chapter 4

1. Geoff Eley, "Labor History, Social History, *Alltagsgeschichte*: Experience, Culture, and the Politics of Everyday—a New Direction for German Social History. Review Article," *Journal of Modern History* 61, no. 2 (June 1989): 658.

2. Michael Schneider, *Kleine Geschichte der Gewerkschaften: Ihre Entwicklung in Deutschland von den Anfängen bis heute* (Bonn: J. H. W. Dietz, 1989), 240–41.

3. Michael Fichter, *Besatzungsmacht und Gewerkschaften. Zur Entwicklung und Anwendung der US-Gewerkschaftspolitik in Deutschland 1944–1948* (Opladen: West-deutscher Verlag, 1982), 211–18; and Siegfried Mielke, "Die Neugründung der Gewerkschaften in den westlichen Besatzungszonen 1945–1949," in *Geschichte der Gewerkschaften in der Bundesrepublik Deutschland: Von den Anfängen bis heute*, ed. Hans-Otto Hemmer and Kurt Thomas Schmitz (Cologne: Bund, 1990), 28–31 and 74–75.

4. For example, Otto Brenner, "Nein zu Notstands- und Notdienstgesetz," *Gewerkschaftliche Monatshefte* 12, no. 2 (February 1961): 70–73; and Irmgard Blät-tel, Ernst Breit, Detlef Hensche, and Adolf Schmidt, "Die grösste Errungen-schaft der Gewerkschaften," *Gewerkschaftliche Monatshefte* 55, no. 3 (March 2004): 136–43.

5. For example, William Carr, *A History of Germany 1815–1985*, 3rd ed. (London: Edward Arnold, 1987), 264.

6. Klaus Schönhoven, "Germany to 1945," in *European Labor Unions*, ed. Joan Campbell (Westport, CT: Greenwood, 1992), 153–54.

7. Frank Deppe, "Der Deutsche Gewerkschaftsbund, 1949–1965," in *Geschichte der deutschen Gewerkschaftsbewegung*, 3rd. ed., ed. Frank Deppe, Georg Fül-berth, and Jürgen Harrer (Cologne: Pahl-Rugenstein, 1981), 320–22; and Theo Pirker, *Die blinde Macht: Die Gewerkschaftsbewegung in der Bundesrepublik*, vol. 1, *Vom "Ende des Kapitalismus" zur Zähmung der Gewerkschaften* (Berlin: Olle & Wolter, 1979), 259–60.

8. Andrei S. Markovits, *The Politics of West German Trade Unions: Strategies of Interest Representation in Growth and Crisis* (Cambridge: Cambridge University Press, 1986), 418–19; and Chris Howell, *The Trade Unions and the State: The Construction of the Industrial Relations Institutions in Britain, 1890–2000* (Princeton: Princeton University Press, 2005).

9. Eberhard Schmidt, *Die verhinderte Neuordnung 1945–1952* (Frankfurt/Main: Europäische Verlagsanstalt, 1977), 41–45.

10. Markovits, *Politics of West German Trade Unions*, 65; and Anne Weiss-Hartmann and Wolfgang Hecker, "Die Entwicklung der Gewerkschaftsbewegung 1945–1949," in *Geschichte der deutschen Gewerkschaftsbewegung*, 3rd. ed., ed. Frank Deppe, Georg Fülberth, and Jürgen Harrer (Cologne: Pahl-Rugenstein, 1981), 282–85.

11. Mielke, "Neugründung der Gewerkschaften," 35–41.

12. Ibid., 41–46; and Schneider, *Kleine Geschichte der Gewerkschaften*, 254–55.

13. Hermann Weber and Siegfried Mielke, eds., *Die Angestelltenfrage 1945–1949: Quellen zur Geschichte der deutschen Gewerkschaftsbewegung im 20. Jahrhundert*, vol. 8 (Cologne: Bund, 1989), 32–40 and 101–7.

14. Mielke, "Neugründung der Gewerkschaften," 45–46.

15. Werner Müller, "Die Gründung des DGB, der Kampf um die Mitbestimmung, programatisches Scheitern und der Übergang zum gewerkschaftlichen Pragmatismus," in Hemmer and Schmitz, *Geschichte der Gewerkschaften*, 87–93. See also Deutscher Gewerkschaftsbund, *"Mittelpunkt ist der arbeitende Mensch": Protokoll Gründungskongress des Deutschen Gewerkschaftsbundes München, 12–14 Oktober 1949*, repr. (Cologne: Bund, 1989).

16. The 1949 DGB constitution allocated the confederation 15% of gross dues. For many years, member unions also paid an additional 0.46% into a "solidarity and action fund" for special campaigns. The 2010 DGB convention ended that payment, which in 2009 totaled €3.6 million, or 2.5% of the DGB's budget (*Frankfurter Allgemeine Zeitung*, 18 May 2010).

17. In the past, the DGB also played a central role in running several nonprofit, labor-owned enterprises. These included the co-op chain of grocery stores, the huge Neue Heimat housing authority, and the Bank für Gemeinwirtschaft. Several of these ventures had roots dating back to the nineteenth century. The original intention was to apply additional competitive pressure on for-profit firms in order to drive down prices for employees' everyday needs. Mismanagement and at times corruption, combined with financial shortfalls within the DGB, led the peak confederation to sell off these holdings during the 1980s and early 1990s.

18. The data in this section on the trade unions, unless otherwise noted, come from the *Geschäftsberichte* (officers' reports) of the Deutscher Gerwerkschaftsbund and its affiliated unions. Economic data, unless otherwise noted, comes from the publications and the website of Germany's Statistisches Bundesamt.

19. The official name of DGB conventions is the "parliament of labor." From 1950 to 1956 it was biennial. From 1956 to 1978 it was triennial. Since 1978 it has been quadrennial.

20. The number of convention delegates is currently four hundred. For more on the institutional architecture and practices of the DGB see http://www.dgb.de/wir and http://www.dgb.de/dgbkongress.

21. In the past, the DGB managing federal executive board had one president and two vice-presidents. As an institutional expression of unitary unionism, at least one of the vice-presidents was always a member of a Christian Democratic party. When the 1994 DGB convention streamlined the board from nine to five members, it eliminated this symbolic post but maintained the practice of having at least one Christian Democrat on it. The 2010 DGB convention cut the number of board members from five to four starting in 2014.

22. Before unification, the DGB had nine "state districts" (*Landesbezirke*). Unification prompted union leaders to add four more in the early 1990s. Decreasing membership led to a reduction back to nine.

23. The original term for the subdistricts was "wards" (*Kreise*). The DGB originally had well over one hundred. The 1994 DGB convention cut the number down to eighty. The 2010 DGB convention set a goal of reducing their number to approximately seventy by 2014.

24. Walther Müller-Jentsch, "Gewerkschaftliche Politik in der Wirtschaftskrise II 1978/79 bis 1982/83," in Hemmer and Schmitz, *Geschichte der Gewerkschaften*, 384.

25. Deutscher Gewerkschaftsbund, *Grundsatzprogramm des Deutschen Gewerkschaftsbundes* (Düsseldorf: DGB, 1963).

26. Markovits, *Politics of West German Trade Unions*, 101.

27. Deutscher Gerwerkschaftsbund, *Grundsatzprogramm des Deutschen Gewerkschaftsbundes* (Düsseldorf: DGB, 1981).

28. Markovits, *Politics of West German Trade Unions*, 11.

29. *VDI Nachrichten*, 7 April 2006; Christliche Gewerkschaft Metall and Ost-Metall, *Phönix im Spiegel der Presse, Mai bis Dezember 1998* (Dresden: OstMetall, 1998); Christliche Gewerkschaft Metall and OstMetall, *Die Metall- und Elektro-Industrie im Wandel: Phönix—eine Chance für den Flächentarifvertrag* (Dresden: OstMetall, 1998); Christliche Gewerkschaft Metall and OstMetall, *Phönix. Das moderne Tarifvertragssystem*, 5th rev. ed. (Dresden: OstMetall, 2006); and CGZP Pressemitteilungen, 7 December 2009.

30. *Frankfurter Allgemeine Zeitung*, 15 December 2010; *Frankfurter Rundschau*, 3 April 2009; *ver.di-Mitteilung*, 25 May 2012; and Manfred Weiss and Marlene Schmidt, *Labour Law and Industrial Relations in Germany*, 4th ed. (Alphen aan den Rijn, Neth.: Kluwer Law International, 2005), 174.

31. Bundesministerium für Arbeit, *Statistisches Taschenbuch* (Bonn/Berlin, various years), series 4.1.

32. Markovits, *Politics of West German Trade Unions*, 114–26; and Stephen J. Silvia, "Public Pension Reform in Germany and the United States," in *Healthcare and Pension Reform*, ed. American Institute for Contemporary German Studies (Washington, DC: AICGS, Johns Hopkins University Press, 2007), 33.

33. *Frankfurter Rundschau*, 27 January 1979.

34. Stephen J. Silvia, "Every Which Way but Loose: German Industrial Relations since 1980," in *The Brave New World of European Labor: European Trade Unions at the Millennium*, ed. Andrew Martin and George Ross (New York: Berghahn, 1999), 75–174.

35. The question of the impact of working-time reduction remains controversial. Studies that find working-time reduction ineffectual include: Axel Börsch-Supan, "Reduction of Working Time: Does It Decrease Unemployment?" paper presented at the Fifth Meeting of the Deutsch-Französisches Wirtschaftspolitisches Forum/Forum Economique Franco-Allemand, Paris, 6–7 July 1999, which summarizes several analyses; and Jennifer Hunt, "Has Work-Sharing Worked in Germany?" *Quarterly Journal of Economics* 114, no. 1 (February 1999): 117–48. The best presentation of the alternative argument is Gerhard Bosch and Steffen Lehndorff, "Working-Time Reduction and Employment: Experiences in Europe and Economic Policy Recommendations," *Cambridge Journal of Economics* 25, no. 2 (March 2001): 209–43. For a discussion of unemployment in eastern Germany, see Stephen J. Silvia, "The Elusive Quest for Normalcy: The German Economy since Unification," *German Politics and Society* 28, no. 2 (Summer 2010): 82–101.

36. *Die Zeit*, 18 May 1984.

37. Stephen J. Silvia, "The West German Labor Law Controversy: A Struggle for the Factory of the Future," *Comparative Politics* 20, no. 2 (January 1988): 155–73.

38. Michael Fichter and Hugo Riester, "Die Gewerkschaften," in *Intermediäre Strukturen in Ostdeutschland*, ed. Oskar Niedermayer (Opladen: Leske & Budrich, 1996), 309–34.

39. The Treuhandanstalt (Trust Holding Agency), which was the official government body responsible for the properties held by the former German Democratic

Republic, rented most of the disputed properties at market rates to the DGB during a protracted legal wrangle over their ownership. The Treuhandanstalt agreed in 1994 to sell fourteen of the disputed eastern properties to the DGB for 46.5 million deutschmarks (i.e., at slightly less than half of the market price). Ten of the fourteen properties required additional renovations that cost an additional 95 million deutschmarks, *Quelle* 47, no. 5 (May 1996).

40. Bruno Köbele, "Interview: 'Das Stimmrecht ist keine Geldfrage,'" *Quelle* 45, no. 4 (April 1994): 13.

41. Klaus Lang, "Das wäre das Ende des DGB," *Quelle* 45, no. 5 (May 1994): 9.

42. Jürgen Hoffmann, Reiner Hoffmann, Ulrich Mückenberger, and Dietrich Lange, eds., *Jenseits der Beschlusslage: Gewerkschaft als Zukunftswerkstatt* (Cologne: Bund, 1990), 17-26.

43. The ten framing *Leitfragen* are: (1) paths to social unity; (2) the future of the welfare state; (3) the structuring of the economy; (4) the future place of work in society; (5) education and training for the future; (6) the emancipation of women; (7) European cooperation; (8) migration and social integration; (9) the environment, peace, and development; and (10) the future of trade union interest representation. Deutscher Gewerkschaftsbund, *Leitfragen zur Programmdebatte*, ed. Abteilung Grundsatz, politische Planung (Düsseldorf: DGB, 1993).

44. For example, Heinz-Werner Meyer, ed., *Aufbrüche—Anstösse: Beiträge zur Reformdiskussion im Deutschen Gewerkschaftsbund und seinen Gewerkschaften*, vol. 1 (Cologne: Bund, 1994).

45. Wolfgang Uellenberg von Dawen, "Organisations- und Programmreform des DGB," in *Gewerkschaften heute 1995*, ed. Michael Kittner (Cologne: Bund, 1995), 97–112.

46. Rudi Schmidt and Rainer Trinczek, "Fusion und Konfusion: Gründe und Hintergründe für die Reorganisation des DGB," in *Reform des DGB: Herausforderungen, Aufbruchspläne und Modernisierungskonzepte*, ed. Thomas Leif, Ansgar Klein, and Hans-Josef Legrand (Cologne: Bund, 1993), 84-85.

47. Deutscher Gewerkschaftsbund, *Protokoll. 5. ausserordentlicher Bundeskongress. Dresden, 13.-16. November 1996* (Düsseldorf: DGB, 1997).

48. Deutscher Gewerkschaftsbund, Bundesvorstand, *Grundsatzprogramm des Deutschen Gewerkschaftsbundes: Entwurf für den ausserordentlichen Bundeskongress—Beschlossen auf der Sitzung des Bundesvorstandes,* 6 March 1996 (Düsseldorf: DGB, 1996), 21.

49. Ibid.

50. *Süddeutsche Zeitung*, 18 November 1996; and *die tageszeitung,* 18 November 1996.

51. Deutscher Gewerkschaftsbund, Bundesvorstand, *Die Zukunft gestalten: Grundsatzprogramm des Deutschen Gewerkschaftsbundes* (Düsseldorf: DGB, 1996).

52. Deutscher Gewerkschaftsbund, *Geschäftsbericht des Bundesvorstandes des Deutschen Gewerkschaftsbunds*, various years.

53. Deutsche Presse Agentur, 8 January 1995; *Focus*, 28 May 1995; *Gewerkschafter*, February 1994; and *ÖTV-Intern*, 18 March 1994.

54. Hermann Rappe, "Wir werden Beispiel setzen: Gespräch mit Hermann Rappe über die Fusionspläne von IG Chemie-Papier-Keramik und IG Bergbau und

Energie," *Gewerkschaftliche Monatshefte* 43, no. 1 (January 1992): 8–13; and Seppel Kraus, "Bausteine für eine DGB Reform," *Gewerkschaftliche Monatshefte* 44, no. 5 (May 1993): 284–93.

55. Hermann Rappe, "Die Rolle der Gewerkschaften in der modernen Industriegesellschaft," in *Für eine Politik der Vernunft: Beiträge zu Demokratie und Sozialpolitik,* ed. Hermann Weber (Cologne: Bund, 1989), 276–84.

56. *Wirtschaftswoche,* 7 September 1990.

57. *Handelsblatt,* 14 May 1993.

58. *Quelle* 44, no. 11 (November 1993): 13; and Michael Fichter, "Trade Union Members: A Vanishing Species in Post-Unification Germany?" *German Studies Review* 20, no. 1 (February 1997): 99.

59. Hans-Hermann Hertle and Jürgen Kädtler, "Die industriepolitische Wende der industriellen Beziehungen: Gewerkschaftspolitik unter dem Primat der Industriepolitik am Beispiel der IG Chemie, Papier, Keramik," *Soziale Welt* 21, no. 2 (1990): 183–205.

60. Gewerkschaft Öffentliche Dienste, Transport und Verkehr; Deutsche Postgewerkschaft, Gewerkschaft der Eisenbahner Deutschlands, Gewerkschaft Erziehung und Wissenschaft, and Gewerkschaft der Polizei, "Kooperation statt Fusion. Zweite gemeinsame Erklärung der Gewerkschaften des öffentlichen Dienstes" [Cooperation instead of merger. Second common declaration of the public-sector unions], Stuttgart, 1 July 1993.

61. Industriegewerkschaft Medien, Gewerkschaft Holz und Kunststoff, Gewerkschaft Nahrung-Genuss-Gaststätten, and Gewerkschaft Textil-Bekleidung, "Eigenständigkeit sichern. Gemeinsame Erklärung zur DGB-Reform" [Secure independence. Common declaration on DGB reform"], Düsseldorf, October 1993.

62. Industriegewerkschaft Metall, *Protokoll. 18. ordentlicher Gewerkschaftstag der IG Metall in Berlin, 29. Oktober bis 4. November 1995* (Frankfurt/Main: Union, 1995), 281.

63. *Quelle* 46, no. 12 (December 1995).

64. Burckard Bösche, Gerhard Kirschgässner, Norbert Trautwein, Wolfgang Rose, and Frank Schmidt, "DGB-Organisationsreform: Verändern ohne Konzept?" *Gewerkschaftliche Monatshefte* 47, no. 1 (January 1996): 17–19.

65. Günter Frech, "Organisationsreform ohne Tabus: Die 'fünf kleinen Tiger' wollen ein neues 'DGB-Bewusstsein,'" *express* 34, no. 4 (April 1996), 3.

66. Deutscher Gewerkschaftsbund, *Geschäftsbericht 1998–2001* (Berlin: 2002), 112–15, http://www.dgb.de/dgbkongress/information1/geschftsbericht4.

67. Industriegewerkschaft Bau-Steine-Erden, *Geschäftsbericht, 1991–1993* (Frankfurt/Main: Union, 1994), 865–67; and Industriegewerkschaft Bauen-Agrar-Umwelt, *Geschäftsbericht, 1994–1996* (Frankfurt/Main: Union, 1997), 47–48.

68. Industriegewerkschaft Chemie-Papier-Keramik, *Geschäftsbericht 1991–1994* (Hanover: Buchdruckwerkstätten Hannover, 1994), 16–17.

69. Industriegewerkschaft Bergbau, Chemie, Energie, *Protokoll der Verhandlungen des 1. Ordentlichen Gewerkschaftskongresses der Industriegewerkschaft Bergbau, Chemie, Energie* (Hanover: Buchdruckwerkstätten, 1997).

70. Frech, "Organisationsreform ohne Tabus," 4.

71. Industriegewerkschaft Metall, *Geschäftsbericht 1995–1998* (Frankfurt/Main: Union, 1999), 45.

72. Bernd Riexinger and Heinz-Günther Lang, "'Megalithkultur': Fusionsprojekt als Antwort auf die gewerkschaftliche und politische Krise?" *express* 36, no. 10 (October 1998), 5.

73. Deutsche Angestellten-Gewerkschaft; Deutsche Post Gewerkschaft; Gewerkschaft Erziehung und Wissenschaft; Gewerkschaft Handel, Banken und Versicherungen; Industriegewerkschaft Medien; and Gewerkschaft öffentliche Dienste, Transport und Verkehr; "Entwurf der 'Politischen Plattform' zur Neustrukturierung der gewerkschaftlichen Interessenvertretung im Dienstleistungsbereich, in der dienstliestungsnahen Industrie, im Medien-, Kultur- und Bildungsbereich durch die Gewerkschaften DAG, DPG, GEW, HBV, IG Medien and ÖTV," Stuttgart, 24 February 1998.

74. For example, Hans-Otto Hemmer, "Am Ende ein Anfang?" *Gewerkschaftliche Monatshefte* 49, no. 5 (May 1998): 267.

75. Ulrich Briefs, "'Plattform': Nomen est omen—GEW-Stimmen zum Mega-Fusionsprojekt," *express* 36, no. 10 (October 1998), 6.

76. Franz Kersjes, "10 Jahre ver.di," *Neue Rheinische Zeitung*, 16 September 2011.

77. For more detailed accounts of the ver.di merger, see Berndt Keller, *Ver.di: Triumphmarsch oder Gefangenenchor?—Neustrukturierung der Interessenvertretung im Dienstleistungssektor* (Hamburg: VSA, 2001); and Hans-Peter Müller, Horst-Udo Niedenhoff, and Manfred Wilke, *Ver.di: Porträt und Positionen* (Cologne: Deutscher Instituts-Verlag, 2002). For more analytical assessments of the merger, see Claire Annesley, "Ver.di and Trade Union Revitalisation in Germany," *Industrial Relations Journal* 37, no. 2 (March 2006): 164–79; and Berndt Keller, "Union Formation through Merger: The Case of Ver.di in Germany," *British Journal of Industrial Relations* 43, no. 2 (June 2005): 209–32. For an assessment ten years after the merger, see Franz Kerjes, "10 Jahre ver.di," *Neue Rheinische Zeitung*, 16 September 2011. Ver.di's archive has posted numerous documents from the merger at: "ver.di-Prozess: Der Weg zu ver.di," http://archiv.verdi.de/verdi/prozess.

78. Deutsche Angestellten-Gewerkschaft; Deutsche Post Gewerkschaft; Gewerkschaft Erziehung und Wissenschaft; Gewerkschaft Handel, Banken und Versicherungen; Industriegewerkschaft Medien; and Gewerkschaft öffentliche Dienste, Transport und Verkehr; "Grundsätze für die Organisationsbeziehungen und die Kooperation der DGB-Gewerkschaften aus Anlass der Gründung von ver.di und der Integration der DAG in den DGB," Berlin, 5 December 2000.

79. *Einblick*, no. 21 (20 November 2000).

80. See http://www.verdi.de/0x0ad00f05_0x0000d9c4 for pdfs documenting the merger.

81. Ulrich Brinkmann and Oliver Nachtwey, "Krise und strategische Neuorientierung der Gewerkschaften," *Aus Politik und Zeitgeschichte*, nos. 13–14 (29 March 2010).

82. For example, Theo Pirker, *Die blinde Macht: Die Gewerkschaftsbewegung in der Bundesrepublik*, 2 vols. (Berlin: Olle & Wolter, 1979); and Heinrich Epskamp, Jürgen Hoffmann, Otto Jacobi, Ulrich Mückenberger, Hinrich Oetjen, Eberhard Schmidt, and

Rainer Zoll, "Schafft den DGB ab!" *Gewerkschaftliche Monatshefte* 43, no. 1 (January 1992).

83. Deutscher Gewerkschaftsbund, *Protokoll. 15. ordentlicher Bundeskongress. Berlin, 13.–17. Juni 1994* (Frankfurt/Main: Union-Druckerei, 1994).

84. Deutscher Gewerkschaftsbund, *Einblick*, no. 03 (1998); *Quelle* 45, nos. 3 and 9, March and September 1994; *Reform Raster*, no. 2 (3 February 1994); and Deutscher Gewerkschaftsbund, *Geschäftsbericht des Bundesvorstandes des Deutschen Gewerkschaftsbunds* (Frankfurt/Main: Union-Druckerei, various years).

85. Keller "Union Formation through Merger," 226–27.

86. *Handelsblatt*, 12 June 1998; *Süddeutsche Zeitung*, 12 June 1998; and Deutscher Gewerkschaftsbund, *Protokoll. 16. ordentlicher Bundeskongress. Düsseldorf, 8.–12. Juni 1998* (Düsseldorf: DGB, 1998).

87. Deutscher Gewerkschaftsbund, *Geschäftsbericht 1998–2001*, 109–10.

88. *Handelsblatt*, 29 May 2002; and *Einblick*, no. 3 (18 February 2002).

89. Cyril Gläser, "Europäische Einheitsgewerkschaft zwischen lähmender Überdehnung und umfassender Repräsentativität: EGB-Strukturen und die Herausforderung der Erweiterung," *Mitteilungsblatt des Instituts für soziale Bewegungen*, no. 42 (2009): 215–34; Wolfgang Kowalsky, "Das Verhältnis von EGB und nationalen Gewerkschaften: Zwischen Europäisierung und Renationalisierung," *Mitteilungsblatt des Instituts für soziale Bewegungen*, no. 42 (2009): 257–83; and Walther Müller-Jentsch, "Die Dekade der Herausforderungen: Deutsche Gewerkschaften zwischen europäischer Integration und nationalstaatlicher Reorganisation in den 1990er Jahren," *Mitteilungsblatt des Instituts für soziale Bewegungen*, no. 42 (2009): 235–56.

90. Hans-Joachim Schabedoth, "Zwischenruf: Europäische Wirtschaftsregierung—Lohndiktate durch die Hintertür?" *Neue Gesellschaft/Frankfurter Hefte* 58, no. 7/8 (July/Aug. 2011): 62–63.

91. *Berliner Zeitung*, 21 September 2011.

92. Anke Hassel, "Sozialpakte: Die Deutschen Gewerkschaften im Bündnis für Arbeit," *Forschungsjournal Neue Soziale Bewegungen*, no. 15 (2/2002): 58–67; and Klaus Zwickel, "Ein Bündnis für Arbeit," *Neue Gesellschaft/Frankfurter Hefte* 42, no. 12 (December 1995): 1066–67.

93. Stephen J. Silvia, "The Causes of Declining Unemployment in Germany: Can the Schröder Government Take Credit?" in *Unemployment Ebbs in Germany: Explanations and Expectations*, ed. Stephen J. Silvia (Washington, DC: AICGS, Johns Hopkins University Press, 2000), 16–19.

94. *Süddeutsche Zeitung*, 5 December 1998.

95. Gemeinsame Erklärung des Bündnisses für Arbeit, Ausbildung und Wettbewerbsfähigkeit, 7 December 1998. The benchmarking group issued a report in 2001: Werner Eichhorst, Stefan Profit, and Eric Thode, *Benchmarking Deutschland: Arbeit und Beschäftigung—Bericht der Arbeitsgruppe Benchmarking und der Bertelsmann Stiftung* (Berlin: Springer, 2001).

96. *Frankfurter Rundschau*, 12 May 1999; *Der Spiegel*, 8 May 1999; and Reinhard Bispinck, "Niedriglöhne und Tarifpolitik. Zehn Thesen zur aktuellen Niedriglohndebatte aus tarifpolitischer Perspektive," in *Perspektiven für mehr Beschäftigung*, ed. Peter Blechschmidt, Uwe Gudowius, Günter Heidorn, Detlev Hensche, and Franziska Wiethold (Hamburg: VSA, 1999), 55–68.

97. BDA and DGB, "Gemeinsame Erklärung von BDA und DGB zum Bündnis für Arbeit, Ausbildung und Wettbewerbsfähigkeit," 6 July 1999.

98. Bündnis für Arbeit, "Gemeinsame Erklärung des Bündnisses zu den Ergebnissen des Spitzengesprächs," 9 January 2000.

99. *Süddeutsche Zeitung*, 10 January 2000.

100. *Berliner Zeitung*, 25 September 2000; and *Frankfurter Rundschau*, 23 November 2000.

101. *Süddeutsche Zeitung*, 5 March 2001.

102. *Frankfurter Allgemeine Zeitung*, 21 July 2001; and Bundesvereinigung der Deutschen Arbeitgeberverbände and Deutscher Gewerkschaftsbund, "Bündnis für Arbeit muss sich weiter bewähren—Gemeinsame Erklärung von BDA und DGB," 20 July 2001.

103. *Frankfurter Rundschau*, 28/30 March 2000.

104. *Frankfurter Rundschau*, 2 May 2002; and Stefan Vossemer, "Job Parade 2001," "Job Parade 2002," "Job Parade 2003," and "Job Parade 2004," at www.youtube.com.

105. *Financial Times Deutschland*, 14 June 2002.

106. http://www.boeckler.de/549_19392.html.

107. Silvia, "Elusive Quest for Normalcy," 86.

108. *Süddeutsche Zeitung*, 23 February and 24 June 2002; Peter Hartz, Norbert Bensel, Jobst Fiedler, Heinz Fischer, Peter Gasse, Werner Jann, Peter Kraljic, Isolde Kunkel-Weber, Klaus Luft, Harald Schartau, Wilhelm Schickler, Hanns-Eberhard Schleyer, Günther Schmid, Wolfgang Tiefensee, and Eggert Voscherau, "Moderne Dienstleistungen am Arbeitsmarkt:Vorschläge der Kommission zum Abbau der Arbeitslosigkeit und zur Umstrukturierung der Bundesanstalt für Arbeit," Berlin, 16 August 2002, http://www.sozialpolitik-aktuell.de/tl_files/sozialpolitik-aktuell/_Politikfelder/Arbeitsmarkt/Dokumente/hartzteil1.pdf.

109. *Süddeutsche Zeitung*, 29 July 2001; and *Die Zeit*, 6 July 2001.

110. Stephen J. Silvia, "Schwarzer Peters? The Implications of Leadership Succession in the German Metalworkers' Union," *AICGS Advisor*, April 2003, www.aicgs.org.

111. *Frankfurter Rundschau*, 17 April 2003; *Handelsblatt*, 18 April 2003; and *Die Welt*, 23 April 2003.

112. *Frankfurter Rundschau*, 14 February 2004.

113. *Frankfurter Rundschau*, 8 May 2003; *Die Welt*, 11 and 17 May 2003; and Geschäftsführender Bundesvorstand des Deutschen Gewerkschaftsbundes, "Mut zum Umsteuern: Für Wachstum, Beschäftigung und soziale Gerechtigkeit. Hintergrundpapier für die wirtschafts- und sozialpolitische Reformagenda des DGB," Berlin, 8 May 2003.

114. *Süddeutsche Zeitung*, 28 May 2003.

115. *Die Welt*, 17 and 21 June 2003; and Geschäftsführender Bundesvorstand des Deutschen Gewerkschaftsbundes, "Mut zum Umsteuern."

116. http://www.boeckler.de/29742_29193.html.

117. *Frankfurter Rundschau*, 3 September and 17 October 2003.

118. *Frankfurter Rundschau*, 13 February 2004; Gerhard Schröder, Regierungserklärung von Bundeskanzler Schröder vor dem Deutschen Bundestag, 14 March 2003,

http://archiv.bundesregierung.de/bpaexport/regierungserklaerung/79/472179/multi.htm.

119. Thomas Haipeter, "Kontrollierte Dezentralisierung? Abweichende Tarif-vereinbarungen in der Metall- und Elektroindustrie," *Industrielle Beziehungen* 16, no. 3 (2009): 232–53.

120. *Frankfurter Rundschau*, 15 November 2004; *Die Zeit*, 6 February 2006; and Antonio Brettscheider, Tabea Bromberg, Thomas Haipeter, and Steffen Lehndorff, "Konzepte gegen die Krise? Chancen und Ambivalenzen betrieblicher 'Besser'-Strategien für Arbeitspolitik und Interessenvertretung," *WSI-Mitteilungen* 63, no. 9 (September 2010): 451–57.

121. Britta Rehder, "Kampagnenpolitik zwischen Siegen und Los Angeles," *Mit-bestimmung* 58, no. 12 (December 2007); Andreas Hamann and Gudrun Giese, *Schwarz Buch Lidl: Billig auf Kosten der Beschäftigten* (Berlin: ver.di gmbh medien buchhandel verlag, 2004); Agnes Schreieder, "Die Lidl-Kampaigne: Eine Zukunftsmodell für Gewerkschaften," in *Never Work Alone: Organizing—eine Zukunftsmodell für Gewerk-schaften*, ed. Peter Bremme, Ulrike Fürniss, and Ulrich Meinecke (Hamburg: VSA, 2007), 153–74; Lowell Turner, "Institutions and Activism: Crisis and Opportunity for a German Labor Movement in Decline," *Industrial and Labor Relations* Review 62, no. 3 (April 2009); and Detlev Wetzel, "Gewerkschaftliche Erneuerung ist möglich," afterward to *Power at Work: Die Rückgewinnung gewerkschaftlicher Macht am Beispiel Australiens*, ed. Michael Crosby (Hamburg: VSA, 2009), 349–62.

122. *Frankfurter Rundschau*, 6 August 2004.

123. Hubertus Schmoldt and Ulrich Freese, open letter, IG BCE, Hanover, July 2004.

124. *Frankfurter Rundschau*, 6 and 7 August 2004.

125. *Frankfurter Rundschau*, 9 and 12 August 2004.

126. *Handelsblatt*, 11 August 2004.

127. *Die Welt*, 14 February 2005.

128. *Frankfurter Rundschau*, 21 June and 10 July 2004.

129. Markovits, *Politics of West German Trade Unions,* 444–45.

130. *Handelsblatt*, 4 January 2005; and *Stern*, 1 August 2009.

131. *Handelsblatt*, 13 July 2004.

132. Deutscher Gewerkschaftsbund, *Geschäftsbericht des Bundesvorstandes des Deutschen Gewerkschaftsbunds, 2002–2005* (Frankfurt/Main: Union Druckerei, 2005), 126–29.

133. Planungsgruppe Weiterentwicklung des DGB, "Turnaround! Vorschläge der Planungsgruppe Weiterentwicklung des DGB—Vorlage für die Klausur DGB-Bundesvorstand, am 25.01.2005 (nur für den internen Gebrauch)" (Berlin: DGB, 2005), 4–5.

134. Planungsgruppe Weiterentwicklung des DGB, "Turnaround!" 4–7.

135. Ibid.

136. *Frankfurter Rundschau*, 26 March 2005.

137. *Die Welt*, 27 January 2005.

138. *Frankfurter Rundschau*, 11 May 2005.

139. Tatjana Fuchs, "Forschungsbericht an die Bundesanstalt für Arbeitsschutz und Arbeitsmedizin. Projektnummer 'Was ist gute Arbeit? Anforderungen aus der

Sicht von Erwerbstätigen' Konzeption & Auswertung einer repräsentativen Unter-suchung," Internationles Institut für Empirische Sozialökonomie, Stadtbergen 2006, http://www.bmas.de/SharedDocs/Downloads/DE/generationpraktikum-forsc hungsbericht-bmas.pdf?__blob=publicationFile; Deutscher Gewerkschaftsbund, *DGB-Index Gute Arbeit: Der Report* (Berlin: DGB, various years); and Dietmar Hexel, "The Good Work Index" (Berlin: DGB, 2008).

140. *Frankfurter Rundschau*, 11 May 2005; and Bundesarbeitgeberverband Chemie and Industrie Gewerkschaft Bergbau, Chemie, Energie, "Gemeinsames Kommuni-qué. Die Tarifautonomie wahren. Sozialpartner lehnen einheitlichen gesetzlichen Mindestlohn ab," BAVC, press release, 11 May 2006.

141. *Direkt*, no. 13 (2009), 1.

142. *Frankfurter Rundschau*, 11 May 2005.

143. *Frankfurter Rundschau*, 27 May 2006.

144. To be sure, wage restraint and fixing exchange rates with other euro mem-bers also contributed to Germany's fall in joblessness. Karl Brenke and Klaus F. Zimmermann, "Reformagenda 2010: Strukturreformen für Wachstum und Be-schäftigung," *Wochenbericht des DIW Berlin*, no. 11 (11 March 2008), 117–24; Tom Krebs and Martin Scheffel, "Macroeconomic Evaluation of Labor Market Reform in Germany," paper presented at the 13th Jacques Polak Annual Research Conference, International Monetary Fund, Washington, DC, 8–9 November 2012; Reinhold Schnabel, "Agenda 2010 und Rentenpolitik: Grosse Erfolge und drohende politische Risiken," *Vierteljahrsheft zur Wirtschaftsforschung* 77, no. 1 (2008): 98–107.

145. *Frankfurter Rundschau*, 6 March 2006; and *Die Welt*, 20 May 2006.

146. Detlev Hensche, "Lokführer als Avantgarde?" *Blätter für deutsche und inter-nationale Politik* 51, no. 9 (September 2007): 1029–32; Hagen Lesch, "Spartengewerk-schaften: Entstehungsmotive und ökonomische Wirkung," *Industrielle Beziehungen* 15, no. 4 (2008); and Wolfgang Schroeder, Viktoria Kallas, and Samuel Greef, *Kleine Gewerkschaften und Berufsverbände im Wandel*, Böckler Forschungsmonitoring 3 (Düs-seldorf: Hans-Böckler-Stiftung, 2008); and Stephen J. Silvia, "The German Rail Strike: The Italianization of German Industrial Relations?" *AICGS Advisor*, 15 No-vember 2007.

147. *Berliner Zeitung*, 17 September 2011; *Süddeutsche Zeitung*, 19 June 2010; Deutsche Feuerwehr-Gewerkschaft, http://www.dfeug.de/; Deutsche Feuerwehr-Gewerkschaft Baden-Württemberg, http://www.baden-wuerttemberg.dfeug.de/ pressespiegel/46-gruendung-einer-feuerwehrgewerkschaft.html; and Wolfgang Schroeder, Viktoria Kalass, and Samuel Greef, *Berufsgewerkschaften in der Offensive: Vom Wandel des deutschen Gewerkschaftsmodells* (Wiesbaden: VS Verlag, 2011).

148. *Frankfurter Allgemeine Zeitung*, 9 February 2007; *Frankfurter Rundschau*, 7 January 2009 and 24 February 2011; and *Die Zeit*, 6 October 2011.

149. *Frankfurter Rundschau*, 11 November 2007.

150. Detlev Wetzel, Jörg Weigand, Sören Niemann-Findeisen, and Tor-sten Lankau, "Organizing: Die mitgliederorientierte Offensivstrategie für die IG Metall—Acht Thesen zur Erneuerung der Gewerkschaftsarbeit," Frankfurt/Main: IG Metall, May 2008, 3–6.

151. Wetzel et al., "Organizing," 6–7.

152. Ibid., 10–15.

153. Martin Behrens, "Die Rolle der Betriebsräte bei der Werbung von Gewerk-schaftsmitgliedern," *WSI-Mitteilungen* 58, no. 6 (June 2005): 329–38.

154. Britta Rehder, "Revitalisierung der Gewerkschaften? Die Grundlagen amerikanischer Organisierungserfolge und ihre Übertragbarkeit auf deutsche Ver-hältnisse," *Berliner Journal für Soziologie* 18, no. 3 (2008): 432–56.

155. Brinkmann and Nachtwey, "Krise."

156. *Direkt*, no. 6 (2009); and *Die Welt*, 10 October 2011.

157. *Handelsblatt*, 30 March 2009; and IG Metall, "Kampagnen. Für ein gutes Leben," www.gutes-leben.de.

158. Industriegewerkschaft Metall, Vorstand, *Projekt IG Metall 2009—Dis-kussionspapier: Sich ändern, um erfolgreich zu sein* (Frankfurt/Main: IG Metall, 2009); Industriegewerkschaft Metall, Vorstand, *Projekt IG Metall 2009—Diskus-sionspapier: Sich ändern, um erfolgreich zu bleiben*, Zweite, überarbeitete Fassung vom 20. Januar 2010 (Frankfurt/Main: IG Metall, 2010); Christian Kuehbauch, "IG Metall 2009: 'Sich ändern, um erfolgreich zu sein,'" PowerPoint presenta-tion (in English), Frankfurt/Main, 2009, http://www.emf-fem.org/Projects/Staff-Networking-Policy-Project/Seminar-on-Networking-on-HR-manage ment-in-trade-unions-in-the-metalworking-sector/Presentations/IG-Metall-Christian-Kuehbauch-IGM-2009_englisch_mk.

159. For example, *Manager Magazin*, 7 December 2009; Thies Gleiss, "IG Metall diskutiert neue Strukturreform," *Sozialistische Zeitung*, no. 12 (2009); and Industriegewerkschaft Metall-Nürnberg, "Diskussionsstand der IG Metall-Betriebsräteversammlung am 3./4.11.2009 in Nürnberg zum Diskussionspapier des Projekts IG Metall 2009," http://labournet.de/diskussion/gewerkschaft/real/igm_nuernberg.pdf.

160. *Die Zeit*, 6 October 2011.

161. Brinkman and Nachtwey, "Krise."

162. *Frankfurter Rundschau*, 11 October 2011.

163. *Junge Welt*, 7 February and 15 March 2011; *Tagesspiegel*, 1 July 2010; *die tageszeitung*, 1 July 2010; Solidaritätskreis, "Solidaritätskreis für vom Ausschluss bedrohte MetallerInnen im Mercedes-Benz-Werk Berlin," http://www.solikreis.blogspot.com; an open letter to Berthold Huber, Detlev Wetzel, Olivier Höbel, Arno Hager, Jörg Hofmann, and Hans Baur, 7 June 2010, http://archiv.labournet.de/diskussion/gewerkschaft/gewdem/ausschluss_igmdc.pdf.

164. Interview, Detlev Wetzel, Frankfurt/Main, 4 June 2009.

165. Thomas Haipeter, "Neue Tarifakteure im Betrieb: Tarifabweichungen und die Mitbestimmung der Betriebsräte—Erfahrungen aus der Chemischen Industrie und der Metallindustrie." (Draft of a final report to the Hans-Böckler-Stiftung). Entwurf des Abschlussberichts an die Hans-Böckler-Stiftung, Duisburg, August 2009, 284, 353, and 372, pdf. file.

166. Ibid.

167. Steffen Lehndorff, "Before the Crisis, in the Crisis, and Beyond: The Upheaval of Collective Bargaining in Germany," *Transfer* 17, no. 3 (August 2011): 342.

168. Bundesministerium für Arbeit und Soziales, "Kurzarbeitergeld plus," press release no. 53, 19 June 2009. It is worth noting that during the Alliance for Jobs

discussions, union officials were unwilling to accept wage subsidies to expand the use of low-wage employment as a means to reduce joblessness. They were, in contrast, proponents of wage subsidies in the form of short-time work to contain unemployment. One possible explanation for this is that in the former case few of the employees benefitting from the subsidies would have been union members, but in the latter instance many of them were.

169. *Frankfurter Rundschau*, 4 March 2009; *Handelsblatt*, 7 April 2009; Martin Allespach, Peter Donath, and Michael Guggemos, "Aktiv aus der Krise," *WSI-Mitteilungen* 63, no. 9 (September 2010): 486–89; and Berthold Huber, "Statement anlässlich der Jahres-Pressekonferenz der IG Metall," Frankfurt/Main, 20 January 2011.

170. *Handelsblatt*, 6 October 2011.

171. *IG BCE Aktuell*, January 2011; and interview, Michael Vassiliadis, 22 May 2012.

172. Ver.di Bundesvorstand, "Chance 2011: Zur Veränderungsarbeit der nächsten Jahren in ver.di: Mitgliederorientierung muss Ziel und Massstab für das gesamte Organisationshandeln werden," Berlin, May 2008, http://labournet.de/diskussion/verdi/chance2011, 3.

173. Ibid., 3–5.

174. Ibid., 6–15.

175. Ibid.; *Ver.di News*, 17 April 2010, 1; and ver.di Abteilung Frauen- und Gleichstellungspolitik, "Checkliste für Geschlechterdemokratie und frauenorientierte Gewerkschaftsarbeit in ver.di," Berlin, September 2009, http://frauen.verdi.de/.

176. *express*, October 2011; *Die Zeit*, 16 September 2011; *die tageszeitung*, 20 September 2011; and Vereinte Dienstleistungsgewerkschaft, *Geschäftsbericht, 2007–2011* (Berlin: ver.di, 2011).

177. *Frankfurter Allgemeine Zeitung*, 17 September 2011.

178. Anja Kirsch, "Union Mergers as a Revitalization Strategy? The Role of Post-Merger Integration," Eighth European Congress of the International Industrial Relations Association, Manchester, UK, University of Manchester, 3–6 September 2007.

179. *Neues Deutschland*, 22 November 2009; *Welt am Sonntag*, 18 September 2011; and Wolfgang Uellenberg van Dawen, "Die Krisenreaktion der Vereinten Dienstleistungsgewerkschaft," *WSI-Mitteilungen* 63, no. 9 (September 2010): 490–92.

180. *Handelsblatt*, 5 November 2008; and *Süddeutsche Zeitung*, 15 May 2009.

Chapter 5

1. See, for example, Wolfgang Schroeder and Bernhard Wessels, eds., *Handbuch Arbeitgeber- und Wirtschaftsverbände in Deutschland* (Wiesbaden: VS, 2010).

2. Philippe C. Schmitter and Wolfgang Streeck, "The Organization of Business Interests: Studying the Associative Action of Business in Advanced Industrial Societies," MPIfG Discussion Paper 99/1, March 1999, esp. 19–45.

3. Ibid., 22–23.

4. Gerard Braunthal, *The Federation of German Industry in Politics* (Ithaca: Cornell University Press, 1965), 4–6; Henry Axel Bueck, *Der Centralverband Deutscher*

Industrieller, 3 vols. (Berlin: Deutscher Verlag, 1902–5); Hartmut Kaelble, *Industrielle Interessenpolitik in der Wilhelminischen Gesellschaft: Centralverband Deutscher Industrieller 1895–1914* (Berlin: Walter de Gruyter, 1967), 3–50; Roswitha Leckebusch, *Entstehung und Wandlungen der Zielsetzung, der Struktur und der Wirkungen von Arbeitgeberverbänden* (Berlin: Duncker & Humblot, 1996); and Hans-Peter Ullmann, *Der Bund der Industriellen. Organisation, Einfluss und Politik klein- und mittelbetrieblicher Industrieller im deutschen Kaiserreich, 1895–1914* (Göttingen: Vandenhoeck and Ruprecht, 1976).

5. Wolfgang Schroeder, "Geschichte und Funktion der deutschen Arbeitgeberverbände," in Schroeder and Wessels, *Handbuch Arbeitgeber- und Wirtschaftsverbände*, 30.

6. Michael Schneider, *Kleine Geschichte der Gewerkschaften: Ihre Entwicklungen in Deutschland von den Anfängen bis heute* (Bonn: Dietz, 1989), 117–26.

7. Gerald D. Feldman and Irmgard Steinisch, *Industrie und Gewerkschaften, 1918–1924: Die überforderte Zentralgemeinschaft* (Stuttgart: Deutsche Verlags-Anstalt, 1985), 136.

8. Ronald F. Bunn, "Employers Associations in the Federal Republic of Germany," in *Employers Associations and Industrial Relations: A Comparative Study*, ed. John P. Windmuller and Alan Gladstone (Oxford: Oxford University Press, 1984), 170–71; and Petra Weber, *Gescheiterte Sozialpartnerschaft–Gefährdete Republik? Industrielle Beziehungen, Arbeitskämpfe, und der Sozialstaat—Deutschland und Frankreich im Vergleich (1918–1933/39)* (Munich: Oldenbourg, 2010).

9. For example, David Abraham, *The Collapse of the Weimar Republic* (New York: Holmes & Meier, 1986); and Henry Ashby Turner, Jr., *German Big Business and the Rise of Hitler* (Oxford: Oxford University Press, 1985).

10. Bunn, "Employers Associations," 173; and Avraham Barkai, *Nazi Economics: Ideology, Theory, and Policy* (New Haven: Yale University Press, 1990), 16.

11. Peter Hayes, *Industry and Ideology: I. G. Farben in the Nazi Era*, 2nd ed. (Cambridge: Cambridge University Press, 2001); Harold James, "The Deutsche Bank and the Dictatorship," in *The Deutsche Bank: 1870–1995*, ed. Lothar Gall, Gerald D. Feldman, Harold James, Carl-Ludwig Holtfrerich, and Hans E. Büschgen (London: Weidenfeld & Nicholson, 1995), 277–356; Stephan H. Lindner, *Inside IG Farben: Hoechst during the Third Reich* (Cambridge: Cambridge University Press, 2008); and Francis R. Nicosia and Jonathan Huener, eds., *Business and Industry in Nazi Germany* (New York: Berghahn, 2004).

12. Braunthal, *Federation of German Industry*, 22; and E. G. Erdmann, "Organisation and Work of Employers Associations in the Federal Republic of Germany," *International Labour Review* 78, no. 6 (December 1958): 542–43.

13. See, for example, United States, Office of Military Government, Germany (Territory under Allied Occupation, 1945–, US Zone) Military Tribunals, *Trials of the War Criminals before the Nuernberg Military Tribunals under Control Council Law No. 10*, vol. 6, "Flick Case"; vols. 7 and 8, "I. G. Farben Case"; and vol. 9, "Krupp Case."

14. Rudolf Herbig, *Notizen: Aus der Sozial-, Wirtschafts- und Gewerkschaftsgeschichte vom 14. Jahrhundert bis zur Gegenwart* (Frankfurt/Main: Union, 1980), 222–23.

15. Eric Owen Smith, *The German Economy* (London: Routledge, 1994), 300.

16. Lutz Niethammer, "Structural Reform and a Compact for Growth," in *The Cold War in Europe: Era of a Divided Continent*, ed. Charles S. Maier, rev. ed. (New York: Marcus Wiener, 1996), 271–311.

17. Braunthal, *Federation of German Industry,* 24; Gabriel A. Almond, "The Politics of German Business," in *West German Leadership and Foreign Policy*, ed. Hans Speier and W. Phillips Davison (Evanston, IL: Row, Peterson and Company, 1957), 198; and Michael Fichter, "Aufbau und Neuordnung: Betriebsräte zwischen Klassensolidarität und Betriebsloyalität," in *Von Stalingrad zur Währungsreform: Zur Sozialgeschichte des Umbruchs in Deutschland*, ed. Martin Broszat, Klaus-Dietmar Henke, and Hans Woller (Munich: R. Oldenbourg, 1988), 469–549.

18. Bunn, "Employers Associations," 172; and Clark Kerr, "Collective Bargaining in Postwar Germany," *Industrial and Labor Relations Review* 5, no. 3 (April 1952): 324–26.

19. Bunn, "Employers Associations," 172; Erdmann, "Organisation and Work," 535; and Arno Krüger, *Walter Raymond: Arbeitgeberpräsident der ersten Stunde*, Kleine Reihe der Walter-Raymond-Stiftung, no. 61 (Cologne: Bachem, 1996).

20. Wolfgang Schroeder, "Arbeitgeberverbände sind nicht gleich: Die Spitzenverbände der Arbeitgeber in der Metall-, Holz- und Textilindustrie," in *Bilanz mit Aussichten: Die neue IG Metall an der Schwelle zum 21. Jahrhundert*, ed. Hans O. Hemmer (Opladen: Westdeutscher Verlag, 1999), 127.

21. Arbeitgeber-Ausschuss Nordrhein-Westfalen, *Deutsche Sozialpolitik in neuem Aufbruch, Bericht über die Jahre 1945–1948* (Düsseldorf: Rechtsverlag, 1949); and Eva Moser, *Bayerns Arbeitgeberverbände im Wiederaufbau: Der Verein der bayrischen Metallindustrie 1947 bis 1962* (Stuttgart: Franz Steiner, 1990).

22. Bunn, "Employers Associations," 183–84; Interview, Hansjörg Döpp, director-general Metall Nordrhein-Westfalen, 20 June 1998; interview, Friedrich Wilhelm Siebel, general manager Collective Bargaining Policy, Gesamtmetall, 20 March 1996; interview, Hugo Stärker, president Bayern Metall, 29 July 1993; and interview, Thomas Vajna, general manager Public Affairs/Economics/Apprenticeships, Gesamtmetall, 29 September 1998.

23. Bunn, "Employers Associations," 176.

24. Stephen J. Silvia, "Mitgliederentwicklung und Organisationsstärke der Arbeitgeberverbände, Wirtschaftsverbände und Industrie- und Handelskammern," in Schroeder and Wessels, *Handbuch Arbeitgeber- und Wirtschaftsverbände*, 169–82.

25. Wolfgang Schroeder and Stephen J. Silvia, "Gewerkschaften und Arbeitgeberverbände," in *Gewerkschaften in Politik und Gesellschaft der Bundesrepublik*, ed. Wolfgang Schroeder and Bernhard Wessels (Opladen: Westdeutscher Verlag, 2003), 245–70.

26. Hansjörg Weitbrecht, *Effektivität und Legitimität der Tarif-Autonomie: Eine soziologische Untersuchung am Beispiel der deutschen Metallindustrie* (Berlin: Duncker & Humblot, 1969).

27. Bundesvereinigung der Deutschen Arbeitgeberverbände, *Gedanken zur Sozialordnung: Grundsatzprogramm der Bundesvereinigung der Deutschen Arbeitgeberverbände* (Bergisch Gladbach: Haider, 1953).

28. For example, Otto Esser, "Das Selbstverständnis der Arbeitgeberverbände von ihrer Bedeutung und Rolle in der Arbeitsverfassung," *Zeitschrift für Arbeitsrecht* 11

(1980): 301–9; and Dieter Hundt, "Weichenstellungen für nachhaltiges Wirtschaften und sozialen Zusammenhalt," Rede vor dem 38th Kolloquium der Walter-Raymond-Stiftung [speech to the 38th Colloquium of the Walter Raymond Foundation], Dresden, 28 March 2000.

29. The concept of a social market economy is a product of the Freiburg school of economists and the intellectual cornerstone of Germany's postwar economic order. Stated briefly, it is a "socially responsible free market economy." Stated more fully, market mechanisms serve as the principal means for allocating goods and services, but the state has an obligation to raise citizens and regions out of poverty through transfer payments. The state also has an obligation to provide "framework conditions" (*Rahmenbedingungen*) conducive to competition and growth, but it should not intervene as an economic actor (e.g., a state-owned firm) or to favor some economic actors over others. For a brief discussion of the idea, see Smith, *German Economy,* 16–18. For a more thorough treatment, see Alan Peacock and Hans Willgerodt, eds., *Germany's Social Market Economy* (New York: St. Martin's, 1989).

30. Bunn, "Employers Associations," 177; and Wolfgang Schroeder, "Gewerkschaften und Arbeitgeberverbände," *Gewerkschaftliche Monatshefte* 47, no. 10 (October 1996): 602.

31. *Frankfurter Rundschau,* 28 June 1955; and Walther Simon, *Macht und Herrschaft der Unternehmerverbände: BDI, BDA und DIHT im ökonomischen und politischen System der BRD* (Cologne: Pahl-Rugenstein, 1976), 114.

32. Andrei S. Markovits, *The Politics of the West German Trade Unions: Stategies of Class and Interest Representation in Growth and Crisis* (Cambridge University Press, 1986), 198–99.

33. Joachim Bergmann, Otto Jacobi, and Walther Müller-Jentsch, *Gewerkschaften in der Bundesrepublik: Gewerkschaftliche Lohnpolitik zwischen Mitgliederinteressen und ökonomischen Systemzwängen* (Frankfurt/Main: Europäische Verlagsanstalt, 1976), 284–94; and Claus Noé, *Gebändigter Klassenkampf: Tarifautonomie in der Bundesrepublik Deutschland—der Konflikt zwischen Gesamtmetall und IG Metall vom Frühjahr 1963* (Berlin: Duncker & Humblot, 1970), 315.

34. The contents of a revised version of the BDA taboo catalog were leaked to the press in 1979: *Frankfurter Rundschau,* 27 January 1979.

35. Arbeitsring der Arbeitgeberverbände der Deutschen Chemischen Industrie, *25 Jahre Arbeitsring Chemie* (Wiesbaden: AADCI, 1974); Hans-Hermann Hertle, Jürgen Kädtler, and Theo Pirker, "'Wir waren immer für Partnerschaft!': Gespräch mit Dr. Karl Molitor," *Berliner Arbeitshefte zur sozialwissenschaftlichen Forschung,* Zentralinstitut für sozialwissenschaftliche Forschung, Freie Universität Berlin, no. 37, July 1990, 12; and Dieter Schlemmer, "Verantwortung und Partnerschaft: Markierungen der Tarifpolitik in der chemischen Industrie," in *Sozialpartnerschaft in der Bewährung: Festschrift für Karl Molitor zum 60. Geburtstag,* ed. Franz Gamillscheg, Bernd Rüthers, and Eugen Stahlhacke (Munich: C. H. Beck'sche Verlagsbuchhandlung, 1988), 315–16.

36. Rolf Seitenzahl, *Einkommenspolitik durch Konzertierte Aktion und Orientierungsdaten* (Cologne: Bund, 1974).

37. Bundesvereinigung der Deutschen Arbeitgeberverbände, *Freiheitliche soziale Ordnung heute und morgen* (Cologne: BDA, 1968).

38. *New York Times*, 20 October 1977.

39. Germany has a set of sectoral industry associations parallel to the employers associations. Industry associations focus on product standards, taxation, trade promotion, and regulations unrelated to employment.

40. *Süddeutsche Zeitung*, 4 and 5 September 2002.

41. Schroeder, "Arbeitgeberverbände sind nicht gleich," 127.

42. For a synopsis of the strike, see Otto Jacobi, "Streik der Chemiearbeiter 1971," in *Gewerkschaften und Klassenkampf: Kritisches Jahrbuch 1972*, ed. Otto Jacobi, Walther Müller-Jentsch, and Eberhard Schmidt (Frankfurt/Main: Fischer, 1972), 28–44.

43. Hertle, Kädtler, and Pirker, "Gespräch mit Dr. Karl Molitor," 1–2; and Kurt Biedenkopf, "Zukunft der Tarifpolitik," in *Zukunft der Tarifpolitik: Eine Podiumsveranstaltung des Bundesarbeitgeberverbandes Chemie*, ed. Bundesarbeitgeberverband Chemie (Wiesbaden: BAVC, 1995), 14–15.

44. Stephen J. Silvia, "Jobs, Trade and Unions: The Politics of Employment and Protectionism in West German and American Unions," PhD thesis, Yale University, 1990.

45. Stephen J. Silvia, "Every Which Way but Loose: German Industrial Relations since 1980," in *The Brave New World of European Labor: European Trade Unions at the Millennium*, ed. Andrew Martin and George Ross (New York: Berghahn, 1999), 87–88.

46. Silvia and Schroeder, "Gewerkschaften und Arbeitgeberverbände," 1433–59.

47. *die tageszeitung*, 13 June 1996.

48. *Frankfurter Allgemeine Zeitung*, 23 April 1987; *Frankfurter Rundschau*, 7 March 1994; *Handelsblatt*, 8 March 1995; *Süddeutsche Zeitung*, 5/6 May 1990; *Wirtschaftswoche*, 24 April 1987; Schroeder, "Arbeitgeberverbände sind nicht gleich," 127; and Wolfgang Schroeder, "Die Unternehmerverbände: Programmatik, Politik, Organisation," in *Gewerkschaftsjahrbuch 1992: Daten–Fakten–Analysen*, ed. Michael Kittner (Bonn: Bund, 1992), 672–73.

49. Arbeitsgemeinschaft selbstständiger Unternehmer, *Mehr Marktwirtschaft am Arbeitsmarkt* (Bonn: ASU, 1990); and Hans-Joachim Selzer, "Auszüge aus dem Bericht des Vorsitzenden des Arbeitgeberverbandes der hessischen Metallindustrie, Bezirksgruppe Mittelhessen e.V. anlässlich der 40. ordentlichen Mitgliedsversammlung der Bezirksgruppe," 10 March 1990.

50. Industriegewerkschaft Chemie-Papier-Keramik, *Der Entgelttarifvertrag im Spiegel der Medien* (Frankfurt/Main: Union Druckerei, 1987); and Jürgen Kädtler and Hans-Hermann Hertle, *Sozialpartnerschaft und Industriepolitik: Strukturwandel im Organisationsbereich der IG Chemie-Papier-Keramik* (Opladen: Westdeutscher Verlag, 1997), 119–67 and 172.

51. Walther Müller-Jentsch, "Arbeitgeberverbände und Sozialpartnerschaft in der chemischen Industrie," in Schroeder and Wessels, *Handbuch Arbeitgeber- und Wirtschaftsverbände*, 404–7.

52. Stephen J. Silvia, "German Unification and Emerging Divisions within German Employers' Associations: Cause or Catalyst?" *Comparative Politics* 29, no. 2 (January 1997): 187–208.

53. Bundesvereinigung der Deutschen Arbeitgeberverbände and Deutscher Gewerkschaftsbund, "Gemeinsame Erklärung zur Wirtschaft der Deutschen

Demokratischen Republik," 9 March 1990; and Bundesvereinigung der Deutschen Arbeitgeberverbände and Deutscher Gewerkschaftsbund, "Für mehr Beschäftigung in der DDR," Gemeinsame Erklärung zur Sozial- und Wirtschaftseinheit Deutschlands [Common Declaration on the Social and Economic Union of Germany], 18 September 1990, printed in *Der Arbeitgeber*, 5 October 1990.

54. Verband der Sächsischen Metall- und Elektroindustrie, *VSME Chronik* (Dresden: Union Druckerei, 2000), 18–21.

55. Stephen J. Silvia, "The Elusive Quest for Normalcy: The German Economy since Unification," *German Politics and Society* 28, no. 2 (Summer 2010): 87.

56. Wolfgang Schroeder, *Das Modell Deutschland auf dem Prüfstand: Zur Entwicklung der industriellen Beziehungen in Ostdeutschand* (Wiesbaden: Westdeutscher Verlag, 2000), 234–40.

57. Thomas Haipeter and Gabi Schilling, "Von der Einfluss- zur Mitgliedschaftslogik: Die Arbeitgeberverbände und das System der industriellen Beziehungen in der Metallindustrie," *Industrielle Beziehungen* 13, no. 1 (2006): 28–29.

58. *Quelle*, June 1995; and Haipeter and Schilling, "Von der Einfluss- zur Mitgliedschaftslogik," 30.

59. *Handelsblatt*, 19 February 1993; Kay Ohl, "Die Ost-West-Tarifangleichung in der Metall- und Elektroindustrie," *WSI-Mitteilungen* 62, no. 11 (November 2009): 627–30; and Stephen J. Silvia, "'Holding the Shop Together': Old and New Challenges to the German System of Industrial Relations in the mid-1990s," *Berliner Arbeitshefte zur sozialwissenschaftlichen Forschung*, no. 83 (July 1993), 18–20.

60. Haipeter and Schilling, "Von der Einfluss- zur Mitgliedschaftslogik," 31.

61. *Handelsblatt*, 8 March 1995.

62. *Fokus*, 24 July 1995; *Frankfurter Allgemeine Zeitung*, 10 March and 31 May 1995; *Handelsblatt*, 9 March 1995; and Thomas Haipeter and Gabi Schilling, *Arbeitgeberverbände in der Metall- und Elektroindustrie. Tarifbindung, Organisationsentwicklung und Strategiebildung* (Hamburg: VSA, 2005).

63. Gesamtmetall, "Freiburger Erklärung–Grundsatzpapier vom Juni 1996," Cologne, 1996, http://www.gesamtmetall.de/gesamtmetall/meonline.nsf/id/041EDA B1B8558FFAC1256BB3004E418D; Gesamtmetall, "Frankfurter Erklärung zur Reform des Flächentarifs," Cologne, 1997, http://www.gesamtmetall.de/gesamtmetall/meonline.nsf/id/A4BCFE4FF92F7CA0C125687800548F91; and Gesamtmetall, "Berliner Erklärung. Positionspapier von Gesamtmetall zu tarifpolitischen Themen des Bündnisses für Arbeit," policy statements, Cologne, 1999, http://www.gesamtmetall.de/gesamtmetall/meonline.nsf/id/359F3C658B939535C1256BB300 4E41A7.

64. Gesamtmetall press release, 25 June 1996; and *Süddeutsche Zeitung*, 28 September 1999.

65. For early assessments of the phenomenon, see Herbert Buchner, "Mitgliedschaft in Arbeitgeberverbänden ohne Tarifbindung," *Neue Zeitschrift für Arbeitsrecht* 11 (January 1994): 2-12; Gottlieb Förster, "Flucht aus Tarifverträgen: Eine aktuelle Gefahr," *Umschau* 46 (March 1994): 13; Axel Langer, "Arbeitgeberverbandsaustritte: Motive, Abläufe und Konsequenten," *Industrielle Beziehungen* 1 (1994), 132–54; and Walther Müller-Jentsch, "Das (Des-)Interesse der Arbeitgeber am Tarifvertragssystem," *WSI-Mitteilungen* 46, no. 8 (August 1993): 496–502.

66. Thomas Haipeter, "OT-Mitgliedschaften und OT-Verbände," in Schroeder and Wessels, *Handbuch Arbeitgeber- und Wirtschaftsverbände*, 209–19; and Martin Völkl, *Der Mittelstand und die Tarifautonomie: Arbeitgeberverbände zwischen Sozialpartnerschaft und Dienstleistungen* (Munich: Hampp, 2002).

67. Schroeder, "Arbeitgeberverbände sind nicht gleich," 137 and 142; Verband der Sächsischen Metall- und Elektroindustrie, *VSME Chronik*, 31; Nicholai Besgen, *Mitgliedschaft im Arbeitgeberverband ohne Tarifbindung: Tarifflucht statt Verbandsflucht* (Baden-Baden: Nomos, 1998); and Markus H. Ostrop, *Mitgliedschaft ohne Tarifbindung: Besondere Gestaltungsformen einer tarifbindungsfreien Mitgliedschaft im Arbeitgeberverband* (Frankfurt/Main: Lang, 1997).

68. Müller-Jentsch, "Arbeitgeberverbände und Sozialpartnerschaft," 408.

69. BAVC, "Information," 18 October 1996.

70. Markovits, *Politics of the West German Trade Unions*, 327–61.

71. *Berliner Morgenpost*, 21 and 27 March 1997.

72. *Berliner Morgenpost*, 11 and 27 July, 1 August, and 17 September 1997; *die tageszeitung*, 14 August 1997; and Zweckverbund Ostdeutscher Bauverbände, http://www.zvob.de/.

73. *Handelsblatt*, 17 August 2008; Chemiesozialpartner, Wittenberg-Prozess, http://www.chemie-sozialpartner.de /wittenberg-prozess/.

74. Reinhard Bahnmüller, "Tarifbewegung als Projektmanagement: Neue Wege bei der Entwicklung eines einheitlichen Entgelttarifvertrags in der Metallindustrie Baden-Württembergs," *WSI-Mitteilungen* 46, no. 12 (December 1993), 821–30; and Dieter Hundt, "Einheitliches Entgelt für Arbeiter und Angestellte in der Elektro- und Metallindustrie," Lecture no. 5, *Analytik '93*, Stuttgart, February 1993.

75. Ulrich Brocker, "Flächentarif—wirklich ein Kartell?" *Forum:* Vortragsreihe des Instituts der deutschen Wirtschaft Köln [Lecture series of the Institut der deutschen Wirtschaft Cologne] 53, no. 45 (4 November 2003); Verband der Metallindustrie Baden-Württemberg, http://www.vmi.de/swm/web.nsf/id/li_de_pressemitteilung_nr_6_aus_2005.html; and Verband der Metallindustrie Baden-Württemberg, http://www.suedwestmetall.de/swm/web.nsf/id/pa_de_era.html.

76. *Handelsblatt*, 23 February and 1 March 2004; and *Die Welt*, 13, 19, and 23 February 2004.

77. Hagen Lesch, "Das Verhältnis zwischen Arbeitgeber-, Wirtschaftsverbänden und Gewerkschaften," in Schroeder and Wessels, *Handbuch Arbeitgeber- und Wirtschaftsverbände*, 327–28.

78. Hansjörg Weitbrecht, "Arbeitgeberverbände in der Tarifpolitik und im tarifpolitischen System der Bundesrepublik," in Schroeder and Wessels, *Handbuch Arbeitgeber- und Wirtschaftsverbände*, 239–42.

79. *Handelsblatt*, 21 May 2005.

80. Jan Stefan Roell, "ERA und Pforzheim-Vereinbarungen haben Praxistest bestanden," 11 July 2007, Südwestmetall, http://www.vmi.de/swm/web.nsf/id/li_de_mitgliederversammlung_2007.html.

81. Gesamtmetall, *OT-Verbände in der M+E-Industrie* (Cologne: Bercker, Kevelaer, 2002).

82. Gesamtmetall, press release, 31 January 2005.

83. Bundesarbeitsgericht, 4 AZR 230/08, 28 May 2006; 4 AZR 261/08, 1 July 2009; and 4 AZR 552/08, 20 October 2010.

84. Melanie Haisch, *Wirtschaft ohne Tarifbindung: Vom Flächentarifvertrag zum OT-Verband* (Marburg: Tectum, 2008); and Melanie Wichmann, *Mitgliedschaft im Arbeitgeberverband ohne Tarifbindung* (Munich: Grin, 2008).

85. *N-TV*, 13 September 2004; and *Süddeutsche Zeitung*, 5 August 2003 and 1 March 2004.

86. Rudolph Speth, "Grenzen der politischen Kommunikation von Unternehmensverbänden," in Schroeder and Wessels, *Handbuch Arbeitgeber- und Wirtschaftsverbände*, 228–30.

87. Berndt Keller, "Arbeitgeberverbände des öffentlichen Sektors," in Schroeder and Wessels, *Handbuch Arbeitgeber- und Wirtschaftsverbände*, 105–23.

88. *Frankfurter Rundschau*, 4 July 2009, 3 January and 18 June 2010; *Tagesspiegel*, 2 January 2010; and WSI-Tarif-archiv, "Tarifrunde 2009: Ein kurzer Überblick," http://www.boeckler.de/wsi-tarifarchiv_2283.htm.

Conclusion

1. European Industrial Relations Observatory, "France: Industrial Relations profile," http://www.eurofound.europa.eu/eiro/country/france_1.htm; Guy Groux, "France: The State, Trade Unions and Collective Bargaining," in *Trade Unionism since 1945: Towards a Global History,* vol. 1, *Western Europe, Eastern Europe, Africa and the Middle East,* ed. Craig Phelan (Oxford: Peter Lang, 2009), 37–64; and Organization for Economic Cooperation and Development, http://stats.oecd.org/Index.aspx?DataSetCode=UN_DEN.

2. Bundesvereinigung der deutschen Arbeitgeberverbände, *Newsletter*, no. 7 (17 July 2008).

3. Jun Imai, *The Transformation of Japanese Employment Relations* (New York: Palgrave, 2011), 17–49; and John Price, *Japan Works: Power and Paradox in Postwar Industrial Relations* (Ithaca: Cornell University Press, 1997).

4. Steve Early, *The Civil Wars in US Labor: Birth of a New Workers' Movement or Death Throes of the Old?* (Chicago: Haymarket Books, 2011).

INDEX

Page numbers followed by letters *f* and *t* refer to figures and tables, respectively.

collective bargaining by, 22, 165–66, 205–6, 213; and employers associations, 204, 205–6; failed strike of June 2003, 152–53; global financial crisis and, 171–72; grassroots organizing by, limits on, 170–71; influence of, 126, 223; membership losses by, 174; merger with GTB, 135–36; minimax strategy of, 123; minimum wage debate and, 160; and multisectoral unionism, 132; new sectors covered by, 138; Pforzheim agreement and, 214; political confrontation by, 7; reform efforts of, 8, 166–72, 177; risks for, 177; size of, 126, 138, 139; and social movement unionism, 3, 8, 154, 222–23; succession crisis of 2003, 150–51; traditionalists vs. reformers in, 150, 166, 169; workweek reduction campaign of, 122
Imperial Germany: collective bargaining in, 18–19; industrial and commercial courts in, 30; labor law in, 4, 13, 14–15; worker committees in, 65
income, personal: in 1950s and 1960s, 118, 119t, 190, 191; in 1970s, 119t, 120, 121; in 1990s, 119t, 147, 203; in 2000s, 119t, 148, 162; adjusted labor share of, 121f. *See also* wages
individualism, rise in, impact on industrial relations, 2, 94–95, 177, 222, 229
industrial relations system, German: actors in, 220, 221–24, 225; codetermination as backbone of, 9; comparison with other countries, 41, 226–29; conflictual partnership in, 51, 53, 60, 71; framework of, 220–21, 224, 225; future of, 3, 229–30; importance of understanding, 11–12; politicians' willingness to preserve, 37; postwar history of, 2–3; previous research on, 10–11; resilience of, 4, 44, 81–82; role in economy, 1–2; role of state in, 4, 9, 13, 18, 41, 77; unification and, 2–3, 124–26, 129–30, 224
industrial unionism *(Industriegewerkschaft)*, principle of, 111–12
industrial union movement, 6, 104, 105–18, 176, 222. *See also* first postwar German trade union movement
INSM (New Social Market Economy Initiative), 216

Jackson, Gregory, 81
Japan, industrial relations in, 228
juridification *(Verrechtlichung)*, 32
just-in-time production, and vulnerability to strikes, 123, 197–98

Kannegiesser, Martin, 172
Kapp, Wolfgang, 107–8
Kersjes, Franz, 137
Keynesian economics, 116, 193
Kiesinger, Kurt, 52
Kohl, Helmut, 27, 40; and Alliance for Jobs, 143; and early retirement campaign, 122; and works council legislation, 75
Köhler, Horst, 212

Lafontaine, Oskar, 144, 161
LAG (state labor courts), 31
Lang, Klaus, 132
last resort *(ultima ratio)*, strike as, 34, 36, 37
law, labor, 13–38; continuity in, 4, 13, 220, 221; Nipperdey criteria and, 33–34; role in industrial relations, 220–21
Left Party: membership in, as measure of labor milieu, 95; origins of, 156–57; and trade unions, 96, 161
Legien, Carl, 16, 182
lockouts: in 1960s, 119t, 191–92; in 1970s, 119t, 195; in 1980s, 119t, 198; BAG decisions regarding, 34–36; offensive *(Angriffsaussperrung)*, 34, 35. *See also* strikes and lockouts
logic of membership vs. logic of influence: employers associations and, 192, 195, 197, 199–200, 211, 212, 215, 217, 219; in theory of organizational behavior, 180–81
Ludendorff, Erich, 15

manufacturing sector: employment in, and union density, 98t, 100; original unions in, 113, 114t; union membership in, 92
Marshall, T. H., 94
mechanical engineering sector, employers associations in, 9, 201–7, 212–15, 223; in 1994–1995 collective bargaining round, 205–6; cancellation of contracts by, 204; chemicals sector compared to, 208, 214–15; construction sector compared to, 209, 210; density declines in, 180, 195f, 199, 200, 201–3, 205, 207, 208–9, 211,

TVöD (Collective Bargaining Agreement for the Public Sector), 24–25, 163, 164

ultima ratio principle, 34, 36, 37
unemployment, in Germany: in 1950s and 1960s, 118, 119*t*; in 1970s, 119*t*, 120; in 1980s, 119*t*, 121, 122; in 1990s, 119*t*, 146, 203; in 2000s, 119*t*, 148, 162, 211; global financial crisis and, 1; and union density, 91, 97, 98*t*; working-time reduction and, 122
unemployment benefits, 39, 40; reform of 2003, 149, 155; strikes and, 93, 123
unification, German: and codetermination, efforts to amend, 55–60; data used to capture impact of, 89; and employers associations, 200–202, 204; impact on industrial relations, 2–3, 124–26, 129–30, 224; and union density, 6, 84, 86, 88, 99–100, 99*t*, 102, 103, 125, 224; and union membership, 84, 86; use of BA funds after, 40
union density (unionization rate): calculation of, 85, 86, 87, 246n8; definition of, 85; as dependent variable, 89; factors influencing, 6, 14, 83–84, 90–97; milieu and, 6, 84, 89, 94–95, 98*t*, 99, 102, 229; as sociological vs. economic phenomenon, 103; trend in, 87–88, 88*f*; unification and, 6, 84, 86, 88, 99–100, 99*t*, 102, 103, 125, 224
unitary collective bargaining *(Tarifenheit),* 111
unitary unionism *(Einheitsgewerkschaft),* 107–10, 252n21
United States: collective bargaining agreements in, 23; decentralized model of unionization in, 111; incorporation of firms in Delaware, 61; industrial relations in, 51, 167–68, 228; social movement unionism in, 154, 167–68, 177, 228, 229; and trade unions in postwar Germany, 106, 107

Vassiliadis, Michael, 172
ver.di (United Service Employees Union), 6; 2011 convention of, 28; aggressive tactics of, 7; creation of, 136–38, 246n6; in DGB, 139, 139*t*, 140; failure to thrive, 223; and federally mandated minimum wage, 160; and fragmentation of labor

movement, 164; global financial crisis and, 175; Hamburg agreement of 2006, 163; matrix structure of, 137, 174, 177; membership losses for, 174–75; new sectors covered by, 138; on one workplace, one union principle, 37; reform efforts of, 172–74, 177; size of, 138, 139; and social movement unionism, 8, 154; teachers union compared to, 165; traditionalists in, 150
Visser, Jelle, 85, 91, 93, 95, 96, 97, 246n8
Vredling, Henk, 78

wages: changes in, and union density, 90, 97, 98*t*, 102, 103, 175; unification and, 200–201; unitary compensation framework agreement and, 212–13. *See also* income; minimum wage
Wallerstein, Michael, 91, 92, 97, 102
warning strikes, 36
Weimar Republic: acrimonious industrial relations in, 63; collective bargaining regime in, 20, 182; employee representation on supervisory boards in, 45; labor courts in, 30, 31, 32; labor law in, 4, 13, 16; state arbitration in, failed experiment with, 230; trade unions in, 67, 107, 108; works councils in, 66–68, 69
welfare state: expenditures in, and union density, 94, 98*t*, 100; tripartite bodies in, 38–41
Werder, Alex von, 56
Wetzel, Detlev, 154, 165, 166, 169, 170
white-collar workers: and blue-collar workers, merging of categories of, 24, 94, 212–13; industrial unionism and, 111–12. *See also* DAG
Wiesehügel, Klaus, 151
wildcat strikes, 36
Wissmann, Hellmut, 58
women: and union density, 93, 98*t*, 100; in ver.di governing committee, 137; works council reform of 2001 and, 77
workday, Stinnes-Legien agreement on, 16
worker committees, early experiments with, 64–65, 182
working-time accounts, 214
workplace agreement *(Betriebsvereinbarung),* 25, 242n93